Siting the Other

Re-visions of Marginality in Australian and English-Canadian Drama

P.I.E.-Peter Lang

Bruxelles · Bern · Berlin · Frankfurt/M · New York · Oxford · Wien

Dramaturgies

Texts, Cultures and Performances

Series Editor

Marc Maufort, *Université Libre de Bruxelles*

Editorial Board

Christopher Balme, *University of Mainz*
Judith E. Barlow, *State University of New York-Albany*
Johan Callens, *Vrije Universiteit Brussel*
Jean Chothia, *Cambridge University*
Harry J. Elam, *Stanford University*
Albert-Reiner Glaap, *University of Düsseldorf*
André Helbo, *Université Libre de Bruxelles*
Ric Knowles, *University of Guelph*
Alain Piette, *École d'interprètes internationaux-Mons/ Université Catholique de Louvain*
John Stokes, *King's College, University of London*
Joanne Tompkins, *University of Queensland-Brisbane*

Editorial Assistant

Franca Bellarsi, *Université Libre de Bruxelles*

Marc MAUFORT & Franca BELLARSI (eds.)

Siting the Other

Re-visions of Marginality in Australian and English-Canadian Drama

Dramaturgies
No.1

Die Deutsche Bibliothek – CIP-Einheitsaufnahme

Siting the other : Re-visions of marginality in Australian and English-Canadian drama / Marc Maufort & Franca Bellarsi (ed.) – Bruxelles ; Bern ; Berlin ; Frankfurt/M. ; New York ; Oxford; Wien : PIE Lang, 2001
(Dramaturgies ; 1)
ISBN 90-5201-934-7

CIP available from the British Library, GB and the Library of Congress, USA.
ISBN 0-8204-4667-X

© P.I.E.-Peter Lang s.a.
Presses Interuniversitaires Européennes
Brussels, 2001
E-mail : info@peterlang.com

No part of this book may be reproduced in any form, by print, photocopy, microfilm or any other means, without prior written permission from the publisher. All rights reserved.

ISSN 1376-3199
ISBN 90-5201-934-7
D/2001/5678/03

Acknowledgements

The sum of my institutional and personal debts in the edition of this book reflects its mosaic-like analysis of otherness in Australian and English-Canadian drama. I can only hope to do justice to them all in this short preface. This project originated in my joint interest in anglophone postcolonial drama and literatures, which I have taught for several years at the *Université Libre de Bruxelles*. The background research which led to this work was facilitated by a generous research grant from the National Fund for Scientific Research-Belgium, which enabled me to consult the theatre documents preserved in various university libraries in Australia. This travel grant gave birth to the idea of a collection of essays on postcolonial drama in Australia and Canada.

First and foremost, I wish to express my gratitude to all the contributors in this collection for their excellent contributions and their patient cooperation in the editorial process. Further, I am most grateful to Mrs. Closson, my editor at P.I.E.-Peter Lang S.A., who in addition to her enthusiasm for this project, gave me the opportunity to edit a new book series on dramatic studies for her press. Financial support for the publication of this book and the creation of the new book series was provided by the Center for Canadian Studies and the *Faculté de Philosophie et Lettres* of the University of Brussels. I therefore wish to express my most sincere gratitude to Professors Ginette Kurgan and Serge Jaumain, respectively President and Director of the Center for Canadian Studies, and to Professor Guy Haarscher, former Dean of the *Faculté de Philosophie et Lettres*. I owe a major debt to my assistant, Franca Bellarsi, who joined this project at an advanced stage as an associate editor. Her scientific advice as well as her wonderful skills as a meticulous copy-editor have been much appreciated. I also wish to express my thanks to Mrs. Kathleen Dassy, my production manager at P.I.E.-Peter Lang, who carefully supervised the preparation of the camera-ready copy.

On a more personal note, editing a collection of essays about identity formation in drama inevitably prompted me to redefine my own cultural roots. The year 2000, during which this book was put together, saw the passing of my maternal grandparents, who certainly played a crucial role in my identity shaping. However, if one's sense of self is firmly rooted in the past, it is also constantly projecting itself into the future. I therefore wish to dedicate this book both to my grandparents, in loving memory, and to my children, Jessica and Quentin, wishing them fulfilling tomorrows.

Marc Maufort

Brussels, November 2000

Table of Contents

Marc Maufort
   Siting the Other: Cross-cultural Re-visions of Marginality................ 1

Marc Maufort
   Forging an "Aboriginal Realism": First Nations Playwriting
   in Australia and Canada 7

Helen Thomson
   Aboriginal Women's Staged Autobiography 23

Helena Grehan
   "Implacement" and Belonging: Dramatising White
   Women's Stories in *Tiger Country* 39

Maryrose Casey
   Siting Themselves: Indigenous Australian Theatre Companies 53

Jacqueline Lo
   Playing the Yellow Lady: Performing Gender and Race 69

Susan Pfisterer
   History and Mystery and Suffragettes on the Australian
   Stage: A Consideration of Women's Suffrage as Presented
   in Australian Theatre 85

Bruce Parr
   Queer/Irony in Nick Enright's Drama 99

Peta Tait
   Queer Circus Bodies in Rock 'n' Roll Circus's *The Dark*
   and Club Swing's *Razor Baby* 115

Tom Burvill
   Urban Theatre Projects: Re-siting Marginal Communities
   in Outer Western Sydney 127

Paul Makeham
> Fear and Desire *Under the Big Sky*: Brink Visual Theatre and
> the Post-colonial Australian Landscape 141

Peter Fitzpatrick
> Spot the Infidel: Aspects of Multiculturalism
> in Mainstream Australian Theatre.. 155

Gerry Turcotte
> "Collaborating with Ghosts": Dispossession in *The Book
> of Jessica* and *The Mudrooroo/Mueller Project* 175

Anne Nothof
> Canadian "Ethnic" Theatre: Fracturing the Mosaic 193

Albert-Reiner Glaap
> Drew Hayden Taylor's Dramatic Career... 217

Robert Appleford
> Making Relations Visible in Native Canadian Performance.......... 233

Ric Knowles
> Translators, Traitors, Mistresses, and Whores:
> Monique Mojica and the Mothers of the Métis Nations 247

Ann Wilson
> *Beatrice Chancy*: Slavery, Martyrdom and the Female Body........ 267

Alan Filewod
> "From Twisted History": Reading *Angélique* 279

Robert Wallace
> Defying Category: Re/viewing John Herbert's *Fortune
> and Men's Eyes* 291

Robert Nunn
> Crackwalking: Judith Thompson's Marginal Characters............... 311

Reid Gilbert
   Escaping the "Savage Slot": Interpellation and Transgression
   in George F. Walker's *Suburban Motel* 325

Joanne Tompkins
   "Fatherlands and Mother-Tongues": Family Histories and Futures
   in Recent Australian and Canadian Multicultural Theatre 347

Appendix 363

Maryrose Casey
   Garden of Drama: Talking to John Harding

Notes on Contributors 371

Siting the Other:
Cross-cultural Re-visions of Marginality

MARC MAUFORT

Université Libre de Bruxelles

As Diana Brydon and Helen Tiffin make abundantly clear in their seminal study *Decolonizing Fictions*,[1] Australia and Canada are prominent instances of settler-invader colonies of the former British Empire which share a number of significant historical, political, cultural and even literary characteristics. In the context of this study, it is particularly relevant to observe that both twentieth-century Australia and Canada have progressively become multicultural countries, in their constant search for a flexible definition of their nationhood. In their very ethnic fragmentation, both countries can be compared to perpetually reconfigured mosaic or kaleidoscopic patterns, differing markedly from the assimilationist model of the American melting pot. The Australian and Canadian forms of post-coloniality are predicated on a continuous negotiation of the boundaries between "Self" and "Other." This reflects the profound crisis of identity encoded in the (post)colonial experience. First, from their very colonial beginnings, Australians' and Canadians' struggle for self-definition was hampered by an acute sense of social and intellectual inferiority towards the centre of the Empire, indeed a form of cultural cringe. Second, both countries are increasingly, at the dawn of this new millennium, faced with contentious internal polarities between First Nations aborigines, various marginal ethnic groups and the mainstream. In other words, social margins are ceaselessly repositioned in these former colonies.

This process of multicultural reinvention of the opposition self/other is especially visible in the field of theatre, which by its very nature constitutes an essentially political form of art. Whereas Australian and Canadian fiction have both achieved a comparable level of international recognition, boasting world-famous authors like Michael Ondaatje or David Malouf, drama still represents an emergent art form in the two

---

[1] Diana Brydon and Helen Tiffin, *Decolonizing Fictions* (Sydney: Dangaroo Press, 1993): 55-76.

countries. It is perhaps not a coincidence that the coming of age of both Australian and Canadian drama should date from the late 1960s/early 1970s, with playwrights such as David French and George Walker in Canada, and the "New Wave" playwrights such as Louis Nowra, David Williamson and Jack Hibberd in Australia. The maturation of drama is concomitant in both countries with the development of a multicultural fabric, which this new body of plays records in its multiple facets. Australian and Canadian drama offer ideal vantage points from which to observe the two countries' struggle to accommodate the pluralism of difference. As the critics in this collection cogently argue, the articulation of otherness forms a central concern in the drama of the two countries. Although this volume does not contain essays on French-Canadian drama—which it was felt would deserve a volume on its own—, it is safe to conjecture that many of the issues characterising multicultural English-Canadian drama also typify Quebec and Acadian drama. In this respect, this collection of essays constitutes a sequel to my previous anthology, *Staging Difference: Cultural Pluralism in American Theatre and Drama*,[2] which gathered essays on multiculturalism in twentieth-century U.S. drama. While American dramatists view the problematics of cultural pluralism within the enduring myth of the American Dream (or possibly nightmare, in the case of First Nations or ethnic minorities), Australian and Canadian postcolonial playwrights regard marginality as a site where it is possible to express a resistance against the legacy of Empire, often through the weapon of what Homi Bhabha has termed subversive mimicry. Viewed from this perspective, Australian and Canadian plays deserve as much recognition as their maturer American or English counterparts.

 The title of this collection suggests a spatial metaphor: contributors offer new readings of the shifting positionings of the "other" in Australian and Canadian theatre arts. The re-visions of the concept of marginality contained here view it as an evolving site of contestation. This volume articulates a new form of comparative poetics, one that seeks to identify divergences from rather than resemblances with the traditional Western canon. It pre-supposes a de-centering of the time-honoured Euro-centric approach. Moreover, Australian and Canadian dramatic texts are used as reflecting mirrors, which give us privileged tools to explore the similarity and otherness that the two countries share. Such a cross-cultural method of investigation is currently widely used in postcolonial studies, following in the wake of Brydon's and Tiffin's study quoted above, to shed light on both the diversity and unity of the

---

[2]   Marc Maufort, ed., *Staging Difference. Cultural Pluralism in American Theatre and Drama* (New York: Peter Lang, 1995).

Introduction

postcolonial experience. The essayists of this anthology have thereby heeded Arun Mukherjee's condemnation of the erasure of "differences between and within diverse post-colonial societies ..." Like Mukherjee, they reject the tendency to homogenise postcolonial literatures through an "assumption of endless substitutability and comparatibility of post-colonial texts."[3] Likewise, they resist the temptation of the touristic gaze, i.e. the tendency to re-appropriate marginality, to re-inscribe colonialism, through facile and spurious celebrations of the colourful diversity of ethnic minorities within the mainstream. On the contrary, they engage the complexity inherent in each marginal form of culture, without masking inner contradictions and conflicts. In other words, they stress the liminality of the post-colonial experience in their delineation of comparable patterns in the dramatic representations of Canada and Australia. Their deconstructing glance at marginality points to the impossibility of actually "placing" the other once and for all, thereby challenging established notions of marginality.

The structure of this collection completes the title's spatial metaphor with a musical-like sequence, which likewise underscores an alternation between similarity and difference. The book opens with my own essay on First Nations drama in Australia and Canada, in an attempt to show the bond between dramatic inscriptions of aboriginality in the two countries. What follows is a sequence of essays devoted solely to Australian drama. Taken together, these essays show the strong interrelation between different types of "marginality," i.e. that of gender, class, ethnicity and aboriginality. In a spirit of experimentation echoing the playwrights' own sense of innovation, the traditional link between centre and margin is reversed and thereby perverted through the sequence in which these essays are arranged: they move from the margins to the centre. While Helen Thomson's, Helena Grehan's and Maryrose Casey's essays deal with aboriginality—sometimes intertwined with feminist issues—, Jacqueline Lo examines stereotypical representations of Asianness in recent Australian drama. Susan Pfisterer and Bruce Parr further explore the theme of marginality in the realm of gender studies (feminism and gay studies). Other forms of marginality are explored by Tom Burvill's, Peta Tait's and Paul Makeham's articles, in their discussions of alternative modes of theatrical representation, which also betray class and gender concerns. Finally, Peter Fitzpatrick's article shows how reminiscences of marginality subsist in mainstream drama. Gerry Turcotte's essay, which focuses on the issue of theatrical collaboration in Australian and Canadian aboriginal drama, serves both

---

[3] Arun Mukherjee, "Whose Post-Colonialism and Whose Postmodernism?", *World Literature Written in English* 30.2 (1990): 7.

as a structuring device echoing the initial essay of the collection and as a turning point, meant to introduce the Canadian section of the anthology. Its theme, "collaboration," illustrates the comparative perspective in which Australian and Canadian plays are studied. While Anne Nothof's essay gives an overview of marginality in multicultural Canadian drama, the subsequent contributions move, like their Australian counterparts, from the margins to the centre in their attempts to pinpoint the link between gender, class, ethnicity and aboriginality. Albert Glaap's, Robert Appleford's, and Ric Knowles' essays examine aboriginal drama; Ann Wilson's and Alan Filewod's contributions deal with African Canadian drama, while Robert Wallace and Robert Nunn focus on gender issues in the drama of John Herbert and Judith Thompson. Finally, echoing Fitzpatrick's contribution, Reid Gilbert analyses marginality in the mainstream drama of George Walker. To recapitulate, Joanne Tompkins' essay concentrates on the issue of family and the crisis of identity common to both the Australian and Canadian playwrights discussed in this anthology. Her essay performs the same structuring role as Gerry Turcotte's and my own: like a leitmotif, it reaffirms the proximity of the Australian and Canadian dramatic renditions of otherness, which lends the book its coda. Maryrose Casey's interview with John Harding, in the appendix, may be regarded as an encore which gives the last word not to the critics but to the playwrights themselves. If, then, this collection emphasises the postcolonial kinship between Australia and Canada, the uniqueness of their respective experiences is also underlined: Ann Wilson's and Alan Filewod's contributions on African Canadian drama contrast sharply, in that respect, with Tom Burvill's, Peta Tait's and Paul Makeham's emphasis on the importance of alternative modes of theatrical production in Australia.

Like its subject-matter, this book resists containment and closure. It does not pretend to offer a definitive re-assessment of marginality in Australian and Canadian drama. Rather, it seeks to open up a new literary debate around the issue of otherness. The many contributions assembled here show how these contemporary, "marginal," playwrights, in their challenges to cultural hegemony, transgress the boundaries of traditional realism and performance, which they refashion through the uniqueness of their outsider status. To paraphrase the title of Fitzpatrick's essay, their dramaturgy forges the new language of the "infidel" in a Bakhtinian, indeed carnivalesque, re-visioning of Western artistic conventions.

Works Cited

Brydon, Diana and Helen Tiffin. *Decolonizing Fictions* (Sydney: Dangaroo Press, 1993).

Maufort, Marc, ed., *Staging Difference. Cultural Pluralism in American Theatre and Drama* (New York: Peter Lang, 1995).

Mukherjee, Arun. "Whose Post-Colonialism and Whose Postmodernism?," *World Literature Written in English* 30.2 (1990): 1-9.

Forging an "Aboriginal Realism": First Nations Playwriting in Australia and Canada

MARC MAUFORT

Université Libre de Bruxelles

The 1970s and 1980s have witnessed the simultaneous emergence of Aboriginal drama in Australia and Canada. Native playwrights have not failed to elicit the attention and praise of critics in both postcolonial countries: in Canada, Daniel David Moses, Drew Hayden Taylor and Tomson Highway are considered accomplished artists; in Australia, Jack Davis, Richard Walley, Bob Maza and Eva Johnson have had their plays published and even anthologised.[1] Their pioneering efforts have resulted in an international recognition of the place of aboriginal drama in the postcolonial literary canon. In the 1990s, more recent native playwrights, such as Ian Ross and Jane Harrison in Canada and Australia respectively, have consolidated the work of these founding fathers. This essay proposes to re-examine the plays of the first generation of aboriginal dramatists in Canada and Australia from a cross-cultural perspective, rejecting conventional national boundaries to emphasise the playwrights' comparable attempts at reinventing literary models inherited from Europe and Britain, the former centre of the Empire. Their works can be regarded as illustrations of the post-colonial desire to cross and reposition the boundaries of traditional Euro-American dramatic realism. Their search for new forms of expression reinforces the links between their geographically distant communities. Through their innovative aesthetics, akin to Mudrooroo Narogin's concept of "aboriginal realism," these dramatists unmistakably share an intellectual common-

---

[1] See Helen Gilbert, *Sightlines. Race, Gender, and Nation in Contemporary Australian Theatre* (Ann Arbor: The U of Michigan P, 1998); Helen Gilbert & Joanne Tompkins, *Post-colonial Drama. Theory, Practice, Politics* (London & New York: Routledge, 1996); Sheila Rabillard, "Absorption, Elimination, and the Hybrid: Some Impure Questions of Gender and Culture in the Trickster Drama of Tomson Highway," *Essays in Theatre* 12.i (November 1993): 3-27.

wealth.² This chapter, while meant as an overview of the generic elements of confluence between two divergent dramatic traditions, especially in their respective representation of otherness, does not liken the Canadian and Australian aboriginal experiences, which differ through sometimes radically antithetical national political and social contexts. This essay seeks to pave the way for further detailed comparative textual studies of the plays of some of the foremost Aboriginal dramatists in Australia and Canada.

I

Aboriginal drama articulates a world vision differing significantly from that of the European literary canon. First and foremost, both Canadian and Australian aboriginal playwrights wish to offer a new perspective on their forgotten history, thus undermining the biased vision of white settlers. These playwrights underscore the contradictions and discontinuities inherent in the colonial discourse. In some moving dramatic moments, they show the horror contingent on the process of colonisation, a process which deprived aboriginals of their identity and land rights. Needless to say, their historical slant also gives these plays a satirical and political bite. They can therefore be regarded as an indictment of the abuses of colonial power. Instances of this thematic thrust abound: Tomson Highway's plays are conceived as part of a cycle—yet to be written—describing Indian life on a Canadian reservation with its concomitant social problems (drinking, drugs etc.)—a situation which manifestly takes its roots in the colonial past; Daniel David Moses' *Almighty Voice and His Wife* dramatises the fate of a nineteenth century Indian chief unable to resist white invasion—the image of the Indigene that emerges from this play being that of a suffering human being rather than that of a stereotype; Shirley Cheechoo's play *Path with No Moccassins*, focusing on the childhood of a female Aborigine, retraces the hardships which Indians had to endure in Canada in the 1950s; Drew Hayden Taylor's *Someday* poignantly recounts the cruelties of the Canadian assimilation policy in the 1950s and 1960s. This inhuman policy resulted in the separation of thousands of native mothers from their children, who were adopted by white foster parents. Taylor subtly shows how such children will forever remain estranged from their roots. One cannot avoid speaking of the future when evoking the past, and this is precisely what Taylor does in his award-winning play *Toronto at*

---

² Quoted in Christopher Balme, "Reading the Signs. A Semiotic Perspective on Aboriginal Theatre," in *Aratjara. Aboriginal Culture and Literature in Australia*, eds. Dieter Riemenschneider & Geoffrey V. Davis (Amsterdam: Rodopi, 1997): 149-64. See in particular p. 153.

Dreamer's Rock. In this work, three Indian boys—from the past, the present and the future—meet at an ancient Indian sacred place, Dreamer's Rock. Eventually, the boy from the present recognises the necessity for Indians to return to their traditional roots, to be proud of their legacy, if they wish to inherit a bright future at all.

In Australia, the contradictions inherent in the white discourse of colonisation, which seeks to erase the sufferings of the conquered First Nations, is perhaps most evident in the plays of Jack Davis. *Kullark* retraces the history of Aborigines in Australia from the beginnings of the colonial enterprise to recent developments in the twentieth century. Davis focuses primarily on the heroic figures of Aborigines who resisted white colonisation, namely Chief Yagan. Further, he dramatises the various stages of discrimination which the political regimes of the Federation enforced, shedding light successively on the resettlement laws of the early twentieth century, which deprived Aborigines of their homes, and on the child adoption policy, which separated numerous black children from their native families. This, then, stresses the similarity of the social background in Canada and Australia, as exemplified in Drew Taylor's *Someday*. Jack Davis's subsequent plays—*The Dreamers*, *Barungin*, and *No Sugar*—deal with the life of Aborigines after they have been displaced in an urban environment. These plays focus on the fate of the Wallitch family up to the present day and, as such, echo the motifs embedded in Tomson Highway's *The Rez Sisters* and *Dry Lips*. Like the Indians of Highway, Davis's characters express nostalgia for a happier Aboriginal past. The playwright's attack against white settlement in Australia is perhaps best summarised in Robert's public lecture in the concluding part of *Barungin*. In this long speech, Robert offers a subversive vision of the history of white settlement and its implications for the black population. He does not hesitate to compare the extermination of Blacks with Auschwitz: "... For you Rottnest is a holiday resort ... For us ... it is what Auschwitz must be for the Jews ... Those who died defending this country in the first war against the invaders died without recognition ... and ... without memorial ..."[3] Similarly, Bob Maza's *The Keepers* concentrates on the relationship between settlers and Indigenes in the nineteenth century, showing how difficult it is to reconcile their cultural differences. Maza powerfully expresses the loss of identity that the Aborigines experience in the colonisation process, particularly in the confiscation of their land rights. Eva Johnson's short but striking play *Murras* also shows how white settlers have "raped" black culture, focusing as she does on the medical tests that were per-

---

[3] Jack Davis, *Barungin* (Sydney: Currency Press, 1989): 55. Subsequent quotations will be noted parenthetically in the text.

formed on black children without the consent of their parents; these experiments caused their sterility. Here, the loss of identity is equated with a lack of fertility. The symbol of rape recurs even more literally in *No Sugar*, in which Mary tells us how some girls were abused by white overseers on the Moore River settlement: "Some of them *guddeeahs* real bad. My friend went last Christmas and then she came back *boodjarri*. She reckons the boss' sons used to belt her up and, you know, force her. Then they kicked her out. And when she had that baby them trackers choked it dead and buried it in the pine plantation."[4] The rape metaphor constitutes one of the most powerful artistic devices enabling Aboriginal playwrights to counter dominant white historical discourses. A sense of parody further derives from this form of challenge: in *No Sugar*, the Aborigines offer only a perversion of the traditional "There is a Happy Land" song. In their version, the Saviour King remains conspicuously absent: "There is a happy land, Far, far away, No sugar in our tea, Bread and Butter we never see. That's why we're gradually Fading away"(98). In short, the course of history has proved devastating for Aboriginals in Canada and Australia. The dramas of Native playwrights seek to document facets of that disaster.

Further, Aboriginal drama asserts a cyclical vision of human history opposed to the linear European one. While European settlers envision history as inevitably leading to "progress," Aboriginals view history as a cyclical return to their mythical roots, in the guise of the Australian Dreamtime or the Canadian Nanabush. The plays considered in this essay never completely resolve the conflict between these two conceptions of history.

II

Inevitably linked with this problematised rendition of history is the native crisis of identity. Even though Canadian and Australian native characters display a strong sense of confidence in the possibilities of life, they nevertheless suffer from a displaced perception of selfhood. They feel crushed between their spiritual heritage and the influence of Western materialism; hence their hybridity. The central characters of Daniel David Moses' *Big Buck City*, for instance, have decided to adopt Western bourgeois values. However, they can never be fully assimilated, and they have completely lost touch with Nature in their new urban environment. Evidence of this is Mrs. Buck's inability to procreate. A similar hesitation between native ethics and the materialistic values of

---

[4] Jack Davis, *No Sugar* (Sydney: Currency Press, 1986): 66. Subsequent quotations will be noted parenthetically in the text.

the West plagues the characters of Tomson Highway's plays; likewise, the displaced Nyoongah characters of Jack Davis's *The Dreamers* long for a return to an idealised Aboriginal setting, connected with the cosmos and Nature, far from the urban imperial rule. The sense of hybrid identity is reinforced when one deals with half-caste characters, who feel it impossible to identify either with the values of their Aboriginal ancestry or with those of the white world. They are not considered as white by European settlers, nor as blacks by Aborigines. Koolbardi, in Richard Walleye's *Coordah*, perfectly illustrates this theme. In Scene IV, Koolbardi is attacked by one of his fellow Aborigines because he adopts white patterns of behaviour, especially in matters of religion: "When you see my people worship the spirits at our sacred places you say it no good. No good to worship the trees and the rocks."[5] A similar motif recurs in Maza's *The Keepers*, as Danny feels only the "black shadow" of his white friend Michael: "You all had me believing that white was right ... the white way is the right way. It's alright if you are white ... like Michael ... my white brother Michael ... confident ... successful ... and author. And what am I? Eh? I'll tell you what I am ... his little black shadow ..."[6] Aboriginal characters can only see themselves through the eyes of their white colonisers.

Canadian and Australian Aboriginal playwrights reject European representations of Native characters. Daniel David Moses deconstructs stereotypes of Natives prevalent in popular Indian medicine shows; in his play *The Indian Medecine Shows*, he dramatises how helpless and suffering a human creature the Indian mowhawk can be. He proposes an alternative image that in no way corresponds to Hollywood or white middle-class representations of the Native Other. In *Princess Pocahontas and the Blue Spots*, Monique Mojica similarly undermines false Hollywood embodiments of the Indian female. In plays by Davis, Walley, Maza and Johnson, the Australian black character is also invested with a psychological depth untypical of white stereotypical misconceptions. Jimmy Chi's musical play *Bran Nue Dae* can even be read as a statement about the multi-faceted and fluid nature of Aboriginal identity. The white characters of this drama, Slippery and Annie, eventually discover that they too have Aboriginal blood: the difference between white and black characters no longer boils down to a matter of

---

[5] Walley, Richard, *Coordah*, in *Plays from Black Australia* (Sydney: Currency Press, 1989): 109-66. This quote is from p. 158. Subsequent quotations will be noted parenthetically in the text.

[6] Bob Maza, *The Keepers*, in *Plays from Black Australia* (Sydney: Currency Press, 1989): 167-229. This quote is from pp. 215-16. Subsequent quotations will be noted parenthetically in the text.

race but rather to a matter of culture.[7] The play celebrates the diversity of Aboriginal identity and culture, as the chorus declares "We are all born black" or as Slippery somewhat extravagantly exclaims: "Ich bin Eine Aborigine!!"[8] In Australian and Canadian Aboriginal drama, the concept of identity becomes a shifting site of contestation and constant renegotiation: not only are stereotypes challenged from the inside, the very binary black/white is superseded by a celebration of "inbetweenness." Thus, siting the Other becomes a problematic enterprise.

III

If, in most of the plays concerned here, the Aboriginal doubt of identity reflects a profound social fracture, more deeply philosophical allusions to the link between the divinity/cosmos and man, i.e. the Natives, also abound. Aborigines often perceive Christian religion as the prime source of their torments, conspiring as it does with the Imperial eradication of black culture. In Tomson Highway's *Dry Lips*, a young female character is raped and stabbed with the crucifix; in Richard Walley's *Coordah*, Brother Davis is depicted as a representative not only of religion but also of white imperial power; however, he seems to understand what whites have done to blacks. He recognises that his people have erased the Native spirit: "They tell me we poisoned your brain. I think we may have removed it" (158). Maza's *The Keepers* proves more ambiguous in its condemnation of Christian religion: it depicts Reverend James Campbell as an honest man who does not hesitate to sacrifice himself for the survival of the Native chief Koonawar. However, Maza makes it clear at the end of the play that this noble gesture did not mean that Campbell really understood black culture. The connection between Christian missions and Imperialism is explicit in Davis's *No Sugar*: this play dramatises the appalling living conditions in which the Aborigines of South Western Australia were left on the infamous Moore River settlement as a consequence of the Australian official Protection policy of Aborigines in the first half of the twentieth century. This is particularly noticeable when Sister Eileen almost forces the natives to admire the wonders of the story of Jesus together with the benefits of British colonisation: "SISTER: It's a hymn I'm sure you all know, and want you to sing in your very best voice, because it is the hymn we'll be singing for Mr Neville in the Australia Day celebrations ... There is a

---

[7] Paul Makeham, "Singing the Landscape: *Bran Nue Dae*," *Australasian Drama Studies* 28 (April 1996): 117-32. See in particular p. 130.

[8] Jimmy Chi & Kuckles, *Bran Nue Dae* (Sydney: Currency Press, 1991): 70-71. Subsequent quotations will be noted parenthetically in the text.

First Nations Playwriting

happy land, Far, far away, Where saints in glory stand ..." (91). In a subsequent scene, Sister Eileen expects the Aborigines to intone the same hymn on the occasion of Australia Day. Her rhetoric ironically contrasts with the scenes depicting the plight of Aborigines:

> It gives me great pleasure to be with you all on this very special day, when we gather together to pledge our allegiance to the king and to celebrate the birth of this wonderful young country that we are so fortunate to be living in. We must remember today not just our country and King, but the King of kings, the Prince of princes, and to give thanks to God for what He has provided for us because our sustenance in life is provided by Him (97).

However, the hymn that the Aborigines start to sing resorts to parody to convey their sense of revolt: "There is a happy land, Far, far away. No sugar in our tea, Bread and butter we never see" (98). The contrast between the idealised view of the hymn and the actual predicament of the natives enacts Davis's biting ironical stance towards the power of the coloniser. Likewise, the opening scene of *Barungin* shows how ludicrous a Christian sermon, invoking the goodness of the Lord on the occasion of a black man's death, may appear for those who, like Aborigines, live in a kind of hell on earth. It is interesting to note how the preacher is interrupted by the muttering and angry aboriginal crowd: "PREACHER: There is no other way to be saved from death but only God's way. SHANE: For Christ's sake, put the man in his grave. PREACHER: And with these few words—SHANE: 'Few words'! ... That was a fuckin' marathon ..."(6). In Jimmy Chi's *Bran Nue Dae*, Father Benedictus is satirised as the German missionary who has deprived Aborigines of their identity and has even shamelessly abused them. While Benedictus delivers sermons on sexual restraint to the young Aborigine Willie, it eventually becomes ironically clear that he is the father of an illegitimate son, Slippery (83).

Native plays posit a radically un-Christian world vision, that of the myths and legends of the Aboriginal world. While Christian religion separates the individual from Nature, the Aboriginal world view presupposes a fundamental link between man, the Creator and the earth, i.e. Nature. The Nanabush present in Highway's *The Rez Sisters* and *Dry Lips Oughta Move to Kapuskasing* is very different from the Christian God, in that it can change its shape: it can easily become an animal. Further, it conflates the comic and the tragic spirit. Indeed, it is also dubbed as a Trickster. This readily indicates the fluidity of the Native cosmology, as compared to the European one. Highway describes the Nanabush in his introduction to the plays in terms that bespeak this lack of fixity:

> The dream world of North American Indian mythology is inhabited by the most fantastic creatures, beings, and events. Foremost among these beings is the "Trickster," as pivotal and important a figure in the Native world as Christ is in the realm of Christian mythology ... (this Trickster) can assume any guise he chooses. Essentially a comic, clownish sort of character, he teaches us about the nature and the meaning of existence on the planet Earth; he straddles the consciousness of man and that of God, the Great Spirit ... Some say that "Nanabush" left this continent when the whiteman came. We believe he is still here among us—albeit a little the worse for wear and tear—having assumed other guises. Without him—and without the spiritual health of this figure—the core of Indian culture would be gone forever.[9]

Highway's plays constitute a plea for the Indians to retrieve the spirit of the Nanabush, the only condition on which they will recapture a sense of identity. The Nanabush is not simply an abstract concept. It has a very theatrical presence in Highway's plays, in which it introduces elements of the supernatural.

Similarly, Aboriginal Australian plays oppose the world of the Dreaming to the Christian world vision. The Dreaming represents the mythical era in which man, animals and the cosmos were one and in which everything was created. Nostalgia for the primaeval unity of the Dreaming is expressed in such plays as Walley's *Coordah*, where allusions to the spirit of the earth typify Jillawara's attack against Koolbardi:

> We say we one with the earth—she my mother. You don't believe that. But you say 'Ashes to Ashes, dust to dust,' same thing. When you see my people worship the spirits at our sacred places you say it no good. No good to worship the trees and the rocks. Yet you cut the trees down and make a building, shape the rocks to make altar, then you worship your spirits (158).

As in Tomson Highway's plays, allusions to the Dreaming time, to the time of legends, are made tangible in theatrical terms, through the presence of a native dancer in the background of Davis's *The Dreamers* and *Barungin*, or in Eva Johnson's *Murras*. In neither case does the presence of the dancer appear realistically motivated, which introduces a fantastic element into the texture of the play.

Exile, dispossession, homelessness, ill-defined identity constitute the dramaturgical expressions of the First Nations predicament. Most interestingly, Australian and Canadian Aboriginal playwrights have sought to develop an innovative form to give shape to their highly original cosmology.

---

[9] Tomson Highway, *The Rez Sisters* (Saskatoon: Fifth House, 1988): p. XII. Subsequent quotations will be noted parenthetically in the text.

IV

Aboriginal culture was undoubtedly influenced by European art, despite the coloniser/colonised antagonism. This is manifest in the hybridity characterising almost all the plays discussed here, particularly as regards language and tonality. The playwrights dealt with use English as their means of communication. It is of course not the language of their ancestors; on the contrary, English bespeaks the imperial power that has crushed their sense of nation and selfhood. Typically, therefore, their plays include whole passages in their native language (for which translations are not always provided). This enables the playwright to express cultural difference: the native tongue is perceived as less rigid and fixed than the language of the invader. Once again, examples of this hybrid technique abound: it can be observed in the two plays that Tomson Highway has published so far, as well as in Drew Taylor's *Toronto at Dreamer's Rock* and Daniel David Moses' *Almighty Voice and His Wife*. Jack Davis resorts to it abundantly in *The Dreamers, No Sugar* and *Barungin*, and so do Walley, Maza and Johnson.

The tonality of Aboriginal plays is equally hybrid: it would be difficult to classify them according to the rigid Western standards of comedy, tragedy, melodrama or farce. Can we speak of tragedies? The classical European rules hardly apply in this case, although we are clearly dealing with a depiction of the intense sufferings of courageous human beings. This lends these plays a tragic mood, although they cannot be labelled tragedies in the Aristotelian sense of the word. Likewise, most of the plays incorporate comic passages, testifying to the positive world vision which Natives have preserved in spite of their oppression. Nevertheless, it would be simplistic to consider these dramas as comedies since they simultaneously deal with tragic themes. A typical example of this hybrid blend of moods characterises the plays of Highway, which combine farcical passages with deeply tragic scenes, expressing the Natives' loss of identity; Daniel David Moses' *Big Buck City* also fuses comic elements with deeper probings into the nature of reality, the rejection of Western materialism and the crisis of identity among urban Indians. Likewise, Jack Davis juxtaposes comic and near-tragic passages in *The Dreamers*, and so does Richard Walley in *Coordah*. This sense of comedy is due to Davis and Walley's characterisation skills: both have developed in these plays strong and exceptional characters, Worru and Nummy.

Hybridity also offers a key to an understanding of the new form/genre evolved by Native dramatists. Aboriginal playwrights borrow the basic realistic form so prevalent in mainstream Australian and Canadian drama and then proceed to modify it with the help of various techniques.

The result is a hybrid form, one that combines elements drawn from Euro-American realism with elements derived from an Aboriginal world vision. This new, extended realism suggests that most of the dramas analysed in this essay cannot be regarded as well-made plays. Aboriginal playwrights have abandoned the linear pattern of the ultra-realistic play. One of the most common characteristics of these Australian and Canadian plays is their fragmentation: most are constructed as a series of short scenes which do not culminate in a well-defined climax or a resolution of conflict. A few Canadian and Australian plays even offer a radical parody of conventional Western dramatic forms: in that respect, Mojica's *Princess Pocahontas and the Blue Spots* and Moses' *Almighty Voice and His Wife* are particularly relevant. In the former, the central character undergoes a number of unrealistic transformations, staged through a series of short, apparently unrelated scenes. This naturally eliminates the conventions of mimesis, as the plot does not move to a neat climax. In *Almighty Voice*, Almighty and his wife transform themselves into actors in the second part of the play, speaking directly to the audience; they announce the various parts that they are impersonating, which introduces some distancing between the characters and the public; the various roles that they perform debunk Western stereotypical prejudices. Thus, the second act of Moses' play can be seen as a parody of the realistic tradition of Western drama, although its first act, which recounts the death of an Almighty pursued by white settlers, is written in that very traditional vein. This sense of parody, while reinforcing the notion of extended realism and hybridity mentioned above, shows a willingness to challenge the rationalism inherent in the Western perception of the world. Moses' use of European metatheatre serves his wish to dramatise a thoroughly Native vision of the universe. Similarly, Jimmy Chi's *Bran Nue Dae* relies heavily on the use of a form of parody closely related to Moses' metatheatrical experiments. As the critic Paul Makeham has indicated, Chi's musical can be regarded as a takeoff of various literary and popular forms of expression: the sentimental Hollywood musical film, romantic love stories and the melodramatic convention of family discoveries. In addition, the play appropriates Western modes of expression and fuses them with typically Aboriginal ones: the Western quest motif is alluded to, but its spiritual overtones are undercut through the highly sexual background of the musical. The play combines these echoes of the quest with allusions to the Aboriginal song cycle, which, according to Makeham, is a re-enactment of "the journeys of heroic dreamtime spirits."[10] The conflation of Western and Aboriginal forms foregrounds a highly parodic and hybrid tone. But it is

---

[10] Makeham, *op.cit.*: 120-21.

precisely through this subversion of Western conventions that renewal is achieved: the Aboriginal cast ascends to heaven by the end of the play (89). As Homi K. Bhabha suggests in *The Location of Culture*, the colonised subject/artist resorts to hybridity/mimicry to unsettle the artistic domination of the Western canon. The colonised artist's use of mimicry is clearly subversive: rather than signalling a form of cultural cringe, it creates a "third hybrid space" which de-stabilises rigid aesthetic Western categories. It projects a desire for a "reformed, recognizable Other, as a subject of difference that is almost the same, but not quite ... mimicry emerges as the representation of a difference that is itself a process of disavowal."[11] Bhabha further comments: "Under cover of camouflage, mimicry, like the fetish, is a part-object that radically revalues the normative knowledges of the priority of race, writing, history. For the fetish mimes the forms of authority at the point at which it deauthorizes them. Similarly, mimicry rearticulates presence in terms of its 'Otherness,' that which it disavows."[12] Further, Mikhail Bakhtin's concept of dialogism indirectly sheds light on the notion of hybridity. Indeed, Bakhtin refers to a "mixture of two social languages within the limits of a single utterance, an encounter, within the arena of an utterance, between two different linguistic consciousnesses, separated from one another by an epoch, by social differentiation or by some other factor."[13] Bakhtin's dialogism reflects the conflictual relationship between colonised/coloniser manifest in Aboriginal drama. These notions of hybridity/mimicry can be extended to matters of referentiality.

The most important innovative formal feature of these plays undoubtedly resides in their use of the fantastic and/or the mythical, which blurs the frontier between the real and the supernatural in an effort to contest the premises of Western materialism and modes of perception. The phrase "magic realism" could be used to describe sporadic disruptions of traditional realism in native drama. The recent theoretical work of the European critic Jeanne Delbaere sheds considerable light on the all too often elusive notion of magic realism. Magic realism, Delbaere argues, is often used by postcolonial or minority writers—marginalised artists as it were—to express a reaction against the centre, against hegemonic society. Magic realism thus reinforces the postmodern concept of the "ex-centric." It serves to designate a "fracture in the real," a sense of crisis. In what Delbaere terms "psychic realism," a variant on magic realism, the "magic" is "almost always a reification of the hero's

---

[11] Homi K. Bhabha, *The Location of Culture* (London: Routledge, 1996): 86.
[12] *Ibid*.: 91.
[13] M.M. Bakhtin, *The Dialogic Imagination. Four Essays*, eds. and trans. Caryl Emerson & Michael Holquist (Austin: U of Texas P, 1981): 358.

inner conflict."[14] This form of magic realism records the character's fissured vision of the real. Delbaere's second subcategory defines a form of "grotesque realism," which tends to even further distort and amplify reality. Delbaere suggests that "grotesque realism" be used "for any sort of hyperbolic distortion that creates a sense of strangeness through the confusion or interpenetration of different realms like animate/inanimate or human/animal."[15] A third sub-category, which Delbaere terms "mythic realism," emanates from the supernatural features of the environment itself rather than from the character's psyche.[16] Magic realism, whose role consists in showing the "interface between realms," offers an appropriate label for a number of the plays analysed in this essay. Tomson Highway's works reflect Delbaere's three sub-categories. Indeed, the figure of the Nanabush is not only an expression of the characters' inner turmoil but also a hybrid, grotesque creature, which evokes the mythical background of Native culture. For reasons of space limitations, this essay deals with only one representative Canadian play, Highway's *The Rez Sisters*, although references to the Nanabush also characterise the plays of Daniel David Moses. Drew Taylor's *Toronto at Dreamer's Rock*, by positing the possibility for the past, the present and the future to be experienced simultaneously, likewise considerably extends the boundaries of Western realism. In *The Rez Sisters*, the Nanabush, defined above as a God-figure from Native mythology, embodies a male spirit, which nags at the women in quest of freedom. The Nanabush is at once a Seagull (and thus appears in white), the Nighthawk (in dark feathers), and the Bingo Master. The capacity of the Nanabush to reconcile various incompatible elements truly points to its magic realist nature: white or dark, animal or human, a mythical creature or a symbol of degraded Western materialism. This clearly exhibits what Delbaere calls "grotesque" realism, especially in the interpenetration of animal and human features. Elements of psychic realism emerge in the characters' relationship with and reaction to the values represented by the Nanabush. Zaboonighan communicates with the bird/Nanabush, when she confesses how she was raped as a child. The Nanabush, upon hearing this, goes through "agonizing contortions" (47-48). Symbolically, it seems that the Spirit vicariously experiences Zaboonighan's painful emotions. In a technique typical of "psychic realism,"

---

[14] Jeanne Delbaere, "Psychic Realism, Mythic Realism, Grotesque Realism: Variations on Magic Realism in Contemporary Literature in English," in *Magical Realism. Theory, History, Community*, eds. Lois Parkinson and Wendy B. Faris (Durham & London: Duke UP, 1995): 249-63. See in particular p. 251.

[15] *Ibid.*: 256.

[16] *Ibid.*: 252-53.

Zaboonighan's nightmares are projected onto the Nanabush. The final ritual scene evokes the third category of magic realism, i.e. "mythic realism." This theatrical moment suggests a return to cultural roots, a fusion of the character with the Nanabush. At the outset of the scene, the Nanabush becomes the Bingo Master. Marie-Adèle, who suffers from an incurable form of cancer, eventually merges with the Nanabush. She is the only character able to achieve this reunification in this play, a fusion that ironically can only take place in death. The Nanabush leads Marie-Adèle to the other world:

> And out of this chaos emerges the calm, silent image of Marie-Adèle waltzing romantically in the arms of the Bingo Master. The Bingo Master says "bingo" into her ear. And the Bingo Master changes, with sudden bird-like movements, into the nighthawk, Nanabush in dark feathers. Marie-Adèle meets Nanabush (103).

The Nanabush symbolises, in a male disguise, the messenger who connects the netherworld with everyday reality, thus evoking "mythic realism."

In the Australian plays which I have selected, the world of magic realism, in which opposites are blurred, assumes a prominent role. It is suggested by songs and spoken allusions in Jack Davis's *The Dreamers*, whose very title refers the Aboriginal myth of the Dreaming. In the opening scene, Worru sings: "Now we who were there who were young, are now old and live in suburbia, and my longing is an echo a re-occurring dream, coming back along the track from where the campfires used to gleam."[17] References to unkind spirits also abound in the narrative: "They come from that way. They was real bad. Round face, an' they was white, jus' like Wetjalas, an' they 'ad red eyes, an' red 'air, an' them scream, an' shout, sing out in the night time, in the pine plantation, jus' like *koolongahs*" (94). Similarly, in *Barungin*, Granny Doll alludes to a legend dating from the Dreamtime: "Well, this koolbardi—that's the magpie—and this wahrdung—that's the crow—they was brothers, see. This was the time of kundum, dreams, see, and they was biiig strong men, and they both had beautiful whiiite feathers"(34). Further, Granny Doll explains the meaning of "barungin" in the hunting days of the Dreamtime: "It means 'to smell the wind,' coz that wind used to talk to him and tell him where the kangaroo and the emus and the ducks were, and the rain and when people were around he learned about barungin from the old people from a long time back" (45). In addition, in Jack Davis's *The Dreamers* and Eva Johnson's *Murras*, "mythic

---

[17] Jack Davis, *Kullark & The Dreamers* (Sydney: Currency Press, 1982): 73. Subsequent references will be noted parenthetically in the text.

realism" yields some psychological resonances. In *The Dreamers* and *Murras*, the constant background presence of a native dancer introduces an element of ritual. It resembles the role of the Nanabush in Highway's works as a remote commentator on the action of the play and constitutes a reminder of the mythic underpinnings of the native community. Thus in *Murras*: "The MIMI SPIRIT sits in a coiled position before the Great Rainbow Serpent motif. The didjeridu begins to play and the MIMI SPIRIT wakes and slides across the stage, awakening the earth spirits. This is the birth dance of the Aboriginal Dreaming."[18] In addition to its mythic dimension, the dancer underscores the characters' psychological throes, caused either by their homelessness and sense of spiritual decay in *The Dreamers* or by their dispossession in *Murras*. In *The Dreamers*, the dancer represents a projection of Worru's mind, as he actually throws the spear that Worru can only dream of throwing: "Didjeridoo crashes in, the lights change. The DANCER appears at front of stage and in stylised rhythmic steps searches for a straight stick, finds it, straightens it, pares and tips it before sprinting up the ramp onto the escarpment and striking the mirrolgah stance against a dramatic sunset as the music climaxes and cuts"(99). The nostalgia for a happy Aboriginal past is embodied in the magical presence of the dancer, which introduces a spiritual dimension into the materialistic world of the colonisers. The dancer also conjures up elements of "grotesque realism," in its conflation of incompatible elements, such as the realistic action of the play and its magical, fantastic framework. In a typically grotesque transformation in *The Dreamers*, the dancer becomes the Featherfoot spirit of death to which Worru has just alluded: "Shafts of cold light fade in revealing the dancer as featherfoot at the front of the stage. He is heavily decorated with leaves and carries two short sticks. He dances slowly across the stage ..."(130). Significantly, in *The Dreamers* and *Murras*, the dancers who both open and close the play symbolise permanence. In a scene reminiscent of Highway's *The Rez Sisters*, Uncle Worru is finally reunited with his Dreaming as the play draws to a close. Like Marie-Adèle who waltzes away with the Nanabush, he merges with the world of his ancestors through his death, which is perceived as spiritual rebirth. Dolly concludes the play with a lyrical song expressing her sorrow at her Uncle's demise: "Stark and white the hospital ward/In the morning sunlight gleaming,/But you are back in the *moodgah* (West Australian Christmas tree) now/Back on the path of your Dreaming./... (Worru) told me the tales of Nyoongah deeds/When the world first woke from dreaming ... I will let you dream—dream on old friend/Of a child

---

[18] Eva Johnson, *Murras*, in *Plays from Black Australia* (Sydney: Currency Press, 1989): 79-107. This quote is from p. 85.

and a man in September,/Of hills and stars and the river's bend;/Alas, that is all to remember"(138-39). While Dolly voices her joy at Worru's encounter with his Dreaming, she simultaneously bemoans the predicament of those who, like her, will have to live on in a world deprived of this mythic dimension.

Both in Canadian and Australian Native drama, the use of sporadic extended/magic realism is meant to decenter the certainties of Western realistic perception. It helps the playwright to question the validity of the Empire's power. Evidently, the very term "magic realism" is problematic. For some, it may in itself reflect a Eurocentric theoretical vision and, as such, may threaten to categorise a fluid native reality from a fixed Western perspective. Therefore, it is tempting to use the phrase suggested by Mudrooroo Narogin, "Aboriginal realism." Through this concept, Mudrooroo expresses the view that Aboriginal drama cannot be reduced to the European categories inherent in stage naturalism. The hybridity of the magic realism that I have delineated in this essay merges with Mudrooroo's definition of "aboriginal realism" as a literary mode apparently predicated on the same codes of referentiality as Euro-American dramatic realism, but which subverts them through reminders of the oppressed culture, such as the use of myth, distortion, abstraction, transformations, story-telling and special sound effects. Thus Mudrooroo: "Aboriginal realism expands European realism by taking in certain supernatural aspects, characters and situations found in Aboriginal storytelling."[19] Mudrooroo refuses to regard the symbolic effects of Aboriginal drama as mere "devices to break down the 'realist' frame, but [sees them] as integral parts pointing to the polysemic nature of Aboriginal drama."[20] I would contend that, in forging such an innovative aboriginal realism, native playwrights seek to reposition the Other and its complexities on the postcolonial stage. Their aesthetic efforts in re-siting Europe's "Others" have lent new vigour to Australia's and Canada's dramatic traditions.

Works Cited

Bakhtin, M.M. *The Dialogic Imagination. Four Essays*, eds. and trans. Caryl Emerson and Michael Holquist (Austin: U of Texas P, 1981).

Balme, Christopher. "Reading the Signs. A Semiotic Perspective on Aboriginal Theatre," in *Aratjara. Aboriginal Culture and Literature in Australia*, eds. Dieter Riemenschneider & Geoffrey V. Davis (Amsterdam: Rodopi, 1997): 149-64.

---

[19] See Balme, *op. cit.*: 153.

[20] *Ibid.*: 153.

Bhabha, Homi K. *The Location of Culture* (London: Routledge, 1994).
Cheechoo, Shirley. *Path With No Moccasins* (West Bay, Ontario: n.p., n.d).
Chi, Jimmy & Kuckles. *Bran Nue Dae* (Sydney: Currency Press, 1991).
Davis, Jack. *Barungin* (Sydney: Currency Press, 1989).
—— *Kullark* and *The Dreamers* (Sydney: Currency Press, 1982).
—— *No Sugar* (Sydney: Currency Press, 1986).
Delbaere, Jeanne. "Psychic Realism, Mythic Realism, Grotesque Realism: Variations on Magic Realism in Contemporary Literature in English," in *Magical Realism. Theory, History, Community*, eds. Lois Parkinson & Wendy B. Faris (Durham & London: Duke UP, 1995): 249-63.
Gilbert, Helen. *Sightlines. Race, Gender, and Nation in Contemporary Australian Theatre* (Ann Arbor: The U of Michigan P, 1998).
—— and Joanne Tompkins. *Post-colonial Drama. Theory, Practice, Politics* (London & New York: Routledge, 1996).
Highway, Tomson. *Dry Lips Oughta Move to Kapuskasing* (Sakatoon: Fifth House, 1989).
—— *The Rez Sisters* (Sakatoon: Fifth House, 1988).
Johnson, Eva. *Murras*. In *Plays from Black Australia* (Sydney: Currency Press, 1989): 79-107.
Makeham, Paul. "Singing the Landscape: *Bran Nue Dae*,"*Australasian Drama Studies* 28 (April 1996): 117-32.
Maza, Bob. *The Keepers,* in *Plays from Black Australia* (Sydney: Currency Press, 1989): 167-229.
Mojica, Monique. *Princess Pocahontas and the Blue Spots. Canadian Theatre Review* 64 (Fall 1990): 67-77.
Moses, Daniel David. *Almighty Voice and His Wife. Canadian Theatre Review* 68 (Fall 1991): 64-80.
—— *Big Buck City* (Toronto: Playwrights Canada Press, 1991).
—— *The Indian Medecine Shows* (Toronto: Exile Editions, 1995).
Rabillard, Sheila. "Absorption, Elimination, and the Hybrid: Some Impure Questions of Gender and Culture in the Trikster Drama of Tomson Highway," *Essays in Theatre* 12.i (November 1993): 3-27.
Taylor, Drew Hayden. *The Bootlegger Blues* (Saskatoon: Fifth House, 1991).
—— *Someday* (Saskatoon: Fifth House, 1993).
—— *Toronto at Dreamer's Rock* (Saskatoon: Fifth House, 1990).
Walley, Richard. *Coordah*. In *Plays from Black Australia* (Sydney: Currency Press, 1989): 109-66.

Aboriginal Women's Staged Autobiography

HELEN THOMSON

Monash University

> You know
> There has always been this grieving,
> grieving for our land, our families.
> our cultures that have been denied us.
> but we have been taught to cry quietly
> where only our eyes betray us with tears.
> but now, we can no longer wait;
> I am scared my heart is hardening.
> I fear I can no longer grieve
> I am so full and know my capacity for grief.
> what can I do but ... perform.
>
> these are my stories.
> these are my people's stories.
> they need to be told.[1]

"No document has a greater chance of challenging the cult of forgetfulness than a black woman's autobiography."[2] Forgetfulness in Australia is a politically charged strategy that has characterised settler history, while revisionism has been insultingly designated "black armband history." Yet, this very term throws the so-called objectivity of post-Enlightenment, humanist history into question. Black women's autobiography declares its gender and race marginality, and likewise claims the truth-value of subjectivity. When it is also publicly performed the challenge is empowered by the vital dynamics governing audience and performer relationships. Joy Hooton was writing about written black women's autobiographies when she described their effect on readers thus: "Speaking with a frankness that cuts like a knife through white ignorance, these narratives capture the imagination, compelling the

---

[1] Wesley Enoch and Deborah Mailman, *The Seven Stages of Grieving* (Brisbane: Playlab Press, 1996): 73.

[2] Joy Hooton, *Stories of Herself When Young: Autobiographies of Childhood by Australian Women* (Melbourne: Oxford UP, 1990): 313.

reader to experience with the narrator the pain, deprivation, and bewildered shame of being black, young and female."[3] The performed life narrative is even more provocative, drawing uniquely upon black as well as white cultural traditions and practices, particularly black oral narratives, emphasising the performative skills of the teller, whose presence asserts a degree of triumphant achievement regardless of the past history which she has endured.

Four young Australian Aboriginal women performers have recently created and performed autobiographical shows that signify the importance of this particular form of drama: Ningali Lawford, Deborah Cheetham, Leah Purcell and Deborah Mailman. Their life narratives constitute a powerful statement from the most marginalised of all social groups in Australia. All stories centre on cultural dispossession, especially on the most notorious of all historical "forgettings" in Australia, that of the Stolen Generations. From the time of first white settlement, Aboriginals have been stolen for various anthropological, Christian and scientific purposes, but when Assimilation was formulated as official policy, beginning in the late nineteenth century and in effect still in operation until the Whitlam government came to power in 1972,[4] generations of Aboriginal children—particularly those of mixed descent—were removed from their families and placed in State care. Their stories are only now beginning to be heard, most significantly the five hundred told in the Human Rights and Equal Opportunity Commission's *Bringing Them Home* report of 1997.

On stage, two of the most powerful retellings of the Stolen Generations stories have been *The Seven Stages of Grieving* and *Stolen*. *The Seven Stages of Grieving*—in which the poem quoted at the beginning of this essay forms the conclusion—was created by Deborah Mailman and Wesley Enoch, director of the Kooemba Jdarra theatre company in Brisbane, and performed by Deborah Mailman. *Stolen*, written by Jane Harrison, was first produced by the Ilbijerri Aboriginal and Torres Strait Islander Theatre Co-Operative.[5]

The Seven Stages of Grieving sophisticatedly meshes Elizabeth Kubler-Ross's five stages of dying—denial and isolation, anger, bargaining, depression and acceptance—with the seven phases of Aboriginal history—dreaming, invasion, genocide, protection, assimilation, self-

---

[3] *Ibid.*

[4] Graeme Davison, John Hirst, Stuart Macintyre, eds., *The Oxford Companion to Australian History* (Melbourne: Oxford UP, 1998): 40.

[5] Wesley Enoch and Deborah Mailman, *The Seven Stages of Grieving* (Brisbane: Playlab Press, 1996); Jane Harrison, *Stolen* (Sydney: Currency Press, 1998).

determination and reconciliation. The play also combines Aboriginal cultural practices with European ones. A smoking ceremony precedes the request for permission to speak the names of the dead, something proscribed in Aboriginal law; their images are projected on the back wall and their photos later entombed in a suitcase, one that must be unpacked by blacks and whites together in order to achieve "wreck, con, silly, nation." (71) The cultural effects of taking children whose potential marriage partners depend on complex "skin" relations is demonstrated in a sand picture, its carefully organised lines swept into a hopelessly mixed strand with one movement. Subtextually this refers to the risk of unknowing incest faced by children whose origins and identities have been deliberately effaced by white officialdom.

Deborah Mailman's performance gives this story, shaped by the historical and cultural processes of loss undergone by all indigenous Australians since 1788, the intimacy of autobiography. The collaborative creation of the work also blurs neat categorisation. No individual Aboriginal autobiography is free from traces of the collective experience of dispossession in all its forms. The play primarily affirms communality and the two histories shaping contemporary Aboriginal individuality: sixty thousand years of traditional Dreaming and two hundred and twelve years of white settlement. All Aboriginal autobiography carries this dual sense of historicity. This represents the first distinguishing characteristic of these dramatic works.

Stolen, also collaboratively created, tells five stories of stolen children. The play employs the first-person mode of fictional autobiography, but makes it more complex by having the actors provide brief "real" autobiographies at the end of the play, narratives all linked to the metanarrative of the Stolen Generations in one way or another. Each actor steps forward briefly to recount her own autobiography: each one shares some of the experiences of the acted autobiographies which they have just performed. This functions as an effective validation of their speaking positions, of the communality of loss and shared racial identity. It blurs white literary distinctions between biography and autobiography in a unique way. The deliberate autobiographical stance and the blurring of acted and "real" roles strengthen the impression that this story is in a sense pan-Aboriginal, that there exists indeed a community of grieving as Deborah Mailman's story had suggested. Certainly the orphanage children of *Stolen* are cause for grief. Bewildered by not knowing the "crime" for which they are punished, desperate for lost love and family members, victimised by bureaucratic cruelty, utterly powerless, each one provides a harrowing testimony of a childhood that leaves them all damaged as adults. The ultimate cruel irony lies in the fact that their adult social problems are seen to reinforce the racist assumptions of inferiority that underlay the original crime of theft from their Aboriginal families. Thus, the drinking, the petty crime, the mental illness, the violence, the despair and suicide, the joblessness—"it's because they're Aboriginal, you see." This work also gives ironic play to notions of home, significantly absent despite the title of Home claimed by the institution that houses them. A child without a home remains homeless forever: the symbolism in terms of indigenous dispossession of land and culture is extremely powerful.

White apologists for assimilationist policies and practices such as child removal still maintain that the improvement in life chances—as conceived by whites—is justification enough for the pain caused. In these terms, Deborah Cheetham would represent a dream product of such social engineering: a beautiful, talented, intelligent, middle-class opera singer, who also happens to be an Aboriginal woman who was adopted by white parents. Yet her autobiographical show *White Baptist Abba Fan*—which demonstrates among other things her outstanding performative skill—aggressively challenges and deconstructs her learned identity and replaces it with a much more complex and less comfortable reality. The adjectives of her show's title are all ironically charged. Each represents an acquired cultural link to white Australia: she was a daughter of white parents, brought up a convinced Baptist Christian, and a devoted Abba fan. Her Conservatorium-trained voice gave her entry into the highest reaches of white culture—opera. Singing in French and Italian, assuming the roles of white heroines from white cultural narratives, Cheetham became an accomplished role player.

Her show deliberately takes us backwards from this pinnacle of personal achievement, courageously stripping away, one by one, the layers of assumed character that constituted a series of false identities. She travels from white to black, high to low culture, heterosexual to homosexual, middle to lower class, then deliberately challenges these binaries with their built-in hierarchies, revealing them to be as patronising as they are false. Yet, Cheetham's odyssey is characterised by no anguished search for her real family, and she at first frankly rejects the country-and-western music of her birth mother and aunt, symbol of the gulf of class and education that divides them. However, as her whiteness, her Christianity, her unthinking acceptance of white culture drop away from her, she celebrates a coming-out that is about her race as well as her sexuality. She discovers, despite the significant absence of blame, the cruelty and injustice suffered by her mother, unjustly treated by professional Christians arrogantly assuming a white superiority and knowledge of what is "best." Nevertheless, while religion is discredited by its hypocrisies, Cheetham's impassioned rendition of "Jerusalem" reveals the emotional power behind it that is not easily relinquished. Her operatic arias, hymns and popular songs encode a series of complex and shifting cultural meanings.

At the end, standing in front of a list of her black family with its many premature deaths recorded, Cheetham forces us to consider the terrible price that has been paid in order to make this white Baptist Abba fan, this perfect product of assimilation. She is not so naïve as to repudiate her white advantages, but in an enormously emotional climax, she sings in public to an audience that includes, for the first time, her mother, "Songs My Mother Taught Me." Music turns out to be the language without racial inflection, and for Cheetham a channel for the mixed and complex emotions experienced in the series of crises in her life. Identity, culture, sexuality—all are contested sites for this dislocated woman. However, her triumph rests on the performed and personal assertion that Cheetham is both an opera singer and an Aborigine, a complex and sophisticated personality who defies conventional categorisation.

The trajectory traced by Leah Purcell in *Box the Pony* might be described as going in the opposite direction to that of Deborah Cheetham's.[6] Hers is a story of moving from childhood poverty marked by maternal drunkenness and neglect, teenage pregnancy, violence and despair on a Queensland Aboriginal mission, to a career in Sydney with all the trappings of white success. Here is a woman who paints the picture of Aboriginal deprivation used so often to justify white policies of social engineering. Yet, Purcell simultaneously asserts it as the source of her identity, not an ideal one, but part of the strength of the character who performs so engagingly in this play. The language, the style, the symbolism, even the jokes appear uncompromisingly individual, as pugnacious as the work-out with the boxing bag and gloves that begins the show. Mum was a drunk, but she loved the daughter who waited night after night outside the pub. Grandmother Daisy is bedridden, but she passes on to her grand-daughter the song "Run Daisy Run," the last words she heard from her mother before she was carried away by the white man on horseback. The subject of domestic violence is shockingly but obliquely raised when we suddenly become aware of the dual meanings of "box": in the local meatworks where she packs meat in boxes, Purcell's rejection of a violent partner is cruelly avenged when her beloved pony is deliberately killed and becomes part of the meat being processed.

---

[6] Scott Rankin and Leah Purcell, *Box the Pony* (Sydney: Hodder Head Line Australia, 1999).

The autobiographical nature of this play is mediated in two ways. The first lies in Purcell's use of a collaborator, a white male, to help write her story. The collaborative nature of many Aboriginal life narratives further blurs biography/autobiography distinctions. The collective nature and ownership of traditional Aboriginal stories challenge the humanist assumptions of individuality that invariably define white autobiography. Rita Felski belongs to the feminist commentators who explore the ways in which gender is a transformative aspect of modern autobiography: "Early critical surveys such as Roy Pascal's *Design and Truth in Autobiography* could posit a normative model of autobiography as a cohesive, chronological, and restrospective account of the author's life centered around a unifying vision of self-identity ...," while in contrast Elizabeth Bruss understands autobiography "as a speech act which makes certain claims rather than as a structure governed by unique formal rules."[7] Felski goes on to claim that feminist confessional literature "explicitly seeks to disclose the most intimate and often traumatic details of the author's life and to elucidate their broader implications."[8] For her, the problem is how to employ such material to achieve feminist political goals. For Australian Aboriginal women autobiographers, however, disclosure of such experience already forms part of a racial politics in which gender issues are embedded, but not necessarily foregrounded.

The second mediation occurs through Purcell's third-person mode of narration, the creation of a character called Steff, who is the subject of the story. The shift to third-person narration represents a transparent but necessary device, which stresses the performative nature, the dramatic aims of the text. Steff becomes both narrator and one of the many characters depicted by Purcell as she plunders a bag of simple props and costumes to indicate the changes of character. At times, some fragments of Aboriginal language (Purcell is a member of the Wakka Wakka tribe) shift cultural paradigms. Alternatively, familiar white cultural narratives, notably the well known Little Black Sambo story, are appropriated and put to ironic and comic use. Finally, Purcell positions herself—courageously and with considerable humour—somewhere between the black world that left her nowhere to go but away from it, and the white world of coffee shops and Chanel suits that she sees as hollow and coldhearted. She is, quite simply, on her way, but she will always position and identify herself as she does at the beginning of this play: "I'm from Queensland ... up'ome'der ... Joh's country ... Murgon ... Barambah

---

[7] Rita Felski, *Beyond Feminist Aesthetics: Feminist Literature and Social Change* (Cambridge, Massachusetts: Harvard UP, 1989): 89.

[8] *Ibid.*, 90.

Mission ... Wakka Wakka Tribe ... BIG family." Once again, we find the form of narrative most distinctively defined in individualist terms here firmly grounded in communal identity.

In a performance simply entitled *Ningali,* Ningali Lawford tells her story, one that also demonstrates why the possession of her own language and culture represents her greatest treasure. Born under a tree on a Western Australian cattle station, only learning English at thirteen, spending some lonely years in a city boarding school, then subsequently exposed to American culture as an exchange student in Alaska, Ningali narrates a life whose trajectory is paradigmatically post-colonial. Her dual language performance emphasises this, the autobiographical material being interspersed with stories, songs and dance, which creates an evocative and engaging picture of Aboriginality as a place of warmth and wisdom. She turns her experiences of alienation and racism into humour and leaves her audience with a sense of optimism for the future. Katharine Brisbane points to Ningali as a prime example of the particular contribution which Aboriginal women have made to Australian theatre, saying: "these women have used performance to focus upon the healing process; they have given their audiences lasting images of power and grace."[9]

These autobiographical works constitute a strong challenge to official versions of Australian history. They create a counter-discourse that contests not only the content of conventional histories, but the so-called objective basis of their methodology, underpinned by humanist assumptions that are hostile to the challenges of otherness and difference. Furthermore, official histories—as Euro-centric accounts of processes of dispossession—form part of the imperialist project itself and are typically gender-blind as well. Aboriginal women's voices challenge the official erasure of members of their race and sex from Australian histories, and the subjectivity of their narratives vindicate the authority of first-hand knowledge as against the claims of so-called rationality and detached objectivity. These voices are further empowered by their seemingly paradoxical combination of individual and collective experience. The cultural hybridity of their performances combines "I" with "we" in reminding us of Aboriginal traditions of oral performance, ritualised practices of storytelling, dancing and singing.

---

[9] Katharine Brisbane, *The Future in Black and White: Aboriginality in Recent Australian Drama,* paper delivered at IDEA '95, 2nd World Congress of Drama/Theatre and Education, repr. in the Currency Press catalogue of Aboriginal drama, *Black and White Australia.* This essay provides an excellent short overview of Aboriginal theatre history.

Kateryna Longley points out that: "[r]ules of authorship, ownership, and authority ... are so differently understood by Aboriginal people that the term *autobiography* is immediately problematized when it is used in an Aboriginal context."[10] She points to the sense of communal life evoked through individual stories, and the intimate relationship with tribal land—yet these concepts in turn appear problematised in stories like that of Deborah Cheetham, whose birth family is urbanised, living in public city housing and enthusiastic in country and western music making. Contemporary celebrations of Aboriginality are often complicated by a mixed-race heritage and cultural identifications far removed from traditional ones. Ground-breaking anthropological studies such as Diane Bell's *Daughters of the Dreaming*, first published in 1983, established the important, autonomous and powerful rituals that belonged to women in Aboriginal societies, as well as the complex taboos that often constrain storytelling, even one's own story.[11] White educated black women such as Deborah Cheetham can rarely have access to such knowledge, yet there may still be silences and absences in their stories that need to be "read" as significant omissions. The first written text that demonstrated this to white readers was probably Sally Morgan's autobiographical work *My Place*, incorporating oral autobiographical narratives of her older relatives in which, for example, the practice of incest is never named.[12] Morgan herself never names it either, but it can be read in the gaps between the stories of three generations of Aboriginal women. Morgan's text lays claim only to traces of the originary culture as she, like Deborah Cheetham, moves backwards from a white upbringing to the discovery of her racial inheritance. Deborah Mailman in *The Seven Stages of Grieving* actually draws our attention to the taboo on speaking the names of the dead, ritually requesting permission before she tells us their stories and reveals their photographed images.

Anthropology embodies a white discourse that explains other cultures in the language of the coloniser. Aboriginal autobiography can reverse this process in challenging ways. Speaking from the margins of white society, Leah Purcell, for example, in *Box the Pony*, demonstrates to her largely white audiences that the negative Aboriginal stereotypes created by white culture are indeed made by whites, not blacks. This is

---

[10] Kateryna Olijnyk Longley, "Autobiographical Storytelling by Australian Aboriginal Women," in *De/colonizing the Subject: The Politics of Gender in Women's Autobiography*, eds. Sidonie Smith and Julia Watson (Minneapolis: U of Minnesota P, 1992): 371.

[11] Diane Bell, *Daughters of the Dreaming* (Melbourne: McPhee Gribble/Allen and Unwin, 1983).

[12] Sally Morgan, *My Place* (Fremantle, W.A.: Fremantle Arts Centre Press, 1987).

Aboriginal Women's Autobiographies

the powerful subtextual message of *Stolen* as well, the orphanage children continually puzzled by white behaviour posited upon racial prejudice which they do not understand. Their treatment in white hands unmistakably leads to their subsequent careers as jobless drunks and troublemakers, as they ironically fulfil the originally false racial judgements made by whites. The dismantling of racial stereotypes can be seen as a primary—if sometimes subtextual—function of these performed autobiographies, as happens in much other Aboriginal literature.

An enormous diversity can be found in the frames of reference employed by Aboriginal storytellers. Cultural dislocation is often recorded by individuals like Sally Morgan and Deborah Mailman, who are urban and have been "white" educated. Occasionally, urban theatre audiences get a glimpse of the traditional practices of an oral culture. In *Ochre and Dust*, an installation performance designed by Batjala artist Fiona Foley and performed by Nura Ward and Nelly Patterson, two elders of the Anangu-Pitjantjara tribe, audiences heard of first-hand colonial violence.[13] These two women are responsible for handing down the law and culture of their people. Sitting on a mound of red sand, speaking in their first language which was translated into English from the side, drawing illustrative sand pictures, they sorrowfully recorded two forms of cultural destruction. One was the removal from their land for the Maralinga nuclear tests, a dispossession made worse by the fragmentation of the tribal groups who were sent to destinations all over the country. Loss of land was exacerbated by loss of language, loss of "skin" groupings vital to marriage, loss of traditional authority. The struggle to reclaim Uluru was the second narrative, but both stories were made vivid by the first-hand account of the effects on the original inhabitants. A grieving record of the loss of their traditional roles and authority was accompanied by descriptions of the substance abuse—alcohol in their children's generation, glue and petrol sniffing in their grandchildren's—destroying the last vestiges of their culture. This was "tribal" autobiography performed in traditional oral form in its original language. It was a measure of the urgency of the situation and the erosion of traditional authority that these dignified, sorrowing women should communicate with white audiences, agents of their destruction but also, in a terrible irony, the only chance of salvation.

The particular vulnerability of Aboriginal women in white society has concerned Australian writers both black and white. Early plays—such as Henrietta Drake-Brockman's *Men Without Wives* (1938) and Katharine Susannah Prichard's *Brumby Innes* (1927)—sympathetically

---

[13] *Ochre and Dust* was performed at the Adelaide Art Gallery at the 2000 Adelaide Festival.

depicted the plight of the sexually exploited Aboriginal woman in outback Western Australia, yet inevitably spoke from the position of the sexually displaced white woman, sharing a gender predicament, indeed sharing the white men sexually at least, yet not otherwise equal. Sally Morgan's *My Place*, by incorporating female Aboriginal autobiographies, those of her mother and her grandmother, gave the black woman's side of this sordid story, made all the more powerful by the dignified reticence of the tellers. Jane Harrison's *Stolen* contains the story of a black female child in the orphanage, selected for the privilege of weekend visits to a white home, where she is sexually molested, an unspoken atrocity in the play signalled by her shamed body language and change of personality, precursor to her subsequent insanity. The sexually colonised body of the black woman coincides with one of the most shameful sites of the Other in Australian history. The theft of the children of these women by other white men amounts to the cruellest of attempted erasures of identity.

Yet the autobiographical genre and the varied modes of performance of the women who tell their own stories on stage are often as optimistic as they are empowering. The source of this power is often grounded in the communality of Aboriginality, but as Joy Hooton points out, while gendered strategies are common to white and black female autobiographies, black writers take them further: "If white women value relatedness, it is a religion for black women; if white women privilege the personal over the public sphere, black women transform the public into the personal; if white women prefer the informal voice of conversation and the discontinuous structure, black women employ these strategies with a fresh spontaneity and conviction."[14] Nowhere is this better demonstrated than in Leah Purcell's iconoclastic *Box the Pony*, where spoken intimacy, aggressive colloquialism, interaction with the audience, uncensored language and a wicked sense of humour stamp her story and personality with a challenging honesty. The candid readiness to claim relatedness to family members and lovers palpably damaged by white culture is transformed into an unlikely triumphalism by an individual who refuses victimhood for herself.

The figure of the mother haunts all these stories. It was black mothers whose children had white fathers who were robbed of their offspring in the name of assimilation. Female stolen children found themselves at particular risk of sexual molestation, so that cycles of sexual exploitation and child theft were repeated over more than one generation, as Sally Morgan's polyvocal text demonstrates. In *Stolen*,

---

[14] Joy Hooton, *op. cit.*: 315.

one orphanage child who never sees her own mother again after she is taken from her, has in turn her own two children taken, and spends twenty-seven years in anguished searching for them. Hers is a relatively happy ending, as she finally discovers grandchildren, babies whom she can at last hold in her own arms. All of the Stolen Generations grieve for their black mothers, and the maternal becomes a particularly privileged site, another reversal of the official hierarchy that denigrated and even demonised the culture and race of these mothers. Eva Johnson's *What Do They Call Me?* (1990) is a three-part monologue centring on a mother mourning the children who were taken from her, and on her two daughters seeking the truth about their past. Yet, the white fathers are almost always absent despite the hegemonic nature of their race and culture, the civilised "norm" to which their children must be—forcibly if necessary—acculturated.

The number of female autobiographical plays and the many written prose versions—such as those of Ruby Langford, Sally Morgan, Margaret Tucker, Elsie Roughsey, Ella Simon and Glenyse Ward—suggest that the gender of the writer or performer is a crucial determinant. It almost appears as if the extremity of social subjugation, occupying the lowest position in Australia's social hierarchy, requires the unmediated subjectivity and powerful claim of truth that is uniquely found in the autobiography. One male Aboriginal performer, however, breaks with this apparently gender-inflected body of work. Tom E. Lewis, musician and actor, has performed two autobiographical plays—*Thumbul* (1996) and *Lift 'Em Up Socks!* (2000)—in which the crucial search is for his white father. In fact, he straddles two tribal cultures, Aboriginal and Welsh. After a brief childhood in his mother's Gulf country, Lewis became a father at thirteen. His schooling truncated, he was discovered by film-maker Fred Schepsi and rocketed to fame as the star of the film of Thomas Keneally's novel *The Chant of Jimmy Blacksmith*. He had by then gone in search of his white father, and his acceptance by him confirmed a sense of belonging to white as well as to black culture. Yet, Lewis might himself have become another tragic Jimmy Blacksmith, and he does not shirk the disclosure of years lost to alcohol. He refuses the victim position, however, the "Poor Bugger Me" syndrome as he calls it, and finds salvation of sorts in music, the didgeridoo of the black man and the guitar of the white. His later play, *Lift 'Em Up Socks!*, provides an interesting contrast in style and subject matter. Here he defines himself much more emphatically as Aboriginal, using an impressionistic series of devices, from a white-painted figure shadowing him around the stage to the "map" of stones on the floor, a dot-painting whose symbolism is gradually revealed to us. Touchingly, he guides an exquisite miniature puppet black boy around the stage, telling, in two languages, the Dreamtime stories that explain languages, the Dreamtime stories that explain the skin relationships, the totems, the family groupings. The "lost" boy represented by the puppet figure must discover, as did Lewis, his genealogy, and this cannot be found from books, but from an oral tradition and from the land itself. Thus he adopts the traditional role of the father, in contrast to his own paternally deprived childhood. His title for the show records the white teacher urging the children to "lift 'em up socks!" on the appearance of an important government visitor. This phrase is a comic representation of white teaching and culture, a whole history of colonial paternalism being suggested by it.

Much of the power of autobiography by female Aboriginals has its source in the dual oppression represented by their gender as well as race. Their narratives—in particular with their challenges in terms of subjectivity and with their deliberate invocation of hybridity—can be read as part of a de-colonising cultural process. In terms of feminist theories, they constitute a radical refusal to accept conventional binaries both of race and gender. It is these traits that mark them as distinct from most male Aboriginal writing for the stage. One of the distinguishing characteristics of this writing can be located in an often ironic appropriation of white-fella strategies, tropes and genres. Thus Jimmy Chi in *Bran Nue Dae* makes a virtue of racial hybridity, a tool of western pop music, and subverts the usual pattern of cultural retrieval with a jokey version of mission Christianity.[15] Richard Whalley in *Munjong* reverses racial stereotypes and employs the figure of the Brer Rabbit type of trickster to snatch victory out of persecution.[16] Mudrooroo in his play *The Aboriginal Protesters Confront the Proclamation of the Australian Republic on 26 January 2001 with a Production of "The Commission" by Heiner Müller* problematises the Republican issue by invoking other colonisations—notably the British colonisation of Jamaica and the abortive French attempt to initiate a revolt and free the slaves—and ends the play with a revolt of the actors who refuse to be made slaves to a white, colonising narrative.[17] In *Up the Road*, John Harding examines the problematical success of assimilation from the Aboriginal point of view, his main character a successful Aboriginal bureaucrat who returns to his community to find himself implicated in their serious social problems.[18] Jack Davis's earlier plays, *Kullark*, *The Dreamers*, *No Sugar*, and *Barungin* appropriate white stage conventions—suitably

---

[15] Jimmy Chi and Kuckles, *Bran Nue Dae* (Sydney: Currency Press, 1989).

[16] First performed 1990.

[17] First performed in 1996.

[18] John Harding, *Up the Road* (Sydney: Currency Press, 1997).

Aboriginal Women's Autobiographies 35

subverted at crucial points with Nyoongah language, music and dancing—in a deliberate black rewriting of white post-settlement history.[19]

These and other male-written Aboriginal plays have played an important part in raising white consciousness of Aboriginal problems, but they do not, of themselves, address the problem of the "gendered subaltern" described by Gyatri Spivak as the ultimate victim of colonial imperialism.[20] Leela Gandhi describes the particular subaltern dilemma, writing of Spivak that she "... argues that the 'gendered subaltern' disappears because we never hear her speak about herself. She is simply the medium through which competing discourses represent their claims."[21] The Australian Aboriginal woman, standing before a theatre audience, telling her own life story, seems a most potent contradiction to this claim. As Bell Hooks says, describing the situation of black American women: "For us, true speaking is not solely an expression of creative power, it is an act of resistance, a political gesture that challenges politics of domination that would render us nameless and voiceless."[22] The staged female Aboriginal autobiography embodies a powerful "talking back," a de-colonising act. The strength of the current Australian post-colonial discourse—a discourse enacted in a variety of academic disciplines, in Parliaments, law courts and on the streets—can be seen at a most basic level in the fact that these women have been given permission to speak. They combine self-representation with self presentation. They contest official imperialist narratives, but also issues of race, gender, class and sexuality. They can tell us about the world at the margins of Australian society, and even more importantly, criticise the mainstream, the "higher" levels of social, gender and racial hierarchies, with devastating deconstructions of assumptions of superiority:

> So now I live in Woollahra, real fuckin' flash, which is nice ... because as Aunty Pauline Hanson says, "Too many people up'ome get paid too much money for sitting around drinking too much port." So Woollahra feels like home.[23]

---

[19] Jack Davis, *Kullark, The Dreamers* (Sydney: Currency Press, 1982); *No Sugar* (Sydney: Currency Press, 1986); *Barungin* (Sydney: Currency Press, 1986).

[20] Gyatri Spivak, "Can the Subaltern Speak?" in *Marxism and the Interpretation of Culture* (London: Macmillan, 1988).

[21] Leela Gandhi, *Postcolonial Theory: A Critical Introduction* (St. Leonards, New South Wales: Allen and Unwin, 1998): 90.

[22] Bell Hooks, *Talking Back: Thinking Feminist: Thinking Black* (Boston, Massachusetts: South End Press, 1989): 8.

[23] Scott Rankin and Leah Purcell, *op. cit.*: 33.

Works Cited

Printed Works

Bell, Diane. *Daughters of the Dreaming* (Melbourne: McPhee/Gribble/Allen and Unwin, 1983).

Brisbane, Katharine. *The Future in Black and White: Aboriginality in Recent Australian Drama*, paper delivered at IDEA '95, 2nd World Congress of Drama/Theatre and Education, repr. in the Currency Press catalogue of Aboriginal drama, *Black and White Australia*.

Chi, Jimmy, and Kuckles. *Bran Nue Dae* (Sydney: Currency Press, 1989).

Davis, Jack. *Kullark, The Dreamers* (Sydney: Currency Press, 1982).

——— *No Sugar* (Sydney: Currency Press, 1986).

——— *Barungin* (Sydney: Currency Press, 1989).

Davison, Graeme, John Hirst, & Stuart Macintyre, eds. *The Oxford Companion to Australian History* (Melbourne: Oxford UP, 1998).

Drake-Brockman, Henrietta. *Men Without Wives and Other Plays* (1938; Sydney: Angus and Robertson, 1955).

Enoch, Wesley, and Mailman, Deborah. *The Seven Stages of Grieving* (Brisbane: Playlab Press, 1996).

Felski, Rita. *Beyond Feminist Aesthetics: Feminist Literature and Social Change* (Cambridge Massachusetts: Harvard University Press, 1989).

Harding, John. *Up the Road* (Sydney: Currency Press, 1997).

Hooton, Joy. *Stories of Herself When Young: Autobiographies of Childhood by Australian Women* (Melbourne: Oxford UP, 1990).

Keneally, Thomas. *The Chant of Jimmie Blacksmith* (Ringwood, Vic.: Penguin Books, 1973).

Longley, Kateryna Olijnyk. "Autobiographical Storytelling by Australian Aboriginal Women," in *De/colonizing the Subect: The Politics of Gender in Women's Autobiography*, eds. Sidonie Smith and Julia Watson (Minneapolis: U of Minnesota P, 1992).

Morgan, Sally. *My Place* (Fremantle, W.A.: Fremantle Arts Centre Press, 1987).

Prichard, Katharine Susannah. *Brumby Innes and Bid Me To Love* (1927; Sydney: Currency Methuen Drama, 1974).

Rankin, Scott and Purcell, Leah. *Box the Pony* (Sydney: Hodder Head Line Australia, 1999).

Spivak, Gyatri. "Can the Subaltern Speak?" in *Marxism and the Interpretation of Culture* (London: Macmillan, 1988).

Performed Works

Lift 'Em Up Socks (2000), Tom E. Lewis.
Mungjong (1990), Richard Whalley.
Ningali (1996), Ningali Lawford.
Ochre and Dust (2000), Nura Ward and Nelly Patterson.

Thumbul (2000), Tom E. Lewis.
The Aboriginal Protesters Confront the Proclamation of the Australian Republic on 26 January 2001 with a Production of "The Commission" by Heiner Müller (1996), Mudrooroo.
What Do They Call Me? (1990), Eva Johnson.
White Baptist Abba Fan (1998), Deborah Cheetham.

"Implacement" and Belonging: Dramatising White Women's Stories in *Tiger Country*

Helena Grehan

Murdoch University

At the Third International Women Playwrights' Conference in Adelaide in 1994, Sarah Cathcart and Andrea Lemon discussed their work in the "New Storytellers" section. They talked about their participation in the development of a new tradition of storytelling in Australia, a tradition which explores the relationship of "Australians" to their surroundings, a tradition which includes people's attempts to read or understand the landscape and their implacement within it. According to Edward Casey, concrete implacement represents for Deleuze and Guattari "their conviction that *where something is situated* has everything to do with *how it is structured.*"[1] This view of implacement is significant as it emphasises the ways in which places may mark or inscribe the subject; it may in addition be useful within the current Australian climate, where a concern with the issues of positionality and locatedness are compounded by the dubious positioning of the Aboriginal and Torres Strait Islander populations. They are on the whole disenfranchised by the dominant cultural forces, and often categorised according to the imposed binaries of "traditional" and "urban"; alternatively, they are ignored and rendered invisible by the politics of an increasingly oppressive (Liberal) government[2] and by non-Aboriginal inhabitants, who exist, in many cases, as

---

[1] Edward Casey, *The Fate of Place: A Philosophical History* (Berkeley: U of California P, 1997): 302.

[2] Human Rights and Equal Opportunities Commission, *Bringing Them Home: National Inquiry into the Separation of Aboriginal and Torres Strait Islander Children from Their Families* (Sydney: Commonwealth of Australia, 1997). This report called upon all Australian Parliaments to "acknowledge" and to work with the Aboriginal and Torres Strait Islander Commission (ATSIC) so as to draft "official apologies to Indigenous individuals, families and communities" (625). Since the publication of this report, the Liberal government has steadfastly refused to apologise, and this month (April 2000) they announced that "the stolen generation" is in fact a myth or a misnomer. This statement, which is considered inaccurate, has had a devastating effect on race relations in this country, to the point where many Austra-

subjects positioned at the interstices of the coloniser/colonised nexus. This is occasioned by virtue of the continuing oppression of Aboriginal and other marginalised groups, and by the complexity of relationships between convicts/settlers and migrants in an uneasily "post"-colonial country. In view of these concerns, several questions become significant when attempting to engage with the concepts of "place" and "belonging." For example, how do we inscribe ourselves onto places, which have, in many cases, been traced over to eliminate the inscriptions of Aboriginal and Torres Strait Islander communities? What are the moral responsibilities of belonging within such a fraught political and social context? Finally, how, if at all, is a balance maintained between the cultural inscriptions, which may have informed past worldviews and current inscriptions? In other words, what processes of translation or negotiation occur among subjects who may consider themselves migrants, exiles, or even nomads?

This desire for a consideration of the importance of the landscape and one's implacement within it is stressed by Andrea Lemon, when she suggests that it is her aim to write plays which resonate with her experiences of growing up "white" in Australia rather than plays which pay homage to distant European traditions.[3]

---

lians feel deeply ashamed of their government and hold grave fears for the future of any meaningful notion of reconciliation.

[3] In their play *The Serpent's Fall* written in 1987, Cathcart and Lemon attempt to deconstruct, through the stories of five women, the Christian creation myth and its relevance to the lives and stories of these "Australian" women. The characters in *The Serpent's Fall* include a Greek and an Aboriginal woman. In preparation for *The Serpent's Fall*, they researched and workshopped extensively, finally producing a play, performed by Sarah Cathcart, which tells the stories, dreams and beliefs of these five women. For the Greek and Aboriginal characters, the performer used accents that could have been read as stereotypical. By adopting these accents in performance, Sarah Cathcart and Andrea Lemon argued that the performer was not attempting to become a Greek or an Aboriginal character but, rather, trying to provide a representation of those women. The motivation, therefore, was one of engagement rather than appropriation, and the focus was on fostering a dialogue. Several participants at the conference objected to the use of accents and what they saw as the homogenisation of the diverse experiences of Greek women by focusing solely on one stereotypical example. However, it must also be noted that *The Serpent's Fall* was written in 1987, at a time when feminist debates were specifically focused on attempting to acknowledge difference and to move beyond the self/other dichotomy. Positioned historically, therefore, *The Serpent's Fall* was attempting to deal with these issues performatively. (See also Susan Bennett's book *Theatre Audiences* (Routledge: London, 1997) for an interesting assessment of this incident in terms of cross-cultural spectatorship). *The Serpent's Fall* was published in Sydney by Currency Press in 1988.

"Implacement" and Belonging in Tiger Country 41

Tiger Country[4] was written by Sarah Cathcart and Andrea Lemon in 1995 and is a play that negotiates the place of four "white" women in the Australian landscape.[5] According to Casey: "[A] landscape seems to exceed the usual parameters of place by continuing without apparent end; nothing contains it, while it contains everything, including discrete places, in its environing embrace."[6] This definition of landscape gives the term a complexity which becomes significant when looking at it in relation to *Tiger Country*: it represents more than a view or stretch of land; it is a surface which encompasses sky, below and above ground. Landscape yields a permeable framework that encapsulates both the known and the unknown. In fact, the flyer for *Tiger Country* reads "Out there is Tiger Country beyond the border where the blue dust rolls across the desert, the sky is huge and the land never forgets."[7]

Through the skilful interweaving of stories, *Tiger Country* invites the reader to engage with the processes which these women go through in navigating their way around the Australian landscape. In *Tiger Country* Sarah Cathcart and Andrea Lemon present a play that attempts to chart the experiences of "white" Australians and to achieve a frame of reference which adequately reflects life here, rather than one which continually relies on foreign or alien traditions.

Tiger Country addresses the issues of place and belonging through the stories of four women: Louisa, a colonial migrant whose journey begins as she sails towards Australia on a ship with her father; Iris, who is an opal miner and the proprietor of the Moonrock Road House in the middle of the desert; Stella, a young girl who lives on a nuclear tracking station surrounded by a fence; and Barb, a young city woman who marries a station owner and moves to the station, a landscape also dominated by a fence. Two of the characters are new arrivals attempting to position themselves in unknown or alien places. The other two find themselves in familiar landscapes, but still, to a certain extent, have not acquired the tools with which to explain their implacement in these surroundings. These women exist in different temporal realms and do not meet at any stage in the play; their only point of contact is that a single performer performs them all.

---

[4] *Tiger Country* remains currently unpublished. In this paper I refer to a script given to me by the writers Sarah Cathcart and Andrea Lemon in 1995.

[5] This focus on "white" women could perhaps have been triggered by the responses to *The Serpent's Fall* at the Third International Women Playwrights' Conference.

[6] Edward Casey, *Getting Back into Place* (Bloomington: Indiana UP, 1993): 25.

[7] The flyer for *Tiger Country* was produced by Deck Chair Theatre in Fremantle in August 1995.

As each of the characters interrogates her place or implacement within the landscape of the play, her interrogation raises questions about the definitions and understandings of place within the context of Australian culture generally. Place as a concept has no static meaning and is associated with ideas of subjectivity, space, time, and memory. It stands for a composite of responses to locations past and present. It is place with which Barb, Stella, Iris and Louisa attempt to come to terms. For each of these characters, place, however liminal and fractured, symbolises something different. As a reader, I respond to their complex relationships to place by questioning my own. My understanding of their attempts to navigate place are mediated by my own diasporic or nomadic alliances to interlocking places, stories and memories. And all of this must be considered as place in the represented world of performance. However, on a larger scale, this representation has ramifications not only for theatrical implacement, but also in terms of cultural implacement for "white" women who are attempting to investigate their own situatedness within Australia. Sarah Cathcart and Andrea Lemon argue that they are trying to see, carve or highlight the place of "white" women in the landscape; and in this regard, Andrea Lemon, in an interview with Anita Gardner, suggested that

> ... the piece is very much about white women's perspective or white people's perspective and is actually about white people's racism, and because the Aboriginal culture is another unknown that they are dealing with and for us the piece is about the unknown. How we deal with the unknown. The landscape is an unknown, the country itself is an unknown ... all these things that challenge our way of actually viewing the world.[8]

I find this concern with "white women's perspective" quite complex and challenging. Although I admire their attempts to tackle the issue of non-Indigenous relationships to land and place, and acknowledge that a more self-reflexive approach to theatre may have been inspired by their experiences at the Third International Women Playwrights' Conference, I believe that attempting to achieve a "white women's" response may not only be homogenising, but may in fact prove impossible. It may be feasible to elucidate elements or fragments of non-Indigenous responses to land. However, so many different ethnic groups and sub- groups exist under the rubric "white" that the label "white women" seems redundant and fraught with as many difficulties as that of "speaking for." As a category, "white" ultimately masks the specificities of cultural, social

---

[8] This interview took place in September 1995 and was subsequently published in *FAR* 10.2 (October/November 1995). The published version is shorter than the original; therefore, any references used here refer to an unpublished transcript given to me by Anita Gardner.

and racial differences, and is, I believe, as problematic as attempting to speak the stories of Aboriginal and Greek women.[9]

Sarah Cathcart and Andrea Lemon's use of their own personal experiences of growing up in Australia as the point of departure for a generalised comment on "white" women and place seems to deny any clearly considered interrogation of the experiential and epistemological basis on which the term "white" rests. In her interview with Anita Gardner, Andrea Lemon stated "... we wanted to look at, I guess, the white women's perspective of Australia."[10] Later on in the same interview, she says "[T]hese characters are us, we are not talking about something that is other, we are these people."[11] Perhaps this approach positions "white" women as an all encompassing category which stands in opposition to those of Aboriginal, ethnic and/or migrant women. But it is, as I have indicated, fraught with problems. Ruth Frankenberg argues that the current "vogue" of interrogating and attempting to make whiteness visible rather than leaving it as an unmarked signifier can often lead to

---

[9] I must acknowledge the complicity of "white" Western women in the oppression of their "non-white" counterparts and their initial unwillingness to recognise this. This issue, theorised as "the politics of difference," dominated much feminist and cultural theory in the late 1980s and early 1990s. For an in-depth understanding of these terms and ideas, see bell hooks, *Yearning: Race, Gender and Cultural Politics* (Boston, MA: South End Press, 1990); Gloria Anzaldua, ed., *Making Face, Making Soul Hacienda Caras: Creative and Critical Perspectives by Feminists of Color* (San Francisco: Aunt Lute Books, 1990); Trinh-T. Minh-ha, *When the Moon Waxes Red: Representation, Gender and Cultural Politics* (New York: Routledge, 1991); Rosemary Hennessy, *Materialist Feminism and the Politics of Discourse* (New York: Routledge, 1993); Ien Ang, "I'm a feminist but ... 'Other' Women and Postnational Feminism," in Barbara Caine and Rosemary Pringle, eds., *Transitions: New Australian Feminisms* (St Leonards: Allen and Unwin, 1995): 57-73; and Chandra Talpade Mohanty, "Introduction: Cartographies of Struggle: Third World Women and the Politics of Feminism," in Chandra Talpade Mohanty, Ann Russo et al., eds., *Third World Women and the Politics of Feminism* (Bloomington: Indiana UP, 1991), amongst others. I suggest, however, that the term "white" is a problematic one that does not allow for the levels of oppression and marginalisation that exist within this category. As a "white" reader, I feel that although I relate to certain aspects of the characters' responses to their surroundings, I do not have a uniform response to, or rapport with, any of them in a singular sense. My responses are informed by my experiences of migration and displacement as well as by personal difficulties with the issue of place. My point is that while "white" women have been complicit in oppression, they do not form an effective group with any singular or unifying motives. Therefore, I feel that to try and speak the experiences of "white" women is a difficult enterprise that raises many questions. For example, who are these women? How does one become white? And how is this represented?

[10] See note 8.

[11] *Ibid.*

the "reification of cultures and the erasure of the processes through which cultures as practices come into being."[12] Frankenberg goes on to hypothesise that cultures can as a result become static and singular concepts which are not seen as "fluid, intersecting realms," but rather "one gleams the image of a toy-merry-go-round, with each bobbing figure representative of a group hermetically sealed from all the others."[13] Although I am not arguing that this is what is happening here, I do believe that an attempt to speak "white" stories does not go far enough in terms of interrogating what Cathcart and Lemon see as the lack in the representational balance. Instead, it can reaffirm the binary self/other, reinforcing essentialist notions of cultural identification rather than examining why the documentation of whiteness is specifically important and what it might achieve. Therefore, whilst I can find fault with the parameters within which Cathcart and Lemon frame their search for a performative mode that could address this representational lack, I believe that their work is important and should be seriously considered, as it begins a process of response whereby non-Indigenous Australian women highlight their relationships to land, place, and belonging, and to the effects of these on their subjectivity. As Jeff Malpas suggests:

> ... the idea of persons as constituted through landscape or place is philosophically intriguing in a way that goes beyond questions of narrative style or literary method. For it is suggestive of a way of seeing human beings that treats them, not as individual creatures who exist in a way independent of their surroundings, independent of the landscape, but as beings who are indeed constituted as the beings they are only within their surroundings, within a landscape, within a place.[14]

Tiger Country plays a significant role in highlighting alternative responses to landscape and place, and the characters are each fundamentally concerned with inscribing themselves, or questioning their inscription on/within the landscape and its concomitant inscription on them.

Of the four characters in *Tiger Country*, Louisa is the one who experiences the most acute sense of displacement. She is constantly attempting to retain the memory of her old place (home) and exists in fear of the new. She encounters the landscape as alien and hostile, and

---

[12] Ruth Frankenberg, "Introduction: Local Whitenesses, Localizing Whiteness," in *Displacing Whiteness: Essays in Social and Cultural Criticism*, ed. Ruth Frankenberg (Durham: Duke UP, 1997): 18.

[13] *Ibid.*

[14] Jeff Malpas, "A Taste of Madeline: Notes Towards a Philosophy of Place," *International Philosophical Quarterly* XXXIV. 4, Issue no. 136 (1994): 433-51.

suffers from a profound sense of homelessness, a sensation which, according to Edward Casey, "... involves a sense of unbearable emptiness. Separation from place is perhaps most poignantly felt in the forced homelessness of the reluctant emigrant, the displaced person, the involuntary exile."[15] From the moment we encounter Louisa, her extreme sense of displacement begins to surface. She constantly refers to and almost always addresses herself to "Edwina."[16] It is as if she is continually in correspondence with her "self." Edwina seems to be used as an anchor or a referent that keeps the character connected to her past, her home, the land from which she is now unwillingly alienated. For Louisa, the struggle does not consist in a balancing between an attempted re-constitution of an old place and the negotiation of the new, because it seems that she is unable to see or ground herself in the landscape which envelops her, and clings to any fragments of "civilization" that she can. "Dear Edwina everything has turned about since we crossed the line."[17] Louisa's narrative is riddled with fear and uncertainty as she journeys closer and closer to the unknown. Even the referents of nature on which she is used to depend no longer offer her guidance, as she says: "I do not know one thing that I have felt so much as the loss of the North Star. Night after night I watch it sinking lower and lower ..." (1). This literal use of cartography reflects Louisa's desire to retain links to her known place. She exhibits a literal desire for belonging, which sees the map as a stable referent in Louisa's increasingly fragmented universe.

As she floats along the ocean of in-betweenness, her fear and worry increase, and when land is in sight, Louisa calls out frantically to Edwina: "This is to be our new home? There are no trees, no port no dock no flotilla of boats to welcome us" (20). Her childlike sense of despair signals her absolute vulnerability. Throughout the play, she seems to be a character who wallows in the void of her displacement. She is tentative and uncertain; she does not like marking the landscape. She cannot participate in a process of inscribing herself onto the land as it continues to be alien to her. When her father beckons her to help prevent the stock from bolting, she gets up and begins to (according to the stage directions) "struggle through the bush"; however, her movement is slow, and she appears reticent and resentful of the chore which she has been assigned. She says: "I could find the countryside almost charming, if only there were something here" (34). When she has recov-

---

[15] Edward Casey, *Getting Back into Place* (Bloomington: Indiana UP, 1993): x.

[16] Edwina is never clearly labelled—it would seem that she is Louisa's best friend.

[17] Sarah Cathcart and Andrea Lemon, *Tiger Country* (Melbourne: unpublished script, 1995): 1. Further references to this work appear parenthetically in the text.

ered from the initial shock of arrival, her fear of the Other begins to take over. Her feelings of apprehension towards the natives is juxtaposed with her desire to lie at home in her "feather bed in our little house across from the park with the lake" (44). She thinks that she will never achieve a "sensation of home" (45) in this new land; it seems as if she is unable to begin the process of navigating her surroundings, as her fear of the unknown and desire to either label or deny its existence remains paramount.

As the play progresses her fear of the natives increases. She becomes frantic as she calls for her Papa to defend her. When they begin to touch the hem of her skirt, Louisa recoils in horror, frozen on the spot. She is offended by their smell and implores Papa for help. When there is no response and the natives touch Louisa's leg, she pushes a woman violently into the fire. The tension created by Louisa reaches a crescendo as she says: "I didn't mean to push her, Edwina, but she fell into the fire and screamed like a banshee!" (59) Her complete alienation becomes evident here, as she describes the cries of a burning woman as those of a "banshee." Thus ends Louisa's last scene in the play. As a character, she does not develop any rapport with the landscape or its inhabitants, and she is framed by her inability to acknowledge her place.

The other character who arrives at an unknown or new place is Barb. She is a city girl who travels to the country to go to the races with her friend Hugh. Barb embodies the antithesis of Louisa: she displays an "up-beat" and cheerful attitude. While she initially appears tentative about her surroundings and continually surprised by what she sees, she embarks on a journey of inquiry during which she is transformed into someone who can navigate her way around with ease; she evolves into a character who can read her environment very closely. This transformation must largely be attributed to her friendship with Lucy, an Aboriginal woman who lives on Hugh's station.

As she arrives at Alagoona siding, Barb exclaims in horror: "Where *is* this place?" (6) She talks excitedly about the races and the ball that she will attend afterwards with Hugh. She was thrilled by Hugh's invitation, and when she asked him where he lived, he replied, "Just get off the train at Alagoona siding, well here I am and it's horrible! We passed the end of the world 500 miles back!" (6) It quickly becomes apparent to Barb that her imagined idea of Hugh's place is radically different from the actual one. She is surrounded by men with loudspeakers, animals, pies, flies and beer, and calls out to Hugh for help.

Things do not improve for Barb as they travel from the races to the homestead where the ball is to be held. As Barb observes the countryside, she asks nervously: "Where are the trees?" (9) Like Louisa she finds the landscape very strange, but she is too concerned with the ball to focus on her surroundings.

As time passes, Barb marries Hugh and moves from the city to the Station. She gets a job as the station cook and is quickly confronted with the realities of cooking for seventy people. As she begins to make mutton stew, there is a noise at the door. "It's an Aborigine! Hugh never said anything about Aborigines!" (22) She does not know how to react to these strangers, and despite her fear, she gives the Aborigines sugar, tentatively introducing herself to them: "Oh hello I'm Barbara, Hugh's new wife, they seem to think that's very funny, I hope they're not taking advantage of me" (22). After a brief interaction, Barb dashes back inside to the comfort and safety of the kitchen and her cooking. Her attitude, although initially tentative, completely differs from Louisa's, as she embraces her fear and attempts to talk to the Other or unknown rather than giving way to panic.

Barb attempts to retain a sense of her past by reading magazines and dancing to her records; she is at this point still unsure of the landscape that surrounds her and feels constrained by the fence. "I feel like I'm drowning. I've never been past the chicken wire fence that surrounds the house" (28). The fence acts as the boundary line separating the known from the unknown. The turning point for Barb occurs in interaction with Lucy. Lucy comes to the fence to talk and eventually invites her outside to attend a *corroboree*. The magic of the event transpires from Barb's description of her experience:

> Lucy said it was a story about how the world began and how the stars are their ancestors. She said a big snake came up out of the earth and moved across the land swishing its tail from side to side creating mountains and trees and valleys and waterholes (37).

Although Barb may not fully understand the significance of the event, her friendship with Lucy teaches her to begin to see the landscape differently. Lucy shares with her some of her vast knowledge about the land, and this knowledge gradually allays Barb's fear. As the play progresses, Barb becomes very settled in her surroundings and she even begins to see the subtle changes in the landscape. She says in an assured tone:

> I've started noticing how the land changes, how there are the gibber plains where it's flat with no trees at all, then all the sandhills and claypans and how the colour of the soil keeps changing, from white to black to red and all the trees in the creek beds and the way the country responds after rain! It just explodes! (50)

Barb's transformation is very important and, for me, one of the most potent aspects of the play. She arrives in an alien landscape totally unable to see or understand her surroundings; through time, experience and the guidance of Lucy, she begins to learn to perceive things differently and to negotiate the terrain. Lucy reminds her that she ultimately remains a foreigner in the landscape, but her (perhaps-partial) implacement is achieved through her ability to move beyond the fence and to embrace her place within that landscape. As Casey points out: "Places, like bodies and landscapes, are something we experience—where *experience* stays true to its etymological origin of 'trying out,' 'making a trial out of it.'"[18] The difference between Barb and Louisa comes from the fact that Barb is a willing participant in her implacement. While initially nervous, she finally moves with the help of her guide into the unknown and reconciles herself to it, whereas Louisa does not seem capable of making that leap.

The other two characters in the play, Stella and Iris, have both stayed in their environments for a long time. This does not necessarily mean, however, that they have acquired the skills to understand their place within the landscape. Stella, a young girl who lives on a nuclear tracking station, takes a "macro" approach to her location. By this I mean that Stella examines her position *vis-à-vis* the stars and the galaxies, measuring distances and imagining other places. She moves out into the imaginary sky and views her town from there, taking an existential approach to the landscape, which still remains an unknown for her, even though she is within it: "If you looked at our town from outer space you'd see rows of tiny silver houses in straight lines in a big square ... in the middle of the desert ..." (12). The stage directions indicate that she speaks in the small voice of a young girl who is excitedly learning about her surroundings. She goes on to say: "When you get to the edge of my town there's just a fence and past the fence is the desert" (12). She points to the markers which delineate her surroundings and, unlike Barb who seems constrained (at least initially) by her fence, is able to move beyond it immediately. "Out there's the line of the creek bed and they're gidgi trees that's where I play after school ... and over there that's my secret place" (12). On a surface or topographical level, Stella appears to know her environment: she is aware of trees, hills, bushes, and other markers; but the symbolic nature of her journey is complex, as she exists within a fenced community, a community where people only stay for three years and then go back to America. Stella says: "[N]obody ever dies in my town because nobody ever grows old" (18). She is alienated by the fact that she and her family are the only people—or so it seems—

---

[18] Edward Casey, *op. cit.*: 30.

who actually live permanently in the town. They are taught American history at school, and exist within a surreal community of people who only stay there for employment. The community is patterned around the nuclear tracking station and filled with lives which do not seem to have specificity or variation.

Stella's process represents one of self-discovery, of finding a place in which she can celebrate her difference from the townsfolk and acknowledge her surroundings. Although her knowledge of the landscape is strong, the denial of it by the people who live around her must make things difficult. She battles to chart her own responses to place, while attempting to digest the dominant American view. Her American schooling does not account for the landscape which surrounds the station. Stella's only knowledge of Aboriginal culture comes from books which she has read. She has no understanding of the cultural significance of the cave paintings which exist, and sees them as a challenging code to be cracked. When she believes to have glimpsed two old Aboriginal women in her secret cave, she is unsure of how to respond to them:

> Yesterday I went to my secret place after school and someone's found my cave! There are two old ladies looking at my paintings and talking and you know what? I think they're Aborigines cos I've seen them in books with big boats and white people lying dead *urgh* on the sand with spears sticking up out of them. S'true. But these two ladies don't look dangerous they just look really old and black (38).

Stella's secret place is the cave and it surprises her that these women also know it. When she approaches them, they leave and she remains alone with her secret code and her *Secret Seven* books. Initially, Stella believes that to live on a nuclear tracking station, and consequently to be a target, is an honour, but she gradually begins to see the irony of such a position and eventually decides that she does not want to die. The Americans can leave quickly in case of an emergency, but Stella does not enjoy that privilege:

> I saw Mrs Jackson kissing mum. She had a suitcase and she was crying. There was a red alert! All the Americans were being airlifted out and we were going to be left behind! (58)

She seems to deal with her lack of power by trying to move beyond her situatedness within the station out into the unknown, the galaxies and the universe. Many of Stella's ponderings on the universe have atomic referents, and she talks about the fact that her hand is a tiny solar system, composed of atoms which, if split, could blow a hole "four miles wide and make this town disappear just like that!" (57)

Stella embodies a complex character. Her role in the play seems unclear. Is she there to present the young (white) person's point of view? What does her participation in the play achieve? On one level, her role seems to point to the difficulties of reading the landscape if you are not schooled or prepared in any way, and on another, her role begins to explore the issues of isolation and fear which accompany living in remote military surroundings.

In contrast to Stella's attempts to understand her relationship with her place, Iris has it all sorted out from the beginning:

> Wal and me built this roadhouse with our own bare hands. Picked up all them moonrocks from out on the moon plains. Slapped it together in a weekend ... Wal and me still sleep in the caravan out the back, have done for 40 years. Bought that van when we left the city to come up this way lookin for opal (4).

I would argue, however, that while Iris seems to comprehend the landscape and her place within it, she actually entertains a very static idea of place. She is in fact so bound up with her place that she cannot see or move beyond it, or contextualise it in any way. Even when she experiences spaceship travel and is given the opportunity to perceive her own position more objectively, she does not grasp the concept of places as interconnected. She has her place and that is that. Anyone coming into her place who cannot be clearly and obviously labelled, becomes the Other, and although she talks about Japanese people and Martians, she has grown oblivious to any differences between them. In some ways, Iris emblematically symbolises the stereotypical remote Australian who is concerned with survival and not with cultural difference: she represents the "real Aussie battler" icon, and this is reinforced by her brusque tone, plain speaking approach, her unsophisticated demeanour, and generally direct attitude throughout the play. Despite the limitations of such a stereotypical representation, the character displays real receptiveness to the beauty in the (immediate) surrounding landscape, an ability not shared by Barb (initially), Louisa or Stella. In her description of the opal fields, for example, Iris says:

> When I first saw the fields it took me breath away. All the saltbush had disappeared and there was nothin but pink and white rubble shinin in the sun ... It was that beautiful I thought I'd landed on the moon (8).

This capacity for observation is not carried through in her mimed interactions with "Martin," a Japanese tourist.[19] Iris lectures Martin about his

---

[19] While Barb's interaction with Lucy provides her with guidance and the tools necessary to see the landscape, Iris's interactions with "Martin" seem to facilitate the

lack of preparation for travelling in the heat. She goes on to tell Martin of the need to be ready for the harsh conditions "out there" and the importance of treating the landscape with respect:

> Now listen up Martin you've only gotta break down out in them sandhills and you'll be sittin out there, no shade coz there's no trees ... Y'gotta find out about the country you're goin into Martin ... y'gotta understand it ... y'gotta treat it with respect (14).

Iris has lived at the Moonrock Roadhouse for forty years and there exists nothing—not even aliens it would seem—that can faze her. Her identity is firmly entrenched in her roadhouse, her dealings with Japanese tourists, or people she perceives to be Japanese, and her search for opals. Her entrepreneurial skills, although they make the reader cringe at times, provide most of the humour in the play. Iris comes across as a real "character." The stage directions indicate that she darts and shuffles around the stage and speaks with a thick Australian drawl. She can provide for herself in whatever form necessary: from short-changing her customers when they buy petrol to gambling on cards with them. She demonstrates through her story that she has learned about the landscape the hard way. She describes the opal mining shafts that litter the landscape and her tying of the children to the van (when they were young) "so they couldn't get too far!" (16) She foregrounds her love of this outdoor lifestyle by describing her exhilaration at the shortages of water and the need to collect the rare rain whenever possible to wash whole bodies with a cupful.

Tourists who enter Iris's domain should conform to the rules of her place. Throughout the play, she displays a racist and condescending attitude, based on her belief that her knowledge of and belonging to the landscape entitle her to treat people who may not be so familiar with the territory as inferior. Even when abducted by aliens and taken up in a spaceship, Iris uses the referent of Japanese tourist to talk to the "Martians" and assumes that they need her in order to find their way around:

> Inside Martin, everythin was made of metal and there were three steering wheels with a pilot chappy sittin at one of em. Hello, do you want me and Wal to steer the bloody thing? Heard about us from one of them Japanese tourist maps ... thought we might be able to show youse around? (43)

Iris's inability to see beyond her specific bounded implacement in the desert functions as a direct counterpoint to Stella's inability to focus on

---

telling of her story. This relationship, therefore, resembles more Louisa's conversations with or appeals to "Edwina."

her immediate surroundings. Stella's attempt to situate herself within a larger "universal" context seems to mask her ability to read her implacement at the tracking station. As a result of this difference, however, these two characters provide some interesting insights into the complexities of surviving in the more remote parts of Australia; they also provide two distinct, if not oppositional, responses to the concept of place and the idea of implacement.

Notwithstanding the concerns I have expressed here about the authors' attempts to create what could be seen as stereotypical characters within the landscape, and my anxiety about the dangers of essentialism inherent in defining or representing "white" women, I do believe that *Tiger Country* is an important social document which begins to redress what Cathcart and Lemon see as a lack in the representational balance. *Tiger Country* depicts the lives of four very different women and interrogates the complexities of their relationships to their surrounding landscapes. Through an engagement with the issues of implacement and belonging, readers are encouraged to question not only the difficulties of inscription that the characters face, but also to reflect upon their own implacement and belonging within this anxiously "post"-colonial nation.

Works Cited

Casey, Edward. *The Fate of Place: A Philosophical History* (Berkeley: U of California P, 1997).

Cathcart, Sarah & Andrea Lemon. *Tiger Country* (Melbourne: unpublished script, 1995).

Frankenberg, Ruth. "Introduction: Local Whitenesses, Localizing Whiteness," in *Displacing Whiteness: Essays in Social and Cultural Criticism*, ed. Ruth Frankenberg (Durham: Duke UP, 1997).

Human Rights and Equal Opportunities Commission. *Bringing Them Home: National Inquiry into the Separation of Aboriginal and Torres Strait Islander Children from Their Families* (Sydney: Commonwealth of Australia, 1997).

Malpas, Jeff. "A Taste of Madeline: Notes Towards a Philosophy of Place," *International Philosophical Quarterly* XXXIV. 4, Issue no. 136 (1994).

Siting Themselves: Indigenous Australian Theatre Companies

Maryrose Casey

La Trobe University

Cultural production by Indigenous Australian artists represents a major industry in Australia. In this essay, I examine some of the terms on which this work is acknowledged. In practice, the critical reception of cultural production by Aboriginal and Torres Strait artists is a site where the political struggles of Aboriginal and Torres Strait people confront the subject and power positions of Eurocentric critical commentary. The cultural constructs underlying the commentary that defines much of the work by Indigenous Australian artists delineates a social history of Australian attitudes more than it delineates the work. The current terms of reference for reception of Indigenous cultural production are usually assumed to have developed more culturally sensitive and open paradigms. Yet Indigenous artists continue to contest the paradigms of analysis and the resulting critical reception.

In September 1997, the Olympic Cultural Committee auspiced the *Festival of the Dreaming* in Sydney. The *Festival* was proclaimed as "a celebration of the art of the world's Indigenous peoples—and especially that of the Australian Aborigines and Torres Strait Islanders." The scheduling of the Indigenous arts festival as the first of the Olympic cultural festivals was meant to demonstrate the recognition of Indigenous artists and their work.[1] The limits of this recognition, specifically in relation to critical reception and commentary, were raised as important and ongoing concerns by the *Festival*'s Artistic Director, Rhoda Roberts, and members of the organising committee such as Lydia Miller, prior to, during and after the *Festival*.[2] These concerns were

---

[1] Rhoda Roberts, *The Festival of The Dreaming: Festival Guide* (September 1997): 15.

[2] Some examples include: Rhoda Roberts, "Sweet Dreams" Review, *Weekend Australian* (13-14 September 1997): 20-21; Louise Adler, "Interview with Rhoda Roberts," Arts National, Radio National ABC Radio (1997); Lydia Miller, 1997 Paperbark Seminar, State Library of New South Wales, Festival of the Dreaming; Rhoda Roberts, "The 1997 Rex Cramphorn Memorial Lecture," *Australasian Drama*

focused on "how [Indigenous cultural production] is judged and how far we have travelled in understanding Indigenous cultural expression."[3]

Cultural specificity has been and continues to be an important factor in ensuring judicial, political and social salience for Aboriginal and Islander communities in relation to the settler/ migrant based Australian institutions and communities. Since the 1970s an active aim within Aboriginal and Islander communities has been "to survive as distinctive social and cultural entities."[4] A history of practices that have certainly been genocidal in effect, and a present as a minority in a predominately settler/migrant based population, where Anglo—and more recently Celt—and multicultural narratives predicate political and social salience, continue to make cultural respect and recognition a priority.

Conversely, the "lack" of culture or cultural viability was used as a reference point in justifications for many repressive policies and the related justifying narratives. The academic disciplines of history and anthropology provided narratives of culture and identity, which have at different times denied or affirmed Indigenous cultural specificity, and still inform debates. These include narratives such as Daisy Bate's "dying pillow"[5] thesis and the concept of *Terra Nullius*[6] as the justification for dispossession over much of Australia's post-invasion

---

Studies 32 (April 1998): 3-20; also published in an abbreviated form in Rhoda Roberts, "A Passion for Ideas: Black Stage," *Dialogue* 34 (March 1998) : 10-11.

[3] Rhoda Roberts, "Sweet Dreams": 20; Rhoda Roberts, "Passion": 11.

[4] Marcia Langton, *Well I Heard It on the Radio and I Saw It on the Television* (Sydney: Australian Film Commission, 1993): 13. The current definition of who is or can identify him/herself as an Aboriginal or Torres Strait Islander "is primarily social." An Aboriginal person is defined as a person who is a descendent of an indigenous inhabitant of Australia, identifies as an Aboriginal, and is recognised as an Aboriginal by members of an Aboriginal community. This definition resulted from a High Court decision and is accepted by the Australian Commonwealth Government and its authorities. It is also the definition preferred by most Aboriginal and Torres Strait Islander People (see Marcia Langton above).

[5] The "dying pillow" thesis was a sentimentalised social Darwinist view current in the late nineteenth and early twentieth centuries. It posited that the Australian Aboriginal population was dying out and that the only humane steps that could be taken was to "smooth the pillow" on their death bed: "Children of the woodland ... the Australian native cannot withstand civilisation ... he loses the will to live, and when the will to live is gone, he dies ... I did what I set out to do—to make their passing easier ... I have tried to tell of their being and their ending." In Daisy Bates, *The Passing of the Aborigine* (Melbourne: John Murray, 1944): 67-68.

[6] *Terra Nullius* refers to the declaration of Australia as an "empty" land. In other words, Aboriginal people might inhabit Australia, but they had no formal claim to or relationship with the land.

history. Indigenous Australian cultures or the "perceived lack" of culture and cultural viability have been used as a platform for racist policies and practices, as well as to buttress the transitions through the "protection," "assimilation," "self-management" and "self-determination" programmes within Australian State and Federal government policies towards Aboriginal communities.

In this context, it is hardly surprising that cultural recognition and respect are understood as primary aspects of reconciliation. The Commonwealth Government Act that established the Council for Aboriginal Reconciliation in 1991 states that one of its major tasks is "to promote a process of reconciliation between Aboriginal and Torres Strait Islanders and the wider Australian community based on an appreciation of Aboriginal and Torres Strait Islander cultures and achievements."[7] There are many factors involved in cultural appreciation and respect. A major factor pertains to the issue of representation of the specific cultures. Representation in all forms of cultural production and the importance of self-representation have been and continue to be a central focus of debate and analysis in a wide range of studies.[8] The process of "stereotyping, iconising and mythologising" Aboriginality as cultural and textural constructions persists within Australian society.[9]

In Australia, a range of contested definitions and assumptions underlie the designation "Indigenous" or "Aboriginal" in reference to the artist's work in its form and content. There are two sides to designations of identity: the elements that are claimed and the elements that are imposed. However, the identity which the artist uses and the identity understood by the external observer do not necessarily coincide. Definitions and assumptions result from a dynamic process operating between self-designation and validation on the one hand, and critical and social designation and validation on the other, these resulting from "the intersubjectivity of black and white in dialogue." Marcia Langton argues that "Aboriginality ... is a field of intersubjectivity ... that is remade over and

---

[7] Council for Aboriginal and Torres Strait Islander Reconciliation Act, Commonwealth Government of Australia (1991): 1.

[8] See Stephen Muecke, *Available Discourses on Aborigines* (1982), Catriona Moore and Stephen Muecke, *Racism and Representation of Aborigines in Film* (1984), Maurie Scott, *Black Consciousness on Stage and Screen* (1986), Kevin Brown, *The Racial Referent* (1988), Terry Goldie, *Fear and Temptation* (1989), J.J. Healy, *Literature and the Aborigine in Australia* (1989), B. Hodge and V. J. Mishra, *The Dark Side of the Dream* (1991), and Marcia Langton, *Well I Heard it on the Radio and I Saw It on the Television* (1993) among others, including recent articles by Allan McKee such as "The Aboriginal Version of Ken Done" (1997).

[9] Langton, *op. cit.*: 34.

over again in a process of dialogue, of imagination, of representation and interpretation."[10] The evolution of the current parameters of critical reception and designations of artists and their work can be traced through—and in part result from—a series of calls and responses, sometimes originating from political activists, sometimes from critics and critical theory, sometimes from specific artists or groups of artists, pushing against the parameters established by imperial and colonial narratives and practices.

These calls and responses emanate from a series of discursive positions, each operating with its own rationalities of power and constructions of truth. Within this context and operating from different power positions, the artists and critics have established and continue to establish relationships between different elements within the artwork and the terms of critical reception. These elements include artistic intention, definitions of culture, the power of influence, the role of originary cultures and social constructs of identity, and the resulting attributions of cultural ownership.

The works of Indigenous artists are valued or devalued by the descriptions and definitions that are produced by these conflicting discourses. These valuations have implications for the production of theatre work and its reception, both at the time of production and as it is perceived within or outside specific cultural positions and artistic traditions. Within the parameters of theatre criticism, what is valorised and/or excluded contributes to the representation of cultures and artists. But this field of representation does not operate in isolation: it is reinforced by and reinforces other social discourses.

Urban Renewal or Cultural Definition?

If these social discourses affect the terms of reception of artists' work, they need to be examined in tandem with the frames of representation implied in the critical reception. In this instance, an account of a battle between two urban events illustrates some of the broader social context that impinges on the reception of artists' work. This is primarily a tale of urban renewal, a situation that occurs in all modern cities, but it is distinguished by layers with specific ramifications for Indigenous Australians and cross-cultural interaction.

St Kilda is a bay side suburb in Melbourne with a colourful history. The suburb started life as a seaside resort in the late nineteenth century. As the decades of the twentieth century rolled on, St Kilda dropped in

---

[10] *Ibid.*: 31-34.

the public's imagination and spending habits, becoming by the 1970s a place to score heroin and go to the Luna Park. St Kilda had changed into a place for sin, police blitzes and current affairs specials.

For those who lived there, however, it was an oasis of tolerance and cheap housing; it attracted single parent families, recent immigrants, and marginalised members of the community. For example, this image of tolerance drew a large gay community—currently represented by the largest gay pride march in Melbourne—and a small Koori population. In the last decades of the twentieth century, St Kilda's fortunes have turned full circle again. The desire for inner city accommodation has transformed the seedy suburb to a desirable address.

St Kilda's streets embody a site for performance. They have always done so. It is a place in which not just to live, but to be seen to live—its history has made it one of the few places in supposedly staid Melbourne where the street acts as part of the lifestyle of residents and visitors alike—a status recognised by the local council, since the third volume of the official, commissioned history of the suburb was entitled "And the Band Played On." For people who have known St Kilda for a long time, to walk down the streets of St Kilda now means to witness an almost accomplished revolution—the gentrification of St Kilda is nearly complete, though a few boarding houses and some less than salubrious hotels still stand. These remaining pockets testify to the unwritten history of St Kilda—the one that is not necessarily present in the official version, and certainly entirely absent from the real estate agent's description.

The events examined here occur in the midst of the contested gentrification of St Kilda—real estate prices are going up and up, local supermarkets are disappearing in favour of more coffee shops per square inch than anywhere outside Lygon St. in Carlton. The performance embodied in the streets of St Kilda is becoming mainstream rather than fringe. Within this scenario, we experience two separate urban events. On the one hand, we find a small strip of grass between a number of roads that is a social gathering place, a focus for performance and visual art for a Koori community. On the other, we have the Grand Prix at Albert Park.

The small triangular island of grass and trees at the end of Fitzroy St. is known as Cleve Gardens. They are about the size of a large glossy café, dominated by two ancient Moreton Bay Figs, which drop fruit and turn the hardened ground purple in season. The Cleve Gardens are located at the intersection of three streets—Fitzroy St., Beaconsfield Parade and Jacka Boulevard. These gardens developed a strong identity over years as an informal meeting place for the local Koori residents.

The people who gathered there constituted a specific community and were locally referred to as the "drinking club."

The Cleve Gardens community consisted of Koori people who regularly met and socialised in the gardens. There was a toilet block on the site, which was heavily decorated with murals by Indigenous artists, and the community interacted socially around fires in old forty-four-gallon drums. There existed a significant core of about forty individuals with a long standing association with the site; the rest of the population remained fluid. Long-term absences were not uncommon, yet individuals would return to reconnect with the community. Generally speaking, there was a sixty-forty split between male and female, and nearly seventy per cent were aged between thirty and fifty.[11] Cleve Gardens widely enjoyed the reputation of a place where a diverse range of Koori people could be sure of making contact with other members of the community and of hearing and passing on news of friends and families. It represented a place where a large number of Indigenous Australians from all over Australia would "drop in." The community was so well established that a number of films made in the late 1980s and early 1990s centred on or featured the community and the gardens.

In 1992, Cleve Gardens were recorded as a significant Aboriginal place on the Aboriginal Affairs of Victoria Aboriginal historic places register. The site is currently protected under the Aboriginal and Torres Strait Islander Heritage Protection Act of 1984. Because of this legal status, any physical changes to Cleve Gardens requires consultation with and the written permission of the Wurundjeri Land Compensation and Heritage Council.

What Happened

Unfortunately, there was no such protection for the members of the community. In 1996, as part of the passion shown by the then Premier of Victoria, Jeff Kennet, for monuments to his greatness, the Grand Prix came to Melbourne—to Albert Park in fact, a couple of suburbs down the line from St Kilda. As part of the campaign to beautify the city of Melbourne for the international tourists who were expected in their thousands, someone decided that the Drinking Club had to go. The local police practised zero tolerance, which meant that any Koori on Fitzroy Street was arrested. There were ugly scenes of forcible evictions of Koori people from squats, and so it went on with increasing virulence. By the time the dust started to rise to the whine of formula one cars, all

---

[11] Julie Peers, *City of Port Phillip Special Needs Report Koori Community*: 19-23.

Indigenous Australian Theatre Companies

signs of the Cleve Gardens community were gone, the mural toilet block was levelled overnight and there subsisted no sign of life.

At the time, moreover, the local council was dissolved and replaced by commissioners to oversee major changes in the structure and responsibilities of local councils in Victoria. The commissioners played a major role in the process of "beautifying" St Kilda, which also enjoyed a degree of support from the Fitzroy Street traders, especially those with new businesses catering for the upmarket clientele. The extent of the hostilities was clearly demonstrated when a nationally acclaimed and awarded Aboriginal singer/musician was asked to leave a cafe in Fitzroy St because he was Aboriginal.

Aftermath

When the dust had finally settled and the Grand Prix had fulfilled its agenda—at least for the Grand Prix Corporation—negotiations began between the Koori community in St Kilda and the newly reinstated council. The council recognised the importance for the Aboriginal community of Cleve Gardens as a meeting place. A committee and working parties were established, and a needs study conducted a couple of years previously under the last council was put on the table.[12]

The discovery of shell deposits briefly drew attention. Archaeological digs were undertaken to establish if the site had significance. The purpose of the dig was to find out whether the deposits were natural or cultural. It was widely acknowledged that if the source had turned out to be cultural, it would have altered the status of the area.[13] The results, however, indicated that the deposit was natural.

The working party on Cleve Gardens recommended that the area should be beautified as a design concept that would include a cultural and memorial marker to be conceived by a Koori artist.[14] The new landscaping and decoration were to have an "Aboriginal flavour."[15] Official

---

[12] The working parties included representatives of the City of Port Phillip Council and representatives and advocates for the Port Phillip Indigenous community, i.e. representatives of the Bunarong language group people, Wurundjeri elders, Wurundjeri Land Compensation and Heritage Council, Ngwula Willumbong Co-operative, ATSIC and the Mirimbiak Native Title Unit.

[13] "Dig reveals Little," Shorts, *Emerald Hills Times* (26 June 1996).

[14] *Strategic Community Planning Conservation and Dev Committee Report* (9 October 1996): 1; *Cleve Gardens Task Group Meeting Minutes* (25 June 1996): 1.

[15] Bill Nicholson, Wurundjeri Chairperson, correspondence to Carol Mayell (18 April 1997); *Strategic Community Planning Conservation and Dev Committee Report* (9 October 1996) : 1.

recognition of the Cleve Gardens community was given in October 1997 through the launch of the redevelopment of the gardens as per the recommendations. The redevelopment, according to the Mayor of Port Phillip, represented "a further stage in the continuing process of reconciliation between Aboriginal people and other Australians in Port Phillip."[16] The upgrade of Cleve gardens would "provide substantial visual benefits to the streetscape character and functionality of the space ... and encourage the use of Cleve Gardens as a cultural public space which celebrates its significance for the Koori community."[17]

However, to be given formal local respect and recognition, this significance depended on the non-occupation of the gardens by the community. There were a number of reasons why that agreement was reached. The needs study that had been undertaken in 1994 found that in terms of support for the Indigenous community St Kilda's record remained well below average in terms of employment opportunities and welfare services. By 1997 nothing had changed. These social issues were used as bargaining chips contributing to the resolution of an issue that was recognised in the working party reports as "sensitive," since "it was difficult to develop a mutually acceptable position."[18] In the end, the council adopted an active policy of improving the services available to the Indigenous community in exchange for the acceptance of the redevelopment and future non-occupation of the site.

It is necessary at this point to focus on the implications of the negotiated terms of cultural respect. Cleve Gardens was the base of a lively community: now it has institutional respect as a contemporary meeting place as long as no one meets there. And no-one does. Since the Koori community was removed, the gardens have become in effect nothing more than a traffic island with a very small cultural marker, declaring it to be culturally respected.

This incident mirrors a range of other instances where institutionalised cultural respect is based on retaining Aboriginal motifs or art whilst excluding people. This transition from the theatricalised visible presence to the respected empty space is not an isolated occurrence. Work by Indigenous artists constitute an important aspect of the physical presentation of Parliament House, but the symbolic representative of the tent embassy had to go. The participation of Indigenous Australians

---

[16] *Launch of Cleve Gardens Redevelopment* (News Release, 17 October 1997): 2.

[17] *Strategic Community Planning Conservation and Dev Committee Report* (9 October 1996): 3.

[18] ATSIC & City of Port Phillip Koori, *Working Party Final Report Review of Outcomes* (November 1996): 6, 10.

turned out to be a major factor in Sydney's application for the Olympics. The SOCOG Cultural Arts Festivals have capitalised on Indigenous participation, yet the Koori Communities in Redfern, Sydney are facing many of the same problems as the Cleve Gardens community on a much larger scale.

Within the terms of the negotiated cultural respect, we are dealing with an image, a representation detached from life, a plaque. This is an acceptable image. It becomes clear that the living presence is unacceptable. Guy Debord explored the concept of situations as an event, as an object or commodity, shaped and structured with a beginning a middle and an end.[19] To me, the pressure on the Cleve Gardens community centres on the uncontrolled nature of the situation, the event. A group of people, a community is continuously changing, constantly evoking different responses, different images, constantly emphasising the plurality of viewpoints, narratives and voices. In the negotiated resolution, cultural respect was actively sought by the council in good faith, but in terms of a controlled situation, a controlled event with tangible limits. A plaque is static. Interpretations of the situation, the event, the place may vary but the object, the commodity has defined limits.

Debord argued that the spectacle "is not a collection of images, but a social relation among people, mediated by images".[20] The resolution, the mediation of the images in the case of Cleve Gardens determines which images are presented and which are not. A qualitative change occurs in the nature of the iconography of the urban landscape through the exclusion of the bodies in the space concerned. The human body in social interaction is an independent representation, potentially at least. In this instance, that image has been removed along with all the complications of its unreliability to present a correct or acceptable one. In the process, it has been replaced with a neutral abstraction. In this context, cultural respect is a definable commodity exchanged for an equally definable commodity—the art, the motifs—without the link to living people. As one of the results, intercultural contact between people takes place through a unilateral intermediary, with the terms of contact strictly limited and defined, namely through a plaque. The Indigenous image is thereby rendered passive. In a cultural war for iconography and social memory of the urban landscape, the power of the body in space, the physical presence and the ownership and legacy of the space in the social memory are perceived as the most affective weapons.

---

[19] Guy Debord, *Society of the Spectacle* (Detroit: Black & Red, 1977): 5.
[20] *Ibid.*

In Debord's analysis, the spectacle is "the omnipresent affirmation of the choice already made," the permanent presence of this justification of the pre-existing system.[21] His argument was focused on the relation to the means of production within capitalism, but here it describes as accurately the role of the controlled spectacle in relation to the social centrality and dominance of narratives of "White Australia" and to a reaffirmation of early repression. Steps were supposedly taken in a new and better direction, yet they confirm earlier narratives, earlier choices. In the narrative of dispossession, "pre and post peoples cannot occupy the same place at the same time, except in a moment of transformation that decrees the demise of the pre and the flourishing of the post."[22] The plaque in combination with the non-presence of the Koori community recognises a separate past without any links to the present. In many ways, this type of cultural respect boils down to a new form of assimilation. I doubt that it marks an improvement on early active assimilationist policies, since this assimilation removes individuals rather than incorporating them.

This exchange of cultural respect for definable motifs of culture raises disturbing questions in terms of reception, expectations and the relationship between the agent or creator, the intermediaries and the consumers. This type of determined exchange easily lends itself to an extension of the "orientalist" fantasy. The indications of the "other" are separate from the here and now with its ambivalences and ambiguities. The past is incorporated in a commodified form and placed as separate from present experience, present prejudices and disadvantages.

The more separation there is between the artist and the consumer, the more important the role of the intermediary becomes, especially in relation to the flow of information. As Nelson Graburn argues, in this situation the mediators control the content and the terms of interpretation.[23] The terms of cultural respect are determined, in a sense owned as a spectacle, as well as defined and controlled by one community alone.

---

[21] *Ibid.*: 6.

[22] Deborah Bird Rose, "Hard Times: An Australian Study," in *Quicksands: Foundational Histories in Australia and Aotearoa New Zealand*, eds. Klaus Neumann, Nicholas Thomas and Hilary Ericksen (Sydney: U of New South Wales P, 1999): 10-11.

[23] Nelson Graburn, "Epilogue: Ethnic and Tourist Arts Revisited," in *Unpacking Culture: Art and Community in Colonial and Postcolonial Worlds*, eds. Ruth B. Phillips and Christopher B. Steiner (Berkeley: U of California P, 1999): 335.

When Does Solidarity and Cultural Respect Become Appropriation?

When the role of the intermediary becomes critical in determining the content of the commodified image of the spectacle as both culture and as respect, there are implications in relation to the reception of artwork.

In the spirit of solidarity and cultural sensitivity, theatre work is often "hijacked" on behalf of the "educative" potential for non-Indigenous audiences inherent in the work. When critics assume the non-Indigenous audience is the primary—often sole—focus of the material they in affect appropriate the work of artists, denying the roles that the work plays in specific communities and downgrading other responses. As the work often means quite different things to Indigenous and non-Indigenous communities this creates a hierarchy of communities' responses in relation to it. If the work is primarily examined and discussed in terms of its relevance to and reception by the non-Indigenous community, then the artists' intentions and desires—as well as the terms of reception of the work by the Indigenous community—are marginalised.

Two main results emerge in this process: firstly, the type of work that is produced by non-Indigenous controlled companies is limited to what is perceived as fulfilling this consciousness-raising function; and secondly, discussions and perceptions of the work are restricted to the ways in which it fulfils this function. This process potentially reinforces and perpetuates the marginal/central binary dynamic in critical reception.

In this context, artistic control of processes and production continues to be of primary importance. The first Indigenous controlled theatre companies were established in the early 1970s; since then there have been a variety of attempts in different cities. In the 1990s three companies that have exhibited more longevity than previous attempts were established in different Australian states. These companies—Yirra Yaakin in Perth, Ilbijerri in Melbourne and Kooemba Jdarra in Brisbane—feature a number of commonalities. Each of these companies is linked to specific Indigenous communities and these constitute the primary audience by active company policy.

For example, Yirra Yaakin was formally established as a professional theatre company in 1997.[24] The company has presented a range of productions, including *Cruel Wild Woman* by Sally Morgan and David Milroy, *King Hit* by David Milroy, and *Head Space* by Maudie Sketchley. Yirra Yaakin was established on the basis of disillusionment

---

[24] Yirra Yaakin means "stand tall" in Noongar languages.

with the lack of artistic control available to Indigenous artists, as well as in reaction to the level of cultural compromise required and the resulting distancing of their work from Indigenous communities. According to David Milroy, Artistic Director of Yirra Yaakin, "We don't see enough control in the hands of Aboriginal artists in developing their theatre. Theatre [for Aboriginal people] is not just about putting a show on stage but about the social political and financial outcomes for the community."[25]

Yirra Yaakin uncompromisingly produces its work for the Noongar people in South-West WA. Other communities are welcome to attend their shows, but they are not the targeted audiences. The framing of work according to its educative function for the non-Indigenous audience appeared all too clearly in some of the reception of *Cruel Wild Woman*, presented at the 1999 Festival of Perth. The company's orientation in its promotional material declared that Yirra Yaakin was "giving Australia the comedy it deserves."[26] The play offers a satirical look at contemporary Australian politics, challenging the philosophy and public posturings of Pauline Hanson and the rise of the One Nation Party—an extreme right-wing party with an explicitly racist platform—which were current at the time.

The critical resistance to the work was based on the contention that the issues were serious and the company should be offering "new insights ... the script gives us nothing of substance to mull over."[27] The writers, Morgan and Milroy, clearly stated that the work was not "an indictment of the current state of Indigenous and non-Indigenous relations in Australia, they were writing a comedy for the communities that lived with racism, they didn't need it explained to them or its ramifications outlined. They were gathering together to laugh at the completely laughable."[28] According to Milroy, "if the [Noongar] community likes it, the critics are guaranteed not to."[29]

The practices and priorities of Indigenous controlled companies create space for Indigenous artists beyond their designated role in relation to the non-Indigenous communities. These companies and the play-

---

[25] Jo Litson, "White Heat Black Stories," *The Weekend Australian* (20-21 May 2000): 18.

[26] *Cruel Wild Woman* Press Release (February 1999); *Cruel Wild Woman* advertising copy (February 1999); *Cruel Wild Woman* Poster.

[27] Jacqueline Molloy, "Wild Woman Soft at Heart," *The West Australian* (12 February 1999): 5.

[28] Ron Banks, "Laughter as a Lifeline," *The West Australian* (4 February 1999): 5.

[29] David Milroy, telephone interview (April 1999).

wrights associated with them adapt, utilise or ignore the different resonances and meanings that the work offers to specific Indigenous communities in contrast with the broader non-Indigenous one. As in the case of *Cruel Wild Woman*, a brief examination of the development and reception of the play *Stolen* demonstrates the different meanings that the work carries for different communities.

Stolen, by Jane Harrison, a descendent of the Muruwari people of New South Wales, was commissioned by Ilbijerri Aboriginal and Torres Strait Islander Theatre Co-operative. The play was produced at the Malthouse in October 1998 by the company in association with Playbox Theatre Centre and the Melbourne International Festival. It was directed by Wesley Enoch, a Murri artist. Ilbijerri was established in Melbourne in 1990 as an Indigenous controlled theatre company. The company was set up with a clear orientation towards the Victorian Koori community, with the production of work by and for Victorian Kooris its priority.[30] In 1991, after the success of the Ilbijerri's inaugural production of *Up the Road* by John Harding, the committee of management decided to initiate work on a play about the "lost children" as members of the Stolen Generations were known at the time.

In 1991, there was little knowledge or understanding of the "lost children" outside the Indigenous communities. The period of development of *Stolen* mirrors an ongoing campaign by Indigenous activists to gain recognition and a voice for the generations of Indigenous Australian children forcibly taken from their families, supposedly in the service of assimilationist policies. In many ways, the six-year journey of "The Lost children" to "Stolen" also corresponds to the journey of placing responsibility publicly where it belonged.

Like the playwright, the members of the Human Rights and Equal Opportunity Commission's National Enquiry into the Separation of Aboriginal and Torres Strait Islander Children from Their Families established in 1995 heard countless stories from stolen children about abuse, about refusal of access to archives and information about their families, about the trauma of parents who were told that their children were dead and of children who were told that their families had died or abandoned them. The Inquiry found that the children had been forcibly removed, institutionalised, denied contact with their Aboriginality, in some cases traumatised and abused, and that the forced separation had caused long lasting disorders.

Ilbijerri's project *Stolen* pursued two major aims. One aim was to give a public voice to these experiences primarily for the Koori commu-

---

[30] Bev Murray, personal interview (Melbourne, 1998).

nity. The other major aim was to produce a play that reflected the variety of Koori stories, experiences and reactions aimed at countering the representations of Koori people as a "homogenous people who all feel the same way."[31] The latter aim has been an ongoing concern for Indigenous artists and companies. Wesley Enoch, when he was Artistic Director of Kooemba Jdarra, argued that "In the same way that there is no homogenous Aboriginal nation (accepting the fact that we are a collection of peoples of this continent but with a diversity of languages, cultural practices and geographies) there is neither a generic Aboriginal experience to write of."[32]

The process of script development for *Stolen* began in 1992 when Harrison was commissioned to write a play about the Stolen Generations. The Inquiry dealt with stories on a national level, the stories Harrison drew on came from the Victorian community.[33] In *Stolen*, Harrison weaves together the stories of five Aboriginal children stolen from their families and institutionalised. On a series of different levels, the narrative traces each child's individual journey and experience of grief and abuse, as they struggle to play as children and live their lives. In production, at the end of the play, each member of the cast steps out of character and tells their own story. Some cast members like the characters in the play, have tragic stories to tell, others do not. This moment in a sense claims ownership of these stories for individuals in the present in a way that breaks the centrality of the dominant non-Indigenous audience.

The fact that the work focuses on grief and its resolution rather than on rage or revenge constantly fascinates the many critics who have written about the play. The idea that the focus of the work was giving voice to shared experiences and grief rather than informing Euro-Australian audiences or abusing them is not acknowledged anywhere. There is no space in the responses of the media for the responses of Indigenous audiences. On the regional tour of Victoria, Indigenous Australian people would come up after the show and share their stories

---

[31] Bev Murray, "A History of the *Stolen*," unpublished typescript (1998).

[32] Wesley Enoch, "Murri Grief," *Dialogue* (27 June 1996): 10. Kooemba Jdarra Indigenous Arts was founded in Brisbane in 1993; Kooemba Jdarra means "good ground" in the Turrabul languages; shows include *The 7 Stages of Grieving* by Wesley Enoch and Deborah Mailman, *Bethel and Maude* by Joanne Close, *A life of Grace and Piety* by Wesley Enoch, *Little White Dress*, revised, *Murri Love* by Cathy Craigie, as well as earlier works by Indigenous writers such as Kevin Gilbert's *The Cherry Pickers* and Jack Davis's *The Dreamers*.

[33] Anna King Murdoch, "Seeing Things in Black and White," *The Age* (13 October 1998): 17.

with the cast. The experience provided an occasion and a forum for healing.

The example of *Stolen* as a co-production with a non-Indigenous company demonstrates the balancing act that Indigenous artists have to perform in order to accommodate the different communities and their responses. In practice, they focused on the Indigenous communities and this was particularly apparent in the tour, but in terms of critical reception the frame was placed from the perspective of the non-Indigenous audience's responses. Indigenous Australian artists are constantly siting themselves—negotiating with the different demands of their work—as individual artists living as Indigenous Australians with their history that has been silenced and with the requirement that their work fulfil a general broad educative function.

In recent years, major steps have been taken to reveal the hidden histories of Australia and to bridge the gaps between Indigenous and non-Indigenous narratives of Australia's past. Yet, the terms of reception on the record, like the terms of the negotiated settlement in relation to Cleve Gardens, generate different narratives for different communities. The mediation of meaning and focus on art as an object and a commodity rather than on the agent widens the gap between narratives and creates new differences.

Works Cited

Adler, Louise. "Interview with Rhoda Roberts," Arts National, Radio National ABC Radio (1997).

ATSIC & City of Port Phillip Koori. *Working Party Final Report Review of Outcomes* (November 1996).

Banks, Ron. "Laughter as a Lifeline," *The West Australian* (4 February, 1999): 5.

Bird Rose, Deborah. "Hard Times: An Australian Study," in *Quicksands: Foundational Histories in Australia and Aotearoa New Zealand*, eds. Klaus Neumann, Nicholas Thomas and Hilary Ericksen (Sydney: U of New South Wales P, 1999): 2-19.

Cleve Gardens Task Group Meeting (Minutes, 25 June 1996).

Council for Aboriginal and Torres Strait Islander Reconciliation Act, Commonwealth Government of Australia (1991).

Cruel Wild Woman Press Release (February 1999).

Cruel Wild Woman advertising copy (February 1999).

Cruel Wild Woman Poster.

Debord, Guy. *Society of the Spectacle* (Detroit: Black & Red, 1977).

"Dig reveals Little," Shorts, *Emerald Hills Times* (26 June 1996).

Enoch, Wesley. "Murri Grief," *Dialogue* (27 June 1996): 10.

Graburn, Nelson. "Epilogue: Ethnic and Tourist Arts Revisited," in *Unpacking Culture: Art and Community in Colonial and Postcolonial Worlds*, eds. Ruth B. Phillips and Christopher B. Steiner (Berkeley: U of California P, 1999): 335-54.

King Murdoch, Anna. "Seeing Things in Black and White," *The Age* (13 October 1998): 17.

Langton, Marcia. *Well I Heard It on the Radio and I Saw It on the Television* (Sydney: Australian Film Commission, 1993).

Launch of Cleve Gardens Redevelopment (News Release, 17 October 1997).

Litson, Jo. "White Heat Black Stories," *The Weekend Australian* (20-21 May 2000): 18.

Miller, Lydia. Paperbark Seminar, State Library of New South Wales, Festival of the Dreaming (September 1997).

Milroy, David. Telephone interview (April 1999).

Molloy, Jacqueline. "Wild Woman Soft at Heart," *The West Australian* (12 February 1999): 5.

Murray, Bev. Personal interview (Melbourne, 1998).

——— "A History of the *Stolen*" (unpublished typescript, 1998).

Nicholson, Bill. Wurundjeri Chairperson, correspondence to Carol Mayell (18 April 1997).

Peers, Julie. *City of Port Phillip Special Needs Report Koori Community*.

Roberts, Rhoda. *The Festival of The Dreaming: Festival Guide* (September 1997).

——— "Sweet Dreams" Review, *Weekend Australian* (13-14 September 1997): 20-21.

——— "The 1997 Rex Cramphorn Memorial Lecture," *Australasian Drama Studies* 32 (April 1998): 3-20.

——— "A Passion for Ideas: Black Stage," *Dialogue* 34 (March 1998): 10-11.

Strategic Community Planning Conservation and Dev Committee Report (9 October 1996).

Playing the Yellow Lady: Performing Gender and Race

JACQUELINE LO

Australian National University

> ...
> And when the moon grew
> round and bright
> Like a coiled dragon, I would
> Put
> Into my breast for sheer
> delight
> Your tiny rose-leaf Chinese
> foot
> While you would sing *Ming's
> Song* and write
> With long pink nails upon my
> skin
> The tender hymn that wailed
> the flight
> Of nights of sin...*our*
> nights of sin.
> ...[1]

The title of this essay alludes to Alison Broinowski's biblio-text, *The Yellow Lady*, which in turn, takes its cue from Norman Lindsay's 1922 painting, "Yellow Lady" and Hugh McCrae's poem in the epigraph above. McCrae's poem exemplifies many typical Orientalist tropes—the subject is the Western male, the object of desire the Oriental woman. She is depicted as delicate, foot-bound, sexually available, and above all, speechless while he alone speaks for and about her. Broinowski's book has been hailed as "pioneering" work, "an indispensable reference book" encapsulating the "history of Australia's aesthetic responses to Asia."[2] Yet for all its impressive bibliographic coverage, the book presents a surprisingly simplistic view of Asian-Australian relations.

---

[1] Hugh McCrae, "The Yellow Lady," in *Idyllia* (Sydney: N.L. Press, 1922).

[2] Blurb on back cover: Alison Broinowski, *The Yellow Lady: Australian Impressions of Asia* (Melbourne: Oxford UP, 1992; second edition, 1996).

The logic of the text is based on "skin colour" and on the projection of Asia as female. The title belies the author's (unsuccessful) attempt at irony and reflexivity. As Foong Ling Kong points out, to write is to "subscribe to particular formations of selfhood ... [and] Broinowski ... has, consciously or otherwise, sexed this space as female ... [and] fixed the Other woman's speaking position."[3] The authorial voice in this text sounds not unlike those which it seeks to critique. The author speaks from the position of the "non-duped," that is, as someone who is able to navigate through the representations of "bad" or "false" Asia and to locate her "truer" selves.[4] But as Rey Chow reminds us: "Because the image, in which the other is often cast, is always distrusted as illusion, deception, and falsehood, attempts to salvage the other often turn into attempts to uphold the other ... as the site of authenticity and true knowledge. Critics who do this also imply that, having absorbed the primal wisdoms, they are the non-duped themselves."[5] Stripped of its rhetoric, this desire to embody the non-duped is exposed as the desire to maintain control and preserve existing power relations.

This essay does not intend to stake any claims on Asian female authenticity from either a position of "objectivity" or as cultural "insider." I am more concerned with teasing out the negotiations that take place in order to perform Asian femininity on the Australian stage. To "play the Yellow Lady" suggests both resistance and subversion, but also complicity and acquiescence. It is within this tension and problematic of difference that I wish to locate my speaking position and the subject of this critique.

The Politics of Yellow

In Australia, the colour yellow has historically been associated with "Orientals"—that is, with people from East and South East Asia. The category of Oriental and "yellowness" implies a more specific subject than the category of "Asian"—the latter corresponding to a wider cate-

---

[3] Foong Ling Kong, "Postcards from a Yellow Lady," in *Asian and Pacific Inscriptions: Identities, Ethnicities, Nationalities*, ed. Suvendrini Perera (Melbourne: Meridien/La Trobe University English Review 14.2, 1995): 87.

[4] The second edition of *The Yellow Lady* includes an additional chapter on cultural production by Australians of Asian descent. But even here, the works are contained within a simplistic discourse of hybridity as fusion and synthesis. Asian-Australian agency and difference are co-opted to serve the emphasis which hegemonic multiculturalism puts on the tolerance of difference rather than on an engagement with the radical potential of cultural diversity.

[5] Rey Chow, *Writing Diaspora: Tactics of Intervention in Contemporary Cultural Studies* (Bloomington and Indianapolis: Indiana UP, 1993): 52.

Performing Gender and Race

gory which includes people from South Asian and Middle Eastern backgrounds.[6] Popular literature of the late nineteenth century such as Kenneth Mackay's *The Yellow Wave: A Romance of the Asiatic Invasion of Australia* (1895) and M.P. Shiel's *The Yellow Danger* (1898) subscribe to the prevalent myth of the yellow peril invading White Australia.[7] More recently of course, Pauline Hanson has revived this myth, most infamously in her debut parliamentary speech warning against being "swamped by Asians."

Projections of Asia as female have led to a representation continuum ranging from the frail lotus blossom (submissive, child-like) to the dragon lady (sexually active, castrative, deceptive). Between these poles lie a range of positions which offer variations on the same theme of ambivalence towards the Other, marked by both desire and disavowal. The fascination of Western opera with Yellow Ladies such as *Madama Butterfly*, *Aida*, *Turandot*, and *Salome*[8] foregrounds the prevalence of the Orient as a racialised, sexualised and gendered site of Western imaginings. It is not surprising that these operas are named after their Oriental heroines—who all suffer tragic deaths. The idea of Western male dominance and Eastern female sacrifice forms part of the teleology of Enlightenment and its discourses of imperialism and colonialism.

The *femme fatale*/dragon lady stereotype arguably reaches its apogee in Australian cultural production with the character of Cynthia in the 1994 film *Priscilla, Queen of the Desert*. The demonic and sexually aberrant Filipina functions in the text as the Other to "real" femininity, as performed by Bernadette, the transvestite character.[9] Race, gender, as well as class figure implicitly in the filmic logic, since Bernadette's White hyper-femininity and gentility triumph in the love-stake, and it is she and not Cynthia with whom audiences empathise. The Asian woman is used purely as sign—to humanise the White male identities in the

---

[6] Until 1990, the Australian Bureau of Statistics included people from the Middle East under the category of Asian. For more information on statistics and migration patterns, see Laksiri Jayasuriya and Kee Pookong, *The Asianisation of Australia? Some Facts about the Myths* (Carlton South: Melbourne UP, 1999).

[7] As David Walker points out, this fear is partly based on colonial Australia's own insecurity at having procured the land through illegitimate means, that is, through invasion and colonisation. Many of the yellow invasion theme-literatures reveal an anxiety that White Australians would be "Aboriginalised" by the yellow hordes. See David Walker, *Anxious Nation: Australia and the Rise of Asia 1850-1939* (St Lucia: Queensland UP, 1999).

[8] These operas feature regularly in the flagship programming of opera in Australia.

[9] For a more detailed critique, see Merlinda Bobis, Helen Gilbert and Jacqueline Lo, "What *Priscilla* Said," *RealTime* 4 (1994): 4-5.

film. Cynthia exists to serve a didactic function by enabling the men (and by extension, the implied viewer) to understand themselves better as White male subjects.

What reading positions do these Orientalist discourses offer the Asian-Australian woman? Kong's criticism of Broinowski's *The Yellow Lady* is instructive:

> I find my self, as a reader, mirrored in Broinowski's text, her specular observations freeze my entry, since the unitary "we" ... admits only certain figures ... [The text] leaves someone like me, a non-Western woman reader, in the field of the gaze ...[10]

Although Orientalism is imbricated in the Asian-Australian woman's modes of self-perception and self-representation, this does not mean that she is rendered totally passive and compliant as object of the will-to-power. As Elizabeth Grosz argues, "Its enmeshment in disciplinary regimes is the condition of the subject's social effectivity, as either conformist or subversive."[11] While I support her claim that agency lies at the point of implication, not outside it, I am troubled by her binaristic depiction of positions available to the disciplined subject—as either "conformist or subversive." This too neat and wishful proposition does not capture the problematic tensions between desire and disavowal, between self and not-self that I read in the performances of Asian-Australian female identities.

The Asian-Australian writer Beth Yahp describes the "Other Asia" as "that ghostly shadow welded to me more closely than my own."[12] She describes the relationship as one of mutual antagonism and desire. Acknowledging the impossibility of escaping from the Other Asia, Yahp comes to realise that she "has her uses too":

> So I sometimes let her in. I give her Illicit Space to reign in ... I let her choose ... In my stories the Other Asia can play seductress, or victim, or oppressed migrant, or schoolgirl swot, but she has to promise me one thing. Never to be just that ... In fiction, as in life, I'd like the Other Asia to juggle her faces, exuberantly, not meekly, and to her own tune and timing. And if those faces crack, or smear in the process—*all is well*. Maybe then she'll acquire new ones—ones that don't sit so heavily or fit so tightly.[13]

Yahp draws attention to the complex negotiation of subject formation, which entails both resistance and complicity, difference and equiva-

---

[10] Kong, *op. cit*.: 88.

[11] Elizabeth Grosz, *Volatile Bodies: Toward A Corporeal Feminism*, (St Leonard's: Allen and Unwin, 1994): 144.

[12] Beth Yahp, "Place Perfect and the Other Asia," *Westerly* (Autumn 1996): 62.

[13] *Ibid*.: 70-71.

lence. There is no "Real Asia" to be revealed, nor is the "Other Asia" merely a mask. Rather, the enacting of roles brings identity into being. Yahp describes identity-formation in processual and performative terms—the "Other Asia" is never fixed in the one role. Hence, for Yahp, agency lies at the uneasy nexus between subjectivity and subjectification, at the interface between Self and Other. This qualified agency foregrounds the ambivalence that lies at the heart of self-representation as both an assertion of sameness and difference, founded on the tension between the recognition of the self as both reproducer of *and* resistor to Orientalism.

Playing the Yellow Lady

Given the political, structural, and economic challenges to the emergence of Asian-Australian cultural production, the popularity of the monodrama form in theatre does not seem surprising. The one-woman monodrama is easier to stage and cheaper to finance; more importantly, the genre enables a form of self-representation which reveals its uncertain but nonetheless determined intervention into the symbolic sphere of national imaginings. These monodramas combine partial autobiography with a strong feminist orientation and interest in the exploration of maternal relationships. *Chinese Take Away* by Anna Yen and *Border Lover* by Merlinda Bobis offer different perspectives on this emerging tradition. I contend that this interest in mapping matrilineal "herstories" is partly inspired by the visibility of diasporic Asian women's writing (particularly from the United States), especially by authors like Jung Chang, Amy Tan, and Maxine Hong Kingston. Although the increasing confidence in exploring personal stories can be read as a progressive move towards the inclusion of ethnic difference, it can also lead to the entrenchment of gender and ethnic stereotypes, and to the preservation of the status quo.

Rey Chow warns that the popularity of "ethnic" cultural production and the dominance of the confessional or life-writing mode may inadvertently serve "the panopticist multicultural gaze."[14] She argues that hegemonic multiculturalism[15] has led to the widely-held belief in "ethnicity" as a kind of repressed truth that awaits liberation through processes such as confessions, biography, autobiography, and storytell-

---

[14] Rey Chow, *Ethics after Idealism: Theory-Culture-Ethnicity-Reading* (Bloomington and Indianapolis: Indiana UP, 1998): 104.

[15] For a more detailed discussion of hegemonic multiculturalism, see Jacqueline Lo, "Beyond Happy Hybridity: Performing Asian-Australian Identities," in *Alter/Asian*. ed. Ien Ang et al. (Annandale: Pluto Press, forthcoming 2000).

ing.[16] Using a Foucauldian model, she argues that institutionally-sanctioned constructions of ethnicity may not be personal liberation but rather disciplinary subject formation:

> Would it be far-fetched to say that precisely those apparatuses that have been instituted to gain access to our "ethnicities" are at the same time accomplishing the goal of an ever-refined, ever-perfected, and ever-expanding system of visuality and visibility ... that is inseparable from discipline and punishment, from the ubiquitous "economy" of sociopolitical control?[17]

While Chow's argument holds some weight, particularly in view of the various multicultural festivals and media productions celebrating Australian multiculturalism,[18] I would suggest that the performance of self by Asian-Australian women like Anna Yen, Merlinda Bobis and Mémé Thorne[19] exceed the confessional frame to unsettle the production of "truth." The pressures are certainly brought to bear by virtue of the institutional positioning of many of these performances: for example, Yen's production had significant support from Arts Queensland, the Australia Council for the Arts, the Sidney Myer Foundation, and the Queensland Performance Arts Trust. Nevertheless, I contend that in live performance, the process of dis/closure is itself problematised by the ambivalent and ironic performance of self. Furthermore, it should be noted that Foucault himself shifted from arguing in the first volume of *The History of Sexuality* that confessions were the key instruments in producing truths through domination to emphasising in volumes two and three the constitution and transformation of the subject in the process of self-revelation. Foucault's later works focus on individuals who recognise themselves as constituted within particular knowledge/power formations, which then become the condition of their agency: "the relation of self with self and the forming of oneself as subject."[20] Chow's intervention serves to remind us of the need to be attentive to the enunciative practices and locations of self-exposition, enunciations which include the spoken as well as the unspoken—the contradictions, ruptures, slippages and silences.

---

[16] Chow, *op. cit.*: 101.

[17] *Ibid.*: 102.

[18] Examples include the New South Wales state-funded Carnivale and the annual National Multicultural Festival in Canberra, as well as television commercials for the celebrations of the 1988 Bicentennial and the 2001 Centenary of Federation.

[19] For more discussion on Bobis and Thorne, see, Jacqueline Lo, "Dis/orientation: Contemporary Asian-Australian Theatre," in *Our Australian Theatre in the 1990s*, ed. Veronica Kelly (Amsterdam: Rodopi, 1998): 53-70.

[20] Michel Foucault, *The Use of Pleasure: The History of Sexuality,* vol. 2, tr. Robert Hurley (New York: Vintage, 1986): 6.

Chinese Take Away

Anna Yen's physical theatre performance show, *Chinese Take Away*, premiered at the Stage X Festival in Brisbane in 1997.[21] The text recuperates Yen's family history as part of subaltern Australian history. Yen stages her grandmother's story of survival the China of the 1930s and colonial Hong Kong, her mother's struggle to belong in the White Australia of the 1960s, and her own grief as a teenager in the 1970s. According to Yen, the production "set out to honour my ancestors ... I strongly wanted the stories of Asian-Australians to be out there, on stage; stories that are rich and not stereotyped."[22] Yen's keen awareness of the need to unsettle dominant preconceptions of Asianness (Chineseness in particular) and of the fetishisation of the figure of the Chinese woman has resulted in a syncretic text which mobilises ambivalence as a source of critique and empowerment.

Given the codes of embodiment that underpin the figuring of the Yellow Lady, the performing body becomes the primary site where the contestation and negotiation between Self and not-Self is played out. There are many kinds of Yellow Ladies in *Chinese Take Away*, including the coquettish showgirl, the child-woman, the wise and wizened old lady, the mad woman, the marriage resistor and the butterfly. Like Yahp, therefore, Yen does not allow one Asia to hold centre stage for long. The performance is marked by a ceaseless fluidity and mobility as the performer's body turns into the site of both self-critique and self-transformation. The performing body becomes both the sign and the subject of contestation between *personae*—most visibly manifest in the scene where the abandoned child struggles against, and eventually gains strength from, the warrior woman. By embodying this struggle through the figure of the solo performer, identity-formation is shown to be agonistically configured in response to changing sociopolitical conditions rather than being reduced to an uncomplicated "morphing" from one subject to another. The foregrounding of the sutures and gaps in the process of self-transformation denaturalises the theatrical experience and unsettles the fixity of the female Asian body as an object of specular desire.

The title, *Chinese Take Away*, also exemplifies the ludic function of ambivalence. Firstly, the title refers to the stereotype of Chinese food: "You want short soup, long soup, fly lice, spling loll, sweet and sour

---

[21] Anna Yen, "Chinese Take Away," in *Three Plays by Asian Australians*, ed. Don Batchelor (Brisbane: Playlab, 2000). Further references to the published text will feature parenthetically in the main discussion.

[22] Anna Yen interviewed by Don Batchelor, *op. cit.*: 33.

chicken?" (63) Not only is gender destabilised by Yen playing her father playing the Chinaman at this point, but the "inscrutable" face of the Chinese cook begins to crack as we discover how Yen's father, like many other "illegal aliens," survived the scrutiny and bigotry of the White Australia Policy by getting involved in the feminised food business. The stereotype within this context functions both as a mode of survival and a strategy for critique.

The title also refers to the family's diasporic history and the impossibility of a teleology of return to an original state of authenticity. As the Cantonese voice-over translated and projected in English onto the back screen at the start of the show states: "Once water is poured on the ground, it is hard to get it back" (41), the performance problematises the idea of fixity and authenticity. Is Anna Yen less Chinese because she was not born in China? How can one reconcile a self that *looks* Chinese but *identifies as* Australian? The grandmother, mother, and Yen herself represent, in chronological order, an increasing geographical and cultural distance from the homeland and fixed notions of Chineseness. In this sense, the title plays on expectations of a voyeuristic consumption of "authentic" Chineseness, only to be confronted with hybridised, diasporic identities, which—like the "fly lice" and "sweet and sour chicken"—are strategically produced to deal with the specific demands of the hostland.

Finally, the title alludes to women's bodies that have been politicised in systems of exchange in both Western and "native" patriarchies. Yen's staging of a matrilineal history foregrounds the abuse (physical, mental, sexual, medical), economic exploitation, and cultural displacement suffered by women in her family in the name of tradition, colonialism, nationalism, and economic advancement. Her grandmother was sold as a child to work as a servant in China, while her mother was tricked by her own parents into leaving Hong Kong as a seventeen-year-old "student" to come to Australia only to be faced with an arranged marriage, which consisted of repeated rape and multiple pregnancies. Her mother's eventual nervous breakdown and suicide perpetuates the legacy of damaged female bodies and the loss of innocence, and young Anna grows up with the burden of not only being born female but also of failing to rescue her mother.

However, the recuperation of agency through the evocation of transgressive female figures—such as the marriage resistors from Chinese history and mythology—help to offset this history of loss and abuse. In particular, Yen calls upon the warrior woman, who has trained in the Wu Shu martial arts, as a source of physical strength and courage. *Chinese Take Away* opens with the figure of the warrior woman "furiously striking out at many invisible enemies" (40). The warrior woman contradicts the more established images in the West of the Asian woman as "lack" and as lotus blossom, dragon lady, mail order bride, and so forth.[23] The physical and mental discipline necessary to perform these dangerous martial arts movements counter the disciplinary techniques (both Western and Chinese) usually exercised on and reproduced through the female body. These contradictory disciplinary histories and ontologies are textualised on the same performing body to effect an embodied ambivalence which supports the contention that the performing body is not only a locus of power/knowledge, but also a site for the articulation of difference and resistance.

Border Lover

As part of the 1996 Carnivale, Merlinda Bobis's *Border Lover* was performed at the "Found in Translation" Playworks Conference. The text consists of monologues and dialogues spoken by the protagonist and her Filipina grandmother. Most of the performance takes place on an extended diving board above the stage. Parallel to this board, running across the stage are three near invisible lines which, in the course of the performance, are used to hang the "pegged ethnicities" which mark the Filipina-Australian woman as Other. These pegged ethnicities—including a wok and ladle, a banana-leaf wrapped chicken leg, ethnic necklace and scarf, native pouch, Filipino pesos, and coconut shells—are positioned between the performer and the audience to suggest a kind of superimposition which mediates the process of viewing the performance and the performing female body.

Like Yen's text, *Border Lover* also focuses on the diaspora's longing for home—in spite of the knowledge of the provisionality of identity and belonging—lived in the tension between lost homelands and new hostlands: "But how is it to land and not land, my wings rearranging themselves for home and not home?"[24] Caught between the "there" and "here," the Self and not-Self, this diasporic subject also performs multiple roles, switching self-consciously between self and grandmother, as well as playing up the academic, the "native" and the dutiful Filipina

---

[23] The recuperation of the warrior woman as a figure of strength and defiance can arguably be linked to Maxine Hong Kingston's pioneering 1975 novel *The Woman Warrior*. While I am not claiming that Yen was consciously alluding to Kingston's text, the resemblance suggests a strong connection between the various Asian diasporic communities in the West, as well as a confluence of developments in gender politics and cultural production.

[24] Merlinda Bobis, *Border Lover* (1996, unpublished manuscript): 2. All further references will feature parenthetically in the text.

grand-daughter. Significantly, the "pegged ethnicities" installation is derived from the performer's body—the items are part of her costume which also includes a capacious backpack. The stripping away of these signifiers of abjectness does not simply amount to an act of disavowal, however, but rather recognises the Asian woman's playful complicity in the production of her own exoticisation:

> Oh yes, I confess I played up my Otherness before, in order to be noticed at all, but it wears the heart out—letting it do a native jig all the time for the sake of an audience who would marvel at my exotic mask ... always post-card pretty ... Ayyyyyyyy ... !
>
> (while she continues the chant above, takes out a colourful ethnic gear from backpack, wraps it around her and dances a native measure on the plank, still chanting)
>
> Ayyyyyyyy!
> Ang lipad ay awit
> Sa apat na hangin
> Ngunit di umaawit
> Ang panlimang hangin ...
> Delightfully exotic indeed but hang on ... Ayyyyyy ...
>
> (breaks into a David Bowie song and a disco dance)
>
> Ayyyyy ... "Let's dance
> Put on your red shoes
> And dance the blues ..."
>
> (pegs costume onto another string, while still singing) (6)

Frank Chin coined the term "food pornography" to describe the conscious exoticisation of one's ethnic foodways as a means of entering into the dominant culture. According to Chin, foods such as those served up by Yen's father in *Chinese Take Away*, are "ingratiating rather than threatening"—it is food that has been "'detoxed,' depoliticised and made safe for recreational consumption."[25] Chin's argument can easily be transposed from food to cultural terms, but as Sau-ling Wong notes, Chin's argument loses impact and nuance because of its polemical tone and tendency towards extremism. Wong argues that because the inclusion of "cultural pornography" is still determined by the dominant culture, this leads to the paradoxical state where these cultural productions simultaneously proclaim and undermine ethnicity and difference.[26] My argument takes up where Wong's stops—at this very point of ambivalence. While Wong sees cultural pornography as problematic and ulti-

---

[25] In Sau-Ling Cynthia Wong, *Reading Asian American Literature: From Necessity to Extravagance* (Princeton, New Jersey: Princeton UP, 1993): 56.

[26] *Ibid.*: 57.

Performing Gender and Race 79

mately, self-defeating, I wish to stress the performative aspects of pornography as a knowing and strategic play with desire.

This knowingness is exactly what Bobis enacts in the pegging on and off of her ethnic markers. The irony and parody mobilised in her performance of various roles and subject positions suggest that she is highly aware of trading her exoticism as a point of entry into the dominant culture. This trade is not allowed to become entrenched however; the performer/protagonist leaves her pegged ethnicities *on the line* at the end of the performance, as she (literally) touches down on Australian land, after a visit "back home." This return to the hostland—minus ethnic costume—signifies a new stage in the continued negotiation between home and not home, Self and not-Self. The text resolutely resists a reading of authenticity—that the Subject is somehow more "truthful" because of having come into contact with "traditional culture" through the grandmother. The fact that this encounter between past and present, tradition and modernity, is negotiated through the body of the performer rebuffs such simplistic binarisms.

One of the most interesting aspects of the performance lies in its interrogation of theoretical discourse to enunciate the First World/Third World and generational divide. The academic granddaughter spouts French psychoanalytic theories of feminism at her grandmother, who in turn cunningly subverts their erasure of cultural and class differences. In place of theoretical speech, the grandmother stuffs the granddaugher's mouth with food: "Thus my discourse is reduced to a chicken leg" (3):

> But I don't allow her to seduce me from my peroration, so I turn to the wall, blackened with a thousand meals from her old stove, and mutter the argument to myself—the semiotic as against the symbolic which is "the logic, coherent syntax and rationality of the adult," and which—
>
> So they also talk with their mouths full in Australia, ha?
>
> The symbolic which "places subjects in their position and makes it possible for them to have identities" ... a rationalised
> self-representation ... well, who am I anyway?
>
> (Pegs the chicken leg onto line. Grandmother is now very impatient)
>
> Ano baya iyan na pigpaparahuringhuding mo diyan, ha? Who are you? Of course you're my granddaughter, who, after flying to your Australia to write—what is it again, a tisis? Ay, sounds like an affliction of the lungs to me—tisis!
>
> Thesis, Grandmother.
>
> Whatever—and now she comes home with a strange tongue which she

practises on her poor Grandmother. Are you turning up your nose on me? (4)

Poststructuralist-deconstruction theory is not demonised as another form of cultural imperialism, however, nor is it presented as the brave new world for the marginalised:

> Yes, so it is the ecstatic collapse of cultural absolutism. In my mind, I have convinced myself this is bliss: I am the border lover, romancing this edge for dear life, for the sake of survival. And who says I am in the margins? I have centre-ed my own space. It is after all an empowering "seam," where a writer can invent new characters, her either-or/neither-nor gods or monsters.
>
> (self-mockery is almost grating)
>
> ...
>
> What a comfort theory is. You almost think it takes you home. And the resolution is so clear, so crystal clear—but only in the mind ... (7)

The opposing views of the grandmother and academic granddaughter as articulated through the performing body yield a moment of disjunction and dissonance between different ontologies. Likewise, the opposition results in the unsettling of both discourses. No absolute position can be subscribed to, no secure "truths" produced. Ambivalence is like "a hollow growing peculiar in [the] breast" (8).

Much has been written by critics such as Homi Bhabha about the radical potential of ambivalence to overthrow colonial authority. I make no such grand claims in this essay. My aim has been to draw attention to the politics and poetics of ambivalence in Asian-Australian women's theatre as a means of teasing out a fuller picture of the complex negotiations which are performed and embodied, "invariably, under constraint, daily and incessantly, with anxiety and pleasure."[27] To this end, Jane Flax's psychoanalytic definition of ambivalence proves particularly useful:

> Ambivalence refers to affective states in which intrinsically contradictory or mutually exclusive desires or ideas are each invested with intense emotional energy. Although one cannot have both simultaneously, one cannot abandon either of them.[28]

Flax maintains that ambivalence does not necessarily amount to a symptom of weakness or confusion but rather, "a strength to resist col-

---

[27] Judith Butler, "Performative Acts and Gender Constitution: An Essay in Phenomenology and Feminist Theory," in *Performing Feminisms: Feminist Critical Theory and Theatre*, ed. Sue-Ellen Case (Baltimore: Johns Hopkins UP, 1990): 282.

[28] Cited by Ien Ang, "The Curse of the Smile: Ambivalence and the 'Asian' Woman in Australian Multiculturalism," *Feminist Review* 52 (1996): 44.

lapsing complex and contradictory material into an orderly whole."[29] In live performance, the female Asian body speaks as both sign and signifier. This doubleness is used as a strategy to decentre notions of fixed identities and to promote a more processual and performative understanding of identity formation.

Homi Bhabha describes the encounter with identity and identification as a disruption which "occurs at the point at which something exceeds the frame of the image, it eludes the eyes, evacuates the self as site of identity and autonomy, and—most importantly—leaves a resistant trace, a stain of the subject, a sign of resistance."[30] An interrogative performance of race and gender aims to test such limits—to exceed the frame—and in the course of doing so, to unfix both gender and race as stable or essential ascriptions of identity. Gender and race are shown in the performance texts discussed above to be constituted in and of the social and the political.

Chela Sandoval's contention that the ambivalent positioning of U.S. Third-World feminists has led to the development of a "differential mode of oppositional consciousness" is also pertinent to Asian-Australian women's performance of self. This mode "depends upon an ability to read the current situation of power and self-consciously choosing and adopting the ideological form best suited to push against its configurations."[31] Sandoval asserts that various subordinated groups have developed a "kinetic and self-conscious mobility of consciousness" which enables a conception of subject-formation as provisional and manipulatable: "a process that at once both *enacts and yet decolonises* the various relations to their real conditions of existence."[32]

My discussion has focused on the ambivalent interplay between discourses of desire and disavowal. The task ahead does not require one to follow in Broinowski's footsteps, to claim the critical high ground as the non-duped, but rather to see this fluidity and in-betweenness as a gamble and a risk—and one in which it proves impossible not to participate. An attentiveness to the politics and poetics of ambivalence reminds one that oppositionality is never pure, outside the system which it wishes to critique, but rather that the condition of oppositionality is founded at the point of implication and effected through play.

---

[29] *Ibid.*: 44.

[30] Homi Bhabha, *The Location of Culture* (London: Routledge, 1994): 49.

[31] Cited in Karen Shimakawa, "'Who's to Say?' Or, Making Space for Gender and Ethnicity in *M. Butterfly*," *Theatre Journal* 45 (1993): 358.

[32] *Ibid.*: 358, emphasis added.

Works Cited

Ang, Ien. "The Curse of the Smile: Ambivalence and the 'Asian' Woman in Australian Multiculturalism," *Feminist Review* 52 (1996): 36-49.

Bhabha, Homi. *The Location of Culture* (London: Routledge, 1994).

Bobis, Merlinda, Helen Gilbert & Jacqueline Lo. "What *Priscilla* Said," *Real-Time* 4 (1994): 4-5.

Bobis, Merlinda. *Border Lover* (1996, unpublished manuscript): 1-9.

Broinowski, Alison. *The Yellow Lady: Australian Impressions of Asia* (Melbourne: Oxford UP, 1992; second edition, 1996).

Butler, Judith. "Performative Acts and Gender Constitution: An Essay in Phenomenology and Feminist Theory," in *Performing Feminisms: Feminist Critical Theory and Theatre*, ed. Sue-Ellen Case (Baltimore: Johns Hopkins UP, 1990).

Chow, Rey. *Writing Diaspora: Tactics of Intervention in Contemporary Cultural Studies* (Bloomington and Indianapolis: Indiana UP, 1993).

—— *Ethics after Idealism: Theory-Culture-Ethnicity-Reading* (Bloomington and Indianapolis: Indiana UP, 1998).

Foucault, Michel. *The Use of Pleasure: The History of Sexuality*, vol. 2, tr. Robert Hurley (New York: Vintage, 1986).

Grosz, Elizabeth. *Volatile Bodies: Toward A Corporeal Feminism* (St Leonard's: Allen and Unwin, 1994).

Jayasuriya, Laksiri & Kee, Pookong. *The Asianisation of Australia? Some Facts about the Myths* (Carlton South: Melbourne UP, 1999).

Kingston, Maxine Hong. *The Woman Warrior: Memoirs of a Girlhood Among Ghosts* (New York: Alfred A. Knopf, 1975).

Kong, Foong Ling. "Postcards from a Yellow Lady," in *Asian and Pacific Inscriptions: Identities, Ethnicities, Nationalities*, ed. Suvendrini Perera (Melbourne: Meridian / *The La Trobe University English Review* 14.2, 1995): 83-97.

Lo, Jacqueline. "Dis/orientation: Contemporary Asia-Australian Theatre," in *Our Australian Theatre in the 1990s*, ed. Veronica Kelly (Amsterdam: Rodopi, 1998): 53-70.

—— "Beyond Happy Hybridity: Performing Asian-Australian Identities," in *Alter/Asian*, ed. Ien Ang et al. (Annandale: Pluto Press, forthcoming).

McCrae, Hugh. "The Yellow Lady," in *Idyllia* (Sydney: N.L. Press, 1922).

Shimakawa, Karen. "'Who's to Say?' Or, Making Space for Gender and Ethnicity in *M. Butterfly*," *Theatre Journal* 45 (1993): 349-61.

Walker, David. *Anxious Nation: Australia and the Rise of Asia 1850-1939* (St Lucia: U of Queensland P, 1999).

Wong, Sau-Ling Cynthia. *Reading Asian American Literature: From Necessity to Extravagance* (Princeton, New Jersey: Princeton UP, 1993).

Yahp, Beth. "Place Perfect and the Other Asia," *Westerly* (Autumn 1996): 61-71.

Yen, Anna. "Chinese Take Away," in *Three Plays by Asian Australians,* ed. Don Batchelor (Brisbane: Playlab, 2000): 32-71.

History and Mystery and Suffragettes on the Australian Stage: A Consideration of Women's Suffrage as Presented in Australian Theatre

SUSAN PFISTERER

Menzies Centre, King's College, University of London

Mahatma Ghandi altered hundreds of years of British rule in India when he started asking his friends to call him "mother" and began fighting like a woman, as distinguished from manly fights which left people brutalised and turned many into enemies for life.[1] In the history of women as modern citizens, which is barely a century old, documenting the feminist/feminine effectiveness of our political ambitions and achievements proves fascinating and important, but so too does being honest about how things stand for women at the beginning of a new century. This essay maps that history through the cultural practice of performance, arguing against the marginalisation of Australian women's experiences from both national and international suffrage and theatre historiography.

Some extraordinary narratives dominate Australian theatre history, as I have argued elsewhere.[2] Crude memories circulate the myth that Australian nationalist theatre, with the odd aberrant exception, was not properly fertilised until the late 1960s. Exuberance and radicalism and the placement of Australian characters centre-stage did indeed characterise this "New Wave," but these elements had long been part of Australian theatrical traditions. Such nationalist histories not only ignore these traditions, but the (now) marginal identities that constructed the more complicated and richer fabric of Australian theatre history than is commonly acknowledged. Women playwrights, for example, achieve a different prominence when one begins to look at what was really happening over the last century.

---

[1] Harriet Rubin, *The Princessa: Machiavelli for Women* (London: Bloomsbury, 1997): 21.
[2] Susan Pfisterer & Carolyn Pickett, *Playing With Ideas: Ausralian Women Playwrights from the Suffragettes to the Sixties* (Sydney: Currency, 1999).

This essay examines Australian suffrage playwrights and more recent examples of suffrage iconography in Australian theatre, and contrasts those feminist images with the ones circulated of Australian political women in other public media such as national newspapers. Completely different stories emerge about the role and significance of these pioneering Australian feminists. This serves to highlight the importance of theatre history as an essential component of cultural and national histories. Investigating the mystery of being written out of history has been a project of feminist dramatic criticism for some time. This examination continues that tradition, and in so doing poses two central questions: is commercial contemporary Australian theatre still largely guilty of perpetuating masculinist traditions that marginalise women; and how important are history plays to a nation's consciousness? To begin to answer those questions, I will look at examples from suffrage drama itself, and explore suffrage iconography in examples from various theatre styles: historical drama, the historical pageant, and contemporary theatre with historical commentary or characters.

Original Margins: Australian Suffrage Theatre and Its Distinctive Citizens

As Australia grapples with becoming a republic and works towards reconciliation, closer attention must be paid to reconciling marginal identities with national mythologies in order to move towards any kind of decent future. Feminist theatre history has an important part to play in that project. Precisely why is feminist remembering so important for postcolonial Australia? Generally, the significance of the suffrage struggle is regarded as a positive but little-known episode in the making of modern Australia. The new woman citizen proclaimed her great expectations, and suffrage drama mapped those feminist desires. On a more specific level, as Ashcroft, Griffiths and Tiffin have noted, "A major feature of postcolonial literatures is the concern with place and displacement."[3] White Australian women during the suffrage era can be classified as emigrants in a colonial world, part yet not-part of the masculinist project of empire, and therefore experiencing a dislocated sense of self that both marginalised and politicised them. Their cultural production constitutes an essential element in understanding our contemporary sense of self as Australians, because "The development of national literatures and criticism is fundamental to the whole enterprise of postcolonial studies. Without such developments at a national level, and

---

[3] Bill Ashcroft, Gareth Griffiths & Helen Tiffin, eds. *The Empire Writes Back: Theory and Practice in Post-colonial Literatures* (London: Routledge, 1989): 8-9.

Suffragettes and the Australian Stage 87

without the comparative studies between national traditions to which these lead, no discourse of the postcolonial could have emerged."[4] In this sense, and because such discourse is essential, Australian suffrage drama and more recent theatre that examines the politics of female suffrage represent important contributions to both contemporary global feminism and postcolonial constructions of Australian identity.

Australian women during the colonial and suffrage eras were distinctive world citizens. They played a unique role in Australian theatre history and, as expatriates, in international feminism and theatre. They left Australia as enfranchised women and went, generally to England and America, where, for decades after the vote was won at home, women did not receive full citizenship entitlements. Historian Marilyn Lake praises the ambassadorial qualities of Australian feminists who championed their reputations overseas as enfranchised women, suggesting that their distinctive status rendered them political exemplars, lending them "an authority as experts on women's citizenship. They travelled, they advised, they consulted. They extended sympathy, advice and assistance to their 'enslaved' British and American sisters."[5] Yet many histories continually neglect the cultural content of this ambassadorship, particularly that of Australian expatriate women writers. Lake argues that "feminist activists should be recognised as pre-eminent among the theorists of citizenship."[6] Arguably, the feminist artistic community which so uniquely articulated those theories in cultural forms should be similarly recognised.

In a 1907 article entitled "Feminism and Theatre," a male critic commented that, having won the vote, "Woman is confidently expected to exert an ennobling and refining influence in politics." He further pondered: "Can we look with confidence for a new excellence in the drama when woman's tastes and inclinations have fully asserted themselves?"[7] A belated answer to that question, offered in this cursory overview, argues for the uniqueness of Australian suffrage theatre history. In brief, Australian suffragette theatre is characterised by its internationalism, as many Australian feminist theatre practitioners were expatriates during this period, and its advanced expressions of "post-suffrage"

---

[4] *Ibid.*: 17
[5] Marilyn Lake, "Between Old Worlds and New: Feminist Citizenship, Nation and Race, and the Destabilisation of Identity," in *Suffrage and Beyond: International Feminist Perspectives*, eds. Caroline Daley & Melanie Nolan (Auckland: Auckland UP, 1994): 278.
[6] *Ibid.*: 280.
[7] Stargazer, "Feminism and Theatre," *Lone Hand* (August 1907).

feminisms. Miles Franklin's dramatic writing is representative of those traditions.

"I have always held out [that] drama should carry an ethical message as well as entertain. It should be one of the greatest modern influences for good." So said Avis, a famous actress and a character in Miles Franklin's play *The Survivors*, written in 1908. Avis was lamenting the sad state of American drama of the day, which she thought was full of "pornographic balderdash for the edification of moneyed degenerates" [27].[8] Franklin's fictional Avis neatly expresses the sentiments of feminist suffragette theatre practitioners who used the stage for the "good influence" which they hoped to achieve with their political and social ambitions.

Australian writer and suffragette Stella Miles Franklin was born in country New South Wales in 1879, and moved to Sydney after the publication of her famous book, *My Brilliant Career*, in 1901. There she was active in literary and feminist circles for a few years before moving to Chicago, USA, in 1905, where she proved an influential figure in women's suffrage and trade union struggles until moving to England in 1914. She returned to live in Australia in 1932. Franklin's (more than twenty) suffrage plays are mostly devoted to presenting the stories and tasks of women's emancipation in an entertaining, wistfully instructive manner. Women's lack of the vote was a cornerstone of offence in all of these explorations and coupled with wider feminist critiques, as the example of *Aunt Sophie Smashes a Triangle* demonstrates.

Aunt Sophie Smashes a Triangle, written in 1913, is set in Chicago and explores the changing role of women through the discussion of such issues as motherhood, financial independence, spinsterhood, marriage, women's mental health, and suffragette politics. The plot is full of melodramatic twists and contrivances. The husband (David) is unfaithful to his wife (Alice) with a young woman of traditional female values. David's suffragette sister (Sophie) and his own "converted" (to feminism) son warn Alice of the affair. She books into a sanatorium to recover her health; coincidentally, so has David's mistress. Unknowing of each other's identity, they become friendly and swap ideas about love and womanhood. Responding to his mistress's telegram, David arrives only to be met by a surprised and flattered Alice, who believes he has hired a private detective to find her. Eventually, the penny drops and the two women work through the problem with the help of Sophie. David's

---

[8] This and all subsequent page references are taken from Franklin's unpublished plays in manuscript held in the Franklin Papers, Mitchell Library, Sydney.

mistress abandons him and becomes a suffragette; as does Alice, to whom he happily returns a different man.

Much of the dialogue is actually conducted between Sophie and her brother David. Dramaturgically, all men who do not sympathise with women's rights lose not only the argument in hand, but also, gradually, physical space on the stage. Conversely, those male characters who are suffragette sympathisers, David's son for example, enjoy a different dramatic space. Whilst it is not unusual for the husband to be represented as uncomfortable in his own home, because that is regarded as the woman's sphere, it is dramaturgically unorthodox that his "male" space within the home, the office, be invaded—as it is in *Aunt Sophie*—by one righteous female after the other. This eventually leads David to retreat and abandon not only his own ideological space, but his real physical world, or its representation on the stage, in a clear example of feminist dramaturgy at work.

Franklin's manipulation of her characters and their subsequent subversion of "stage" space mirrors and/or inspires a subversion of "real" space. Significantly, not all of the play's conflict is male/female. David and his suffragette son clash forcibly, as do Sophie and Alice. Here speaks pre-conversion Alice, sick of Sophie's feminist advice:

> ALICE: Oh it's easy for you to talk and have such cool sense. You've never been married. You know nothing about marriage and what the tie means.
> SOPHIE: [resignedly] A spinster has to endure that venerable wheeze at least once every day. There is not enough sense or truth in it to break an eggshell.
> ALICE: [wailing afresh] You've never been married—you don't ...
> SOPHIE: Now Alice, don't you ever say that again. I've been made as big a fool of as if I had, if that will serve to raise me to your level [12-13].

It is significant that Franklin labelled *Aunt Sophie* "A Comedy of Domesticity." As this extract exemplifies, the subject of exploration has to do with countering claims of womanhood. The changing role of women, female independence, both emotional and financial, spinsterhood, marriage, women's mental health, and the suffragette cause are all explored in an attempt to promote a feminist vision of womanhood.

This play contains Franklin's most sophisticated commentary on women's emancipation, presented through multi-dimensional, complex characters and delivered with wit and authority. She does not shrink from confronting important feminist issues. Here Sophie explains to Alice how and why she converted to feminism:

> SOPHIE: ... when I had regained my sense and health it was too late. I was past the age of attracting another lover.
> ALICE: ... I suppose that's why you took to suffrage?

SOPHIE: I took to suffrage because in the light of common sense it seemed the nearest thing to get out of the way, not to replace love by it as some nincompoops imagine. I want the women of the future to have a wider outlook, to have more interests so that when love goes astray they will have some healthy outlet and not have to sit down and let neurasthenia devour them ... I'm a silly, sentimental sort of a person, that's why I have taken to civic work. I want things to turn out right and people to live happy ever after, and as that is not possible under present circumstances, some of us are determined to make different circumstances, different human nature [43].

Whether or not her plays dealt directly with the fight for the vote, Franklin's work was at all stages informed by this quest, and comments on the struggle or the inclusion of the odd suffragette activist can be found in almost all of her plays. Cultural history is a crucial element in the renewed and frenzied quest for identity by Australians, as it always has been for feminist practitioners. Australian women's theatre history significantly contributes to that quest, including the feminist theatre of suffrage playwrights.

Historical Narratives Performing Identity

There are significant implications for change in Australian theatre, and indeed to Australian history in general, represented in the challenges of leadership offered by the female dramatic tradition of the history play. In a similar manner, literary critic and historian Susan Sheridan has argued that the novel is recognised as being a form well-suited to "addressing the nation." Further, she insists that the work of women fiction writers who produced historical studies proved particularly valuable as "a key determinant of the meanings of Australian History in circulation," especially during a period when the academic study of Australian History remained in its infancy.[9] This valuable insight would achieve a different dignity altogether if the work of women playwrights was also taken into account, as these plays offer arguably even bolder perspectives to those searching for meaning in or through Australian History.

Discussing women novelists of the 1920s and 1930s who wrote about earlier periods of Australian History, Sheridan claims that their work "can be read as revisions of dominant historical narratives, with women writers setting their own agendas." It is this very effort which revises historical understanding. She lists those agendas in their full variety, covering feminist, anti-racist concerns, and participating in the "male tradition of attacking class privilege." Sheridan reaches an inter-

---

[9] Susan Sheridan, *Along the Faultines: Sex, Race and Nation in Australian Women's Writing* (Sydney: Allen & Unwin, 1995): 156.

esting conclusion: "But whatever their politics, they can be read for signs of the ambiguous position of women writers as members of the dominant class and race—but not quite full members."[10] How much better, or how differently, was that ambiguous status represented through the medium of drama, considerably more confronting in the spoken performance than on the written page?

Historical dramas represent a peculiar genre, because playwrights assert authority over a whole range of higher truths about our past than historians are able or dare to, and in this sense they become surrogate custodians of our past. Women playwrights have long contested that custodianship, because their treatment of the past as subject matter is remarkably different from that of their male counterparts. Such plays operate not only as important documents for historians and theatre practitioners alike, but demonstrate that feminist memory has an important role to play in the formation of our historical consciousness. It can be argued that the way in which historical women have been treated by many Australian historians is neither accurate nor flattering,[11] and that not enough attention is paid in the study of Australian history to the role of women. Oriel Gray's *The Torrents* (1955) and the pageant held for Adelaide's Sesquicentenary Celebrations in 1936 are explored here as examples that revise that marginalisation, revealing women playwrights forcefully confronting their own history. Their sense of place and local knowledge combine to create a unique vision of Australia's past.

Oriel Gray's *The Torrents* shared first prize in the Playwright's Advisory Board 1954 competition with *The Summer of the Seventeenth Doll*. While Lawler's play was performed and went on to become the *cause célèbre* of Australian drama, *The Torrents* languished until it was finally staged by the New Theatre in 1958.[12] Set in a newspaper office in the Western Australia of 1890, the new employee, chosen for excellent on-paper qualifications, arrives: it is unexpectedly a woman, Jenny Milford. The play deals with women gaining professional acceptance from colleagues in a male dominated profession, a problem specific to the real New Woman (the older sister of the suffragette) of the 1890s, but particularly pertinent to women in the post-war workforce of the 1950s in Australia, the time of the play's gestation. There is also a fairly

---

[10] *Ibid.*, p. 157.

[11] See for example Susan Pfisterer, "The Louisa Factor: The Historical Treatment of Louisa Lawson," in *Louisa Lawson: Collected Poems With Selected Critical Commentary*, eds. Leonie Rutherford & Megan Roughley (Armidale: Centre for Australian Literature and Language Studies, 1996): 275-85.

[12] For an account of this, see Michelle Yarrow, "The Play That Time Forgot," *Good Weekend Magazine* (9 December 1995): 37-40.

predictable love plot secondary to the main action of the play, which revolves around a conflict about the future development of a frontier town.

A critic belittled the work as being "a play of 'ideas' in which no-one now has the slightest interest," also arguing that the "question of whether women should take their place in offices and whether or not they lost femininity in the process have surely been settled for some time." Further, the critic found the play's theme boring, because, as he insisted, "history has already decided Australia's position as a pastoral rather than a gold mining country."[13] Both of these criticisms, perhaps fair, are ignorant of the fact that the play reveals through dramatic conflict the process of how these historical decisions were made. The play presents perhaps even more interest for today's Australians, who are less familiar with their own past than Australians of the 1950s.

The Torrents itself abounds in historical reflection, the male characters discussing frontier life and the Eureka Stockade, and all those main things of the era. Then in walks Jenny, and suddenly the discussion shifts to the "feminine" subject of female emancipation and the virtue of Victorian versus Edwardian morals. These ideas irrigate the intellectual streams of the play. As Jenny says, arguing to keep her job: "I'm as much of a soldier as any of your Irish heroes. I fight for the things I believe in ... and it's a desolate thing sometimes to seem to be the one woman alone on such a new battleground."[14]

Oriel Gray has cunningly juxtaposed a masculinist view of our past with feminist intervention—the New Woman—which quietly contests traditional ideas of our own history. Her ridicule of our pioneering legends is tongue in cheek, inoffensive only because it is so very subtle. Her championing of the feminist traditions in our history is firm but gentle. *The Torrents* seems a valuable play for many reasons, not the least of which being that it features a New Woman as the lead character.

Many other women playwrights embraced intriguing questions about Australian history and national identity as themes and subjects in their work. Consequently, they found themselves writing historical dramas. They were guided by leading questions such as "what happened?"; "why are we like we are?"; and "how come things are like this?" In offering their answers, that they chose to do so through theatrical performance is in itself a testimony to the hopes invested in this very public medium to influence opinions long or perhaps wrongly held about Aus-

---

[13] *The Guardian* 896 (20 February 1958): n.p.

[14] Oriel Gray, "The Torrents," in *The Penguin Anthology of Australian Women's Writing*, ed. Dale Spender (Melbourne: Penguin, 1988): 883.

tralian History. *The Torrents* offers an engaging example of feminist contestation of received historical knowledge.

Ownership of history, or the manipulation of its stories for specific purposes, is an oft exercised option in the desire to influence and control popular thought. Championing positive images of historical women may seem a dated feminist critical exercise, but given the condition of Australian historiography this empirical work is still essential. If, for example, one consults a history book in order to locate a pictorial image of the Australian New Woman or suffragette, one can usually guarantee that the evidence provided is a cartoon, a historical visual of ridicule. Often these images lack the appropriate caption underneath explaining that this is how such women were represented in the popular press of the time, and do not in fact amount to accurate representations of how women, or indeed others, may have seen themselves at that time in history.

When such images remain the dominant iconography of suffragettes, for example, offered for circulation in the creation of historical consciousness—particularly in educational textbooks—the recruitment of positive images in the campaign to reinvigorate Australian History becomes an imperative. In this spirit, an understanding of the function of the historical pageant in society offers some interesting insights into readings of how Australians have imagined their past. Thelma Afford's sketches for the pageant held for Adelaide's Sesquicentenary Celebrations in 1936 are explored here further to assess women theatre practitioner's contribution to positive renderings of Australian historical women.

The historical pageant is a theatre spectacle of enormous social import, a community celebration attended en masse by a population that may not have normally enjoyed or had the opportunity to participate in theatrical events. Thelma Afford was a trained artist, and worked as an actress, school teacher, and costume designer. The Adelaide pageant was produced by Heather Gell in collaboration with Ellinor Walker who wrote the historical script. Gell wanted to "present not only a historical pageant but a great, picturesque production which will appeal to the public ... the pageant will be essentially a theatrical production in which ... history will be intermingled."[15]

Walker's script provides a stylised chronological history of South Australia. The story begins before white settlement, covers the major explorers like Flinders and Sturt, and documents the colony's founda-

---

[15] A clipping from the *Adelaide Mail*, PRG 689/1, held in the Mortlack Library, Adelaide.

tion and the first emigrants. The pageant continues to chart the development of the state, incorporating dream scenes and mime to explore the work of women pioneers, Aborigines and politicians up to 1936. Afford's costume designs are essential to the spirit of the pageant and tell their own stories. They demonstrate the great beauty and dignity bestowed by her costumes on these pioneering South Australian feminists. As Gell said,

> This pageant cannot be a mere turning of leaves in a historical book. It must express the spirit of the people and the country, and this can only be done on the stage through rhythm and music, combined with effective stage management, extravagant and picturesque costumes, which catch not only the eye but the heart of the audience.[16]

Afford's costuming of historic women characters appear true to this spirit. Her suffragette costumes script the characters as beautiful, sophisticated, and socially desirable women, in distinct contrast to masculinist representations of the suffragette to be found in leading national publications such as the *Bulletin*, which was fond of satirising feminist militancy. Unfortunately, such rich theatrical images of women are not generally included in Australian cultural histories. Afford's and Gell's work emphasises the unique contribution that theatre history adds to Australian History in general. To historians and students of Australian culture, the inclusion of this dramatic perspective, which has long benefited from explorations of women novelists and artists, serves only to enrich historical appreciations.

Performing Memory: The Past in Contemporary Women's Theatre

The past continues to occupy the imaginative terrain of contemporary women playwrights, and there exist various examples of recent feminist theatre that explores feminine consciousness and politics of the suffrage era, or includes suffragette characters. Jennifer Compton's *Crossfire* (1976) is one such worthwhile example, but this essay concentrates on the more recent one of Beatrix Christian's erotic and operatic play *Blue Murder* (1994).

Blue Murder, which features a suffragette as a major character, is a contemporary play using historical characters to inform the present. Christian describes the play as being about a young woman, Eva, who has tried to live heroically. She leaves her home town of Nyngan in rural Australia, her parents dead, and moves to Sydney with her boyfriend,

---

[16] *Ibid.*

Suffragettes and the Australian Stage 95

whom she abandons to secure a live-in job as an assistant to a children's book writer. This writer, Blue, or the devil, rapidly becomes her lover and husband. On her journey, Eve travels through that love to discover the ghosts of his murdered wives. These three women eventually help Eve to save herself, and she murders Blue. The play has an uneasy resolution for some, because Eve seems to have suffered this liberating journey only to return to her boyfriend, who "loves me, a young man who wants life for me as much as he wants it for himself."[17] While not entirely an easy feminist closure, this particular analysis of the play focuses on the theatrical representation of the suffragette character, Leura McKenzie, one of three female ghosts and a central character in the dramatic action.

Christian's characterisation of Leura is a thematic and dramatic delight. Never before has Australian theatre seen such a mature, complex, suffragette (or even feminist) on the stage. By this I mean that Christian does not give the audience a nice, sanitised, laudable character. Leura is a selfish bitch, complex and contradictory, but a feminist to her core, who ultimately rises to the defence and protection of women so that they may lead their own full lives. In this sense, Christian has come closer than any other playwright, veracity wise, to an honest representation of Australian suffragettes: the suffrage movement was full of such self-serving women, who constantly bickered with and were jealous of each other's gains. Just as recent feminist history of the suffrage period has tired of promoting puritan ideas about the beauty, flawless politics and sisterhood of first-wave feminism, Christian perfectly captures that same temperament in her characterisation of Leura.

This is achieved without detracting from the heart of Leura's feminism, which serves the dramatic purpose of reminding Eve—and the audience—that history has not been kind to women, nor taught them anything much because their memory deserts them. But Leura successfully conveys this message, and provides Eve with both the murderous spirit and the murder weapon to release her from her oppression. Leura's most telling line goes: "… only the dead hold history—in their mouths. The living must lie."[18] This is reminiscent of ideas that criticise the social construction of all history—who can after all speak the truth about the past except those who can no longer speak? While much postmodern theorisation has released many from the need to pursue truth with a capital T, the desire to make life-altering decisions often rests on a need such as knowing absolute truth. It is Leura who most forcefully

---

[17] Beatrix Christian, *Blue Murder* (Sydney, Currency, 1994): 48.
[18] *Ibid.*: 47.

makes Eve choose her destiny and embrace her past in order to free herself from its tragedy so that she can, in Leura's words, "Live. Again and again."[19]

Christian has achieved much with her loopholed realism, and her adventures with theatrical form were much admired during the production run. Her sophisticated grasp of innovative form creates a drama far removed from the "prison-house" of realism, and works most viciously to reveal the workings of patriarchal ideology. Crucial to the feminist agenda of *Blue Murder*, however, is the act of remembering, and while experimental form populates the stage with ghosts, it is what those characters say that counts most. When Eve is making her final, liberating decision, she calls on these female "ancestors" to give her the bedrock of memory that wisdom ultimately resides in, and which funds her actions: "Rosemary Allen. Angel Brokowski. Leura McKenzie. Help me know and I'll never forget you."[20] Christian's experiments with form only added to *Blue Murder*'s success, and contributed to the development of an Australian feminist theatre that remembers historical women as tempestuous, sexual, politically effective human beings, offering challenging perspectives instead of conventional renderings of suffragettes.

Inconclusive

The last word perhaps best belongs to Miles Franklin's character Avis from *The Survivors*, the actress and heiress who gave all her money to the suffrage campaign and who is about to star in a play which at long last has something "real" to say for women. "This play," says Alice, "is appealing to the deeper nature of the audience. It is teaching a wonderful lesson. Just listen to the applause" [50]. Has this applause fallen on deaf ears, or are these feminist experiences marginalised in Australian history and contemporary consciousness? Visual images of suffragettes are collective rememberings of the past that fertilise Australians' sense of citizenship today, so it is imperative that suffrage cultural history should not be forgotten, but instead be allowed to contribute to that contemporary sense of self. As other historians have argued, "Memories link us to place, to time, and to nation: they enable us to place value on our individual and social experiences, and they enable us to inhabit our own country."[21] Huge shifts have recently occurred in

---

[19] *Ibid.*: 49.

[20] *Ibid.*: 48.

[21] Kate Darian-Smith and Paula Hamilton, eds. "Introduction," in *Memory and History in Twentieth Century Australia* (Melbourne: OUP, 1994): 1.

Suffragettes and the Australian Stage

understanding what constitutes our past. Just as it remains essential to acknowledge how organised structures of forgetting have affected Indigenous Australians and contributed to their marginalisation, it seems equally important to remember that patriarchal histories have long disenfranchised women's experiences. Embracing history in its fullness should not be mystery to any nation seeking a mature move into the twenty-first century.

The inclusion of American Indian women's history is currently rewriting United States suffrage history. I searched diligently for examples of Aboriginal women's participation in the struggle for female franchise in Australia, and found no cultural evidence. I was, however, looking for the same kind of evidence that white women had left me, suffrage theatre and its performance history. But I now believe that I need to look for a different kind of participation and evidence, like that revealed in the US example. It appears that that well known figure in American suffrage history, Elizabeth Cady Stanton, had a mentor who spent considerable time with women of the Iroquois Nation, women who had been participating in elections for centuries. The white suffragists at the 1848 Seneca Falls convention were apparently very well aware of this, and hoped to reorganise their own nation's governmental structure accordingly. Their Declaration of Sentiments from this convention acknowledged that Indigenous women were far better off under Iroquois than white law. Little of this history is documented; even less does it play a core part in the history of citizenship in the Western world as it arguably should. As scholar Paula Gunn Allen notes, however, it is there for us to use, we must only "search the memories and lore of the tribal peoples ... the evidence is all around us."[22] As a feminist scholar committed to the politics of reconciliation, it is therefore time to reconsider my "completed" Australian suffrage history. I am now obliged to move backwards, to use different research techniques, and in effect to begin again, in order to avoid marginalising Indigenous voices further amongst the already long silenced. And to (in)conclude, I have to say that this is only the story so far, bearing always in mind the real mystery of this saga: that almost a century after women won the suffrage the "applause" remains so tentative. It appears that the appeals to our "deeper nature" require continued vigilance.

---

[22] Quoted in Jacqueline Keeler, "PBS Omission: What the Suffragettes Owed the Iroquois," *Pacific News Service* (23 November 1999) <www.first_nations@home.ease.lsoft.com>

Works Cited

Adelaide Mail PRG 689/1(held in the Mortlack Library, Adelaide).

Ashcroft, Bill, Gareth Griffiths & Helen Tiffin, eds. *The Empire Writes Back: Theory and Practice in Post-Colonial Literatures* (London: Routledge, 1989).

Christian, Beatrix. *Blue Murder* (Sydney: Currency, 1994).

Franklin, Miles. *Aunt Sophie Smashes a Triangle* (unpublished play held in manuscript in the Franklin Papers, Mitchell Library, Sydney).

—— *The Survivors* (unpublished play held in manuscript in the Franklin Papers, Mitchell Library, Sydney).

Darian-Smith, Kate & Paula Hamilton, eds. *Memory and History in Twentieth Century Australia* (Melbourne: OUP, 1994).

Eldershaw, F., ed. *The Peaceful Army,* 1938 (Penguin, 1988).

Gardner, Vivien & Susan Rutherford, eds. *The New Woman and Her Sisters: Feminism and Theatre 1850-1914* (London: Harvester/Wheatsheaf, 1992).

Gray, Oriel. "The Torrents," in *The Penguin Anthology of Australian Women's Writing*, ed. Dale Spender (Melbourne: Penguin, 1988): 791-865.

Keeler, Jaqueline. "PBS Omission: What the Suffragettes Owed the Iroquois," *Pacific News Service* (23 November 1999) <http://www.first_nations @home.ease.lsoft.com>

Lake, Marilyn. "Between Old Worlds and New: Feminist Citizenship, Nation and Race, and the Destabilisation of Identity," in *Suffrage and Beyond: International Feminist Perspectives*, eds. Caroline Daley & Melanie Nolan (Auckland: Auckland UP, 1994): 277-94.

Pfisterer, Susan & Carolyn Pickett. *Playing With Ideas: Australian Women Playwrights from the Suffragettes to the Sixties* (Sydney: Currency, 1999).

Pfisterer, Susan. "The Louisa Factor: The Historical Treatment of Louisa Lawson," in *Louisa Lawson: Collected Poems With Selected Critical Commentary*, eds. Leonie Rutherford & Megan Roughley (Armidale: Centre for Australian Literature and Language Studies, 1996): 275-85.

Review of *The Torrents*, *The Guardian* 896 (20 February 1958): n.p.

Rubin, Harriet. *The Princessa: Machiavelli for Women* (London: Bloomsbury, 1997).

Sheridan, Susan. *Along the Faultines: Sex, Race and Nation in Australian Women's Writing* (Sydney: Allen & Unwin, 1995).

Spender, Dale & Carol Hayman, eds. *How The Vote Was Won and Other Suffragette Plays* (London: Methuen, 1985).

Stargazer, "Feminism and Theatre," *Lone Hand* (August 1907).

Yarrow, Michelle. "The Play That Time Forgot," *Good Weekend Magazine* (9 December 1995): 37-40.

Queer/Irony in Nick Enright's Drama

BRUCE PARR

University of Queensland

Whereas many of Nick Enright's late twentieth-century plays concern themselves to some marginal degree with homosexuality, it is *Mongrels* (1991), *Good Works* (1994), and *Playgrounds* (1996) which clearly explore homosexuality in the lives of major characters. While it may prove difficult to classify these three playworks as "gay," they can be usefully aligned with the concept of "queer." My use of "queer" includes its meanings of "odd" and "strange" as well as "a host of sexual possibilities that play havoc with the conventional distinction between normal and pathological, heterosexual and homosexual, masculine and feminine."[1] Queer theory's strength depends on its resistance to appropriation by those who find disturbing its marginal status and its lack of definability.[2] Interpreting Judith Butler's musings on queer, Gregory W. Bredbeck stresses the impreciseness of the concept: "[Q]ueer *potentially* creates an identity ... but does so in a way that does not *necessarily* reinscribe opposition."[3] I argue that Enright utilises (homo)sexuality to create a recognisably queer theatre, one which proposes and promotes (a queer) undecidability by deploying the rhetorical/philosophical device of irony, as theorised by John Evan Seery, in conjunction with specific alienation effects relating to doubling and multiple role playing. By addressing these connections primarily in *Playgrounds*, it will be shown that Enright employs a technique common to all three works. In so doing, he successfully incorporates the marginal into the mainstream.

Enright was arguably Australia's most consistently successful theatre writer during the 1990s. After David Williamson, he perhaps currently

---

[1] Ellis Hanson, "The Telephone and Its Queerness," in *Cruising the Performative: Interventions into the Representation of Ethnicity, Nationality, and Sexuality*, eds. Sue-Ellen Case, Philip Brett, and Susan Leigh Foster (Bloomington: Indiana UP, 1995): 56.

[2] See Annamarie Jagose, *Queer Theory* (Carlton South: Melbourne UP, 1996).

[3] Gregory W. Bredbeck, "The Ridiculous Sound of One Hand Clapping: Placing Ludlam's 'Gay' Theatre in Space and Time," *Modern Drama* 39.1 (1996): 82 (emphases added).

ranks as the best-known playwright. Dubbed "Mr Versatile of the Australian theatre"[4] for his variety of output, he contributed the book for the musical *The Boy from Oz*, based on the life of Peter Allen, which ran throughout Australia from 1998 to 2000. With Justin Monjo he adapted novelist Tim Winton's *Cloudstreet* for the stage. Neil Armfields's production opened to critical acclaim and has toured nationally and internationally since 1998. As a screenwriter, Enright's *Lorenzo's Oil* and his adaptation of his play *Blackrock*, first produced on the stage in 1995, have garnered awards and award nominations. Diana Simmonds described *Playgrounds* in the national magazine *The Bulletin* as "one of the richest, most complex, most ambitious, funny and moving depictions of modern Australia yet put to paper and staged."[5] Firmly established then as a mainstream writer, Enright's work cannot be read as a clear declaration of his openly-avowed homosexuality.[6] Nonetheless the sexualities—multilayered, multifaceted, complex, elusive—he deploys in the plays considered here contribute to a queerness infrequently experienced in mainstream theatre. Enright facilitates reflection on the boundaries between sexualities commonly (but reductively) thought of as "major" and "minor," mainstream and marginalised.

Irony suggests itself as an appropriate companion device to queer as, according to Seery, it "involves some sense of a declination from the presumed 'straight' reading of a text."[7] It also inclines towards the humour and the playfulness—its mock-seriousness about not taking itself too seriously—to which queer subscribes. Irony, like queer, has no agreed meaning or definition, and embodies, according to Seery, a sensibility, "an outlook, a worldview, a mode of consciousness, a way of thinking," an elusive, "complex, interactive process."[8] Irony is an act of double-voicing where "covert and literal layers play off one another,"[9] and ambiguity results. However, irony can be taken "in a positive direc-

---

[4] Sandra Hall, "The Enright Stuff," *Weekend Australian* (10-11 June 1998): Magazine 34. For a comprehensive bibliography of Enright's works for theatre, film, television, and radio up to 1993-94, see Veronica Kelly, "'A Form of Music': An Interview with Nick Enright," *Australasian Drama Studies* 24 (1994): 75-76.

[5] Diana Simmonds, "Laughter, Tears at *Playgrounds*," *Bulletin* (16 July 1996): 76.

[6] See, for example, Enright's speech at the launch of the 1994 Sydney Gay and Lesbian Mardi Gras Festival. Nick Enright, "Happy Birthday, Happy Mardi Gras," *Sydney Star Observer* (11 February 1994): 6.

[7] John Evan Seery, *Political Returns: Irony in Politics and Theory from Plato to the Antinuclear Movement* (Boulder: Westview, 1990): 174.

[8] *Ibid.*: 169.

[9] *Ibid.*: 197.

tion, signifying an ethos ... a spirit, that tends toward politics and the political."[10] Seery asks:

> Why is politics implicitly "ironic?" Politics involves an affirmation of the idea of human community, but that affirmation grows out of, or is attendant upon, a profound awareness of human difference, as well as human tragedy. Such an affirmation requires, I suggest, the kind of reversal of expectations typically associated with the concept of irony. To choose to affirm human community in the face of human mortality, to seek order against the background of chaos, to hold out for worldly justice even though death ultimately defeats or mocks all such efforts, to be dedicated when one is also deeply doubtful—all of this suggests a philosophical stance that involves a double perspective on things, though a stance in which one's affirmative side finally (if barely) triumphs over, that is, partially reverses, one's cynical expectations. Given a deep appreciation of tragedy, one would expect cynicism, skepticism, fatalism, even nihilism, to reign. That instead one affirms human association at all—human difference notwithstanding—entails what I think is best called an ironical attitude.[11]

This approach to irony suits an engagement with the complexities of identity in Enright's use of the alienation devices of doubling (in all three works), of his presentation of one single character at different ages (in *Good Works* and *Playgrounds*), and of his reliance on adult actors to play children or adolescents (in all three works). One of Enright's key "political" investigations focuses on the construction of masculinities which is a subject that sociologist R.W. Connell also investigates. Connell has recently detailed the complexities of their construction according to

> differences and tensions between hegemonic and complicit masculinities; oppositions between hegemonic masculinity and subordinated and marginalized masculinities. Each of these configurations of practice is internally divided, not least by the layering of personality described by psychoanalysis, the contradictions in gender at the level of personality. Their realization in social life differs ... according to the interplay of gender with class relations, race relations and the forces of globalization.[12]

Enright confronts these complexities ironically by juxtaposing different types of masculinities in one single actor's range of characters, signifying the fluidity of identity and infinite possibilities for different lives.

---

[10] *Ibid.*: 62.

[11] *Ibid.*: 343.

[12] R.W. Connell, *Masculinities* (St. Leonards: Allen and Unwin, 1995): 242. According to Connell, complicit masculinities are "constructed in ways that realize the patriarchal dividend, without the tensions or risks of being the frontline troops of patriarchy" (79).

In *Good Works*, actors play Tim and Shane at various stages of their lives from the ages of six to thirty, and in addition, most productions so far mounted have followed the premiere's lead by having the actor playing Tim also playing Shane's father, and the actor playing Shane also playing Tim's father. This ironic, dialectical interplay results in an emphasis on the multi-dimensionality of subjectivities, endless potentialities for good or bad. The boys and men all disappear into one another, become interchangeable, indistinguishable, hence susceptible to reconstruction. In *Mongrels*, we might juxtapose the playwrights, Burke and O'Hara, with the myriad of traits exhibited by the range of contradictory subjectivities displayed by the one actor who plays Craig Sheridan, a sort of "mongrel" son of Burke and O'Hara, as well as a variety of characters from the plays-within-the-play. From this amalgam of blurring characteristics, the audience of *Mongrels* is left the task of constructing, ironically—that is, without the expectation of resolution— some notion of artistic and personal conduct and integrity. All three works refer to what Connell terms "the crisis in [the] gender order"[13] and, given the complexities of that crisis, the plays also offer ironic juxtapositions and convergences as a means of negotiating the necessary "reconfiguration and transformation of masculinities."[14]

Playgrounds consists of two one-act plays, *The Way I Was*, first seen early in 1995 as part of the Sydney Theatre Company programme Sydney Stories, and *Where Are We Now?*[15] Both plays are set in and around two high schools in the western suburbs of Sydney, and are connected by the presence in each of a female teacher who observes her ethnically mixed students over the period stretching from 1974 to 1996. One of her students is a sensitive, effeminate, fourteen-year-old Turkish boy, Timur, who is driven out of school in the first play, and whose spirit haunts the second. *Where Are We Now?* has thirteen characters played by nine actors in the Sydney Theatre Company production. Enright specifies only one essential double: supporting characters, Darrell and Tom, father and son, should be played by the same actor.[16]

---

[13] *Ibid.*: 84.

[14] *Ibid.*: 243.

[15] In its first production for the Sydney Theatre Company in January 1995, *The Way I Was* was directed by Wayne Harrison. *Playgrounds* was first presented by the STC in July 1996. *The Way I Was* was again directed by Harrison, and Marion Potts directed *Where Are We Now?*

[16] I wish to thank Nick Enright for allowing me to refer to and quote from the unpublished typescripts of *Where Are We Now?* and *The Way I Was*. Further citations from *Where Are We Now?* appear parenthetically in the text. The typescript page listing the characters and original cast is not numbered.

Apart from the obvious reason of utilising the device of mistaken identity, why does Enright specify this doubling and what significance does it have?

Darrell is seen at two stages of his life: at seventeen, in his final year at high school in 1977, and at thirty-six in 1996. Tom is seventeen in 1996, in *his* final year at the same school. The title *Where Are We Now?* obviously invites us to juxtapose "where were we then?" with "where are we now?" This juxtaposition then necessitates the question of "how far have we come—culturally—since then?" In attempting to answer that question at least partly, we see both father and son, each at seventeen, in the same geographical location, but at two very different historical periods. This difference is reflected in the contrasting behaviours of the two young men, particularly in their attitudes to their ethnicity and cultural heritage. In fact, Darrell's real name is Mustafa Habib. As a Lebanese Arab born in Mecca and wanting so badly to be accepted as an Australian "white bread" (4), he re-named himself Darrell, taking the name from a well-known brand of chocolate, Darrell Lea. But as his *bête noire*, the fiery Greek effeminate student, Dionisos Fotopoulos, goads him: "Darrell's a big blond with blue eyes. What are your chances, Mustafa?" (17) Nineteen years later, Darrell's son, Tom, shows pride in his heritage, speaking Arabic and valuing its contribution to a multicultural Australia. The actor who plays Darrell and Tom is thus required to portray cultural shame alongside cultural pride. This represents but one of Enright's exercises in ironic juxtaposition in *Playgrounds*.

Continuing to probe this doubling of Darrell and Tom, there is a moment near the end of the play—a moment emblematic of the play's appeal for the negotiation of differences—when, in 1996, Darrell, this not-quite-quintessential Aussie, despite his best efforts of the "How are you, mate?" (43) variety, dances his old enemy Dionisos Fotopoulos across the playground and out of the play. That this constitutes a "queer," almost surreal moment does not discount its believability within the realistic framework of the play's structure and logic. On the surface two very different men dance together at a school reunion, symbolising harmony after strife. This might be seen as yet another exercise in ironic juxtaposition.

Other meanings can be found beneath the surface of this strange dance of Darrell and Dionisos across the playground Who exactly is dancing with whom? Two Australian men of thirty-six who hated each other as schoolboys? A Greek and an Arab, Dionisos and Mustafa? Two schoolboys who had sex every Wednesday after sport during year ten? (Dionisos says he closed his eyes and turned Darrell into Robert

Redford [18]). An effeminate Greek/Australian who now identifies himself as Destinee and an Arab/Australian who still insists on being known as Darrell? Two drag queens—Destinee and Darrell Lea? And surely Tom, whom Destinee calls "such a sweetie" (43), has not disappeared altogether. Perhaps Destinee is dancing with young Tom as well, introducing further complexities into the sexual dynamics. These are all possibilities—besides others—because we have at some stage seen these two actors playing an assortment of characters, at different ages, in one case (Darrell) related by blood, in another (Dionisos) in drag—on his last day of school, the "muck-up day" (28), Dionisos appears in a black dress. We see multiple identities, ambiguity, contradictions, queerness, all in what might be termed ironic juxtaposition.

Other possibilities present themselves through the characters played in *The Way I Was* by the same actors appearing as Darrell and Dionisos, according to Enright's suggested doubling pattern (1996: n.p.).[17] The year is 1974, at a different high school, and Timur, the Turkish boy (the double of Dionisos), is persecuted by a group of "Anglos," one of whom is Brett (the double of Darrell/Tom). Timur embodies one of those sissies who are recognised as gay—or more specifically as a "wog poofter" (1994: 29)—by his male, straight-identified classmates before he understands his own sexuality, and certainly before he has ever had a same-sex encounter. In *The Way I Was*, Enright examines the Australian equivalent of what Bradley Boney considers "one of the great open secrets of [American] culture": "[t]he abusive treatment of proto-queer teenagers."[18] The dance in *Where Are We Now?* also carries with it the resonances of the brutalities unleashed upon Timur by the likes of Brett in the companion play.

The central point of interest in *The Way I Was* lies in the attraction between Vangelis[19] and Timur, an attraction which highlights the queerness that Enright is exploring in these plays. The romance between the two fourteen-year-old boys, one Greek, the other Turkish, begins with Van's "fascination" (1996: 4) with Timur's singing as if, as one version of the script states, he were "a star of his own TV special" (1994: 5). Van is attracted by what appears to him the mysterious mixture of the masculine and the feminine in Timur; the attraction is understood by

---

[17] My analysis of *The Way I Was* draws freely from both the 1994 and 1996 versions of the unpublished typescript.

[18] Bradley Boney, "The Lavender Brick Road: Paul Bonin-Rodriguez and the Sissy Bo(d)y," *Theatre Journal* 48 (1996): 35.

[19] Vangelis is called Arky in the 1994 version, an acknowledgement that the character is based upon a story by Arky Michael, the actor who played Arky and Vangelis in both the 1995 and 1996 productions.

neither of the sexually inexperienced boys. They grow closer through their passionate debates on the beauty of their respective screen goddesses, Van's idol, the Greek star, Aliki Vouyouglaki, and Timur's Turkish beauty, Turkan Soray, both of whom appear on stage conjured by Timur's imagination (which also represents his gift to Van). Timur in juxtaposition with Barbra Streisand signals the way in which Van remembers his lost friend; her song, *The Way We Were*, resonates both literally and figuratively throughout the play. It is in imitation of Turkan that Timur performs his belly-dance, which Van experiences as "the most erotic thing [he] has ever seen" (1994: 27). The boys come close to kissing, but no physical contact eventuates. Once their romance is discovered, Van betrays his friend, and the effeminate one is driven out of school, further "abusive treatment" of the type Boney describes. The sexual energies generated by their relationship remain elusive and difficult to define. They come across as more recognisably queer than homosexual or gay.

The play's queerness operates on another level too, one that complicates it further. The parts of Van and Timur—and all the children in the play—are played by adult actors. While an audience may be willing to suspend disbelief, the materiality of the adult bodies on the stage permanently undercuts the implied representation of an innocent or naive sexuality, and consigns it irrevocably to the realm of undecidability. As the separation of actor and role is always in motion despite the realist theatre often pretending otherwise, so too the interconnections of the erotic play of adults and of children are always apparent in a performance of *The Way I Was*. Enright sets up a "queer" conversation between what is happening on stage and what is implied to be happening on stage. This provides another example of his use of ironic juxtaposition.

By juxtaposing difference in *Where Are We Now?*—in the one case of an actor playing two contrasting, though related characters, Darrell and Tom, in the other of the "queer" dance—Enright calls into conversation the elements or variables which make up those differences, in these instances, history, education, family, genetics, generations, sexuality. From the conversations come not solutions but questions about change: for example, how do broad-minded and moderate sons succeed bigoted, cruel, self-hating fathers? What of the fathers becomes lost or found in the sons? What of the sons lies unexpressed or confined in the fathers? Given that Dionisos looks at Tom and sees Mustafa (33), could the fathers be the sons, the sons the fathers? How can difference be accepted in a society made up of many cultures? How can those who do not conform to dominant gender expectations be free of ridicule and persecution? These (political/social) questions about progress and change cannot be simply answered through the play. They are thrown up for circulation in juxtaposition with the queer energies which the play generates. The questions and the queer are interconnected in that they occupy the space of undecidability during the performance. Bredbeck observes: "At the heart of queer theory is an intense unwillingness to privilege the logic of division and classification, the type of binary thinking that always attends the standard of 'the normal.'"[20] *Playgrounds* exhibits the characteristics that the concept of queer would wish to claim as its own: indefinable, elusive, seductive, polymorphous, perverse, abnormal, ironic. In *Where Are We Now?*, Dionisos is asked at one stage: "You really are gay?" He replies: "I'm Maria Callas" (18). This illustrates yet another of Enright's ironic juxtapositions which produces new meanings and resists resolution: a queer moment. Enright's "queer moment" can be traced back to *Mongrels*, the play which made him such "a commanding national figure."[21]

It is well documented that *Mongrels* was partly inspired by two Australian playwrights of the 1970s, Jim McNeil and Peter Kenna, whose friendly acquaintance in actuality is transformed into venomous rivalry in the play.[22] It can hardly be coincidental that Enright has named his playwrights, O'Hara (the Kenna figure) and Burke (McNeil), recalling Robert O'Hara Burke, the leader of the ill-fated expedition which set out to cross Australia from Melbourne to the Gulf of Carpentaria in 1860-61. As Veronica Kelly has noted, O'Hara and Burke "make up a composite personality."[23] This intriguing ploy perhaps points to many other puzzles and questions which the play proffers, not least in the title itself. For example, to what extent is the third playwright, Craig Sheridan, the "mongrel" composite of O'Hara and Burke, and how can this interpretation complement a "queer" reading of the play? Referring to Burke's play, "A Dog's Life," O'Hara describes it as "the kid's play ... He's the one we watch."[24] Although that comment is disputed by Burke, a possi-

---

[20] Gregory W. Bredbeck, *op. cit.*: 82.

[21] Veronica Kelly, "Old Patterns, New Energies," in *Our Australian Theatre in the 1990s*, ed. Kelly (Amsterdam: Rodopi, 1998): 4.

[22] See Veronica Kelly, "Enright's *Mongrels* as Intervention in the Canon of Contemporary Australian Drama," *Southerly* 54.2 (1994): 5-22, and Katharine Brisbane, "Close Associations," in *Mongrels* by Nick Enright: vii-xi.

[23] Kelly, *ibid.*: 6.

[24] Nick Enright, *Mongrels* (Sydney: Currency Press, 1994): 36. Further citations appear parenthetically in the text. *Mongrels* was first produced by the Ensemble Theatre, Sydney, in November 1991 under the direction of Rhys McConnochie. It should be noted that parts of *Mongrels* were rewritten for the Sydney Theatre Company's revival in 1997.

ble answer to this question may lie in what is one of Enright's metadramatic hints about *Mongrels* itself.

Operating in the tension between text and subtext, surface meaning and theatrical device, *Mongrels* can be considered a play about crossings, the word "mongrel" itself indicating the crossing of different breeds or kinds, resulting in neither one thing nor the other. The interplay of differences and apparent oppositions, ironic juxtapositions, is integral to *Mongrels* which, as metadrama, foregrounds its own hybridity and resists precise labelling and definition. The concept of queer likewise displays its self-referentiality in crossing the space between straight and gay, in toying with the gaps and tensions between the "real" and the imagined, between what is said and what is done, between identities and practices, and in exploring the regimes of power around which these tensions are played out. Like *Playgrounds*, *Mongrels* exhibits the characteristics outlined above that the concept of queer would wish to claim as its own: indefinable, elusive, seductive, polymorphous, perverse, ironic, abnormal. In doing so, it raises questions, invites scrutiny, and enters into a dialogue with the audience about other than surface meanings. *Mongrels'* metatheatricality requires its consideration as a work of stagecraft as well as a dramatic text. A play about playwrights and playwriting, it appropriately foregrounds its own complex construction.

While Burke and O'Hara battle it out for supremacy, Craig Sheridan quietly acquires the knowledge that will eventually contribute to his success as a playwright. At varying times, both O'Hara and Burke act as his mentors. He repays them by incorporating "resonances" (63) of their lives and relationship into his "surreal" (63) play through the characters of Maureen and Doggo. This "mongrel" play points to a consideration of Sheridan as the "mongrel son" of Burke and O'Hara, and the play's key "sexual mongrel" (35).[25] On another level, Sheridan's play refers to *Mongrels* itself utilising "now a 'McNeil' and now a 'Kenna' scene or situation"[26] to create Enright's own "mongrel"—although quite distinctive—work. Enright may be suggesting that there is a degree of mongrelisation in all creative composition as an artist borrows and "steals" from many sources to construct a work which then masquerades as an original.

---

[25] Peter Kenna first used the term, "sexual mongrel." See Frank Wells, "The Drama of Peter Kenna," *Campaign* 32 (May 1978): 16.

[26] Kelly, "Enright's *Mongrels* as Intervention in the Canon of Contemporary Australian Drama," *Southerly* 54.2 (1994): 6.

Craig Sheridan might be thought of as the unique result of mixing the characteristics of an O'Hara and a Burke to form a composite personality: their "mongrel" son. This result occupies not the extremes represented by the two formidable, unbending playwrights, but rather an indeterminate, undecidable space suggestive of versatility and flexibility. This is also a "queer" space where Sheridan typifies a pragmatic masculinity tailored to his needs moment by moment. This pragmatic masculinity is reflected metatheatrically in the number and nature of roles played by the Craig Sheridan actor following Enright's suggested doubling pattern (xiv). In addition to Sheridan, he is seen as the young prisoner Ross who also plays Rose (both in and out of a dress) in Burke's prison play, and in a dizzying assortment of other roles in the plays-within-the-play. Such an array of masculinities projected by the one actor has the effect of blurring the distinctive features of any one of them. Through the many roles played by this one actor, we witness the "oppositions between hegemonic masculinity and subordinated and marginalized masculinities,"[27] as outlined by Connell.

Nothing in *Mongrels* suggests that Enright favours one particular style of masculinity or one (fictional) playwright over another, or advocates a particular approach—professional or personal—for attaining success. In the march of history, the new generation typified by Sheridan merely supersedes the older. Nadia Fletcher finds that the play offers the task of "extrapolat[ing] about the generic Playwright when we put the three examples together."[28] What can be discerned from this exercise is the artistic (and personal) need for malleability, pragmatism, and a certain cold-bloodedness. Limitations represent obstacles to self-construction. Creativity may perhaps be directly related to the degree of mongrelisation imagined and exercised. What is clear, however, is that in a work in which, like Seery's irony, "covert and literal layers play off one another" (197), Enright appears at his most queerly ironic.

Like *Mongrels, Good Works* also operates daringly on a variety of levels and juxtapositions, with four actors, two men and two women, playing their main character at various ages between the years 1928 and 1981. In addition, the actors who play Tim and Shane at various stages of their lives from the ages of six to thirty, have also in most productions followed the premiere's lead by playing their opposite's father.[29] The

---

[27] R.W. Connell, *op. cit.*: 242.

[28] Nadia Fletcher, Review of *Mongrels, Australasian Drama Studies* 27 (Oct. 1995): 160.

[29] Productions of *Good Works* in Sydney (Q Theatre 1994), Canberra (Eureka! 1995), Melbourne (Playbox 1995), and Wellington, New Zealand (Downstage 1995) used six actors, three men and three women, playing thirteen parts, whereas the

actor playing the gentle, effeminate boy, Tim Donovan, thus doubles as the criminal tough, Eddie Grogan, while the street-wise boy, Shane Grogan, is doubled with the uptight, unhappy lawyer, Neil Donovan. The overall effect produces a juxtaposition of naturalism and non-naturalism, childhood and adulthood, city and country, sacred and profane, straight and queer, fathers and sons, hegemonic masculinity and marginalised masculinity, which can create for the audience a mystifying though also pleasurable blur, like a dream recollected. Enright contributes to this obfuscatory sensation by concluding the play with fragments of dream/memory amongst which Tim at twelve years encounters his mother Mary Margaret at six. As with his use of Craig Sheridan in *Mongrels*, Enright in *Good Works* offers a myriad of possibilities through his manipulation of many characters in the one person depicted at different stages of life, as well as through the demands of intersecting, contrasting fathers and sons played here necessarily by actors of paramount versatility. Jack Hibberd comments on the Playbox Theatre production: "The constricted ability of some of the actors to sharply transform age or character sometimes adds confusion." He goes on to state that the male actors "were most adept at the transformational leaps demanded."[30] While keeping cast sizes to a minimum and juxtaposing life affirmation and deep cynicism, Enright exploits this casting imperative in demonstrating, with the ironical attitude that Seery defines, human association in all its complexity.

Good Works testifies to Enright's conspicuous and continuing effort, following *Mongrels*, to bring a queer practice to the mainstream stage. Setting the pivotal scene in a gay bar amounts to a daring act. Blatant, extroverted effeminacy, an abundance of camp banter, and men coming on to other men so soon after the play's opening, might unsettle some audiences and suggest that they have stumbled upon a "gay play," as varied as understandings of that term might be. They also know that the play will keep returning to this scene, as the historical re-enactments detail the shaping of Tim and Shane for their handling of the present confusions of this unanticipated reunion in 1981. There is danger in the air, and considerably more danger for those not relishing the prospect of the "queer production of the year,"[31] as *Good Works* was dubbed by sections of the gay press in Sydney in 1994. "Queer" is here used loosely as a synonym for "gay," but it would perhaps be more accurate

---

Queensland Theatre Company production (1995) employed a fourth male actor. For a more lengthy analysis of the play, see Bruce Parr, Review of *Good Works*, *Australasian Drama Studies* 29 (Oct. 1996): 216-20.

[30] Jack Hibberd, Review of *Good Works*, *Australian* (16 June 1995): 10.

[31] Stephen Dunne, "So That's That Then," *Sydney Star Observer* (28 Dec. 1994): 27.

to consider the play queer in the sense that it offers a multiplicity of desires, of sexualities in uncontainable circulation, of which homosexuality represents but, interrelatedly, one of many. Enright's calculated risk seems to have paid off, with *Good Works* uniformly welcomed and praised by both mainstream audiences and the gay and lesbian "community." The play therefore contributes to the complexities and tensions in the continuing debate on what constitutes or can be defined as gay and/or lesbian identity or art. While *Good Works* both is and is not a gay play, its designation as queer seems less problematical. Whatever the case, the very controversy of its categorisation immediately invites the intervention of gay and lesbian theatre studies in these debates.[32]

Good Works stands out as a "problem play" in the most complimentary sense of that term. It does not provide answers or resolutions, but figuratively takes us inside the snow-dome which is a central motif of the play, shakes it up, and leaves us reeling from the weight of meanings contained in so small an artefact. "Truth" and fiction compete without any chance of success for either, but the play's real achievement lies in its ability to delineate so successfully the coherence in incoherence, the importance of striving for continuity and stability when resolution is endlessly deferred, as Seery's work on irony suggests. We recall that the title of the first play in *Playgrounds*, also about childhood cruelties, is *The Way I Was*. The final line in *Good Works* is "Just the way it was."[33] Such titles and lines almost compel the addition of "not" which undercuts any attempt at an unwavering finality in these dramatic representations. "Did it have to be this way?" "What other way might it have been?" are questions that we seem obliged to ask, followed by "If only it might have been otherwise." Because *Good Works* is replete with such alienation effects, "the way it was" becomes a type of dream or fantasy of only one of many possibilities. Its design and structure preclude any identification with one single point of view. The title itself gives a clue to the mysteries of the play. "Don't worry, Mary Marg, you'd go straight to heaven, wouldn't you? All those good works" (52), Rita, Shane's mother, tells her. The central "good work" is the dogged attempt of Mary Margaret to take Rita's child away from her. The play is so bound

---

[32] For a theorisation of gay and lesbian theatre studies, see Bruce Parr, "Gay and Lesbian Theatre Studies: Sex(uality) in the Classroom," in *Queer in the 21st Century: Perspectives on Assimilation and Integration*, eds. John Argus and Stephen Cox (Fortitude Valley: Gay and Lesbian Welfare Association, 1999): 15-28.

[33] Nick Enright, *Good Works* (Sydney: Currency Press Current Theatre Series, 1995): 57. Further citations appear parenthetically in the text. *Good Works* was first produced by the Q Theatre, Penrith, in July 1994 under the direction of Adam Cook.

up with such ironies that all surfaces become suspect. *Good Works* thereby refutes its own capacity for staging the "truth."

In *Mongrels*, the actress, Hazel, gently chides Craig Sheridan for not writing parts for women: "Only one woman in the whole show and she turns out to be a man ... Remember the girls next time" (63-64). Enright takes this advice on board himself in both *Good Works* and *Playgrounds*, and creates female characters whose personal journeys equal the men's. *Good Works* features a moment between Mary Margaret and Rita which captures the intensity of these instances in all three plays where physical contact releases energies both erotic and nebulous. The passionate, consummated sexual relationship in *Good Works* occurs between Rita and Neil Donovan, conducted on stage entirely through correspondence with Neil at boarding school or at war. There is a moment when they come physically together, a moment—like that of the dance between Darrell and Dionisos in *Where Are We Now?*—which both combines and confuses dream and reality. While Rita and Mary Margaret are talking about the absent Neil, the stage direction has him "pass[ing] between them, close enough to kiss." In actuality, it is Rita who kisses Mary Margaret "on the lips" (10), an instance which hints at deeper feelings beyond the formalities of friendship. This moment proves ironic in the commonly understood sense of irony as "a subtly humorous perception of inconsistency."[34] However, it could also be thought of as a moment of ironic convergence, when differences conjoin, releasing "energies, excitations, impulses," some of the stuff of sexuality and desire, as Elizabeth Grosz interprets it.[35] It is at these moments in Enright's plays that irony and queer themselves stand in ironic juxtaposition, bodies or parts of bodies coming together, releasing "eros or libido"[36] both uncontainable and ambiguous.

The same ironic, erotic, queer intensities could apply to the brief cheek kisses exchanged between Craig Sheridan and O'Hara in *Mongrels*, or those moments of physical force between the powerful Burke and the fragile O'Hara in the same play. They likewise apply to the near kiss of Vangelis and Timur in *The Way I Was*, which Enright tantalisingly describes as follows: "Timur pulls up his school jumper and shirt and starts to dance. Van stares. Timur becomes bolder. The music builds. Van wants to kiss Timur. Perhaps he even gets close."

---

[34] Chris Baldick, *The Concise Oxford Dictionary of Literary Terms* (Oxford: Oxford UP, 1991): 114.

[35] Elizabeth Grosz, "Refiguring Lesbian Desire," in *Space, Time, and Perversion: Essays on the Politics of Bodies* by Elizabeth Grosz (New York: Routledge, 1995): 182.

[36] *Ibid.*

(1996: 20). "Perhaps" encapsulates the queer undecidability and the ironic potentialities in these works of a playwright who acknowledges his homosexuality as crucial to his creativity.[37] Enright's remarkable achievement lies in his means of engaging (homo)sexuality with an ironic interplay of the masculine and the feminine within character and between characters, and the myriad possibilities these encounters reveal. That he reduces boundaries between different sexualities in mainstream Australian theatre is all the more remarkable.

Works Cited

Baldick, Chris. *The Concise Oxford Dictionary of Literary Terms* (Oxford: Oxford UP, 1991).

Boney, Bradley. "The Lavender Brick Road: Paul Bonin-Rodriguez and the Sissy Bo(d)y," *Theatre Journal* 48 (1996): 35.

Bredbeck, Gregory W. "The Ridiculous Sound of One Hand Clapping: Placing Ludlam's 'Gay' Theatre in Space and Time," *Modern Drama* 39.1 (1996): 64-83.

Brisbane, Katharine. "Close Associations," in *Mongrels* by Nick Enright: vii-xi.

Connell, R.W. *Masculinities* (St. Leonards: Allen and Unwin, 1995).

Dunne, Stephen. "So That's That Then," *Sydney Star Observer* (28 Dec. 1994): 27.

Enright, Nick. "Happy Birthday, Happy Mardi Gras," *Sydney Star Observer* (11 Feb. 1994): 6.

—— *Mongrels* (Sydney: Currency Press, 1994).

—— *The Way I Was* (Unpublished Typescript, Draft 1, 1994).

—— *Good Works* (Sydney: Currency Current Theatre Series, 1995).

—— *The Way I Was* (Unpublished Typescript, 1996).

—— *Where Are We Now?* (Unpublished Typescript, 1996).

Fletcher, Nadia. Review of *Mongrels*, *Australasian Drama Studies* 27 (Oct. 1995): 156-61.

Grosz, Elizabeth. "Refiguring Lesbian Desire," in *Space, Time, and Perversion: Essays on the Politics of Bodies* by Elizabeth Grosz (New York: Routledge, 1995): 173-85.

Hall, Sandra. "The Enright Stuff," *Weekend Australian* (10-11 June 1998): Magazine 34-38.

Hanson, Ellis. "The Telephone and Its Queerness," in *Cruising the Performative: Interventions into the Representation of Ethnicity, Nationality, and Sexuality*, eds. Sue-Ellen Case, Philip Brett, and Susan Leigh Foster (Bloomington: Indiana UP, 1995): 34-58.

Hibberd, Jack. Review of *Good Works*, *Australian* (16 June 1995): 10.

---

[37] Veronica Kelly, "'A Form of Music': An Interview with Nick Enright", *Australasian Drama Studies* 24 (1994): 72.

Jagose, Annamarie. *Queer Theory* (Carlton South: Melbourne UP, 1996).
Kelly, Veronica. "'A Form of Music': An Interview with Nick Enright," *Australasian Drama Studies* 24 (1994): 58-76.
—— "Enright's *Mongrels* as Intervention in the Canon of Contemporary Australian Drama," *Southerly* 54.2 (1994): 5-22.
—— "Old Patterns, New Energies," *Our Australian Theatre in the 1990s*, ed. Kelly (Amsterdam: Rodopi, 1998): 1-19.
Parr, Bruce. Review of *Good Works*, *Australasian Drama Studies* 29 (Oct. 1996): 216-20.
—— "Gay and Lesbian Theatre Studies: Sex(uality) in the Classroom," *Queer in the 21st Century: Perspectives on Assimilation and Integration*, eds. John Argus and Stephen Cox (Fortitude Valley: Gay and Lesbian Welfare Association, 1999): 15-28.
Seery, John Evan. *Political Returns: Irony in Politics and Theory from Plato to the Antinuclear Movement* (Boulder: Westview, 1990).
Simmonds, Diana. "Laughter, Tears at *Playgrounds*," *Bulletin* (16 July 1996): 76.
Wells, Frank. "The Drama of Peter Kenna," *Campaign* 32 (May 1978): 15-16, 58.

Queer Circus Bodies in Rock 'n' Roll Circus's *The Dark* and Club Swing's *Razor Baby*

PETA TAIT

La Trobe University

> "[T]he postmodern condition in its most basic aspect: the orientation towards alterity."[1]

Australian performers have developed an international reputation for innovation in new circus and physical theatre based on circus skills. Gail Kelly's direction of physical theatre is representative of the current experimentation with a theatre of heightened physical action. Two of her Australian new circus productions, *The Dark* (1996) and *Razor Baby* (1999) are discussed here. These subvert assumptions about the sexual identity of bodies and sexualise the action of circus acts. Kelly directed the award-winning production of *The Dark* for the Brisbane-based Rock 'n' Roll Circus company in 1995. This production toured to the 1996 Melbourne International Festival and the company put on an extra show when it sold out at its Malthouse theatre venue.[2] The enthusiastic response from audiences—some shows had three curtain calls—clearly outweighed a mixed critical reception in Melbourne. Some reviewers praised the circus acts, but criticised the production's theatrical elements, such as the linking images of bizarreness, darkness and madness.[3] Melbourne is the home-base of Circus Oz and has a tradition of polemical new circus that dates back to the 1970s. Queer texts in physi-

---

[1] Thomas Docherty, *After Theory* (Edinburgh: Edinburgh University Press, 1996): 23.

[2] This discussion of *The Dark* refers to performances seen at the Malthouse Theatre, Melbourne, 30 October to 2 November 1996, which were a reworked version of the show first performed in Brisbane. The original production team included Hilary Beaton (dramaturg), Greg Clarke (designer), Joanne Paterson (costumes) and Matt Scott (lighting).

[3] See *Australian and New Zealand Theatre Record* University of New South Wales (October 1996): 26, Fiona Scott-Norman, *The Age,* (1 November 1996), Jessica Nicholas, *Herald Sun* (1 November 1996). Reviews were more uniformly favourable in Adelaide and Brisbane, where the show won an award from theatre critics.

cal theatre, however, first emerged in Sydney in the late 1980s with the performance work of Kelly and her collaborators in the company Legs on the Wall. Perhaps regional differences in the Australian experimentation with new circus and physical theatre influenced *The Dark*'s reception.

The Dark's popularity with audiences, however, might be attributed in part to their familiarity with traditional circus, and to the novelty of viewing its reinvention as an adults-only experience. The show used random images and juxtapositions akin to rock music videos. This postmodern pastiche of references to popular entertainment spanned cinema to circus. Such additions to the conventional circus form became even more explicit with *Razor Baby*. Audience recognition of these elements must have contributed to the extremely enthusiastic responses to *The Dark* and *Razor Baby*.

The Dark consisted of sexualised bodies engaged in circus acts linked by theatrical and cultural metaphors of darkness. The tone ranged from comic silliness to serious *angst*. This exemplified new circus at its best. In keeping with the way that traditional circus is associated with fun, *The Dark* did not render psychological darkness but parodied cultural representations of darkness. The physicality of the performing bodies appeared exaggerated, underscored by generic visual gags from B-grade horror films. The dominance of the visual text and the rejection of narrative—words and songs were used as soundscapes rather than for their meaning—aligned it with postmodern texts. In form, however, *The Dark* was circus. Circus does not use narrative and signs cultural identity on the surfaces of acrobatic bodies in a programme of unrelated acts.

As is the case for many Australian new circus/physical theatre productions, the issue of where aesthetically to locate *The Dark* and *Razor Baby* in relation to either its theatricality or circus origins appears confused, because this emerging genre eschews the conventions of spoken theatre, despite being most often performed in theatrical venues. Invariably, this invites comparisons with theatre rather than circus, which is performed in a tent or a similar spatial configuration. New circus and physical theatre display bodies engaged in physical actions and tricks as central to the performance. The genre strips away the naming of the spoken text that marks the body socially, and the distracting elements of the *mise-en-scène* that obscure the staging of bodily action. The absence of dramatic speech makes the meanings of the text contingent on watching bodies doing actions. For this reason, Australian physical theatre and new circus should be recognised as innovative for both theatre and circus. However, extracting meaning from the action of nonverbal bodies can be a complex process.

This hybridisation of forms, a postmodern strategy, makes the reception of new circus problematic. I contend that not all spectators are comfortable with meanings that have to be interpreted bodily from visual cues, especially if this new experience must be framed in words.[4] Moreover, circus is generally assumed to be devoid of cultural meanings. In *The Dark* and *Razor Baby,* the fluidity of form was further complicated because the gender identity of the performing bodies was destabilised by their physical action and sexual behaviour.

Club Swing's *Razor Baby* was presented as part of the 1999 Melbourne gay and lesbian Midsumma and Sydney's Gay and Lesbian Mardi Gras festivals.[5] It was well attended by audiences and consistently praised by reviewers for its conceptualisation. Interestingly, the overtly labelled "queer" *Razor Baby*—decidedly a more sexually outrageous show—was reviewed more favourably in Melbourne than the very popular *The Dark* with its predominantly heterosexual dynamics between bodies. *Razor Baby* was particularly popular with younger audiences, some of whom would not attend theatre regularly. Was the reception of *The Dark* more problematic because it delivered unsettling depictions of gender identity without attaching the label of "queer" to its performing bodies? Audiences did not appear to mind; perhaps circus continues to be associated with transgressive social identity in the popular imagination. It could be argued that *The Dark*'s parodic horror comedy destabilised what is considered the natural order of sexed difference in ways that are comparable to the queered interactions of *Razor Baby*. The cultural assumption that the physicality of bodies reveals gender difference was revoked in a text of physical action in which strong, muscular female bodies, costumed as feminine, performed what are considered masculine acts of aggression. When the action of these bodies was also sexualised, their identity became queered.

In collaboration with the performers (and composer/performer Brett Parker for *The Dark*), Gail Kelly created texts that illustrate a continuity in her own quirky, visual style of directing. If gender identity is ultimately enforced by the belief that female bodies are less physically aggressive than males, then this can be challenged in performance not only by revoking the costumed appearances of identity with drag, but

---

[4] See Peta Tait, "Fleshed Muscular Phenomenologies: Across Sexed and Queer Circus Bodies," in *Body Show/s: Australian Viewings of Live Performance*, ed. Peta Tait (Amsterdam: Rodopi, 2001): 60-78.

[5] I am discussing *Razor Baby* as I saw it performed at the North Melbourne Town Hall on 14 January 1999 with Kathryn Niesche and with Simone O'Brien (lighting by Margie Medlin and rigging by Clytie Smith). My comments about this show are also informed by conversations with the performers at that time.

also through acrobatic interactions between bodies, through body-to-body engagements that contravene sexually marked physicality. Circus acrobatic acts can deliver a text in which males and females perform interchangeable acts of strength and muscularity. When their actions are sexualised, bodies that are visually coded as feminine seem masculinised—and therefore unnatural—when engaging in sexual aggression. Importantly, it is the physical action in question that makes bodies seem unnatural.

In *The Dark*, circus bodies appeared out of the darkness of the performing space, a darkness which helped to suggest a literal notion of dreams or nightmares, or perhaps cinematic dark spaces. Females conveyed murderous intent. If clues about horror were overtly delivered in the visual text, danger also covertly featured in the performance form, as bodies involved in risky tricks fell from a height. At the beginning of *The Dark*, Terese Casu suddenly dropped out of the darkness of the stage to hang in mid-air on a harness; she sang a haunting refrain, then laughed dementedly. Lowered to the stage, she ran towards the audience, flying out over them, clutching a suitcase as if she had left somewhere or someone behind. By inference, she was penetrating the spectators' safety zone and disrupted their comfort of being unseen in surrounding darkness.

The tone shifted abruptly as Matt Wilson tumbled down on an aerial bungy apparatus, singing a corny, 1960s-style love song to Annabelle Lines, who was dressed in an ultra-kitsch, psychedelic bodysuit. They simulated horizontal sex positions in a comic routine in which Wilson rebounded on elasticised bungy ropes high above her. At the climax she chopped off his hand: perhaps this represented a punishment for stealing her heart or merely a displacement of an implied castration. Blood sprayed over them. Acrobatic skeletons—white bones painted onto black bodysuits—appeared tumbling together, suggesting the live action of dead bones in a sexually bizarre but comic orgy, which finished with a collective group grope on a bicycle.

The mood mellowed when Kareena Oates entered, smoking, and began the first of three routines of attraction and seduction with Rudi Mineur. These three *adagio* routines depicted mutual seduction with sensuous body balances, acrobatic holds and turns, intimate moments of sustained contact and dismissive releases.[6] The sexually explicit ex-

---

[6] Traditional *adagio* acts involve a duo executing fairly slow, flowing, graceful acrobatic balances and holds, sometimes with tumbling. Australian *adagio* work probably evolved out of circus acts adapted to the early vaudeville stage, and became part of the club entertainment circuit in Australia from the 1950s through to the 1980s

Queer Circus Bodies

changes of the lovers culminated in action on the trapeze. There was a disturbing tension, however, in this display of erotic tenderness by these two similarly muscular bodies: a caressing gesture would suddenly become the rough grabbing of the other's body, as if the physical engagement of love-making could flip over suddenly and become a violent struggle initiated by either lover. They appeared and reappeared in subsequent acts, either watching like voyeurs or participating in sexualised acrobatic routines with other performers.

The circus grotesque exaggerated by the skeleton clowns mimicking the clowning dead and the serious tone, which characterised the three erotic acts by Oates and Mineur, combined to challenge both the emotional limitations and masking of sexuality found in traditional circus acrobatics. The evocative beauty of the sequences between Oates and Mineur captured an intensity of emotion, which in some respects alters the circus form more than the comic parody provided by the clowns.[7] Given the preceding action, the trapeze act between Mineur and Oates delivered a striking and original piece of sustained sexual tension defying the constraints of gravity. The only comparable performance that I subsequently saw was the beautiful and compelling full-length *Deadly*, staged by the London-based No Ordinary Angels at the 1999 Edinburgh Festival. These highly skilled aerial performers, ex-New Zealander Deborah Pope and Brazilian Rodrigo Matheus, communicate an intense awareness of the other's physical presence, as they depict the intimacy and destructiveness of a love affair.

Oates and Mineur executed tropes of desiring that became almost tangible because of each performer's complete focus on the movement and the action of the other body. The compulsion of this desire was realised in moments of prolonged body-to-body athleticism. The trapeze was set low at the front of the stage, so that some of the audience could see the more subtle muscular movements of their almost-naked flesh. In this particular instance, they were framed more like dancers than aerialists, although dancers on harness do not accomplish aerial tricks of this calibre.[8] The trapeze act between Oates and Mineur belonged completely within circus aerial work, while at the same time pushing the parameters of form into emotional exchanges usually associated with

---

(conversation with Celia White, 4 November 1996). The tone of traditional *adagio* is non-violent and sexually covert.

[7] In the late 1980s the mostly male The Flying Cranes from Russia became world famous for an emotionally charged—although asexual—act about a dying soldier.

[8] Physical theatre is often linked to dance outside Australia, as for example in the pioneering work of ex-Australian Lloyd Newsom with the London-based company DV8.

dance and/or theatre. Most of Oates's and Mineur's aerial tricks were recognisable, although one turning movement in which their outstretched, backwardly bent bodies formed a complete circle around the trapeze bar remains memorable: Mineur was in a back balance across the bar and Oates linked to him from below, feet to hands, in what they call a Shanghai moon.

The tone of the routine between Oates and Mineur was moreover connected with an *adagio* between Mineur and Wilson, which implicitly suggested eroticism and tenderness. This combination of sexualised emotional engagement is generally not found in traditional circus, although France's new circus Archaos pioneered eroticism between male performers in the early 1990s. These *adagio* routines and the comically grotesque sexual bodies in other acts challenged the prescriptiveness of circus performance while retaining the skilful execution of tricks.

The juxtaposition of emotional intensity with comic images of sexualised behaviour and horror set up an awkward internal tension in the text. Casu sang in Latin about the dark aspects of loving. She passed a book or maybe a mirror to Mineur, and the book/mirror was circulated around and "read." Wilson parried with Lines, who was dressed in a sexually titillating nurse's uniform while carrying a cake of multiple breasts. In a reversal of their previous interaction, Lines appeared in a wheelchair with her head in a magic box, and Wilson operated on it with a drill. He made her head disappear into the image of a skull, thereby symbolically transforming her into a dead head on a live body. In the first version of what would become her signature act by 1999, Oates first spun hoola-hoops around her waist as she stood on the ground, then burning hoola-hoops as she was lifted up into the air. The flaming wheels of an earlier act with a lone rider on a bicycle were echoed in the turning circles of fire around Oates's semi-naked body.

Unlike the exaggerated interaction and parodic queerness of some of Gail Kelly's physical theatre work since 1990, this Rock'n'Roll Circus production only hinted at queer sexuality. A kiss between Wilson and Mineur was fleeting, as if whispered. The text seemed to unravel the physicality of gender difference through interchanging engagements between bodies in heterosexual play. A weirdly polymorphous, multi-armed female figure was created as two performers stood behind a third, wearing sexy, black, Madonna-like underwear and black blindfolds. They held up and licked shining silver cleavers, threatening violent acts. This figure satirised cultural notions of the desiring sexual Woman as self-contained entity, that is, as monster, which Mary Russo has delineated in her discussion of the female other as grotesque.[9] While this exacerbated playful representation mimicked the automatic gasp of horror at female sexuality as a figure of consuming deviancy, it was also an iconoclastic reference to the sideshow display of freak bodies outside the circus ring.[10]

The Dark parodied cultural representations of the desiring female as unnatural by making her grossly grotesque, even zombie-like at times. The circus form added an extra dimension, because it allowed for the display of strong female bodies knocking male bodies to the ground and walking over them. If the female *personae* were tough and brutish, the males appeared overly sentimental and their muscular strength reduced to an ineffectual defence. While *The Dark* parodied some of the darkest fears of masculine projection about the consequences of unleashed female sexuality—abjection was framed as comic absurdity—contradictorily, the physical action underscored the need to remain wary around such physically powerful female bodies.

Bodies in *The Dark* were very clearly and conventionally sexed. Female performers wore costumes characterised by the style and exaggerated features of gender stereotypes such as high heel shoes. The male performers were dressed in conventionally masculine dark suits, albeit with flashes of silver glitter. *The Dark* might have seemed like a warning about the threats to maleness, since the male *personae*, singing of romantic love, fell into fearful spaces where female figures were out to castrate and mutilate them. At the end of the show, amidst fireworks and explosions, Wilson tumbled straight down from above the stage into an enormous soft, red heart where a female figure lurked in shadow. Throughout *The Dark* this comic thread parodied dark fears about unleashed violence between the sexes, but because these *clichés* were delivered acrobatically, the threat seemed to retain some power.

Traditional circus is a cultural space in which the costumed coding of masculinity and femininity is temporarily reversed during acts, although stance and gesture usually reinstate it at the end. It sets up a space in which the cultural categories of sexed, muscular bodies can be reconfigured, at least in the illusions of performance. Similarly in *The Dark*, the female body was rendered as physically strong, like its male counterpart. If, while aligning femininity with a fearful, unknown darkness, the show seemed to present a metaphoric masculine search for

---

[9] See Mary Russo, *The Female Grotesque* (London: Routledge, 1994): 1-6, 29.

[10] By mistakenly collapsing sideshow into circus, extreme physical differences between performing bodies that include animals are obliterated.

emotionally intimate encounters, such a quest became delusionary when sexualised actions shifted continually into violence or its symbols.

Razor Baby featured physicalised pantomimes of same-sex desiring and queer antics. The sensory spill of costumes self-consciously evoked elegant cabaret display and the anonymity of underground sex clubs. The performing bodies dressed in the visually exciting, unique imaginative designs of Angus Strathie juxtaposed glamorous fringed gowns with Grace Lau-inspired studded leather bondage outfits. The show, locating itself in a club, had a continuous techno music soundscape orchestrated by DJ Barbara Clare, who also sung live accompanied by Liberty Kerr and Kevin McClaer.

Razor Baby began with the pre-show mingling of the performers among the audience watching and listening to trash drag queen "Sera Pax,"[11] clad in green and moving up the triangular staircase of the set in outrageously high heels. Whereupon the performers followed her under the spotlights. Jeremy Robins, a guest performer from England, in corset and tights, danced on *pointe* and crawled up the staircase after the disappearing drag queen. Was he seeking the performed *persona* or the physical body, or were these one and the same? He encountered the female *personae* of Anni Davey, Kathryn Niesche, Simone O'Brien, Celia White and Kareena Oates as trouble-shooting American television series *Charlie's Angels'* lookalikes, who were pausing in a *tableau* to the music of Isaac Haye's *Shaft*, their finger-guns pointed skywards, their plastic pistols tucked into the front of their skin-tight outfits. These stylised poses were *Razor Baby*'s running gag, gestures that mimicked pseudo-female toughness and signed nostalgia for the fantasies of 1960s feminine heroism. This was the era of popular culture when fantasy females executing dangerous stunts became more numerous, confounding the social idea that women were naturally weaker and more helpless than men. In *Razor Baby*, these parodic representations of muscular *femmes* seemed as suggestive of queer identity as the brief enactment of a kiss and caress between two women high up on the aerial rig later in the show.

At one point, the metal truss-stairway turned indeed into a very large aerial rig, which had been specially designed for the show and could accommodate seven performers and two riggers. The front section, initially the staircase, was winched up on chains until it hung parallel with the roof, and in the show's second part the performers remained off the ground, even when they were not engaged in acrobatic tricks on other apparatus.

---

[11] Ironically, "Sera Pax" refers to a tranquilliser in Australia.

The ensuing televisual search and rescue motif—the search for the fake *femme* (the drag queen) by Robins and the tough-fisted *femmes*—provided visual links in the action of the show, but did not cohere into a narrative. *Razor Baby* borrowed heavily from formulaic television serials, which progress for extraneous reasons and the substance of the show is action for its own sake, including violent action. The same point might be made about circus skills: they also involve action for its own sake. Sequences with the five tough *femmes* alternated with the appearances of bad-girl guerrilla Kareena Oates in pig-tails, who duelled acrobatically in an *adagio* with Robins on the ground. Four figures in leather bodysuits and hoods dropped down on ropes: these could have been sadomasochists and/or cinematic hangmen. At the same time the performers' gestures prefigured how televisual bodies remain invincible to injurious attacks in a fantasy world where characters playfully smile their way through terrifying ordeals, seemingly without psychological consequences and with only minor physical effects.

Four *tissus* (lengths of lycra fabric) as apparatus dropped from the aerial rig, and routines on these shifted the tone of the show to a gentler sensuality that provided a lull in the leather and steel machismo imagery, perhaps also evoking a 1960s textual combination. Four female *personae* unfurled down and rolled up *tissus* in choreographed unison. A series of spectacular solo pieces followed: as mentioned earlier, Oates performed her acclaimed act of whirling up to forty hoola-hoops around her near-naked body, an act that culminated as she ascended in flaming hoops, and O'Brien descended on a chain with one boot on fire. Hundreds of pink-coloured drinking water bottles fell from roof nets onto Davey playing Narciss-Puss and delivering a very funny monologue—the only spoken text—about rave parties and the loss of her purse, symptomatic of her loss of mind. Niesche swung backwards and forwards on a cloud swing (single looped rope), turning and falling lengthways. White swung out wildly, anarchistically from the rig on an elastic (bungy) rope, high above the whole audience, followed by Davey from the other side of the rig. This action was dazzling and some spectators gasped at the very fast momentum of the swing, which seemed capable of deviating from its diagonal trajectory and jeopardising the performers' safe return to the rig.

While the acts in *Razor Baby* were not discrete entities like those in *The Dark*, they merged together in one ongoing sequence of action. Even lulls were enjoyable; as Jeremy Vincent explains, the pauses seemed "as if the performers, impatient, [were] spinning the radio dial in search of a new sense of energy."[12] Helen Thomson describes this as "comic-book circus," except that these are performers in actual space.[13] In this particular case, the circus form mimics the television stunt: both use risk and danger as sources of viewing pleasure. The voyeuristic appeal of risk in *Razor Baby* is overlayed with an eroticised playfulness. If the dangers of performing these acts were actual—both Niesche and O'Brien suffered injuries during the run of this show that put them out of it—the bodily risks of their physical action were incurred as games that were inseparable from the comic parody of identity fakeness.

Both *The Dark* and *Razor Baby* delivered texts that ironically played with sexual identity while disrupting beliefs about the naturalness of the body's gender identity. Whereas *The Dark* showed action impacting on bodies violently, physical action became another source of parodic play in *Razor Baby*. These two productions exemplify how physical theatre and new circus texts demand perceptual responses from spectators to the performers' actions. Movements can be registered bodily as much as cognitively. The body of the performer as "other" in physical theatre—a moving body in the phenomenal field—is received across sensory and visceral observing spectators' bodies. The performance invites bodily interpretations of social identity. Physical movement and spatiality in physical theatre yield a field of bodily meaning comparable to the cultural significances found in verbal languages. Strong female bodies doing violent acts undermine ideas of the social dominance of male physicality, and erotic play combined with physical risks overturns social beliefs about the physical limitations of female bodies. Spectators can view these challenges to orthodox beliefs bodily within physical theatre and new circus.

Works Cited

Australia and New Zealand Theatre Record, University of New South Wales (October 1996): 26, Nicholas, Jessica. Review of *The Dark, Herald Sun* (1 November 1996), Scott-Norman, Fiona. Review of *The Dark, The Age* (1 November 1996).

Docherty, Thomas. *After Theory* (Edinburgh: Edinburgh University Press, 1996).

Russo, Marie. *The Female Grotesque* (London: Routledge, 1994).

---

[12] Jeremy Vincent, "Razor is Energy on a Knife-edge," *The Australian* (18 January 1999): 17.

[13] Helen Thomson, "Queer Politics Hits the Heights," *The Age* (19 January 1999): 15.

Tait, Peta. "Fleshed Muscular Phenomenologies: Across Sexed and Queer Circus Bodies," in *Body Show/s: Australian Viewings of Live Performance*, ed. Peta Tait (Amsterdam: Rodopi, 2001): 60-78.

Thomson, Helen. "Queer Politics Hits the Heights," *The Age* (19 January 1999): 15.

Vincent, Jeremy. "Razor is Energy on a Knife-edge," *The Australian* (18 January 1999): 17.

Urban Theatre Projects:
Re-siting Marginal Communities
in Outer Western Sydney

TOM BURVILL

Macquarie University

"... other voices speak in (the work of) Urban Theatre Projects."[1]

The "other voices" made to speak in the work of Urban Theatre Projects are those of the people residing in Sydney's stigmatised "Western Suburbs." In the context of popular mythology and media (mis-) representation, this area of the city has become so effectively othered as usually to silence its own voices altogether. The Urban Theatre Projects company turns to the youth and communities of Western Sydney to make new works emphasising the performance of subculture, class marginality, and "multicultural" identity. This theatrical group embodies the continuation of Death Defying Theatre (DDT), which had existed since at least 1981 and been located in various places in Western Sydney since the mid-1980s. As Urban Theatre Projects (UTP), the company signed its name to three large-scale productions in the years 1997 to 1999. These productions, which are set in different parts of the "Western Suburbs" and called "intimate spectacles," develop distinctive methods for working with the many voices of the neighbourhood in question. In addition to its loose literal reference to a sprawling and vaguely bounded area of greater Sydney—an area which spreads some thirty-plus kilometres to the West and South-West of the city centre and is home to perhaps half of Sydney's four and a half million people—the phrase "Western Suburbs" signifies a "problem" part of Australia's largest urban body. Paradoxically, these areas have been stigmatised for their supposed banality and lack of culture, as well as for their alleged tendency to hide pockets of culture antagonistic not only to dominant Anglo-Australian middle-class norms, but also dangerous to public safety, with regular tabloid panics about "streets of fear" and "ethnic

---

[1] Urban Theatre Projects 2000 Programme brochure <www.ozemail.com/~urbantp/page2b.html>.

enclaves," youth gang violence and "Asian drug dealing." These layers of confused and contradictory "knowledges" have become the prevailing general "truth" about the large and differentiated number of citizens to whom this spreading area of the city is home.

Diane Powell writes in *Out West*, her pioneering study of the construction of the image of the West and "Westies":

> The mass media have played a significant role in the emergence of Western Sydney as the "other" side of a social boundary, one which contains several groups of society's "others." The west is seen as the repository for all of those social groups and cultures which are outside the prevailing cultural ideal: the poor, the working class, juvenile delinquents, single mothers, welfare recipients, public housing tenants, Aborigines, immigrants from anywhere but particularly Arabs and Asians ... All are cast out to the margins, to the "outer" of the reconstructed city.[2]

There exists moreover a tradition of stigmatising "suburbia" in Australian writing. Commenting from a Kristevan psychoanalytic perspective, Joan Kirkby analyses some recent Australian literature to conclude that "suburbia—as one of the hideous progeny spawned by modern industrialisation ... is represented as a site of repulsion and disgust, a zone of abomination ... [there is a] demonisation of suburbia and the everyday ..." As Kirkby points out, the suburban is anxiously rejected as "... suburban, not fully urban-like sub-human, not fully human."[3] The still-spreading western and south-western working class suburbs present a contradictory image. On the one hand, there is their unfashionable dormitory mundanity and (allegedly) undifferentiated homogeneity. On the other, they have been attributed a capacity—especially in the imaginary of the tabloid media—to contain and hide ethnic/crime/drug trade/ juvenile delinquent "black spots" on the psychic map of the city.

The works of Urban Theatre Projects to be discussed here correspond to those which the company calls "intimate spectacles." These include *TrackWork* (1997), *Speed Street* (1998) and *<subtopia>* (1999). They represent large-scale outdoor communal performance events held in various parts of the "Western Suburbs"—or in the case of *TrackWork* on the trains and at the stations of the main western commuter railway line. These productions have all seen the day since 1997, when the company took on John Baylis as artistic director and changed their name to

---

[2] Diane Powell, *Out West—Perceptions of Sydney's Western Suburbs* (Sydney: Allen and Unwin,1993): xviii.

[3] Joan Kirkby, "The Pursuit of Oblivion: in Flight from Suburbia," in *Writing the Everyday, Australian Literature and the Limits of Suburbia. Australian Literary Studies* 18. 8 (1998): 3.

Urban Theatre Projects. The name was originally coined to describe *Speed Street*, which was advertised as "an intimate spectacle, the world in a street." This concept is glossed in publicity material by nearby phrases such as "close up on the horizon" and "a stranger whispers in your ear," which poetically encode the paradox of the distant apparently become close, the other grown almost familiar, the unknown glimpsed as if known. The metaphor of siting and re-siting is especially appropriate to these works of UTP, as the company identifies community in the first instance as locality. In other words, a voice is effectively given to a place. Because the locations actually chosen to work in are urban/suburban spaces of a particular kind, this means that the voices of marginalised communities are heard:

> Working in and with the various sites of Western Sydney has become a defining characteristic of Urban Theatre Projects' opus, and it is our goal to develop our expertise in this area. This expertise is not just logistical (though this is very important), but also aesthetic. We want to explore how spaces themselves can be performed, and what are things that spaces can made to say through performance.[4]

As John Baylis, UTP artistic director, explains, the company has developed a process for its "intimate spectacles" which centres on place. "First comes the idea of a particular place, then we develop an angle or a slant on that place, a way of working with it as a performance site, and then we approach the residents, or relevant community and invite their participation."[5] The group has developed an aesthetic of place rather than of political commitment to communities of class, gender, disability, ethnicity, recent migration, or other markers of social marginality, as was often the case with the 1980s community theatre movement in Australia.[6] This can be read as an attempt to avoid pre-determining what is to be spoken, of resisting the temptation to ventriloquise the voices of those who are (re) presented. Indeed, the group's working methods do not assume that there exists a pre-established community to "be voiced,"

---

[4] *Urban Theatre Projects 1999 Annual Report* (Urban Theatre Projects, December 1999): n.p.

[5] Personal interview with John Baylis (14 April 2000). Taking seriously the fragile contingencies of arts funding and the Australia Council's encouragement of export initiatives, the company is in fact offering to take its process to other places, including internationally. They are having preliminary discussions with the Performance Research Centre in Aberystwyth, Wales to make a work in a Welsh village.

[6] For accounts of the 1980s community theatre movement, see Richard Fotheringham, ed., *Community Theatre in Australia* (Sydney: Methuen Australia,1987); Tom Burvill, "Sidetrack: Finding The Theatricality of Community," *New Theatre Quarterly* 11. 5 (1986): 80-89.

or a contrary and therefore more truthful picture to be directly opposed to the media image of conflict and danger. Their approach is more sophisticated: as "streetwise dramaturgs,"[7] not only do they remain aware that stories, performances, expressive activities will be "found" in any area; they also recognise that the character of their own activity calls certain modes of voicing into being, that by having certain kinds of questions and performance forms in mind, they summon particular types of stories and self-presentation into being. The activity of "making a show" in contemporary performance form for community cultural development in itself encourages given kinds of occurrences. All these shows entail a major shaping of what the community offers in the processes by which the material is chosen, curated and logistically managed, activities central to the creation of *TrackWork* and *<subtopia>* as shows made up of a collection of individual acts.

Besides including actual members of groups in the communities as performers, UTP works draw on local and subcultural forms and styles, for instance youth music styles like hip-hop and rap, traditional Vietnamese dance theatre etc. The performances are held in the places about which they speak and played back to the people who inspired them. The group can therefore be seen as an inheritor of the project of Death Defying Theatre and of the community theatre movement of the 1980s. The company's current theoretical and aesthetic strategies, however, differ for the most part from the latter's. The current work of UTP can usefully be construed as "post-contemporary" community theatre, striving to find ways to work with community "post" the high moment of experimental postmodern performance work usually referred to in Sydney as "contemporary performance." The productions of Sydney Front—the group of which John Baylis, the new artistic director of UTP, was a leading member—are often regarded as emblematic of this approach. The current creations of UTP "come after" the work of Sydney Front and others to the extent that certain artistic lessons are carried over from the one style to the other. In the broadest sense, this involves strategies to provoke non-passivity in the audience and the accompanying inscription of multiple perspectives into the work and its experience by the theatre-goers. Not only is there no central narrative to provide a thematic map or continuing characters with whom to identify, but multiple and even simultaneous actions can occur in different parts of the performance site. The works of UTP in question not only require the audience to travel to the performance location, which coincides with a public place, but to continue to move about once there, without necessarily

---

[7] The phrase is taken from the title of the review article by Keith Gallasch in the Sydney (and WWW) contemporary arts magazine *RealTime* 33.

expecting to see everything or the same things. In <subtopia> *a subcultural themepark*, participants were, for instance, led about to take in the sights in a particular order—depending on the "tour group" to which they had been assigned—and perhaps missed some events about which they only heard afterwards. In *Speed Street*, members of the audience were asked to move in the dark as part of a large group milling down the street, without being always able to see or know where to look. In *Trackwork*, spectators would catch different mini-performances and/or different angles on what was happening, depending on where they were seated or standing in the train, or in which direction in particular they happened to look while at various platforms.

The map or cartography invoking representations of place, but also the act or fact of travelling—perhaps a reference to both suburban commuting and the audience travelling "out" to the shows—becomes often foregrounded in the company's self-presentation. In a widely distributed publicity brochure, the cover image shows a section of a road map of Western Sydney and features the names of some typical suburbs. Superimposed on the image is the trace of a white highway centre-line, and inserted in the bottom right hand corner are three black and white photo-images. These show a railway platform destination indicator displaying the stops for the next train as Redfern, Auburn, Tripoli, Lidcombe, Sarajevo. The alert Sydneysider will recognise three actual station names and two place names evoking migration, the dangerous elsewhere, stories of exile, and refugee status. Those with more detailed knowledge of the social/ethnic composition of the "Western Suburbs" will identify Auburn as a heavily Arabic suburb, and may wonder about the appropriateness of conjoining Lidcombe and Sarajevo. The strong co-implication of the global and the local—brought about by migrations both exilic and non-exilic to these areas—is evoked swiftly and visually. The next "frame" shows a supermarket hopping trolley at a precarious angle, being pushed by a figure who cannot clearly be made out; in all probability, however, since it seems to be outdoors and does not contain any groceries in it, it represents a rogue trolley, liberated from its normal duties for the sake of a performance. For what could signify the mundane everyday consumer aspect of the suburbs better than the supermarket shopping trolley? And of course, such trolleys did figure in a backyard choreography of massed trolleys in *Speed Street*.

As far as the actual contents of each "intimate spectacle" are concerned, *TrackWork* took place on regular scheduled CityRail trains and on platforms in Western Sydney. The work was performed on four afternoons over two weekends in November and December 1997. It was co-directed by Fiona Winning, artistic director of DDT, and new artistic coordinator of UTP, John Baylis. The box office was situated at Redfern station, close to the centre of the city train network and thus centrally located for many of the inner-city performance-goers. Redfern also coincides with the departure station for the main western and south-western Sydney suburban lines. At this site, the paying audience received their ticket and a small brightly coloured suitcase, a miniature version of the one that a child might take to school. Inside were a bottle of water—presumably to counter the hot weather in the early summer afternoon—and an apple. It felt like preparation for at least a small adventure. The audience members also appeared a little conspicuous with their tiny cases amongst the weekend shopping crowds on their way home. Throughout the journey, groups of uniformed young performers on board the trains announced themselves as the "On Board Carriage Activities Coordinators." Just like good airline cabin crew, they informed participants of the safety features of the train, sang songs, and told stories. These young people considerably puzzled some of the other passengers as the former made their announcements and entertained the audience. Moreover, on particular sections of the journey, an Italian-Australian women's choir energetically sang from their seats; at different times still, so-called "invisible performers" bopped loudly to the music from their Walkman or enacted other slightly exaggerated versions of typical commuter behaviour. I found one particular feature of the on-board part of the show particularly engaging, perhaps because it came across as so un-theatrical in this mundane and indeed uncongenial setting of a rattling, crowded train carriage. Individual members of the "On-Board Entertainment" teams approached groups of participants and invited them to listen to their stories of the domestic everyday of family life, partly supported by the showing family photographs. Members of these teams had pictures temporarily stuck inside the train windows with adhesive tape to illustrate their dog or cat, their favourite aunty, the inside of their homes, or still "the people in my life, the people I share my life with" etc. The stories sounded anything but spectacular, but being unobtrusively entrusted with them, quietly in the middle of the crowded train carriage, generated a moving and beautiful experience.

 This contrasted in style with some other splendid aspects of the piece, in particular a mini-drama of surreal incidents which the company refers to as "the tragic dumping of the brides." Several young "brides" in full white gowns and veils and clutching bunches of flowers accompanied the participants on the train. The young brides were looking somewhat wistful and appeared to have trouble finding their grooms. At a particular station, two of them climbed into the back seat of a white limousine and were driven off. At a station further down the line, while members of the audience were waiting for a connecting train, two brides could be seen sitting and sobbing in the gutter outside some unsuspecting person's house. Moreover, the participants' attention was suddenly caught by a large white car approaching fast in the street nearby the railway. It screeched to a halt and unceremoniously discharged two other beautifully dressed brides onto the road, leaving them calling disconsolately after the rapidly departing vehicle. They did not appear physically hurt, but seemed understandably upset; they moreover looked wonderfully incongruous, sitting at first on the kerb and then attempting to climb the low wire fence towards the railway, while little groups of local residents came out of their houses to stare and wonder. The story was never explained or resolved, the performance-goers never discovered who was driving the car, but in fact they themselves had to desert the brides as the audience boarded the train for the next leg of the trip. The same enigmatic character of events "seen in passing" invested many of the "sights" at various railway station. At Auburn station, while changing trains, the participants could glimpse strange things happening outside the shops across the street—some people were holding bunches of balloons, others cooking something steaming in woks on the pavement. Had these events all been staged, or did they actually represent local everyday life occurrences that appeared unfamiliar to the participants as outsiders—how unusual were they?

At each station pieces more easily recognisable as performance were also awaiting the arrival of the audience. Before the audience boarded the trains at Redfern, they were entertained by a funk dance by ten-to twelve-year-old females from a youth refuge for girls at risk. At Lidcombe, participants were treated to the following: a rendition of "Begin the Beguine" by elegant septuagenarian crooner Terry Woo, a ballroom dancing exhibition on the platform by members of local dance schools, Turkish music from a high school group, and a Tai Chi performance by a wonderfully graceful older gentleman with a large sword, a member of the West Sydney Elderly Chinese Association. At Cabramatta, the audience left the relatively secure environment of the trains and were led through the shopping centre to a small plaza, where they enjoyed a dance theatre performance of a Vietnamese legend by the Vietnamese Community in Australia and Citymoon Youth Theatre. The sights at Granville station presented a particularly wide span of cultural practices. These included hip hop performances (break dancing, rap, DJ-ing) by youth groups 3 MCs, 2Indij, and South West Syndicate. The lyrics of 2Indij, a duo of young indigenous women, commented directly on contemporary politics of race. On the same platform, one could see an abstract postmodern piece involving manic manipulation in unison of large white sheets by five carefully choreographed men in black, the inner-city performance group Gravity Feed. *TrackWork* perhaps most clearly combines the independent creativity and variety of the actual expressive cultures of "the West" with a very clever form for presenting them in the process of enticing audiences simply to travel into the suburbs like most people who actually live there. This was a performance journey inside a series of normal commuter journeys.

The next work to be examined is *Speed Street*, created in 1998. This site-specific show was located in the street by the same name in the south-western suburb of Liverpool. After much negotiation with local officials, they agreed to close this normally busy street to through-traffic for the four evenings required by the production. The show, which started in late afternoon and continued into the dark, involved not only lighting performance areas within the street and its environs, but also video projection onto buildings and amplified sound. As a consequence, the audience moved along the street accompanied by a large mobile scaffolding tower carrying lighting, sound, and video equipment. This tower itself became a dominant visual design feature, transforming the street by its mere incongruous presence. The show began with a literal bang: as the audience gathered in a vacant lot on one side of the street, John Baylis began to welcome them with a *spiel* about how the work embodied a series of events about the collisions of the global and the local; when he got approximately to "collisions," a car came up the road at high speed and crashed loudly into another one parked opposite. The hit-and-run-driver quickly got out of his vehicle and disappeared. A "TV News team" arrived soon afterwards and the "presenter" began one of those portentous pieces to camera about this all-too-common sort of incident on these dangerous Liverpool streets.

As reviewer Stephen Dunne wrote, "With the car culture and amphetamine overtones of its name, the street becomes an arena in which mainstream stereotypes of Western Sydney are put up, played with and knocked down."[8] The show moved beyond stereotyped images both by satirising them—as in the case of the TV News—and by presenting other ordinary moments of suburban life. One young performer told the the audience about the old man reputed to live in one of the last remaining single storey houses. "He owns two hundred cats," she said, "and knew *all* their names ... or most of them, anyway." Some stories were shown as video, including images which looked like an amateur video of police hassling local kids, and which were replayed through several monitors set up in a dimly lit sub-floor parking basement with concrete walls and floor. In addition, the performance included lyrical and poignant memories of homelands and journeys of exile and migration. People argued about what is was like to live on the street. The

---

[8] Stephen Dunne, "Play in the Traffic: Its Good for You," *Sydney Morning Herald* (8 December 1998).

participants were also reminded of the fears shared by so many women of being stalked or followed at night: to this effect, a young Asian woman spoke a monologue while walking to the amplified background of footsteps, which walked or shuffled when she walked, stopped when she stopped. The audience walked with her when she walked, but could not share her fears beyond being simple onlookers. Other moments were more surreal, as shopping trolleys danced in formation, or video sequences were projected onto the sides of the housing blocks themselves. These images were not always easy to see, but they came across as eery in their incongruity and in their very lack of the usual high definition of broadcast television. This performance took the audience through a darkened street in one of the areas which the media love to paint as dangerous: the participants thereby experienced not only the fears that existed even amongst the residents themselves, but also the warmth and ordinariness that could likewise characterise the streets at other times.

The valuable perspective which Ian Maxwell has articulated on *Speed Street* could extend to the work of Urban Theatre Projects as a whole. He argues that it is not relevant to look for a coherent dramaturgical expression of a community in *Speed Street*, to which he prefers to refer as an "event." Rather, he writes, "*Speed Street* set out to reinscribe interpretations of the west of Sydney, making a play (in the sense of a move in a game) within a political struggle about what it is to represent ..."[9] Maxwell sees the show not so much as a representation of the street as an interpretative process and, therefore, as an "open" creative act. The show does more than reveal conflicting feelings about living in Speed Street: for the idea that the reality portrayed and the terms used to convey it represent a direct expression of what the residents felt actually misses the importance of the processes of mediation whereby a diversity of images and actions are enacted. Nor can the significance of the show simply be reduced to an expression of what the street *is* or is thought to be, since it consists of a series of performative events provoked by responses to the place. The production process admittedly began with resident workshops at which personal stories were told and recorded; however, this material was then distilled by writer Rose Nakad and woven into the texts to be spoken by a cast whose members certainly came from the "Western Suburbs," but were not drawn from the street itself. The image of a community directly "speaking itself" oversimplifies how this event "voiced" the place called Speed Street.

Each of these shows "voiced" or made the "Western suburbs" speak differently. The third of the "intimate spectacles," <subtopia> *a sub-*

---

[9] Ian Maxwell, "Promenading Deepest Suburbia, On Collapsing Theatre and the Real," *Postwest* 15 (1999): 59.

culture themepark, consisted of a series of performance sites clustered around the shopping centre of the suburb of Bankstown, where the office of UTP happens to be located. These sites operated as performance "stations," at each of which different "subcultures" performed colourful scenes presented as typical of their behaviour. The audience witnessed melancholy *nouveau*-Beat poets in punk gear reciting what sounded like pastiche modernist poetry of existential *angst* and inviting them to smash TV sets with large hammers. Participants could even take away a copy of their poetry zine, *The Last Head*. Carefully period-dressed and hairstyled Rocker look-alikes were moreover jiving to good live rockabilly music and somewhat tamely recalling the aggressive sexual politics of the 1950s gang scene. The subculture site that became legendary was the female Gothics, as the audience were led into a darkened set of derelict rooms where an elaborately costumed lesbian drama of adolescence and identity with sado-masochistic overtones was acted out.

As subcultures are by definition always performative, these shows produced an odd "double staging" effect. Although style and fashion basically underlie subculture, the staging of these cultures as exotic, as "to-be-looked-at" realities, courted the danger of turning them into exotic cultural commodities. Approximately half way through their circuit around the performance stations, spectators were collected back in the Bankstown Town Square, where two of the rap/hip-hop groups also seen in *TrackWork*, namely 2Indij and South West Syndicate, were performing once more. Thereby, a contrast was generated by the fact that a subculture was not exhibited as entertainment, but as the political appropriation of U.S. cultural idiom for local identity and youth politics.

2Indij consists of two young women—of Aboriginal and Pacific Islander background—who speak directly in their work of the present racism and the denial of history in contemporary Australian society and politics. South West Syndicate includes a mix of indigenous, Anglo-Australian, and young people of other extraction, including Lebanese-Australians. 2Indij performed their political rap called "Pauline Hanson Sucks," attacking the racial slurs and misinformation recently made famous by the speeches of populist politician Pauline Hanson and her One Nation party. "The message goes back, and two hundred years ago, my people lived peacefully/Until they were invaded by people/With nothing in their mind except genocide ... Open up your mind, and pay attention (Repeat) ..." The song was addressed rhetorically both to Hanson herself and to the white population as a whole.

South West Syndicate in turn set up a resounding call to solidarity addressed to the different areas of the "Western Suburbs": in their stigmatisation as "Westies," their inhabitants were perceived as fellows sharing the band members' plight of working class Aboriginal, migrant or Anglo-Australian youth of unemployment. To the questions of "Bankstown, Are you with us out there?/Lakemba, Are you with us out there?," the crowd chanted back the affirmative response of "Yeah!"

The contrast between these two groups and the other subcultures underscored the difference between subcultures of style and play and those of conscious criticism and resistance. In that sense, these groups were incongruous in this show of fantasy identities. The two young women of 2Indij, in particular, reminded their listeners of the pain of Aboriginal and Islander identity in a still-racist society. To quote from the <subtopia> *Visitor Guide*:

> Behind the apparent uniformity of suburban space are diverse world views and cultural practices. While many are established by ethnicity, class or religion, others are chosen through conscious acts of self-definition. Hip hop, goths, ravers etc: all specific spaces carved out of mass culture for the declaration of difference and identity, separated from each other and from other social *personae* only by a leap of faith, a commitment, a choice.[10]

Although it makes a valid claim about subcultural identities as such, the above nevertheless becomes more problematic when referring to what are said to be subcultures performing themselves in ten-minute bursts for revolving groups of audience. Subculture—at least in the tradition of Stuart Hall and Dick Hebdidge—has also been theorised as the enacting of resistance through ritual.[11] It is a phenomenon of the subordinated. On the one hand, subcultural "style" embodies a way of distinguishing oneself; on the other, it declares solidarity with others against the dominant culture and expresses a refusal, often through transgression of accepted behavioural norms. Subculture is also said to reveal in part what the dominant culture censures or represses. The message that <subtopia> contributes to the theme of re-siting the Western suburbs is perhaps this: the variety of life styles to be found in that area actually corresponds to a playful, creative, and—for many—primarily recreational adoption of the styles of a range of past subcultures based on mass culture. Therefore, to press too hard on whether many of the

---

[10] John Baylis and Alicia Talbot, "About <subtopia>," in <subtopia> *Visitor Guide, This Week in Subtopia* (Bankstown: Urban Theatre Projects, 1999). Performance programme, n.p.

[11] My reference to Hall and Hebdidge is meant to be a general one to arguments that they made throughout two works from the 1970s; see Dick Hebdidge, *Subculture: The Meaning of Style* (London: Methuen, 1979) and Stuart Hall and Tony Jefferson, eds., *Resistance through Rituals: Youth Subcultures in Postwar Britain* (London: Hutchinson, 1976).

activities on display were "real" or authentic subcultures probably misses the point.

An unexpected insight yielded by UTP's work in Western Sydney concerns its positive articulation of specific aspects of globalisation. Not only do immigrants, exiles, and refugees bring with them diverse cultural practices from their homelands to be re-negotiated within Australia's "multicultural mosaic." In a phenomenon highlighted by Homi K. Bhaba's writing on the postcolonial moment within modernity, but ostensibly undervalued by some forms of official multiculturalism, young people appropriate new cultural forms existing as part of Australia's imbrication in global culture as forms to be actively hybridised and for the purpose of developing new identities. Bhaba refers to those forms of alterity which are "... political identities in the process of being formed, cultural enunciations in the act of hybridity, in the process of translating and transvaluating cultural differences."[12] The hybrid forms of expression and identity of subculture together with the hyphenated ethnicity shown by UTP productions to be part of the cultural vitality of the "Western Suburbs" may represent emergent oppositional forms in the sense that they are only on their way to becoming dominant, or may even remain more transient than that. What UTP find/provoke/concentrate and to some extent re-make into their own hybrid "intimate spectacles"—which cannot readily be categorised as "theatre" in some traditional ways, but certainly always involve the liveness of performance—is very far from victim narratives of marginalisation or exclusion. The locally creative appropriation of that globalisation actually corresponds to what they find/provoke/re-site and performatively hyperlink into unique performance events. However, UTP work also highlights that there exists no single picture to which to attend, and—by implication—no such thing as that undifferentiated other, "the West:" when people speak, they do not all say the same things or speak with the same voice. UTP's productions open up in detail the specificity and variety of people's everyday lives: these "intimate spectacles" involve a wide range of registers and modes of performance, from personal stories to public identity rap, from gentle or satiric humour to anger, including some of that fear and loathing which obsess the media.

UTP speak of "... activating the audience, moving them physically through a space, taking them on a metaphorical journey."[13] This in fact means that the majority of their audience will have to take a physical

---

[12] Homi K. Bhaba, *The Location of Culture* (London: Routledge, 1994): 252.

[13] Urban Theatre Projects 2000 programme brochure, *op. cit.* The company also displays a wealth of information, including excerpts of reviews and reports on the Web at <www.ozemail.com.au/~urbantp>.

journey well before they reach the site of the actual performance journey to be made through the particular present history of Liverpool Street, or through the suburban maze of Bankstown. Most of the participants have to travel from the inner city, home to most of the serious theatre-goers in the Sydney population: thereby, they are also required to embark upon a class journey across social boundaries. To be included in the audience, theatre-goers are asked to venture to "unknown" and certainly untrendy parts of the city. They need to re-site themselves physically away from the "café society" of the usual performance venues. The cultural relocation involved in seeing the "Western Suburbs" as the site and location for "art," moreover, appears significant in another respect: not only the mainstage bourgeois theatres, but the alternative and experimental venues as well are securely located within a few kilometres of the centre of Sydney.

Urban Theatre Projects' "intimate spectacles" aim to combine community theatre, community cultural development, and contemporary performance strategies, in order to enable voices to speak which are "Voices rarely heard or heard only in other contexts."[14] To this end, UTP's productions create new performance forms which also afford new ways of working with community. It is in this sense that the company culturally re-sites Sydney's West, treating it as central to its concerns, re-positioning the people of this major population area in terms of the imaginary of the city. No longer dimly pictured as obscure and frightening areas on the margins of culture, in these works "the Western Suburbs" become an array of vital centres.

Works Cited

Bhaba, Homi K. *The Location of Culture* (London: Routledge, 1994).

Burvill, Tom. "Sidetrack: Finding the Theatricality of Community," *New Theatre Quarterly* 11. 5 (1 987): 80-89.

Dunne, Stephen. "Play in the Traffic: Its Good for You," *Sydney Morning Herald* (8 December 1998).

Fotheringham, Richard, ed. *Community Theatre in Australia* (Sydney: Methuen Australia, 1987).

Gallasch, Keith. "Street-wise Dramaturgs," *RealTime* 33 (1999), <www.rtimearts.com/~opencity/rt33/talbot.html>.

Hall, Stuart & Tony Jefferson, eds. *Resistance through Rituals: Youth Subcultures in Postwar Britain* (London: Hutchinson, 1976).

Hebdidge, Dick. *Subculture: The Meaning of Style* (London: Methuen, 1979).

---

[14] *Ibid.*

Kirkby, Joan. "The Pursuit of Oblivion: in Flight from Suburbia," in *Writing the Everyday, Australian Literature and the Limits of Suburbia. Australian Literary Studies* 18. 8 (1998):1-15.

Maxwell, Ian. "Promenading Deepest Suburbia, On Collapsing Theatre and the Real," *Postwest* 15 (1999): 55-59.

Powell , Diane. *Out West—Perceptions of Sydney's Western Suburbs* (Sydney: Allen and Unwin,1993).

Urban Theatre Projects 1999 Annual Report (Urban Theatre Projects, December 1999): n.p.

Urban Theatre Projects 2000 Programme brochure at <www.ozemail.com/~urbantp/page2b.html>.

Fear and Desire *Under the Big Sky*: Brink Visual Theatre and the Post-colonial Australian Landscape

PAUL MAKEHAM

Queensland University of Technology

A woman in a long white dress moves precariously across the top of a cliff face, thirty metres above the ground. She might be a nineteenth-century settler, perhaps a suburban mum. Starkly illuminated, and to the night-time music of crickets and mosquitoes (sounds augmented by an underscore of Aboriginal song), the woman carries a rustic basket filled with washing. Reaching out across the darkness to peg her clothes, she is swept up by a great wind, and left suspended, horizontal, grimly clutching her clothes line ...

She is blown away. As she falls, her dress transforms to become an expanse of white cloth, unfurling and settling against a section of the cliff's vertical plane. Projected onto it, and onto the rock wall below, comes an array of nostalgic images: turn-of-the-century schoolchildren; swirling ocean waves; the silhouette of a windmill on an Australian farm; ANZAC troops; immigrant settlers ...

A First Fleet tall ship glides over the projected sea ...

An explorer-surveyor, armed with theodolite and map, swings dangerously upside down, across and against the jagged rock face. The map falls from his hands. Parched, he goes to drink from his canteen, but out pours a stream of dry sand. The surface gives way beneath him; he falls ...

Sounds and images like these combine in a pastiche of pioneer narratives, the settlers' labours standing metaphorically for the heroic march towards nationhood in determined acts of colonial will and imagination. But these vignettes are also vivid in evoking the fragility and provisional nature of Europeans' tenure in the Australian landscape ...[1]

Few historical forces can be as powerful as the colonial desire to imagine a nation into being. For "the nation as imagined [is] the basis for nationalism, perhaps the most forceful politico-cultural ideology of

---

[1] This text is mine and based on a video copy which I have of *Under the Big Sky*. This extended epigraph is meant to give readers a sense of what the show looked like before they embark on their reading of this essay.

modern history."[2] In seeking to define and express an Australian nationalism, European settler-invaders and their descendants have always interpreted their experiences, fears and desires through reference to the landscape, that complex space at once physical and cultural, actual and mythic. As Robert Kenny has claimed, in other words, Australian history "has been related mainly as landscape."[3] This is not to suggest that European responses to the Australian environment have ever been singular or uniform: the continent has been ambivalently encountered throughout the history of white Australia as a canvas upon which have been projected contradictory feelings, clustered around the poles of attraction and repulsion. Accordingly, the landscape—and by an imperial habit of conflation, its indigenous inhabitants—become simultaneously objects of desire and the national "Other," idealised and demonised at the same time. The colonialist urge "to conquer" and "to settle," then, is paradoxically accompanied by the nationalist need to exalt and to idealise.

A key site in this struggle for national identity in Australia has been theatre and performance, where colonialist ideology and post-colonial critique have evolved alongside one another, generating highly productive tensions. Some of these tensions have recently been explored in the work of Brink, the Brisbane-based Visual Theatre company whose aesthetic engagement with post-colonialism and the Australian landscape draws fascinatingly upon the contemporary influences of physical theatre, digital technology and site-specific performance. Through reference to Brink's outdoor production *Under The Big Sky* (1997), it will be shown that the tenuous nature of white occupation suggested in their work is counterpointed by a subtly asserted acknowledgment of Aboriginal ways of seeing. In order to contextualise this production, though, the first part of this essay provides a broader commentary on landscape and post-coloniality in Australia, and considers some of the ways in which landscapes function as semic economies in Australian culture.

Whilst "land" exists *a priori* as a material entity, "landscape" forms a set of representations or discursive practices. To encounter a landscape is always, in the end, to encounter a human sensibility. Rendering land-

---

[2] Tony Fry and Anne-Marie Willis, "Criticism Against The Current," *Meanjin* 48.2 (1988): 223.

[3] Robert Kenny, "A Secret Australia," epilogue essay in *A Secret Australia* by Ken Taylor (Melbourne: Rigmarole, 1984): 92.

scape, whether as words, objects or images, thus becomes the practice of altering the "disposition of Nature to ... [a particular] point of view."[4]

> A landscape is a cultural image ... [It] may be represented in a variety of materials and on many surfaces—in paint on canvas, in writing on paper, in earth, stone, water, and vegetation on the ground. A landscape park is no more real, nor less imaginary, than a landscape painting or poem.[5]

In a larger historical and political sense, the entire process of Australian colonisation was dependent upon the textualisation of the land: invasion proceeded as a series of linguistic, material and ideological (re)inscriptions. "To live in a place and give it a name is to know it, and to claim it as one's own. This was the political practice of the colonizers of Australia; ownership tended to proceed de facto through the practice of renaming, of *writing over* the original names of the country."[6] Systems of social and economic organisation—notably land clearance and farming—were brought to Australia from Europe, altering the environment and producing a new text, inscribed over the old. However, to judge by the public forms of colonial discourse, many colonists apprehended New South Wales as though it were completely new, untextualised, a space at the beginning of history. According to Ross Gibson, the explorer Thomas Mitchell did "not intend to read the country as if it were a thoroughly edited text that already contained lessons for survival; rather, he [saw] it as a pristine surface receptive to the stories brought from the established systems of Old World thought and behaviour."[7]

This colonial conception of Australia as an unwritten text, whilst perhaps a necessary adjunct to the imperial enterprise, was born of a combination of ignorance and arrogance. For it has become clear in the period since invasion that the country was already densely textualised when the Europeans arrived. "For Aborigines, every part of the country they occupied, every mark and feature, was numinous with meaning":[8]

> As for the emptiness of Australian space, we have learned, mostly from the contrary experience of Aboriginal people, to be wary of assuming that a

---

[4] Raymond Williams, *The Country and the City* (London: Chatto and Windus, 1975): 123. Cited in Susan Keogh, "Land, Landscape and *Such Is Life*," *Southerly* 49.1 (March 1989): 55.

[5] D. Cosgrove and S. Daniels, eds., *The Iconography of Landscape* (Cambridge: Cambridge UP, 1988): 1.

[6] Stephen Muecke, *Textual Spaces: Aboriginality and Cultural Studies* (Sydney: New South Wales UP, 1992): 6.

[7] Ross Gibson, *South of the West: Postcolonialism and the Narrative Construction of Australia* (Indianapolis: Indiana UP, 1992): 15.

[8] Judith Wright, "Landscape and Dreaming," *Daedalus* 114.1 (1985): 31.

landscape is empty only because it does not contain what our European eyes have been trained to find there. A place may be crowded with meanings we do not apprehend because they are in a language we have not learned.[9]

In the century or so after 1788, European settlers collectively re-enacted what Anne McClintock identifies as "a recurrent, almost ritualistic moment in the colonial narrative: the moment of visual and verbal crisis as the colonial intruder stands dumbfounded before an inexpressible landscape ... The effort to give voice to a landscape that is unspeakable because it inhabits a different history creates a deep confusion."[10] Overwhelmingly, novels, poems, paintings, letters and journals from this period figure the colonial experience through reference to the "new" landscape, which is defined in terms of its difference from the familiar landscapes of Home—that is, Europe, and usually England. Anthony J. Hassall observes that many Australian novelists since have either "turned back from Australia to the landscape of 'home' in Europe, or plunged into its arid interior in the hope of solving their alienation by immersion."[11]

"The Landscape" remains the most complex figurative system deployed in constructions of Australianness. It serves as the canvas of our group imagination, "the projective screen for a persistent national neurosis deriving from the fear and fascination of a preternatural continent ... [T]he idea of the intractability of Australian nature is essential to the national ethos."[12] Images of the outback in particular function as a generalised metaphor for a presumed authentic Australia, invoked within a myriad of social, political, and economic activities.[13] One of the most

---

[9] David Malouf, "Making Better Australians," *The Australian* (17-18 September 1994): 29.

[10] Anne McClintock, "Unspeakable Secrets: The Ideology of Landscape in Conrad's *Heart of Darkness*," *Journal of the Midwest Modern Language Association* 17 (1984): 42.

[11] Anthony J. Hassall, "Quests," in *The Penguin* New *Literary History of Australia*, ed. Laurie Hergenhan (Ringwood: Penguin, 1988): 396.

[12] Ross Gibson, "Camera Natura: Landscape in Australian Feature Films," in *Australian Cultural Studies: A Reader*, eds. John Frow and Meaghan Morris (Sydney: Allen and Unwin, 1993): 211-12.

[13] J. Douglas Porteous, commenting upon the wide-ranging metaphoric associations of landscape, observes that "the very word landscape has superseded the previously overused 'situation' in mediaspeak; we are asked, for example, to visualize the effects of an event upon the existing 'political landscape.' Also commonly invoked are cultural, intellectual, and economic landscapes, while the specific notion of 'scape' extends to townscapes, cityscapes, Van Gogh's wheatscapes, L.S. Lowry's seascapes, Freud's dreamscapes, and so on". See J. Douglas Porteous, *Landscapes of the Mind* (Toronto: University of Toronto Press, 1990): 3-4.

vigorous and contentious analyses of the functions of landscape discourses in Australian culture is proffered by Tony Fry and Anne-Marie Willis,[14] who state that the "figure of landscape has pervaded both high and popular culture in Australia for nearly a century, dominating discussions of national identity." In the absence of a fully developed political nationalism in Australia, a cultural nationalist discourse—relying centrally on images of landscape—has become *de facto* the nation's primary medium of political and economic power: "'Australia' and landscape have become indivisible. Nation becomes synonymous with landmass ..."

As suggested above, the discursive construction of landscape, central to the nationalist project, has often involved a conflation of physical space—specifically the outback—with the nation's indigenous peoples. A characteristic of Australian popular culture—including advertising, film, the media and tourism—is its tendency to align Aborigines so closely with ideas of "The Bush" that each becomes, in effect, a manifestation of the other. "To many Australians, Aborigines still represent a kind of atavistic vestige of ancient Australia, the past re-emerged in the present; this notion is particularly apparent in popular images which associate Aborigines with the outback."[15] Accordingly, those dualities which attend images of landscape can also govern representations of Aborigines: images of the uncivilised primitive, for example, compete with Romantic idealisations of the Noble Savage. As in other postcolonial societies, then, representations of "the indigene" in Australia have been contained within a limited field of signifiers, especially the sexual, the violent, and the mystical:

> All these facets are shaped by the needs of the white text, often in some exploration of the relationship between white culture and the indigene as manifestation of nature. The treacherous redskin and the Indian maiden, the embodiments of violence and sex, are also the embodiments of the emo-

---

[14] Tony Fry and Anne-Marie Willis, "Criticism Against The Current," *Meanjin* 48.2 (1988): 223-40. The quotations from this article cited here are from pp. 223-226. It is worth noting that several commentators have challenged aspects of Fry's and Willis's arguments. See for example Grahame Griffin, "Landscape and the Representation of Space in Australian Popular Culture: A Study in Cultural Geography," in *Australian Cultural Studies Conference 1990 Proceedings* (Sydney: Faculty of Humanities and Social Sciences, University of Western Sydney/Nepean, 1991): 171; and Stephen Muecke, *Textual Spaces: Aboriginality and Cultural Studies* (Sydney: New South Wales UP, 1992): 164-66.

[15] Paul Makeham, "Singing the landscape: *Bran Nue Dae*," *Australasian Drama Studies* 28 (1996): 119.

tional signs of fear and temptation, of the white repulsion from and attraction to the land.[16]

The national fascination with landscape, of course, constitutes one of the key preoccupations in modern Australian drama. Theatrical depictions of the physical environment extend as far back as the earliest local melodramas, and continue through the nationalist projects of Louis Esson and the Pioneer Players in the 1920s, the great "bush dramas" of the 1930s and 1940s, the stylistically innovative works of Patrick White and Dorothy Hewett from the 1960s onward, and, more recently, plays by writers as diverse as Louis Nowra, Janis Balodis, Nicholas Parsons, and many others. Probably the most important dramatic voices to have spoken in recent decades are Aboriginal: since the first works of Kevin Gilbert and Robert Merritt were staged thirty years ago, indigenous actors, dancers, writers, directors and others have created amongst the most powerful and innovative drama to have emerged from any Australian context. Katharine Brisbane claims that "[t]oday Aboriginal drama is ... the most important new Australian voice and one which will, in due course, be the most widely heard in other countries."[17]

Historically, though, all these dramatists have been challenged to overcome the practical and ideological constraints imposed on "staging Australia" by realist dramaturgy. "On the one hand, we yearn to explore our psychic connection with space; on the other, we've tended to be 'cabin'd, cribb'd, confined' by the signature design of the realist room, our epic vision immured."[18] As Peter Fitzpatrick observes of Australian theatre up until the 1970s:

> ... the rich evocations of the outback, and the archetypal conflicts of fire, flood and famine which could fill the wide screen, proved resistant to the naturalistic conventions and proscenium stages which constituted the dominant dramatic tradition.[19]

A burgeoning of Australian theatre and performance since the "New Wave" of the 1970s, however, has prompted developments in all aspects

---

[16] Terry Goldie, "Indigenous Stages: The Indigene in Canadian, New Zealand and Australian Drama," *Australasian Drama Studies* 9 (1986): 6.

[17] Katharine Brisbane in "White Heat, Black Stories" by Jo Litson, *The Weekend Australian* (20-21 May 1994): 17.

[18] Paul Makeham, "Narrative Structure and the BLURRED Landscape," in *Blurred: Creating Performance for Young People*, eds. Louise Gough and Judith McLean (Brisbane: Playlab Press, 1999): 21.

[19] Peter Fitzpatrick, "Views of the Harbour: The Empty City in Contemporary Australian Drama," in *Populous Places: Australian Cities and Towns*, ed. Anna Rutherford (Sydney: Dangaroo Press, 1992): 48-49.

of production, including fundamental challenges to that "dominant dramatic tradition." New voices, bold experiments with process and form, technological advances and a post-modern poetics are all characteristic of the most significant new work. Various lines of development have converged in a range of contemporary practitioners and events to provide dynamic new perspectives on landscape, post-colonialism and the "national imaginary." Some of this practice actively resists even the basic tenets of conventional narrative and mimesis; in 1999, for instance, performer-choreographer Tess de Quincey conducted a "BodyWeather Laboratory" at Hamilton Downs in the Central Desert of the Northern Territory. This was the first in a series of three annual workshops, collectively titled *Triple Alice*:

> *Triple Alice* seeks to explore relationships between bodies, place and space. In developing her work's engagement with Australian landscapes, de Quincey wants to draw participants into a set of considerations about, in the first instance, the place of contemporary performance practice in the age of digital reproduction. More than this, in placing her practice in the centre of this continent—a place de Quincey wants to call *"a burning point"*: an intersection of "prehistory, Indigenous history, post-colonial history and the perspective of global futures which forms contemporary reality" — de Quincey is asking a range of questions about our (individual and collective) relationship to land, to culture and identity.[20]

Such experiments eschew representation in any traditional sense. "Gregory Ulmer's claim that contemporary legibility is a legibility 'beyond representation'—in short, a category of the ontologically unspoken—was a powerful provocation" in the BodyWeather experiment. Indeed, there was no "theme" as such, but through physical training, workshops and discussions, "there was a version, enormously dispersed and many-sided, of a living 'topo-analysis' occurring."[21]

Since 1995, the Brisbane-based Visual Theatre company Brink has been making its own distinctive investigations into the post-colonial Australian psyche, its history and geography. Using digitised sound and image together with and large-scale physical theatre forms as basic modes of expression, the company has been "excavating the white occupation of Australia" in a series of spectacular site-specific works around Brisbane. The company's "radically collaborative, multi-artist construction method"[22] involves the core team of Jessica Wilson and

---

[20] Ian Maxwell, personal e-mail correspondence with the author (11 August 1999). See also the internet website <http://www.triplealice.net/>.

[21] Martin Harrison, "Edge, Desert, Reticulation, Information," *RealTime* 35 (2000): 9.

[22] Christine Comans and Rod Wissler, "Brink Visual Theatre: A Case Study of Theatre Form and Drama Education," in *Industrial Relations: Proceedings From the 1999*

Ainsley Burdell, who co-founded the company and who devise, direct and design the productions, usually in collaboration with Rodolphe Blois (composer) and Randall Wood (film maker). Operating within the generic conventions of Visual Theatre, and identifying particularly with the work of Philippe Genty and Robert Wilson, Brink is also influenced by the more diverse lineages of performance and video art.

The "visual potency that characterizes Brink's work [is] often presented in a complex relationship of puppetry, projection, soundscape, gadgetry, performers and space."[23] A wonderfully dry sense of humour is also woven throughout their shows, drawing largely upon the mundane imagery of suburban life: garden sheds and Hills Hoist clothes lines; lawn ornaments which transform into avenging spirits; picket fences and nosy neighbours. *Henry's Shadow* (1995), staged outdoors at the abandoned Teneriffe dock, was the company's first major show, and depicted "a whimsical journey into the nostalgia bred of isolation in contemporary Australia."[24] *Paper Crown* (1996), staged in the one-hundred-year-old Princess Theatre in Woolloongabba, satirised Australian social ritual in the form of a Friday night party. In 1998, the company presented *Brittle* at the Old Queensland Museum, exposing the "mutable boundaries of savagery" as the central suburban couple battle their mortgage, and their "reclaimed land that refuses to yield to human intervention."[25]

Under The Big Sky was co-produced by Brink and the Queensland Performing Arts Trust for the inaugural Stage X Festival for Young People in 1997. Four performers (Larissa Chen, Giuliano Perez Reyes, Lynne Kent and Matt Wilson) presented it on the thirty-metre-high cliff face at the Howard Smith Wharf under Brisbane's landmark Story Bridge, on the bank of the Brisbane River. This site-specific location allowed "large-scale transformations of perspective by way of projection and performer, which in turn gave a proportionate sense of the relationship of European values to an ancient land."[26] The physical size of the cliff, its mass and solidity, generated profound juxtapositions in texture and scale between the stark grandeur of the rock face and the hi-tech

---

QUT/Australasian Drama Studies Association Conference (Brisbane: Theatre and Teaching Studies, Queensland University of Technology, 1999): 53.

[23] Maryanne Lynch, "Push-pull," *RealTime* 28 (1999): n.p.

[24] Christine Comans and Rod Wissler, *op. cit.*: 51.

[25] Maryanne Lynch, *op. cit.*: n.p. The company has recently completed the creative development phase of a new project, inspired by the millennial frenzy generated by the infamous Y2K bug.

[26] *Ibid.*

play of images projected onto it. This was a very suggestive meeting of surfaces: the cliff, monumental and timeless, the projections, virtual and illusory, dependent upon the wall for their very perceptibility. Similarly, the movements in space and time of the performers, puppets and props seemed fragile and, at times, futile against the immensity of the rock face.

The performance text engaged thematics familiar in other theatrical explorations of post-colonial history and geography, but particularly the nature-culture dialectic which "lies at the heart of imperialism."[27] The influence of this ideological opposition on modern history is clear: the ethos of "progress," for example, is dependent upon a belief in the "improvement" of nature through culture. "For several millennia now, the Western tradition has been dominated by various human-centred views of the cosmos. Nature has progressively been defined as ever more distant from human culture."[28] In Australia, this "primitive dialectic of nature and culture"[29] has been particularly powerful, and the national life remains highly attuned to it.

Of particular interest with regard to *Under The Big Sky*, though, are the means by which notions of European "culture" and Australian "nature" were juxtaposed, and through which narrative and meaning were forged. In the first instance, the production created complex and evocative, but highly impressionistic, sound and image texts, without resorting to the more familiar paradigm of characters speaking dialogue. What resulted was a "sometimes cryptic poetry"[30] which, rather than offering a mimetic or iconic rendering of the dramatic world, made spectators complicit in the text's production of meanings, which were "written" even as they were being "read." Moreover, the use of various forms of suspension technology—harnesses, cables, rigging—not only

---

[27] Helen Gilbert, "Fish or Fowl: Post-Colonial Approaches to Australian Drama," *Australian-Canadian Studies* 10.2 (1992): 134. Ross Gibson remarks that the "nature/culture dialectic is necessarily the one that has shaped the history of land in modern Australia. For white Australia is a product of the Renaissance mentality that is predicated on the notion of an environment that is other than and external to the individual ego. This is the mentality that the English colonial office sent to the continent." See Ross Gibson, *South of the West: Postcolonialism and the Narrative Construction of Australia* (Indianapolis: Indiana UP, 1992): 8.

[28] Deborah Bird Rose, "Exploring An Aboriginal Land Ethic," *Meanjin* 47.3 (1988): 379.

[29] Ross Gibson, "Camera Natura: Landscape in Australian Feature Films," in *Australian Cultural Studies: A Reader*, eds. John Frow and Meaghan Morris (Sydney: Allen and Unwin, 1993): 216.

[30] Christine Comans and Rod Wissler, *op. cit.*: 52.

invested the production with a theatrical immediacy and intensity, but also contributed to its abstracted processes of signification. The performance text metaphorically posited the sheer cliff face

> ... as the Australian continent, stark and forbidding but not without grandeur. The danger of the performance site and its moonlit beauty provide a subliminal but key thematic tension. Watching the performers actually performing up, down and across the cliff face while harnessed to cables rigged from above provided a theatrical excitement that combined the best of the roman colosseum, the high trapeze, and added a dose of extreme sports.[31]

This quality of risk, too, worked metaphorically to underscore both the anxieties inherent in colonial exploration, and the dangers of that type of imperial *hubris* by which colonialism is often impelled. Most of the "characters" (cyphers, rather, or emblems), writing themselves into the new landscape, seemed intent on some form of conquest.

Whilst the dramatic structure of *Under The Big Sky* was open and fragmentary, the particular journeys of the explorer-surveyor figure and the woman dressed in white could loosely be regarded as organising narratives. Their movements—beginning at the top of the cliff and progressing down its surfaces—suggested a passage from continental edge to interior. In this progression, too, was a type of questing for knowledge and belonging, attained to some extent by the man, but finally eluding the woman. These two journeys may be illustrated by fuller accounts of some of the production's key sequences.

The surveyor is seen alone at first, attempting to read the barren landscape. His sole point of reference, the map, represents his tradition of knowing, an epistemology which allows him a merely cartographic relationship to space. When the map falls from his hands, he becomes entirely lost. Soon, though, he encounters a different type of explorer, a water diviner, whose function in the drama is somewhat complex and warrants some attention. Sensitive to the problematic nature of representing the indigenous "Other," but wishing to engage ideas of Ab-originality, Brink avoided the portrayal of "an Aboriginal character" as such. Referencing instead the "water diviner" figures in Randolph Stow's novel *Tourmaline*[32] and Dorothy Hewett's play *The Man From Mukinupin*,[33] the company introduced the water diviner as "a white version of 'Ab-originality,' or of an authentic relationship with the landscape." Ainsley Burdell, who worked primarily as dramaturge on this production, acknowledges the complex systems of knowledge and

---

[31] *Ibid.*: 51.

[32] Randolph Stow, *Tourmaline* (Harmondsworth: Penguin, 1965).

[33] Dorothy Hewett, *The Man From Mukinupin* (Sydney: Currency Press, 1979).

the unique relationships that Aborigines have traditionally had with the landscape.[34] One of the ideas investigated in *Under The Big Sky* was that desire of many European descendants to forge a similarly integrated set of relationships with Australian space. Sensing new possible ways of seeing in the water diviner, the explorer-surveyor advances some way towards such a condition of being. He drinks the water offered to him, and as his image is transformed into a giant projection, he is shown diving through an expanse of water, becoming immersed and finally re-surfacing.

The woman dressed in white re-appears. Disoriented now in a Gothic forest of craggy ghost gums, projected images of shrieking birds crowding in on her, she becomes overwhelmed by the landscape. Her terrified submission to the "weird melancholy" of the forest works self-reflexively, evoking a tradition of stereotypically feminised responses to the Australian bush, especially familiar in film: the apparent Assumption into Nature of Miranda in Peter Weir's *Picnic at Hanging Rock* (1975), for example; and the ecstatic bush writhings of the heroine in Charles Chauvel's classic *Jedda* (1955). "One of the Gothic fears that white Australians have about the landscape is becoming dissolved into it, losing your whole sense of Self into the landscape."[35] Women in particular have characteristically been shown stoically battling the landscape, only to submit, finally—sometimes orgasmically—to its dark power. This episode in *Under The Big Sky* interrogates that tendency, but leaves it unredeemed, and the woman gives in to her fear by blasting at her own reflected image with a shotgun.

In the concluding sequence, twentieth century suburbia is imaged as a form of alien invasion. A garishly lit model house flies in over the cliff top like a space ship, nestling into a section of the surface, picket fence and lawn set proudly out in front. Here is a contemporary manifestation of that colonial imperative to write over the continent. What the original European settlers saw "when they confronted the landscape of Australia was how much work would have to be done. It was a landscape that was in their terms meaningless and would remain so till they had changed

---

[34] Ainsley Burdell, personal interview with the author (29 June 2000). David J. Tacey observes: "Aboriginal consciousness and landscape are intimately bound; in fact, Aboriginal spirituality is primarily a spirituality of place ... [F]or Aboriginal consciousness, ecological and theophanic awareness go hand in hand; the actual earth itself, its physical features, is their way to the Dreaming." See David J. Tacey, "Australia's Otherworld: Aboriginality, Landscape and the Imagination," *Meridian* 8.1 (1989): 57.

[35] *Ibid.*

and shaped and humanised it."[36] Such a conquest of wilderness was both picturesque and comforting: "Early arrivals here came with an image in their heads of what a real landscape should be. One, that is, that had been redeemed from wildness by the efforts of man. It should be cleared, fenced, ploughed, [and] made fruitful ..."[37] Finally, the woman retreats into a Gold Coast world of jacuzzis and headsets, cocooned from the reality of her environment. For the explorer-surveyor, though, the journey into the soul of the country continues, and he is seen walking, resolute and hopeful, up the surface of the cliff.

Under The Big Sky explored the problems of alienation and integration in a landscape which is simultaneously feared and desired. Its innovative theatrical languages enabled Brink Visual Theatre to extend, in complex and suggestive ways, the tradition of post-colonial performance in Australia. The company engaged its audiences with an ingenious synthesis of sound and spectacle, high-risk performance strategies and contemporary technology. Many Australians share the attitudes, the anxieties and imaginings of their colonial forebears, and the national agenda is crowded with issues—reconciliation, republicanism, environmental politics—which have remained contentious and unresolved for well over a century. Innovative performance practices such as those which characterise Brink's theatre open up an important cultural space for the continued interrogation of the post-colonial Australian psyche.

Works Cited

Printed Works

Burdell, Ainsley. Personal interview with the author (29 June 2000).

Comans, Christine and Rod Wissler. "Brink Visual Theatre: A Case Study of Theatre Form and Drama Education," in *Industrial Relations: Proceedings From the 1999 QUT/Australasian Drama Studies Association Conference* (Brisbane: Theatre and Teaching Studies, Queensland University of Technology, 1999): 51-69.

Cosgrove, D. & S. Daniels, eds. *The Iconography of Landscape* (Cambridge: Cambridge UP, 1988).

de Quincey, Tess. *Triple Alice* <http://www.triplealice.net/>

Fitzpatrick, Peter. "Views of the Harbour: The Empty City in Contemporary Australian Drama," in *Populous Places: Australian Cities and Towns*, ed. Anna Rutherford (Sydney: Dangaroo Press, 1992): 520-34.

---

[36] David Malouf, *op. cit.*: 29

[37] *Ibid.*

Fry, Tony and Anne-Marie Willis. "Criticism Against The Current," *Meanjin* 48.2 (1988): 223-40.
Gibson, Ross. "Camera Natura: Landscape in Australian Feature Films," in *Australian Cultural Studies: A Reader*, eds. John Frow and Meaghan Morris (Sydney: Allen and Unwin, 1993): 209-21.
—— *South of the West: Postcolonialism and the Narrative Construction of Australia* (Indianapolis: Indiana UP, 1992).
Gilbert, Helen. "Fish or Fowl: Post-Colonial Approaches to Australian Drama," *Australian-Canadian Studies* 10.2 (1992): 131-35.
Goldie, Terry. "Indigenous Stages: The Indigene in Canadian, New Zealand and Australian Drama," *Australasian Drama Studies* 9 (1986): 5-20.
Griffin, Grahame. "Landscape and the Representation of Space in Australian Popular Culture: A Study in Cultural Geography," in *Australian Cultural Studies Conference 1990 Proceedings* (Sydney: Faculty of Humanities and Social Sciences, University of Western Sydney/Nepean, 1991): 170-80.
Harrison, Martin. "Edge, Desert, Reticulation, Information," *RealTime* 35 (2000): 9.
Hassall, Anthony J. "Quests," in *The Penguin New Literary History of Australia*, ed. Laurie Hergenhan (Ringwood: Penguin, 1988): 390-408.
Hewett, Dorothy. *The Man From Mukinupin* (Sydney: Currency Press, 1979).
Kenny, Robert. "A Secret Australia," epilogue essay in *A Secret Australia* by Ken Taylor (Melbourne: Rigmarole, 1984): 85-95.
Keogh, Susan. "Land, Landscape and *Such Is Life*," *Southerly* 49.1 (March 1989): 54-63.
Litson, Jo. "White Heat, Black Stories," *The Weekend Australian* (20-21 May 1994): 16-18.
Makeham, Paul. "Singing the Landscape: *Bran Nue Dae*," *Australasian Drama Studies* 28 (1996): 117-32.
—— "Narrative Structure and the BLURRED Landscape," in *Blurred: Creating Performance for Young People*, eds. Louise Gough and Judith McLean (Brisbane: Playlab Press, 1999): 19-22.
Malouf, David. "Making Better Australians," *The Australian* (17-18 September 1994): 29.
Maryanne Lynch. "Push-pull," *RealTime* 28 (1999): n.p.
Maxwell, Ian. Personal e-mail correspondence with the author (11 August 1999).
McClintock, Anne. "Unspeakable Secrets: The Ideology of Landscape in Conrad's *Heart of Darkness*," *Journal of the Midwest Modern Language Association* 17 (1984): 42.
Muecke, Stephen. *Textual Spaces: Aboriginality and Cultural Studies* (Sydney: New South Wales UP, 1992).
Porteous, J. Douglas. *Landscapes of the Mind* (Toronto: U of Toronto P, 1990).
Rose, Deborah Bird. "Exploring An Aboriginal Land Ethic," *Meanjin* 47.3 (1988): 378-87.

Stow, Randolph. *Tourmaline* (Harmondsworth: Penguin, 1965).
Tacey, David J. "Australia's Otherworld: Aboriginality, Landscape and the Imagination," *Meridian* 8.1 (1989): 57-65.
Williams, Raymond. *The Country and the City* (London: Chatto and Windus, 1975).
Wright, Judith. "Landscape and Dreaming," *Daedalus* 114.1 (1985): 29-56.

Performed Works

de Quincey, Tess. *Triple Alice. Part I: BodyWeather* (1999).
——— *Triple Alice. Part II* (forthcoming).
——— *Triple Alice. Part III* (forthcoming).
Brink. *Henry's Shadow* (1995).
——— *Paper Crown* (1996).
——— *Under the Big Sky* (1997).
——— *Brittle* (1998).

Spot the Infidel: Aspects of Multiculturalism in Mainstream Australian Theatre

PETER FITZPATRICK

Monash University

The title is borrowed from Michael Gurr's *Sex Diary of an Infidel* (1992),[1] a work that will play a more substantial role later in this discussion; its use here assumes that the notion of the infidel—the non-believer, the person vilified, demeaned or simply excluded on grounds of cultural difference—will have something to offer the treatment of multiculturalism in Australian theatre and will broaden the conceptual frameworks on which contemporary discourses in post-colonialism are based.

The "Other" is the most familiar term in these debates, of course, and it has proved a very useful one. But it brings with it, from feminist and orientalist sources as well as intercultural ones, associations of profound—even permanent—binary oppositions. Since the sense of difference in these areas is characteristically both strikingly visible and related to fundamental psychic and imaginative mythologies, that rigidity often does not pose a problem at all. In a post-colonial multicultural society like Australia, however, it does. And even a less mythic proposition such as the "outsider" tends to connote a degree of alienation that makes for a similar rigidity.

Theories built on notions of non-negotiable oppositions will always find it difficult to adapt to the shifting patterns of accommodation that mark post-colonial communities in the phases that follow the initial assertion against the coloniser. Australia offers a quite distinctive case. What happens when a society moves from a form of dual colonisation—the imposition of British imperial rule on a largely unrecognised indigenous culture and on an outcast Anglo-Celtic society which speaks the language of its rulers, but is increasingly conscious of its distinctiveness—to something like a serial form of that process? In other words,

---

[1] Michael Gurr, *Sex Diary of an Infidel* (Sydney: Currency Press, 1993). Throughout this essay, the date of a play's first production appears in parentheses in the text.

what happens when that outcast society assumes mastery in its own right, replicates the suppression of its indigenous population, and is faced with successive waves of immigration from other established cultures, which become first objects and subsequently agents of the expression of cultural dominance? Siting the Other appears reasonably unproblematic in the preliminary phases of post-colonialism, but can become very tricky when the shape of the determinative culture is in a state of continual renegotiation.

In seeking a more evolutionary model of post-colonialism, the concept of the infidel has an appropriately conditional, as well as loosely exotic, quality. Its adaptability is not just a matter of changing historical paradigms, but of coexistent alternative perspectives too. The same applies, of course, to Gurr's play, which contains a series of studies in ambivalence. Tony, the Filipino male prostitute, might be declared an infidel on racial or conventional moral grounds; Toni, the Filipino transsexual, would qualify on both counts as a result of his evasion or confusion of the primary physical and behavioural codes by which society classifies almost all individuals as either male of female. In both characters, however, Gurr invokes preconceptions of the archetypal Other in order to subvert or confute them. From another perspective—not just that of Tony and Toni, but also from the point of view of fairly entrenched humanist understandings of moral and cultural exploitation—the apparently normative figures of Jean and Martin, the Anglo-Australian tourists, might seem at least equally to be the infidels. They certainly have no claim to moral superiority. Jean, in her eagerness for an award-winning story, is as predatory as the Australian sex tourists whom she longs to expose; Martin the photographer, who recognises that about her, is disabled from acting on his knowledge by his incapacity to engage emotionally with the subjects of his pictures. The things that Martin likes to watch, Jean likes to touch, in a spirit of erotic loathing. Moreover, their infidel status is supported by the fact that they are outsiders in Manila and people of no particular faith. As cultural tourists on the make, they have no sustaining belief; Toni, who prays to the Virgin for the operation that will reconcile him to his body, and Tony, who has at least a sense of the ethics of hire, are both, in their different ways, believers. Jean and Martin look for all the world like insiders, like us, and that is how they carry us into the action of the play; but they end up as infidels, with no home. While, for both of them, siting the Other would be an exercise in reflex recognition, for Gurr's audience spotting the infidel becomes a challenge of real moral complexity.

Sex Diary of an Infidel is material to this discussion for more than its provision of a partial title. It represents an advanced stage of adaptation to the previously excluded perspectives of the cultural outsider, to the point where the discourse of the jokey, sophisticated, sceptical Anglo-Australian, who dominated the aggressively nationalist Australian theatre of the 1970s, is, suddenly and disconcertingly, made strange. It marks, therefore, a late stage of the serial and complex development of post-colonial Australia.

That post-colonial narrative might crudely be divided into three chapters. The first involves the formation of a nationalist—or at least nationally self-conscious—tradition; it concerns the self-assertion of the outpost Anglo-culture against its British and American imperial masters, as well as the dramatisation of a distinctive mythology. The second entails the recasting of the colonial outcasts as colonisers and defiantly counter-asserts the indigenous culture which that mythology sought to efface. The third implies the adaptation of the ostensibly monocultural and monolingual Anglo-Celtic mainstream to the waves of post-war European immigration and to more recent and "different" settlers from parts of Asia.

All these phases have their representations in Australian theatre of the last thirty years, both on its experimental margins and—with a usually predictable logic—as an accepted and increasingly promoted current in the mainstream. That process of accommodation has mirrored fairly precisely in theatrical terms the wider community debates about the relative virtues of policies of assimilation (which assumed the desirability of social homogeneity) and multiculturalism (which proclaimed the celebration of diversity as an index of social health as well as a fundamental right). The debate has proved more sensitive and clearly articulated in relation to the new arrivals, of course, than it ever did for the oldest inhabitants.

In assessing the impact of these successive phases of post-colonial adaptation on recent Australian theatre, my focus will fairly narrowly centre on a small group of plays that were written for, or have found their way to, a mainstream audience. The latter term is, in some discussions, as problematic as "multicultural"; Joanne Tompkins, one of the critics of contemporary Australian theatre who has drawn attention to the reductiveness of the concept as currently understood, proposes a model of fluidity that makes its customary antithesis "mainstream" either too rigid or meaningless, depending on your emphasis.[2] But de-

---

[2] Joanne Tompkins, "Inter-referentiality: Interrogating Multicultural Australian Drama," in *Our Australian Theatre in the 1990s*, ed. Veronica Kelly (Amsterdam: Rodopi, 1998). Tompkins proposes "polynationalism" as a replacement for multi-

fining the mainstage in Australia turns out to be, these days, a relatively straightforward matter. "Mainstage" refers to a theatre characterised by heavy subsidy, the expectation of professionalism, and a subscription-based audience, which in socio-economic and educational terms demonstrably corresponds to a cultural elite. That elite is still commonly perceived as monocultural and monolingual, however much its actual composition may have been complicated by the considerable changes happening in the wider community; these theatre-goers are not likely to see themselves as infidels—or as anybody's Other. The repertoire that is played before them has a direct, almost routine, connection with the processes of script publication, which gives it a fair head-start on the way to a place in the canon.

"The mainstage" embodies a theatrical environment that looks intrinsically conservative, or gradualist at best. In examining how and how far it has been persuaded to widen its cultural perspectives in a manner that makes siting Others and spotting infidels a complex process, there are obvious inferences to be drawn about the nature and success of such accommodations in the wider society. The few cases considered in what follows are exemplary, but do not provide that kind of evidence. They do, however, raise questions about the links between new ways of seeing and the familiar models of language and dramatic structure that articulate the experience of the mainstream.

For the purposes of this discussion, then, I shall not concern myself with the phenomenon of the creation of multicultural theatre, generally defined by the wide range of theatre events adjacent to the mainstream, events that represent particular cultural and ethnic minorities, and which are targeted to a specific audience through the distinctive verbal and other codes that express that culture. That would be a separate subject, equally important as this one in every respect, but running by quite different sets of social and theatrical "rules." Nor shall I be looking closely at contemporary theatre about indigenous Australia, though it too is of obvious importance to the redefining of post-colonial approaches to our theatre; that area, at least, has recently received considerable critical attention.[3]

---

culturalism on the grounds that the term is both more flexible and less suggestive of binary opposition. For her, the current political orthodoxy of the term "multicultural" denies more diversity than it admits.

[3] See, for example, Helen Gilbert's work in this field, especially her *Sightlines: Race, Gender and Nation in Contemporary Australian Theatre* (Ann Arbor: U of Michigan P, 1998). Gilbert investigates the notion of conceptual slippage and the erosion of cultural distinctiveness that comes with the fact of performance, especially to an audience of characteristically different background; she cites Bhabha's view that per-

Multiculturalism in Mainstream Australian Theatre 159

This essay focuses instead on the neglected third phase of the story of post-colonialism in Australian theatre: recent treatments of the cultural outsider in plays that conform to the conventions and understandings of establishment theatre, and that are written primarily for its audience. The discussion will be conducted on two fronts in particular, namely representations of the non-Anglo European on the one hand, and dramatisations of the Asian on the other. For that notional mainstream audience, ignorance of the native language of both these generic figures represents an obvious problem, though it may not prove equally so; in the case of the former, shared gestic and cultural codes are likely to make the experience of the character more accessible to the mainstream spectator. But both generic figures, in a theatre which takes for granted the sophisticated use of the English language, are on the face of it significantly disadvantaged.

Language remains so fundamental to the expression of culture that the choice of English for the non-native English speaker constitutes in itself a political act. The most graphic instance of the implications of particular decisions of this kind in script and performance can probably be found in Jack Davis's *Kullark*,[4] which demonstrates the erosion of the culture of the Nyoongah people precisely through the loss of their dialect. In the first-contact scene between the comic opera colonisers, Fraser and Stirling, and the three "savages," Yagan, Mitjitjooroo and Moyarahn, all the communicative advantages are with the interloper: Fraser and Stirling are defined by name, rank and temperament within the first few lines—and of course they speak "our" language. The unintelligibility of the Nyoongah dialect works against any individuation of that kind. Two clear options exist in performance. One is to try to overcome that inaccessibility by working through gesture to provide a semi-translation and to emphasise the distinctive reactions of the three Nyoongahs; the other is to confirm the audience's exclusion, at the risk of leaving them with a limited or generic reading of the "savages," in order to challenge their ownership of the performance space and to simulate the perplexity and dispossession of the original owners of the land. Both strategies have their attractions, though the second is likely to be the more telling; the sustaining irony of the play, which prefers in its title the unfamiliarity of "Kullark" to the familiar resonances of "Home," is that the more available the Nyoongah experience becomes to

---

formance ensures that "the meaning and symbols of culture have no primordial unity or fixity; that even the same signs can be appropriated, translated, re-historicised and read anew" (107).

[4] Jack Davis, *Kullark* and *The Dreamers* (Sydney: Currency Press, 1982).

160   *Siting the Other*

its middle-class Anglo audience, the more their oppression is confirmed, and the less their distinctive integrity survives.

The processes of familiarisation in *Kullark* as in other plays by Davis risk indulging conventional judgements and familiar stereotypes; as a dramatic antidote, naturalism is intermittently disrupted by verse, song and dance to disturb those routine ways of seeing and the assumptions of cultural superiority to which they tend to lead.[5] Treatments of the European who is not a native English speaker run a similar risk, but have fewer codes of obvious difference with which to assert cultural integrity. It is in this area that recent plays in the mainstream theatre repertoire seem to have been least influenced by serial migration, and to recapitulate the reading processes of an earlier generation shaped by explicit assumptions about the importance of assimilation and social homogeneity.

Graham Pitts's wonderfully good-hearted and immensely successful piece *Emma* (1991)[6] runs exactly this risk. The strength of *Emma* lies in the elements of community celebration that frame the experiences of its central character—the generous banquets of pasta and the gusto of the women's choirs that punctuate its scenes with Italian songs. The weakness lies in the articulation of that central experience, in an English which often seems a little too close to parody:

> EMMA Scusati, scusati. Allora. Courage is the price life desires before you have peace. My own life been a list of battles. If you want to survive, you must fight. If you want not to be poor, you fight. If you want a good home, fight. And if you want a good marriage ... then don't fight (2).

The odd bit of Italian that spices the dialogue is nicely judged to give the mainstream audience no trouble; the verbal style reinforces the resilience in Emma's little homilies to her audience, in which the quaintness of the syntax gives a warmly comic inflection to everything she says. And all this is overlaid with broader cultural stereotype—the bustle of the Momma, the histrionics of the Mediterranean temperament. The songs are all in Italian, of course, but there seems no need to know

---

[5] Davis shows a particular cleverness in the sequencing of performance styles in order to exploit the particular shifts in knowledge and perspective which they invoke. In *Kullark*, the kitchen-sink contemporary opening—with all its capacity to evoke negative stereotyping—is quickly subverted by Yagan's ceremonial dance of dispossession and the first-contact; *The Dreamers* plays this intersection of modes quite differently, prefacing the naturalistic family scene with the timeless image of the tribal crossing of the escarpment and with Uncle Worru's startlingly affirmative memories of mission life.

[6] Graham Pitts, *Emma. Celebrazione!* (Sydney: Currency Press, 1996).

the lyrics; the melodies promote a generic emotion to reinforce that in the characterisation.

The world needs its feel-good plays, of course, and the point here is not that *Emma* should have been another kind of play. The contention is that cultural stereotype, in language and manner, not only self-replicates and seemingly self-verifies, but also represents an obstacle to a genuine sense of difference. *Emma*, published with the sub-title *Celebrazione!*, seems to be celebrating not only a gutsy heroine but a multicultural Australia, a place where now we can enjoy Italian choirs and do wonderful things with eggplant. But it remains a theatrical cuisine for an Anglo-Celtic palate, confirming once again that Italians are cute, flamboyant and funny, as we always wanted them to be and always knew they were. In this sense, the depiction of Emma and her husband Peter advances little beyond the similarly endearing caricatures of Momma and Poppa Bianchi in Richard Beynon's *The Shifting Heart* (1957).[7] There are the same charmingly stilted speech rhythms, the same decorative interpolations of Italian words and phrases that a non-Italian can understand; though when Poppa pronounces "Italia finito," he does not offer the comic touch that Peter does when, after throwing down his accordion, he apologetically translates "La musica is finito" for us, just in case.

Perhaps the most meaningful sign of change in this area is that reflected in David Williamson's *Face to Face* (1999).[8] Williamson, as Australia's most popular mainstream playwright over the last three decades, serves as an obvious barometer to measure both theatrical and cultural change. He is absolutely a playwright of conversations, of course; there is no room in the jokey middle-class dialogue for the mediating or complicating codes of dance or song. Characteristically, then, the person who uses the English language clumsily or too earnestly is marginalised; most women and the few men who are unable to compete in the games of send-up and put-down, have been condemned in his work to providing cues for more entertaining companions. In a league like this, spotting the infidel has always proved easy. The cultural outsider is marked for difference, and that becomes his primary character note.

In Williamson's first twenty plays, only two such aliens appear—the German Gunter in *What If You Died Tomorrow* (1973)[9] and the

---

[7] Richard Beynon, *The Shifting Heart* (1960; Adelaide: Angus and Robertson, 1992).

[8] David Williamson, *Face to Face/Corporate Vibes* (Sydney: Currency Press, 1999).

[9] David Williamson, *What If You Died Tomorrow* (Sydney: Currency Press, 1974).

Dutchman Erik in *The Perfectionist* (1982).[10] To the comic potential offered by their difficulties with the English language, Williamson adds in each case a single fixation: Gunter is a hysterical melancholic, Erik a slightly obsolete counter-cultural Marxist. Both visitors bring with them extremities of behaviour which the local ironists would never dream of engaging in, but they are only passing through, and their function consists in acting as simple catalysts in the complex relationships of others. The stereotypes are too impenetrable to sustain an interest in what makes Gunter anguished or Erik cool, even if the playwright had been motivated to ask such questions.

In *Face to Face*, however, a great deal has changed, and the reconciliatory logic of the grievance hearing which constitutes the action of the play might almost be taken as a metaphor for a turn-of-the-century Australia. The plot revolves around two acts of vengeful frustration. Glen, a simple lad, has reacted against dismissal from his job as a builder's labourer by ramming the Mercedes that his ex-boss Greg had just acquired; his dismissal has followed the last in a series of incidents with workmates, in which Glen had responded badly to being made the butt of jokes by his mates.

As in all Williamson's plays, control of language functions as the key to status. Glen is an Aussie, but not a very articulate one, and when words run out, he smashes things—just as Constable Ross did in *The Removalists* (1971),[11] or, for that matter, as another phlegmatic Old Australian Roo does in Ray Lawler's *The Summer of the Seventeenth Doll* (1955).[12] But there are some interesting developments in *Face to Face* when it comes to who has access to the power of words. The ringleader of the blokes who enjoy picking on Glen is Luka Mitrovic, a Serb by birth, but quite clearly very thoroughly assimilated; he even defines the rules of the game—"everyone takes the piss out of everyone all the bloody time ... You take it and give back as good as you get" (92). Luka appears to be no cultural outsider, then, but very much at home. On the other hand, it has not always been like that—there were plenty of jokes about Serbian killers and rapists in the past, and clearly making a fool of Glen represents a tactic to get in first. Luka may have lived in Australia since the age of eight, but he still has a funny name and a different background. He complains to Jack the mediator "I eat pies and shit just like the rest of them and they say I eat stinking wog food" (93).

---

[10] David Williamson, *The Perfectionist* (Sydney: Currency Press, 1983).

[11] David Williamson, *The Removalists* (Sydney: Currency Press, 1972).

[12] Ray Lawler, *The Summer of the Seventeenth Doll* (Melbourne: Angus and Robertson, 1957).

Luka's sensitivity to that kind of prejudice is resolved, at least temporarily, by the process of mediation, along with the other conflicts on the agenda. In a world where a person can always be picked on for something, the play confirms the importance of a modest sensitivity and understanding—and, of course, a sense of humour. It implies the reasonably successful evolution of a hybrid culture on those kinds of terms. Greg, the well-heeled employer, is the product of an earlier phase of "fitting in"; his name, Baldoni, evokes the wave of Italian migration that brought the Bianchis of Beynon's play to Australia in the 1950s and, later, Emma and her husband Peter. Luka's family formed part of a later wave still, and while the Baldonis presumably do not have to suffer witticisms about wog food any more, the Mitrovics still endure the process.

Face to Face might, however, be read as a more historically exact, and more disturbing, cultural metaphor than that: the revenge of the Glens of this world against those empowered Baldonis and Mitrovics might suggest the backlash against a supposed dispossession—by migrants, especially from Asia, and, in a bizarre paradox, by Aboriginal people privileged by government grants—that soured Australian politics in the 1990s. But its predominant mood comes across as conciliatory, even celebratory, and the absorption into the mainstream culture of these people who were once outsiders is confirmed by their adaptation to the communicative codes of the mainstream theatre. In both respects, it is presented as a triumph of assimilation. Spotting the infidel, as a matter of simple cultural discrimination, has by definition now become so complex a process as to be hardly worth the effort.

Sex Diary of an Infidel takes that for granted, of course, in directing its audience to more significant kinds of discrimination. Tony and Toni use English perfectly well for their purposes, even if in the service of systems of value that do not appear so familiar. They are the products of a cultural imperialism so advanced that nobody could know how to begin unravelling it. American influence, understood now as the powerful logic of globalisation, is a fact of life in Gurr's Manila; images of Mickey Mouse and Coca-Cola establish it from the outset. But that homogenising process is not really the subject of the obvious critique; it works as the precondition for the kind of knowledge that enables judgements about who, in moral terms, is truly the infidel.

In the monolingual play, what becomes of multiculturalism and the recognition of the distinctiveness of individual cultures? Does the only alternative to accommodation within the language, structures, and stereotypes of the dominant theatre culture necessarily imply the relative marginalisation implicit in a place on the "fringe" of community theatre? If the word embodies the key to power and attention, what is the status of languages other than English on the "main stage"? If a genuinely bilingual theatre self-evidently sounds like a commercially unthinkable prospect for that theatre, what other options remain for successfully communicating unfamiliar experiences in an unfamiliar way?

It is, oddly, in the depiction of the Asian outsider that the task of spotting the infidel has been made most interestingly problematic; "oddly," that is, given a difference in cultural values and behaviour, and in language and physicality, which has encouraged a conception of the Other as that of an implicit polar opposite. In 1984, I wrote an article on stereotypes of Asianness that appeared in *Australian Literary Studies* and explored the depiction of the Asian as generically and inscrutably Other.[13] The adjective "Asian" then seemed not only legitimate (with the obvious qualifications) but critically useful, precisely because the binary between the markers that constituted Australian identity and those which were self-evidently not part of it seemed so stable. Now, clearly, the label requires multiple reclassifications. This is partly because of what this form of multiculturalism brings to the mainstream theatre. The term can no longer function as a measure whereby to define who "we" are against what we are not, or simply to confirm local insularities and cultural complacencies. In the work of mainstream playwrights like Nowra and Sewell, the term "Asianness" now offers myths of extremity (of genocide in Cambodia, or colonial oppression in East Timor, and so on) which problematise the processes of resettlement and transform the "host" society.

For the most part, the theatrical treatments of the Asian outsider in Australian theatre have reaffirmed the stereotype of inscrutability. Often they managed to neutralise the threat of the unknown and unreadable by making it comic (the "stage Chinaman"), as so many early representations of the Aborigine were inclined to do. Occasionally this process of representing difference was offered for implicit critique, as in John Romeril's *The Floating World* (1975),[14] which focuses on the delayed post-war trauma of Les Harding, once a prisoner of war of the Japanese, now returning there as a tourist on the Women's Weekly Cherry Blossom Cruise. In Les's conflation of past and present and revisiting of old horrors, the memory of the Japanese prison guard absorbs and replaces all the people whom he defines as Asian; the Malay waiter on the boat is transformed into the ubiquitous Oriental figure of threat. The

---

[13] Peter Fitzpatrick, "Asian Stereotypes in Recent Australian Plays," *Australian Literary Studies* 12.1: 35-46.

[14] John Romeril, *The Floating World* (Sydney: Currency Press, 1975).

process which in Les is driven by unresolved obsession has its cosy counterpart in the ignorant insularity of Les's wife Irene, who appears very inclined to the larger generalisations:

> IRENE: I must say they're very polite though, aren't they? They're very polite, the Asians. Yes, madam, no, madam, has madam made up her mind? ... One thing they're not good at, though, and that's toast. You can't beat the toast you make yourself (23).

Irene learns a little, though, unlike Les, who continues to see the Cherry Blossom Cruise as "full of foreigners and ignoramuses." She becomes quite taken with distinguishing different kinds of "Asian":

> IRENE: Real cosmopolitan, isn't it?
> LES: Yeah. What?
> IRENE: The ship. They're Filipinos that do the cabin.
> LES: They'd work for sixpence, those jokers.
> IRENE: Chinese cooks, and Malays and Gherkins (46).

For Les, all Asians are one. He treats them with amused contempt. The nexus between the racist's sense of superiority and the racist's fear, however, is very immediate for Les; it crystallises in the dehumanising oppression of the prisoner-of-war camp, producing in him a hostility that tries to pay back in kind, but disintegrates in the terrors of his dreams and in the helplessness of his breakdown.

But while the mental habits of stereotyping and universalising were exposed in *The Floating World* as signs of psychosis or plain silliness, their representation in a play built on conversations ran a considerable and permanent risk; there was no Other way of knowing the Other. It was perfectly possible to interpret the play, even after allowing for Les's mental breakdown and Irene's mental bumbling, as a partial reinforcement of the failure to read racial difference. The fact that the play placed the Cherry Blossom Tour in a context of Japanese economic expansion encouraged that reading. Les and Irene Harding in 1974, or Australia's racist demagogue Pauline Hanson more recently, might equally find that context decisive in its suggestion that the Second World War had only recently come to an end, with a completely different result from the one apparently conceded in 1945.

It is in the area of cross-cultural transactions between Australia and Japan—a major economic and imaginative influence on Australian culture, if not so far a particularly significant source of migrants to this country—that the most profound shifts have occurred in the ways in which we are invited not only to spot infidels, but to learn about and know them. The critical element has been the appropriation of languages in performance that move beyond the word. In 1984, my paper could find only one instance of the invocation of Japanese theatre methods in the attempt to scrutinise the other. This was Vincent O'Sullivan's *Shuriken* (1981),[15] a play dealing with the reversal of Antipodean stereotype, namely with the experience of Japanese interned as prisoners of war in New Zealand. The Japanese prisoners were given a physical language based on *Noh*, supported by some music played on traditional Japanese instruments; their New Zealand captors spoke a version of the acerbic Ocker vernacular that then dominated both Australian theatre and its less developed New Zealand equivalent. In its reading of the Other, the effect of *Shuriken* proved for its Antipodean audience as alienating as Romeril's depiction of the mysterious Malay/Filipino/Japanese in *The Floating World*, in spite of all the ways in which it insistently drew attention to our complacent and ignorant parochialism. For the idiom of the generally amiable captors remained ingratiatingly familiar; the expressive movement of their Japanese prisoners was essentially unreadable, though it carried all the signs of a discourse that seemed in some indefinable way superior, by appealing to ritualised emotion and to an apparently timeless theatre culture for that purpose.

The line between inscrutability and irreducibility is a hard one to draw in practice. Inscrutability on the whole confirms negative stereotype. It implies the recognition of the unfamiliar physical or verbal codes, and implicitly blames the Other for the poverty of his/her translation; it often assumes a political motive for the obfuscation of feeling and purpose. On the other hand, no such comfortable judgement applies to irreducibility. It suggests a profound ambiguity or complexity in the object, as well as the likelihood of profound limitation in the viewing subject; it leaves open the possibility of a symbolic meaning too deep for words. The former presumes some kind of superiority, the latter a cultural inadequacy of the sort that colonial societies are all too ready to concede.

Both *The Floating World* and *Shuriken*, while evidently rejecting the hostile or simplistic perceptions of racial difference, inevitably confirmed the biases of the framing culture. In production, these might produce very different emphases: they might treat the alien with contempt or greet it with a kow-tow, but the response would be conditioned by the need to affirm or repudiate the known culture. The Other, even when presented in terms of its own codes, its own theatre rituals, remained by definition unknown, a neutral quantity to be invested with

---

[15] A published text of *Shuriken* is not available.

whatever antithetical value a post-colonial self-consciousness placed on it.

Considerable changes have occurred. The iconography of the Orient has not necessarily grown more easily readable, but the Australian playwright who draws on it can no longer plead the kind of justified ignorance that fosters a sense of possibly meaningful mystery. Theatre students in Australian universities have become as familiar with the basic principles of *Butoh* as they are with those of Stanislavski; they are probably more likely to know what is implied by a reference to *Kabuki* than by the phrase "English repertory." There can be very few actors in Australia who have not stomped or slid their way through a workshop in one of the traditional Japanese theatre methods or in one of their modern derivatives.

This has meant a spectacular transformation for Australian theatre culture, not only at its margins but at its centre as well. In plays like Daniel Keene's *Cho Cho San* (1993)[16] and Therese Radic's *The Emperor Regrets* (1992),[17] the production style of the Melbourne-based Playbox Company has heightened the focus on Japanese culture in the written texts. In 1995, its staging of an impressive revival of *The Floating World* by Sato Makoto's Black Tent Theatre with an entirely Japanese cast suggested one promising new direction for theatre that challenged racial and cultural preconceptions. As an act of *Verfremdung*, of making strange, the juxtaposition of Australian script and Japanese cast proved predictably rich. The overtly anti-Japanese sentiments in Les Harding's lines were given a new dimension when they came from the mouth of a Japanese Les, and the danger that the xenophobia of the central character might taint the whole play was neatly evaded and subverted.

But there may exist another model of interculturalism, a model less subject to these niceties of political history and less likely to lead to a simple corroboration of difference. It may be, paradoxically, much less dependent on the pursuit of deep knowledge of the Other, and less determinedly considerate of the source of the borrowing. Richard Schechner, the major apostle of interculturalism, rejoiced in 1982 about the way in which the theatrical imagination could leap lightly over national boundaries:

---

[16] Daniel Keene, *Cho Cho San* (Sydney: Currency Press, 1993).

[17] Radic, Therese. *The Emperor Regrets* (Sydney: Currency Press, 1992).

> There was something simply celebratory about discovering how diverse the
> world was, how many performance genres there were, and how much we
> could enrich our own experience by borrowing, stealing, exchanging.[18]

His terms came across as shamelessly self-educative; it was "our own experience" that was to be enlarged by the transaction, and the notion of "exchange" feels a little like an afterthought in the wake of the borrowing and the stealing. This was of course before Rustom Bharucha[19] spoiled the party by complaining about the cultural ignorance and insensitivity that for him lay behind Brook's *Mahabharatha* project, and made the whole thing sound like a version of the Cherry Blossom Cruise. Bharucha was at pains to clarify that he was not complaining about a failure or poverty of imitation. He objected to what he perceived as Brook's failure to base his adaptation on the principles of the original; indeed Bharucha's criticism that the characters were "presented in outline, with their inner energies and fire missing" implied Brook's excessive fascination with superficialities at the expense of the soul of the piece. Bharucha's argument about the impossibility of genuine translation has moral as well as intellectual authority, but it leaves invitingly open the creative potential in the borrowing (or stealing, or exchange) of style, not substance: in this sense, he provides some underpinning for Schechner's exhilaration at the diversity of the world and its performance genres, though he might want a more discriminating approach to adaptation, as well as an appreciation of those underlying principles.

Theatrical transactions between Australia and Japan are not encumbered by the post-colonial baggage that bedevilled Brook's ransacking of the great myths of India, or Schechner's own freewheeling through the tribal rituals of Africa, or, for that matter, Anglo-Celtic Australian adaptations of Aboriginal subjects. Such "borrowings" are necessarily circumscribed by their audiences' distinctive understandings of forms of narrative and orders of realism; and cross-cultural journeys will always be impeded by the difficulty of reading small differences within the larger ones. However, for Australian writers and performers, adaptations of specifically Japanese theatre models offer the possibility of new ways of knowing.

Another of John Romeril's plays about intersections with Japan was staged by the Playbox company in 1998; it suggested very excitingly the

---

[18] Richard Schechner, *The End of Humanism* (New York: Performing Arts Journal Publications, 1982): 19.

[19] Rustom Bharucha, *Theatre and the World: Performance and the Politics of Culture* (London: Routledge, 1993).

way in which reciprocal gestures might be given substance by a self-conscious adaptation of style. Ostensibly, *Love Suicides*[20] was a free translation from Chikamatsu, but this adaptation involved more an act of homage with something of the spirit of the master in it than a direct reframing of the original. The double suicide which concludes Romeril's play does not in itself represent a familiar cultural motif to Australian audiences, but its method—a rubber tube running into the cabin from the exhaust of an old Holden—has a distinctively local touch. And the telling of the story—the doomed love of a failed Perth businessman and the wealthy young Japanese woman whose world tastes only of ashes—draws freely on the two modes in which Chikamatsu wrote his powerful secular tragedies of love in the contemporary city—*Kabuki* and *Bunraku*.

The degree of accuracy with which Romeril translated the idiom, or even the procedures, of Chikamatsu's theatre does not appear particularly important here. It is not clear—though it would be interesting to find out—how significant an element it would prove in the response of a Japanese audience to Romeril's play. The primary issue concerns the dramatic value of those formal borrowings and thefts for the Australian audience for whom the play was written. And in *Love Suicides*, the structures and conventions lifted rather cavalierly from *Kabuki* and *Bunraku* theatre methods constitute much more than exotic novelties.

Schechner talked about exchanges, as well as borrowed or stolen goods, and here the exchanges occur not only between the two theatre cultures, but between a number of distinctive codes from both of them. The Japanese theatre modes feature as just some of the elements of a play which constantly crosses boundaries and continually redefines its central terms. *Love Suicides* is a musical play too, the operatic self-revelation being the complete hybrid juxtaposed with country-and-western self-absorption. Paris and Ohatsu might sing intensely about love, or more often about sex, but the model of the suicide in the Holden is also anticipated in a pastiche of the melancholy yodeller:

> At no miles per hour he thumbs the lighter in,
> There's lots he couldn't figure,
> And soon it will pop out,
> It's time to pull the trigger.
> The radio it's coming on,
> Top sound but it's a snigger.
> What does it matter this is the end,
> You're going much too fast through a hairpin bend,

---

[20] John Romeril, *Love Suicides* (Sydney: Currency Press, 1998).

No-one will miss you, you never had a friend,
They loved you for your car,
They loved you for your car (31).

One form comments on another in terms of the kinds of things it reveals or conceals, and the doomed love of the central couple is seen from multiple perspectives and through shifting frames.

Paris, the shady businessman whose hard-boiled cynicism is a mask for self-loathing and for a moral revulsion from what seems an irretrievably dirty world, plays a number of roles, and it is hard to tell which, if any, are real. Ohatsu, driven by a host of elaborate proprieties about what it means to be Japanese and a woman, yet in a state of permanent spiritual revolt against them all, comes across as similarly complex and divided. Their moves through different *personae* are staged in a number of exchanges of identity, in which the self is sometimes represented by the puppet self for which the narrator speaks, sometimes by the physical self understood to be the "real" character, sometimes by a puppet for whom that embodied character becomes narrator; frequently any two of these selves will coexist within a given sequence of dialogue.

In the process a number of complex possibilities are explored. Some of these look like the traditional preserves of naturalism. The psychological subtext is frequently narrated, running social behaviour against declared motive. But it is not simply a case of truth underlying public fiction: the ambiguous status of the narrators deprives the audience of those kinds of easy satisfaction. The validity of these revelations of the thought-track does not necessarily exceed that of the dangerous disclosures which Paris and Ohatsu make to one another in their regular game, "What thinking?"; the subtext which they confess to each other then is as likely to function strategically as any other conversational ploy, whether it carries an invitation to share in erotic fantasy or a claim to be liked, loathed or pitied. Increasingly, though, the characters speak for people whom we might call "themselves," suggesting the abandonment of pretences as the plot spirals toward the double love suicide.

But the exchanges between the codes of *Kabuki, Bunraku* and a familiar Australian blend of naturalism with satire complicate even those defined identities. Having a female narrator—doubled in the action with the role of Minh (an employee of the Perth hotel) and a female dancer (the ghost of Keiko, Ohatsu's murdered friend)—dance much of the story which she narrates problematises the depiction of Paris's inner life; so much of his verbal fencing with Ohatsu in the real world is based on the exaggerated playing of gender roles that it becomes a shock and a liberation to see those behavioural *clichés* destabilised in this way. And a powerful element in the character-narrator's role turns out to be the uncertainty about the extent to which they are actually not there, remain participants or detached observers, or might be observing in the process of participation. The style of performance borrows from Suzuki exercises an emphasis on the actor's self-contemplation—the observation projected outside the body—as a crucial stage in developing a representation that is aesthetically true.

Love Suicides, in its extraordinary eclecticism, suggests that exchanges of style between cultures might prove more productive than exchanges of substance. The evidence thus far remains slender, but it is suggestive. The ethics of interculturalism, as mediated through postcolonialism, have fostered a conscientious wariness of adaptation which can diminish the value of the process by producing a worthy exercise in tourism at home, a kind of Cherry Blossom Cruise without the Cruise.

While great myths and narratives might well prove beyond adequate translation, theatre forms are thoroughly exportable. By suggesting new ways of looking and knowing, they may well assist mutual understanding, while promoting in the culture an enlarged understanding of itself. Richard Schechner's recommendation of a blissfully unselfconscious magpie approach to the business of "borrowing, stealing and exchange," despite its apparent insensitivity, might after all offer an emphasis preferable to that of the painfully polite imitation. *Love Suicides*, respecting its sources profoundly though it plunders them mercilessly, points in this direction and represents a watershed in Australian theatre; it is a direction that might be followed by any culture which sees imaginative growth as having more to do with creative interchange than replication.

Significantly too, this exercise in cultural hybridity produces a corresponding hybridity of form. As a means to a different way of knowing, songs are central to *Love Suicides*. In crossing the conventional boundaries of genre, musical theatre and dance drama open up different avenues for the expression of multiculturalism, whether its emphasis rests on the irreversibility of difference or simply on the complex and continual negotiations implicit in new cultural "unions." In mainstream Australian theatre, the evidence so far suggests that the dominant dialogue-driven traditions of "straight" theatre inevitably make degrees of assimilation a subject in itself. The treatment of the figure who does not or cannot share the discourse of the Anglo-Celtic insider can only reinforce marginality, or impose on the subject a celebratory myth of achieved adaptation, as Williamson does in *Face to Face*. This represents one side of the story; spotting the infidel is problematic in this context because of the degree to which those who were once marginal have taken on the social and verbal habits of the centre. So, in *Sex Diary of an*

Infidel, the responsible reading of cultural difference is less a subject in itself than a means to moral discriminations in areas where Gurr's real interests in ambiguity and alienness are seen to lie.

The other side of the story requires that more and different ways be developed to tell it. Song provides no guarantee of a genuine broadening of perspective; the case of *Emma*, where not much more is offered than a highly pleasurable exercise in exotic decor, appears instructive in this respect. But works like *Love Suicides*, and even Darryl Emmerson's *Martin and Gina* (2000)[21] and Anthony Crowley's *Nathanael Storm* (1997),[22] suggest that the representation of multicultural complexity—in which spotting the infidel is made difficult by the range of cultural positions to which audiences are given emotional access— depends on the development of liminal forms. The fact that both methologies—the models of assimilation and diversity—retain such strong claims to attention in our theatre in itself betokens the complexity of the ways in which Australian society in the late twentieth century has evolved.

Works Cited

Beynon, Richard. *The Shifting Heart* (1960; Adelaide: Angus and Robertson, 1992).

Bharucha, Rustom. *Theatre and the World: Performance and the Politics of Culture* (London: Routledge, 1993).

Crowley, Anthony. *Nathanael Storm* (unpublished manuscript).

Davis, Jack. *Kullark* and *The Dreamers* (Sydney: Currency Press, 1982).

Emmerson, Darryl. *Martin and Gina* (unpublished manuscript).

Fitzpatrick, Peter. "Asian Stereotypes in Recent Australian Plays," *Australian Literary Studies* 12.1: 35-46.

Gilbert, Helen. *Sightlines: Race, Gender and Nation in Contemporary Australian Theatre* (Ann Arbor: U of Michigan P, 1998).

Gurr, Michael, *Sex Diary of an Infidel* (Sydney: Currency Press, 1993).

Keene, Daniel. *Cho Cho San* (Sydney: Currency Press, 1993).

---

[21] A published text of *Martin and Gina* is not available. The play, first performed at Monash University in 2000, deals with multiculturalism in the context of the Snowy Mountains Scheme in the 1950's. Gina, an Italian woman, and Martin, a German man, are reunited in Cooma after a long separation. Both struggle a little with the English language: in Gina's case, emotional revelation is aided by her singing in a Neapolitan style; Martin's musical frame is less appositely that of the American pop ballad.

[22] *Nathanael Storm*, first performed at NIDA in 1997, deals with indigenous experience through a score that adapts and quotes, but does not seek to replicate Aboriginal musical form.

Lawler, Ray. *The Summer of the Seventeenth Doll* (Melbourne: Angus and Robertson, 1957).
O' Sullivan, Vincent. *Shuriken* (unpublished manuscript, 1981).
Pitts, Graham. *Emma. Celebrazione!* (Sydney: Currency Press, 1996).
Radic, Therese. *The Emperor Regrets* (Sydney: Currency Press, 1992).
Romeril, John. *The Floating World* (Sydney: Currency Press, 1975).
—— *Love Suicides* (Sydney: Currency Press, 1998).
Schechner, Richard. *The End of Humanism* (New York: Performing Arts Journal Publications, 1982).
Tompkins, Joanne. "Inter-referentiality: Interrogating Multicultural Australian Drama," in *Our Australian Theatre in the 1990s*, ed. Veronica Kelly (Amsterdam: Rodopi Press, 1998).
Williamson, David. *The Removalists* (Sydney: Currency Press, 1972).
—— *What If You Died Tomorrow* (Sydney; Currency Press, 1974).
—— *The Perfectionist* (Sydney: Currency Press, 1983).
—— *Face to Face/Corporate Vibes* (Sydney: Currency Press, 1999).

Collaborating with Ghosts: Dis/possession in *The Book of Jessica* and *The Mudrooroo/Müller Project*

GERRY TURCOTTE

University of Wollongong

> It doesn't fit. It's like doing a corroboree
> in Martin Place.[1]

> You know it's dangerous to mix up
> different kinds of power ...[2]

Setting the Scene

This paper looks at the notion of "dis/possession" in many of its myriad forms, and at the strategies which Indigenous writers adopt in order to avoid being subsumed into majority spaces, or "up-staged" by the performance of imperialisms or neo-colonialisms, specifically through the medium—the *act*—of collaboration. The stage for this reading will be two collaborative works, *The Book of Jessica* and *The Mudrooroo/ Müller Project*, the first a well-known and rather exhaustively analysed "Canadian" text, the other a somewhat neglected "Australian" bricolage of texts, both about the process of collaboratively producing a play.[3]

What is striking about both "casebooks," however, is that they each go to great pains to signal in their very shape the fraught—some would even insist the hopeless—nature of the task. The books are fragmented, contradictory and inconclusive. Ironically, however, and this perhaps reflects the divided nature of the project, the "editors" also work hard to

---

[1] Bob in *The Aboriginal Protesters* from *The Mudrooroo/Müller Project. A Theatrical Casebook*, ed. by Gerhard Fischer (Sydney: New South Wales UP: 1993): 120. Further references to this work appear parenthetically in the text.

[2] Bear in *Jessica* from *The Book of Jessica: A Theatrical Transformation* by Linda Griffiths and Maria Campbell (Toronto: The Coach House Press, 1989): 123. Further references to this work appear parenthetically in the text.

[3] My reading here will focus on the collaborative document rather than on the plays specifically, which are the subject of the respective casebooks.

impose a sense of order—or at least a structured disorder—upon the initiative, anticipating the demands for a type of cohesion from the white, academic, publishing environment to which these books will ultimately cater. Finally, each project summons up, in one sense or another, the notion of a historical-*cum*-spiritual invasion of land and text—and hence the spectre of metaphoric or actual haunting—making the imperialist dimensions of the project undeniable.

Collaborations, inevitably, entail compromises. They are also usually unequal. It rarely happens for projects to emerge spontaneously to each party involved, to derive from the same space, or to reflect the same motives. Collaborations which cross significant lines of power are particularly fraught, and to deny that such inequities exist is either a strategy, ignorance or malice. Pellegrini, citing Koestenbaum, insists that collaboration "is notoriously double-edged ... It invites the happy scene of individuals making common cause—*identifying*—with each other. But collaboration also conjures up the troubling spectre of the double agent, that treasonous representative of misplaced identifications."[4] Collaborations between Indigenous and non-Indigenous writers in particular can only ever be bound in a complex nexus of institutionalised structures which invariably (though perhaps not always) reproduce (and perpetuate) dominant systems of control.

Despite this, collaborations occur, and it would be useful to ask why this might be, given the usually grim prognosis which precedes any such venture. One answer has to be good will: that writers from different communities see an opportunity to re-write, to re-visit, to re-draft a relationship that they perceive as unequal. Some may even feel that the small-scale collaboration can become emblematic of a larger—read national—coming together.[5] This is not to deny that there may be vested interests from both sides—of breaking into the mainstream, of securing a publication, of "redeeming" oneself, of assuaging guilt—but a sense of positive potential is often foreshadowed by collaborative projects. Too often, however, the intercultural project parasitises the Indigenous experience, feeding the Imperial power's "ravenous" appetite for exoticism, exoneration and/or lifeblood. And if my metaphors summon up ghosts of the cannibalistic, or vampiric, it is certainly not accidental.

The Book of Jessica and *The Mudrooroo/Müller Project* represent fascinating texts, because they make clear the "good intentions" of the

---

[4] Ann Pellegrini, *Performance Anxieties: Staging Psychoanalysis, Staging Race* (New York: Routledge, 1997): 9.

[5] *The Book of Jessica* is actually referred to as a "treaty/collaboration" on the back cover blurb.

project initiators—Linda Griffiths and Gerhard Fischer—but they also chart the systemic mechanisms embedded in colonialist and institutional frameworks which eventually militate against the project's success. Neither text outlines clearly what the grounds for reading success might be, but each comments on a perceived failure of the project, and I will return to this issue at the close of this analysis.

Caught in the Act

The Book of Jessica began as a play—*Jessica*—co-written by Linda Griffiths and Maria Campbell, which was loosely based on Campbell's autobiography *Halfbreed*.[6] The play was first produced in 1981. *The Book of Jessica*, published in 1989, is styled as a collaboration which incorporates the play, but which is prefaced by three sections recounting the "tale" of this "theatrical transformation" (as the subtitle puts it). The cover of the 1989 Coach House Press edition features a superimposed image of Campbell's and Griffiths's faces, one over the other, one green eye ghosted beside a blue eye, so that the effect is of one face moving, imperfectly captured by the photograph, or of two faces, each struggling to take over the other. This slightly grotesque image invokes a type of Jekyll and Hyde transformation, but one caught in the act, so that the viewer is unsure which way the transformation is going. It is indeed an apt visual metaphor for the book itself, which charts, in my reading, Linda Griffiths's attempts to exorcise the demons of a collaboration which at times threatened to break her physically and emotionally.

Whilst the play—and the book itself—can be read as Campbell's, in the sense that, as Helen Hoy has argued, "It is her idea initially [and, of course, her life!]. The very substance and format of the book are determined by her ethos of mutual self-disclosure as fundamental to any true collaboration,"[7] it is also true to say that the project is Griffiths's. And without buying into the at times ferocious attacks on Griffiths's initiative, it is important to note that much of the book does take on the aspect of an anthropologised exercise that proves at once therapeutic and opportunistic for Griffiths. Indeed, Campbell's role is frequently delineated pedagogically so that she is there to teach Campbell how to see. In a telling moment in the book, Griffiths discusses her "sibylling" of

---

[6] Griffiths makes the point, however, that the "proposed play was not to be an adaptation of the book, but was to explore what had happened to her since its publication" (19).

[7] Helen Hoy, "'When You Admit You're a Thief, Then You Can Be Honourable': Native/Non-Native Collaboration in *The Book of Jessica*," *Canadian Literature* 136 (Spring 1993): 34.

Campbell and notes that "I was taught that you could open yourself to anything, anyone, let the energy pour through you, and something would happen. I was ravenous for those moments" (14). There is no question that Griffiths, under the guise of her theatrical method, attempts to consume her subject, whatever her motives.

Griffiths, as Hoy has pointed out, controls this product editorially, even suggesting that the book will be produced with or without Campbell's input. She places herself as an interpreter of Indigenous culture to the "outside" world—"I'll make an audience understand" (21);[8] she darkens her skin so that she can pass for Métis (both in the actual community and also on the stage); and she participates in—and partially discloses—a secret ceremony, whilst defending the need to preserve such "dying" moments.[9] To her credit, Griffiths also goes out of her way to signal this aspect of her involvement in the story. She structures the book so that, though she is "driving" the narrative, Campbell frequently intercedes, calling out contradictory directions, disagreeing with Griffiths, or editorialising about Griffiths's academicised discourse. "It just sounds so ... so much like a white professor introducing me at a convention of anthropologists" (18).

What cannot be elided, however, is the fact that Campbell remains a reluctant passenger for much of this journey. Or, put another way, she appears furiously resistant to the type of vehicle which the text continually threatens to become. For Campbell, there is much at stake. As she makes clear later in the book, the entire process revolves around performance, and at some stage, it will take place before an audience. And Campbell, more than Griffiths, will be called to account by her Métis community for what she has disclosed, for whom she has identified with. Her audience will judge whether the collaboration was an act of treason, of double agency. As Paul Thompson, the play's director explains to Griffiths, "She lives here, you'll go back to Toronto, to a to-

---

[8] Also see Hoy, *op. cit.*: 32.

[9] More specifically, when Griffiths begins to describe a ceremony which she has agreed not to discuss, Campbell interrupts her: "I don't believe you're doing this!" (27). Griffiths justifies herself by invoking the famous episode of the photograph of the Sun Dance, a photograph which was illegally obtained by someone who snuck into the ceremony and then published. When Campbell points out that Griffiths was "offended" by the photograph, the latter corrects her: "I wasn't offended by that picture, it inspired and touched me ... Those guys that snuck in and painted pictures and tape-recorded ... were recording something that was dying ..." (28).

tally different life, and she'll take the repercussions of what we do. You have to understand the enormity of her risk" (48).[10]

Wrestling with White Spirits

The Mudrooroo/Müller Project is also promoted as a cross-cultural collaboration, but unlike *The Book of Jessica*, it is presented clearly and more grandiosely as a "battle against white/European cultural hegemony" (back cover), rather than as a "tale of personal, political, and spiritual growth" (as on the back cover of *Book*). First published in 1993, *Project* was the brainchild of historian and literary scholar Gerhard Fischer, who invited Mudrooroo to "Aboriginalise" Heiner Müller's *Der Auftrag* in the context of White Australia's Republican debate. The project began in 1987 as Australia was preparing for its Bicentennial celebrations, and the connecting link is found in the Bicentennial of the French Revolution of 1789, a year after the landing of the First Fleet in Australia. Müller's play, about the betrayal of the Indigenous peoples by representatives of the French Revolution sent to Jamaica to emancipate the slaves, offers an intriguing subtext for the revision, one which is signalled in the volume's cover art.

The front cover reproduces Anselm Kiefer's Auschwitz painting, "Twilight of the West," and an inset of Trevor Nickolls's painting "Wrestling with White Spirit," a series which Nickolls likens to "going on walkabout, on a journey" in order "to come to terms with myself and the white spirit."[11] J.J. Healey has suggested that the juxtaposition pulls "the deathscape universe of Kieferdom into agencies and histories of Australia that ha[ve] distinct Aboriginal references."[12] On the back cover, tucked away almost as an afterthought, is a small playing card featuring an armed slave and bearing the words "Courage" and "Egalité de couleurs." In this respect, at least, the non-Indigenous representation "frames"—contains—the other.

Inside the book, a Preface and a reproduction of the invitation to the Belvoire Street Theatre's staged reading of the Mudrooroo play give

---

[10] See Campbell's comment that "you've gone through hell and high water writing it, because of what you think I've done to you, but I go through hell and high water with that play every time it comes up, my family goes through hell and high water" (81-82).

[11] Trevor Nickolls, "Wrestling with White Spirit," *Seeing Australia Posterbook* (Sydney: Piper Press, 1994): n.p.

[12] J.J. Healy, "*Wrestling with White Spirits*: The Uses and Limits of Modernism and Postmodernism in Aboriginal and Native American Literary Contexts," *Australian and New Zealand Studies in Canada* 12 (December 1994): 47.

way to five separate sections—Concept, Müller, Mudrooroo, Workshop, Politics. An appendix returns us to Fischer's opening voice, re/presenting the "original concept," and then Fischer's synopsis of Müller's play. More importantly, both plays—Müller's and Mudrooroo's—are included.

It is probably fair to say that this complex structure, which divides into numerous further subsections within each section, betrays the editor's inability to hold the project together, or to mould it into anything approaching his own vision. As Gale MacLauchlin and Ian Reid put it, "Every aspect of the book's circumtext seems charged with cross-cultural tensions ... With all its layerings and positionings, such a format announces the difficulty of achieving any intertextual equilibrium" (1994, 110). Healey notes that, "Gerhardt (*sic*) Fischer, with chagrined but very genuine persistence, kept asking Bryon Syron what went wrong: was it me? was it Müller? was it lack of time to workshop the project? was it Müller's text?"[13] In the end, *Project* "records the collaboration that never quite worked, but that still turned up a lot of interesting Aboriginal and Mudrooroo-specific reactions that would otherwise have remained dormant or unexpressed."[14]

Black Skin, White Masks

In some ways *Project* can be understood as emerging out of the failure of the European imagination. Fischer initially planned to write a personal a play about George Forster, "the child prodigy of the European Enlightenment who accompanied Cook on his second journey and who wrote the first article in German on the foundation of the penal colony at New Holland" (4). But the project "leads nowhere." Instead, Fischer turns to Müller's *Der Auftrag*, "the story of the export of the French Revolution to the island of Jamaica, which follows the example of the uprising of the slaves in Haiti" (4). It is a play about the failure of Enlightenment ideals, as well as about the betrayal of Indigenous peoples. Fischer, the "historian," sets about preparing a detailed "*exposé*" of the future project, mapping out his intentions to have Aboriginal actors perform the play. He describes a vision that he has for the performance:

> There are clapsticks and didgeridoos, three of the performers take up position in the middle of the circle ... they begin to put on the clothes of white people while the others watch and assist ... Finally white masks are put on to complete the metamorphosis. It is a vision of Aboriginal performers ap-

---

[13] *Ibid*.: 41.
[14] *Ibid*.: 41.

propriating for themselves the roles/personae of the white masters/liberators (5).

Readers familiar with Mudrooroo's writing will recognise the echo here of Jangamuttuk in *Master of the Ghost Dreaming*, who literally encourages his people to paint the costumes of the European invaders on their bodies in order to enter and possess the White Dreaming—to understand, inhabit, and hopefully to counter the White illness that is killing his people. In case that connection is missed, however, Mudrooroo reproduces the scene almost mid-way through *The Mudrooroo/Müller Project* as a way of contextualising his own forthcoming intervention. "He, the shaman, and purported Master of the Ghost Dreaming, was about to undertake entry into the realm of the ghosts. Not only was he to attempt the act of possession, but he hoped to bring all of his people into contact with the ghost realm so that they could capture the essence of health and well-being, and then break safely into their own culture and society. This was the purpose of the ceremony" (74). The excerpt concludes: "They edged into the time, feeling out the possibilities of the play as the rhythm bounced the shaman towards possession and his people into a new kind of dance" (74). This passage ends the section entitled "Mudrooroo," and introduces part three, the Aboriginalised play: *The Aboriginal Protesters Confront the Declaration of the Australian Republic on 26 January 2001 with the Production of "The Commission" by Heiner Müller*.

Standing on the Edge (of the Set)

In her review essay on *Project*, Helen Daniel borrows Fischer's term "shadow-boxing" to describe the collaborative nature of the "theatrical contest between the two plays."[15] There is a danger in this metaphor which can be read to suggest that the opponent is "unreal," or imaginary, unless of course one pushes the analogy into the area of the ghostly, a trope which Mudrooroo has frequently mobilised in his fiction to re/present Europeans. In *Dr. Wooreddy's Prescription for Enduring the Ending of the World*, Europeans are *num*, ghosts, revenants who are literalised as vampires in his most recent trilogy.

Daniel makes the connection between the middle volume of Mudrooroo's first trilogy, *Doin Wildcat*, and *Project*. In the former, the character Wildcat "is at once novelist, scriptwriter and first-person narrator of *Doin Wildcat*. Standing on the edge of the set where actors play out old versions of his past, Wildcat attempts to disentangle reality from

---

[15] Helen Daniel, "Shadow Boxing," *Island* 55 (Winter 1993): 44.

the rival versions contained in novel and script."[16] It is difficult, in reading this, not to think of both Mudrooroo's efforts to "hijack" Müller's text, but also of Maria Campbell's position *vis-à-vis* her "role" in the writing/making of *Jessica*. Wildcat, like Campbell, "is in a peculiar plight of self-consciousness, at once spectator and protagonist, across the intervening memories ... [where] the narrative keeps crossing the lines between author and character, past and present, actor and spectator, actor and role."[17]

One of the undeniable differences between the positions of the Indigenous participants in this project is precisely that Mudrooroo reverses the parasitical relationship to the institutional aspect of the theatrical: he hijacks Müller's text, whereas Campbell is both the subject/object of the drama. To hijack her own story, therefore, has very different consequences. This is neither to deny author agency, nor to refute what Bhabha has highlighted in the colonial relationship—that is, the ambiguity of the moment of cross-contact which goes both ways—but it is to signal that unequal relations of power can be shifted, and to do so changes the results of the collaborative effort.

The Problem of Collaboration

For Mudrooroo, Indigenous/non-Indigenous collaboration is flawed, because frequently the exercise becomes "assimilationist rather than reconciliationist."[18] But even the latter is not ideal, since the "reconciliatory text" frequently boils down to a compromised text that has elided the "Indigeneity" of the work to make it palatable to a mainstream (that is, White) readership. For Mudrooroo, "The problem of collaboration" is most acutely felt "where the editor enters as co-author."[19] His argument here and the example he uses are particularly

---

[16] *Ibid*.: 45.

[17] *Ibid*.: 45. Since the writing of this work, Mudrooroo's "Aboriginality" has been questioned by both Aboriginal and non-Indigenous groups. In more recent fictions, such as the "Vampire" trilogy which includes *The Undying*, *The Underground* and *The Promised Land*, this self-reflexive gesture has become quite prominent. My own reading here of Mudrooroo as Aboriginal is based on the large community of Aboriginal Australians who continue to accept him as Indigenous, and on a refusal to disregard Mudrooroo's socialisation as an Aboriginal man throughout his life. For a useful study of this "debate" see Maggie Nolan, "Authenticity and Betrayal: The Subjection of Mudrooroo," in *Appreciating Difference: Writing Poscolonial Literary History*, eds. Brian Edwards and Wenche Ommundsen (Geelong: Deakin UP, 1998).

[18] Mudrooroo. *Milli Milli Wanka: The Indigenous Literature of Australia* (Melbourne: Hyland House, 1997): 185.

[19] *Ibid*.: 185.

The Book of Jessica *and* The Mudrooro/Müller Project 183

illuminating in reading what many have seen as the "failure" of *The Book of Jessica*. Without reproducing Mudrooroo's at times misogynistic reading of what he calls "new age feminism," his point that white editors-*cum*-authors invariably seek to transform themselves through the Indigenous experience is right. That Europeans (male and female) have frequently turned to Indigenous spirituality to validate or renew their own sense of cultural decay or loss amounts to a commonplace which needs not be debated here. Daryl Chin's view that the "idea of interculturalism as simply a way of joining disparate cultural artefacts together has a hidden agenda of imperialism,"[20] should nevertheless be kept in mind.

Mudrooroo cites Margaret Somerville's collaboration with Patsy Cohen on *Ingelba and the Five Black Matriarchs* (1991) as an example of his greatest fears about the process of Indigenous/non-Indigenous partnership, which returns us to the opening metaphors of this paper. In reflecting on the editorial process, Somerville notes that it proved "easier to overcome the silences imposed on the written form in the case of finding a voice for Patsy than it was in finding a voice for myself."[21] She goes on to say that

> In traditional histories, the writer herself is absent, a ghost writer. Patsy spoke loud and clear within her own oral discourse. However I still needed to be able to answer the question "Who am I?" in relation to this text ... I could no longer be the conventional 'ghost' writer of life history. The telling of Patsy's life was created out of the particular context of our relationship so I needed to be present in the text.[22]

As Mudrooroo points out, however, "that is how many Indigenous people once saw European people—as 'ghosts'—and so now we have a ghost refusing to be a ghost, or denying her ghosthood. 'I too am human,' she cries."[23] Mudrooroo is correct when he insists that Somerville's

> refusal to be silent, her refusal to let an Indigenous voice speak ... In effect ... in dictating the terms about what is an authentic Indigenous text,

---

[20] Daryl, Chin, "Interculturalism, Postmodernism, Pluralism", in *Interculturalism and Performance: Writings from* PAJ, eds. Bonnie Marranca and Gautam Dasgupta (New York: New York Performing Arts Journal Publications, 1991): 87.

[21] Cited in Mudrooroo, *op. cit.*: 186.

[22] *Ibid.*: 186-87.

[23] *Ibid.*: 187.

[Somerville] has found herself and become the "ghost" matriarch stressing her claims at the expense of Patsy Cohen.[24]

Spectralising the Aboriginal

Ironically, Fischer's "vision" to choreograph this collaborative venture corresponds with the process of "spectralising" the Aboriginal, or at least of invoking one set of phantoms to replace/generate another. In his explanation about how difficult it was to initiate the project, he unwittingly mobilises a phantom Aboriginal theatre. He repeats many times that such a theatre "barely exists" (5), so that "the historian who has metamorphosed into dramaturg becomes a would-be producer who sets out to find the Aboriginal Theatre company that does not exist." Fischer, then, must "figure" the Aboriginal as insubstantial to justify his own desire to create—his section is called genesis after all—a valid Aboriginal site. When he sends the proposal for the collaboration to the Aboriginal National Theatre Trust (ANTT), the concept is rejected. "It is a policy decision: their priority is Aboriginal theatre, done by and for Aborigines, with Aboriginal writers, directors, performers, reflecting Aboriginal concerns, directed towards the Aboriginal community" (6). Fischer "understands" and "sympathises with the professed aims and priorities," but "he wonders about whether a strategy of 'going it alone' and 'doing our own thing' can be successful" (6). He goes on to rationalise that "Theatre in Australia is too much of a minority affair already; trying to set up an Aboriginal theatre without realistically addressing the question of an available audience, the dramaturg fears, will be perpetuating the constraints of a marginal existence, on the fringe of a fringe" (6-7). This insight is borne out, we are reassured, by Fischer's comment that "Later the dramaturg discovers that ANTT is in disarray, soon to be *dissolved*" (7, emphasis added).

As a result of this Indigenous insubstantiality, then, Susanne Abegg of the Sydney Goethe Institute—and Fischer—realise that "an Aboriginal theatre company will have to be set up and incorporated, if only on paper" (9). A further irony here is that he tells this story whilst also explaining that the director, Bryon Syron, is frustrated by his dealings with the Australian Film Institute, which has rejected his own separate film project as insufficiently—or not appropriately—Aboriginal. "It is not the kind of film the AFC wants to see: they have told him to make a movie about Aboriginal 'causes' ... white people who have the power and the money telling him how to make an Aboriginal movie" (10). He then moves on to discuss Mudrooroo's *Doin Wildcat*, "about a writer

---

[24] *Ibid.*: 187.

who witnesses his first novel being made into a movie, and his search for power, input, control, watching at the periphery of the shooting, reliving his work and seeing it transformed into something else, into somebody else's work" (11). Without wishing to be too harsh, since the dynamics of collaborations are so difficult and so fraught, it seems necessary to point out that Fischer does not appear to be aware of the resonant ironies which his own role involves, nor of the overdeterministic nature of his own vision. He discusses Mudrooroo's academic writing, noting that the latter has "mastered and appropriated for himself the critical jargon of the 'European' academic," but it is in his "novels that I find what *I am looking for*" (11, emphasis added).

Mudrooroo, however, refuses to be so pliable. Fischer's "Genesis" narrative ends with a comment that says as much: Mudrooroo "has dissected the Müller text more radically, breaking it up to a point that threatens the coherence of the story while the Aboriginal characters still remain thin, shadowy. But Mudrooroo does not want to discuss it: he's had enough of me and from me; he needs Aboriginal input and feedback" (17). Strange that Fischer considers his construction of an insubstantial—a phantom—Aboriginality as unproblematic, but that he feels Mudrooroo's shadowy figures to be so.

An Assembly of Phantoms

For reasons of space, it is impossible to provide a detailed reading of Müller's text, or of the other narratives that take place here.[25] Let me, for the sake of brevity, reinvoke what constitutes a central metaphor throughout this study. For Fischer, Müller's play combines Artaud's theatre of cruelty and Brecht's *Lehrstück* "in the phantasmagoria of a theatrical work that is unique, and uniquely Müller's" (6). Built into this representational spectralisation, of course, is Müller's own explanation about what he had to do before he could "envision" his play about Jamaica: he can only begin to write about the other—in this case the Jamaican slaves—after he has visited "Mexico and Puerto Rico" (40). For Müller, the "Third World" coincides with an orientalised, essentialised space, entirely undifferentiated, so that Mexico and Puerto Rico can stand in for any "remote village" peopled by "dark figures," who are themselves only understandable via their representation in European demonisations. The dark figures, then, who as emblems elicit terror in him, can be imagined only in the context of "a painting by Goya" in what is "A walk through fear through the Third World" (40). The Greek term phantasmagoria can be translated literally to mean an assembly of

---

[25] See Dunstone and Healy for detailed readings of the play itself.

phantasms—of ghosts. This "exhibition of optical illusions," this "shifting series of phantasms, illusions, or deceptive appearances"[26] precisely represents what Mudrooroo is up against, what he must dispossess.

To do this, then, Mudrooroo uses the frame of a play-within-a-play, featured on the page with Müller's corresponding text, fragmented and shaded in, under erasure as it were. The players constantly interrupt the process of rehearsing the play in order to editorialise. As Bill Dunstone has argued,

> the Aboriginal "rehearsal" text articulates the politics of black identification and black sovereignty as confrontationist, processual and performative ... Mudrooroo's key strategies for re-working the politics of the "stage-world" metaphor are to deny the illusionist privileging of performance (as visible product) over rehearsal (as concealed process), and to mobilize the politics of both rehearsal and performance as modes of theorization and political activation ... His play disrupts notions that the rehearsal is a transparent, fundamentally mimetic progress towards a fixed and finished performance.[27]

The ironically named King George, at one stage, comments that what is needed is not what "that academic bloke" wants, but "a theatre of black-fella business. Proper theatre" (100). And throughout, the *Djangara*—"proper" Aboriginal spirits—haunt and disrupt the show, suggesting that "a theatre of blackfella business" can only be proper when it resists being "finished off" by white dramaturgical means.

The Theatre Gods

Spirits similarly haunt the *Jessica* project. The opening page of the first section, "Spiritual Things," comments on the "spookiness" of the collaboration, though this is contextualised by Linda Griffiths through her own ghosts: "I had some kind of connection with the spirits, we called them 'the theatre gods'" (13). Griffiths's practice of ravenously sibylling "other people's psyches"—where she literally possesses the other—is not as effortlessly managed as her past experience has suggested. Previous possessions, which include the Prime Minister of Canada, the head of nation, have never been present during the "feeding" process. But with Jessica, Campbell was there to argue, refuse access, and resist incorporation. "Then the old, half-digested, theatrical gods met Maria and her Native spirits, and all hell broke loose" (14).

---

[26] *Macquarie Dictionary*: 1275.

[27] Bill Dunstone, "Mudrooroo: The Politics of Aboriginal Performance and Aboriginal Sovereignty," in *(Post)Colonial Stages: Critical and Creative Views on Drama, Theatre and Performance*, ed. Helen Gilbert (London: Dangaroo Press, 1999): 95.

Whilst Griffiths contextualises the process in terms of her own victimization—"Nobody approved of me, even though I worked my guts out" (14)—Campbell locates the process, fittingly, by appropriating—indeed vampirising—a Judeo-Christian metaphor:

> She always looked like the Virgin Mary ... She walked around like a missionary, begging for something with one hand—give it to me, tell me about it—just bleeding all of me dry. She made me think of those stupid stories in the *National Enquirer*: "Virgin Mary Bleeds as Visitors Watch in Horror" ... and I'd stand there feeling like she'd stolen my thoughts. She'd just take it all (15).

Perhaps not surprisingly, Linda Griffiths and Paul Thompson, who directed the play, both determine, *à la* Fischer, what the play should be about. In a scene which is reminiscent of Thomas King's satiric "One Good Story, That One," in which a group of anthropologists refuse to hear a story of everyday life from *their* Native Informant, asking instead for a "real Indian story," Campbell is made to feel that she must assume a "spiritual" mantle when what she really wants to talk about is the story of "a woman struggling with two cultures, and how she got them balanced" (17). For Campbell, the spiritual and the human remain inseparable. Griffiths, however, considers that "Under Paul's guidance, we were to make up a woman who was Maria, but not really" (19).

Ghosts Are in Purgatory

In "Autobiography as Collaboration," Kathleen Boardman notes that "Autobiographies with two or more collaborators include not only the ghostwritten versions omnipresent in popular culture, but also the many 'as-told-to' life stories produced by Native narrators and white ethnographers since the nineteenth century."[28] Boardman quite rightly examines *The Book of Jessica* through the prism of the autobiographical procedure, since so much of the book concerns each "collaborator's" attempt to write her*self*. For Boardman, this "collaborative process ... breaks down, or nearly does."[29] The possible breakdown results in part from the baggage which Campbell is willing to carry and which—Campbell feels—Griffiths is not.

Campbell resists Griffiths's cultural appropriation, particularly in the way that the latter constantly attempts to embody Native spirituality at the expense of recognising/owning her own. Much of the drama, then, is

---

[28] Kathleen A. Boardman, "Autobiography as Collaboration: *The Book of Jessica*," *Textual Studies in Canada* 4 (1994): 28.

[29] Ibid.: 29.

enacted around the theme of totemic animals/spirits, Griffiths's eventual performance of the Wolverine character, and her creation of a Unicorn figure, which represents the Celtic side of her life/story. Without embracing this part of her own history, the story cannot be exchanged. Collaboration cannot take place. As Chester and Dudoward put it, "In order to collaborate, one must first communicate."[30]

Campbell, on the other hand, constantly faces up to her own spirituality, refusing to allow the individual/personal history to be separate from the social/community history. Indeed, she illuminates the very process of collaborative exchange *via* the prism of cultural *métissage*—literally. Campbell insists that the Métis people, as mixed bloods, are themselves the example and the product of collaboration—between white and Native nations. And in that respect, they are emblematic of the difficulty of the collaborative effort:

> I told her I'd always felt a kind of historical guilt because we had been (when I say "we," I mean Metis people, Halfbreed people, mixed-blood people) the link between Indians and whites. We had acted as interpreters in treaties, we had walked ahead of the explorers and showed them the way. In the course of trying to deal with that guilt, I had come to the realization, on both sides, that it wasn't my guilt. That garbage belonged to both those two peoples, not to my people (20).

The process, then, of false collaboration, of negotiation in bad faith, of broken treaties leads to the dispossession of the Métis, "until we were just like a band of gypsies moving around, landless" (20). For Campbell, the journey of the collaboration represents an attempt to "replace the negative with things from both peoples that were precious and beautiful" (20); indeed, one has a sense that the theatrical space can lead to what Mudrooroo called "the Theatre of Reality ... out there in that mass of signs we declare to be the real world" (31).

Ironically, for Griffiths, the journey—though similar—leads in the opposite direction. She is unable for much of the book to realise the baggage of her European ancestry which she too carries. In a statement which summons up the ghosts of Northrop Frye, Griffiths refuses to see the ghosts of her own past, seeking redemption *via* the absorption of Native spirituality instead. In a section called "Community Canada," Griffiths goes on to speak about the non-Indigenous feeling of dispossession—of landlessness—somehow managing to "appropriate" even the Métis experience, the Native reality of dispossession. To be Canadian is to be a "wishy-washy ... ghost-like people ... sometimes I feel

---

[30] Blanca Chester and Valerie Dudoward, "Journeys and Transformations," *Textual Studies in Canada* 1 (1991): 158.

like we're ghosts with this losing battle ... I feel like a ghost ... The lack of a sense of place makes you feel ghostly. Why do I still cling to the theatre: Because it's the only ground I feel I have" (94). Campbell rejects the fallacy of this conclusion: "as long as you refuse to look at that history, of course you'll be ghosts, because you have no place to come from. Ghosts are in purgatory, they're someplace in between" (95). She goes on to say "Using the word ghost is good because that's what the old people say when they talk about white people in this country: 'Ghosts trying to find their clothes.' And to me they're ghosts because I don't understand where they're coming from" (96).

The Show Can't Go On

I have chosen to "read" these collaborative projects together because they illustrate much about the dangers of collaborative work. The sheer number of similarities between these texts can be discounted, on the one hand, as coincidences. However, I think that, without resorting to special pleading, some case can be made for a commensurability which emerges because they share a common point of conflict—the *act* of collaboration—reflecting on the process of Indigenous/non-Indigenous interaction. How, then, does one act out a collaboration? Which of these texts best "performs" its exchange?

In one way, it may be possible to argue that the plays can be measured in inverse proportion to their success on stage. While it is dangerous to argue that the "whiteness" of form militates against the message in *Jessica*, or that its rave reception suggests a certain failure, I am nevertheless keen to suggest that Mudrooroo's unperformability is somewhat more of a sign of its radical resistance to the framework which is attempting to incorporate it. Mudrooroo reverses the polarity—it is Fischer who cannot participate.

In what I hope will not be considered an unforgiveable pun, and by way of mobilising one final time the prevailing metaphor of this paper, the medium is often the message. Hence, when I suggested, at the beginning of this article, that Indigenous writers often found themselves working against absorption through the medium of collaboration, I mean, in one sense, that in the act of collaboration, Indigenous "partners," relegated to the status of Native Informant, have their energies and stories channelled—sybilled—in the service of a non-Indigenous vision. However powerful that product may end up being, the question of possession is paramount. The success of *The Book of Jessica* can be measured instead in the way Campbell overturns the traditional power relationship between ghost writer and subject. Campbell haunts Griffiths: she takes possession of the story and switches the channel, so that Griffiths's rather than Campbell's story appears groundless. Despite the odds stacked against her—white forms, white modes of production, white director, white editor, white contract—Campbell refuses to allow the book to become a figment of the white imagination. When Linda Griffiths accusingly tells Campbell that she would have let the project die, Hoy perceptively points out that that may not—necessarily—be a bad thing. It depends on whom the spirit is living for—and whom it serves.

Certainly, Campbell sets the pace, and the narrative is written over a much longer period than Griffiths would have wished. And when Campbell attempts to claim the right of first refusal for subsequent performances, so that she can continue to repossess the character of Jessica for each performance, Griffiths quite rightly reads this as a breach of contract—indeed, she never sees this part of the contract until after it is signed by Campbell and Paul Thompson. "I read it and the contract said that you would have first refusal rights on who would play Jessica. But you and I had already said that after this time Jessica would have to be played by a Native woman ... The ugliest part of the contract was that I had never been consulted, and it reminded me of the treaties ... and I didn't even get the right of an interpreter" (105-06). In the end, though, Jessica is performed by a number of Indigenous actors, and Griffiths relinquishes her claim to ground that was, arguably, never hers to begin with.

The Book of Jessica, for all its problematic contextualisation, is a testament to the courage of both collaborators. The book brutally exposes the weaknesses and strengths of both women, as well as the fraught landscape of this exhilarating contested spirit world, and suggests a way forward for the possibility of future collaborations.

The *Project*, on the other hand, ends with Fischer's almost desperate plea to have the play performed. For him, the marker of successful performativity is clearly enacted on the stage, before an audience, and such a result would act out his vision. The point of the *Project* publication, in fact, is "meant as a challenge to theatre practitioners in Australia to realise this project on stage" (vii). But Mudrooroo's points of reference differ. "And was the play successful? The success was in the workshopping, was in the strengthening of our Aboriginality." He goes on to say, "We were confronted by the Other and managed to contain the Otherness of that text. How is success to be gathered? Is it in putting on a black play in a bourgeois theatre for a mainly white audience, or is it in working and performing for our own people?" (143). The answer to this question, for many would-be collaborators, *must be* dispiriting in every sense.

Works Cited

Andrews, Jennifer. "Framing *The Book of Jessica*: Transformation and the Collaborative Process in Canadian Theatre," *English Studies in Canada* 22.3 (September1996): 297-313.
Boardman, Kathleen A. "Autobiography as Collaboration: *The Book of Jessica*," *Textual Studies in Canada* 4 (1994): 28-39.
Chester, Blanca, and Valerie Dudoward. "Journeys and Transformations," *Textual Studies in Canada* 1 (1991): 156-77.
Chin, Daryl, "Interculturalism, Postmodernism, Pluralism," *Interculturalism and Performance: Writings from PAJ*, eds. Bonnie Marranca and Gautam Dasgupta (New York: New York Performing Arts Journal Publications, 1991): 83-95.
Daniel, Helen. "Shadow Boxing," *Island* 55 (Winter 1993): 44-47.
Dunstone, Bill. "Mudrooroo: The Politics of Aboriginal Performance and Aboriginal Sovereignty," in *(Post)Colonial Stages: Critical and Creative Views on Drama, Theatre and Performance*, ed. Helen Gilbert (London: Dangaroo Press, 1999): 89-99.
Egan, Sasanna. "*The Book of Jessica*: The Healing Circle of a Woman's Autobiography," *Canadian Literature* 144 (Spring 1995): 10-26.
Fischer, Gerhard, ed. *The Mudrooroo/Müller Project: A Theatrical Casebook* (Sydney: New South Wales UP, 1993).
Griffiths, Linda, and Maria Campbell. The Book of Jessica*: A Theatrical Transformation* (Toronto: The Coach House Press, 1989).
Healy, J.J. "*Wrestling with White Spirits*: The Uses and Limits of Modernism and Postmodernism in Aboriginal and Native American Literary Contexts," *Australian and New Zealand Studies in Canada* 12 (December 1994): 31-50.
Hoy, Helen. "'When You Admit You're a Thief, Then You Can Be Honourable': Native/Non-Native Collaboration in *The Book of Jessica*," *Canadian Literature* 136 (Spring 1993): 24-39.
Koestenbaum, Wayne. *Double Talk: The Erotics of Male Literary Collaboration* (New York: Routledge, 1989).
MacLauchlin, Gale and Ian Reid. *Framing and Interpretation* (Melbourne: Melbourne UP, 1994).
Macquarie Dictionary (Sydney: Macquaries Library & Griffin Press, 1985, revised ed.)
Mudrooroo. *Milli Milli Wanka: The Indigenous Literature of Australia* (Melbourne: Hyland House, 1997).
Nickolls, Trevor. "Wrestling with White Spirit," *Seeing Australia Posterbook* (Sydney: Piper Press, 1994): n.p.
Nolan, Maggie. "Authenticity and Betrayal: The Subjection of Mudrooroo," in *Appreciating Difference: Writing Poscolonial Literary History*, eds. Brian Edwards and Wenche Ommundsen (Geelong: Deakin UP, 1998).

Pellegrini, Ann. *Performance Anxieties: Staging Psychoanalysis, Staging Race* (New York: Routledge, 1997).

Tompkins, Joanne. "Infinitely Rehearsing Performance and Identity: *Africa Solo* and *The Book of Jessica*," *Canadian Theatre Review* 74 (Spring 1993): 35-39.

Canadian "Ethnic" Theatre: Fracturing the Mosaic

ANNE NOTHOF

Athabasca University

The comfortable myth of the "cultural mosaic" is an imaginative construct that reifies the Canadian self-concept of tolerance, freedom, and diversity. It configures social harmony as a pleasing aesthetic pattern: the juxtaposition of many differently-coloured pieces. However, a mosaic imagined as a social metaphor assumes that each piece occupies a specific place that is proportionate to the grand design. Even though in Canada such a construction of "national character" resists the notion of "assimilation," diversity and distinctiveness are tolerated—even encouraged—only when they are perceived as indicators of a rich and colourful social fabric, without subversive or threatening implications. Moreover, from the perspective of immigrants, the cultural mosaic may not be a benign metaphor: they may resist the way in which they are placed in the grand design—usually on the edges. They may also fear that their traditions and history may be lost, that their children will become so integrated with the pattern that they will forget their connections with their heritage and their language.

In the English-Canadian construction of the cultural mosaic, those who are perceived as not constituting the post-colonial matrix of an "Anglo" society are designated as "ethnic"—an exotic "other" differentiated by race, language, culture. The term "ethnicity" may evoke colourful images of folk dances, traditional costumes, an accented English, but it also has racist underpinnings. The Greek root word for "ethnicity," *ethnikos*, means "heathen"—one who is unenlightened, lacking in culture or moral principles. Any group that departs from the "norm" of anglophone, "Western" culture is typically cast as a foreign element that may be threatening until integrated with the whole. However, when the "ethnic" element confronts these assumptions and resists definition in terms of the majority culture, then there exists also the possibility of the displacement of the traditional historical construction of Canada as bilingual and bicultural:

> Ethnicity as a representational politics pushes against the boundaries of cultural containment and becomes a site of pedagogical struggle in which the legacies of dominant histories, codes and relations become unsettled and thus open to being challenged and rewritten.[1]

Canadian history as conceived by political historian J. L. Granatstein is being "killed" by "multicultural mania."[2]

Canadian minority writing constitutes "a primary cultural site for the discussion of plural, cross-boundary, and intersecting concerns."[3] Furthermore, the inclusiveness facilitated by a greater openness to a multicultural climate "coincides with the turn towards postmodernism and post-colonialism, traditionally seen as marked by the demise of unifying narratives of history; the aesthetics of multiplicity, heterogeneity, and fragmentation; as well as the increased political mobilization of the oppressed peoples."[4] However, "the intersection of ethnicity, race, gender, and class ... is precisely where the mosaic cracks."[5] These cracks in the mosaic are particularly evident in a Canadian ethnic theatre in which self-representation challenges the characterisations of the cultural majority.

The strategies in the deconstruction of the master narrative of the cultural mosaic have been varied: one response has been made in terms of identity politics—basing the theatrical event on the cultural and social practices of the minority community in order to validate or to critique them. Another has been iconoclastic—fracturing the cultural and political construction of the mosaic by exposing racist attitudes and actions. A third strategy has represented an attempt at transcultural communication through a performance of self in terms of heritage and future possibilities for a composite identity—an attempt to inhabit the border zones. A fourth strategy has consisted in establishing an intercultural dialogue, in which the limitations and potentialities of majority and minority cultures are explored through self-reflexive and ironic metatheatrical prac-

---

[1] A. Henry Giroux, "Living Dangerously: Identity Politics and the New Cultural Racism: Towards a Critical Pedagogy of Representation," *Cultural Studies* 7.1 (1993): 23.

[2] J. L. Granatstein, *Who Killed Canadian History?* (Toronto: Harper Perennial, 1998): 79.

[3] Enoch Padolsky, "Ethnicity and Race: Canadian Minority Writing at the Crossroads," in *Literary Pluralities*, ed. Christl Verduyn (Peterborough: Broadview Press, 1998): 22.

[4] Eva Karpinski, "Multicultural 'Gift(s)': Immigrant Women's Life Writing and the Politics of Anthologized Difference," in *Literary Pluralities*, ed. Christl Verduyn (Peterborough: Broadview Press, 1998): 112.

[5] *Ibid.*: 112.

tices. By challenging the point of view inherent in the construct of the Canadian cultural mosaic, these ethnic plays allow for other ways of seeing and a fuller participation in the imaginative life of the country. Although ethnicity "is likely to be in the twenty-first century what class was to the twentieth—a major source of social tensions and political conflicts," it can also be a "source of creation and diversification."[6]

This paper will consider examples of these four expressions of Canadian ethnic theatre: "community" plays such as those written by Sadhu Binning for Vancouver Sath theatre; the *agit-prop* plays of Rahul Varma and Rana Bose written for Teesri Duniya and Montreal Serai theatres; the "autobio-mythographies" of Guillermo Verdecchia and Djanet Sears; and the cross-cultural comedies of Padma Viswanathan and Marty Chan. It will also interrogate audience reception: whom do these plays address—the minority groups or the dominant culture? Does a multicultural content become an "exotic" form of entertainment for a predominantly "white" audience?

Community Theatre

East Asian theatre has a long history in Canada. It is based on the structure and style of protest theatre in India, which reflected the Marxist movement of the early 1920s, and it specifically addresses community issues. The plays developed by theatres such as Vancouver Sath and Teesri Duniya in Montreal typically portray the conflict between minority South Asian workers and the "white" dominant society, or conflicts within the community itself. Self-representation primarily occurs through the employment of identity politics; the plays are usually polemical and the characterisation representational. Conflicts are simply stated and politicised; plots are skeletal. In Toronto, however, South Asian theatre has been developed through the agency of such multivalent theatres as Cahoots, which has a mandate to "develop theatre representative of Canada's diverse cultural mosaic"; Tarragon Theatre, which has developed and produced new Canadian plays since 1974; and Nightwood, which develops primarily feminist drama. Typically, plays developed at these theatres attempt to reach a wider audience and to move outside of a specific community.

Vancouver Sath was founded in 1982 by a group of Punjabi writers and community activists whose aim was to address the social inequities in their community. The first plays were collectively created and performed in Punjabi, but after 1986 they were also staged in English, and

---

[6] J.W. Berry and J.A. Laponce, eds., *Ethnicity and Culture in Canada: The Research Landscape* (Toronto: U of Toronto P, 1994): 3.

written primarily by Sadhu Binning: *Picket-Line* (1984) is about a women's strike against their Punjabi employers on a mushroom farm; *Ghost that Can Only Be Handled with Force* (1985) focuses on the abuse of a woman forced to sponsor relatives; *Mansions and Parks* (1987) deals with the problems of Punjabi elderly; *Whose Marriage* (1987) questions parents' attitudes about arranged marriages; *Different Age Same Cage* (1987) portrays three different stages of a woman's life, the favouritism of sons over daughters, wife-beating, and the abuse of elderly parents; *A Crop of Poison* (1988) attacks the use of pesticides on British Columbia farms; *A Lesson of a Different Kind* (1989) examines the exploitative situation of immigrant janitorial workers; and *Not a Small Matter* (1989) looks at violence against women.[7] There is no simple ethical alignment in terms of race or origins. Vancouver Sath hangs up the community's dirty laundry, sometimes occasioning accusations of betrayal from within.

According to critic and playwright, Uma Parameswaran, South Asian theatres are also engaged in a larger project: "We are in the process of forging a new national cultural identity in Canada, an identity that will be a composite of many heritage cultures ... Perhaps that culture will be a seamless coat of many colours rather than the patchwork quilt that is today's multiculturalism."[8] This more integrative ambition is shared by two theatres in Montreal, Teesri Duniya and Montreal Serai; however, their means of achieving it are cathartic—exposing the poison before the healing can begin.

Protest Theatre

Teesri Duniya Theatre—which translates as "Third World" Theatre—was founded in 1981 by Rahul Varma and Rana Bose. According to Uma Parameswaran, "unlike the Sath that is motivated by forces within the community, [Teesri Duniya] was motivated by the patterns of racism endemic to the Canadian system and ... react[ed] to forces generated by structures outside [its] heritage and culture."[9] Although it used multiracial casts, its focus lay initially on the South Asian Canadian experience. Until 1985, it produced plays in Hindi, then in English, beginning with *The Great Celestial Cow* (1985) and *On the Double* (1986). Following

---

[7] Sadhu Binning, "Vancouver Sath: South Asian Canadian Theatre in Vancouver," *Canadian Theatre Review* 94 (Spring 1998): 14.

[8] Uma Parameswaran, "Protest for a Better Future: South Asian Canadian Theatre's March to the Centre," in *Contemporary Issues in Canadian Drama*, ed. Per Brask (Winnipeg: Blizzard, 1995): 117.

[9] Sadhu Binning, *op. cit.*: 124.

an ideological split, Bose broke away from Teesri Duniya to form Montreal Serai, developing plays which reflected the influence of the Western tradition—a theatre of ideas—whereas Teesri Duniya has retained its Marxist orientation and its agit-prop style. Its aim is to protest and to educate. Plays are developed to address specific social problems or issues and are collectively workshopped. The artistic director, Rahul Varma, functions as *dramaturg* or playwright, shaping the material for final production and/or publication. His many collaborations include *Job Stealer* (1987); *Isolated Incident* (1988); *Equal Wages* (1989); *Land Where the Trees Talk* (1990), produced at Montreal's Centaur Theatre; *No Man's Land* (1992); *For You Jafroon* (1995), presented as part of *Women's Rights in Pakistan*, a conference organised by CERAS, Montreal; and *Counter Offence*, produced at Tessri Duniya in 1996 and co-produced with Black Theatre Workshop in 1997.

Teesri Duniya theatre has expanded its original aim—"to provide actors of South Asian descent with a voice"[10]—to promote the concept of "diversity," which, according to Rahul Varma, represents "a shift from monoculturalism, biculturalism and xenophobia, and towards ... multiplicity and multiculturalism."[11] The theatre now positions itself "as a culturally inclusive theatre company where the minority and mainstream artists could share the same stage."[12] The mission statement reflects this broad inclusiveness: "to provide opportunities to theatre artists of diverse cultural and ethnic backgrounds to work together ... The company's stage reflects the country: colourful, multiracial and multicultural."[13]

In 1998, Teesri Duniya launched a multi-faceted Cross-Cultural Play Development programme entitled "Making Sparks," headed by company *dramaturg* Shelley Tepperman. The plays nurtured by the playwrights' unit were presented in a showcase entitled "Fireworks," which afforded an opportunity for Montreal audiences "to experience recent intercultural works from elsewhere in the country." Auxiliary programmes have included "Other Fires," "a series of staged readings of eight outstanding plays from cultures rarely depicted on our stages."[14]

---

[10] Rahul Varma, "Contributing to Canadian Theatre," *Canadian Theatre Review* 94 (Spring 1998): 25.

[11] Rahul Varma, "Diversity: Its Promise and its Potential" <http://www.aei.ca/~tduniya/alt.theatre/diversity.htm>.

[12] *Ibid.*

[13] Rahul Varma, "Mission and History" <http:/www.aei.ca/~tduniya/backstage.htm>.

[14] Shelley Tepperman, "At Teesri Tuniya" <http:/www.aei.ca/~tduniya/alt.theatre/at_teesri_duniya.htm>.

The writers come from a wide range of cultural backgrounds—Portuguese, Salvadorean, Iraqi—but they have in common the experiences of marginalisation and stereotyping. Most of the playwrights in the programme write in English as a second language.

However, although the theatre increasingly reflects Canada's ethnic diversity, most of the plays have been a consideration of the immigrant experience as victimisation: the newcomers are systematically exploited by the capitalist social system, or marginalised economically and socially. For example, Varma's *No Man's Land* bleakly portrays the materialism that infects Canadian society and those who attempt to survive on its terms. The title—taken from the mediaeval expression which denotes the place where the dead were abandoned outside the city walls in times of plague, and reinstated to describe the killing fields of World War I—becomes an indicator of dispossession and dislocation.

A Muslim family, driven out of India during the bloody partition of India and Pakistan by the British, attempts to relocate in Canada, and for the father, the evidence of the success of that relocation is a house:

> Look at this house. Two stories, balcony, a lawn and a backyard, two car garage and a church within two blocks ... But still the price did not hit the sky. Thank you, God.[15]

As a reminder of his mission in Canada, he has brought with him a charred brick from his destroyed ancestral home, but the end subsumes the means, as he sacrifices the health and happiness of his wife, who must work in a "sweat shop" in order to pay off the large mortgage. The wife finally abandons the family when she realises that she has worked all of her life for a family nest and has had no time to live in it.

Satiric comments on racism in Canada—practised by the majority culture against minorities, and by minorities amongst themselves—are provided by a Sikh "friend" of the Muslim family, who guides them through the initial culture shock, but who also exploits their naiveté. The daughter, Samreen, provides the viewpoint of a more "integrated" second generation: she rejects the limiting traditions of her culture, in particular those propounded by the local Mullah, who claims that Muslim women should remain in "*purdah*." A stereotypical "redneck" white factory worker articulates the more virulent racist attitudes:

---

[15] Rahul Varma, *No Man's Land*, in *Canadian Mosaic: 6 Plays*, ed. Aviva Ravel (Toronto: Simon & Pierre, 1995): 167. Further references to this play appear parenthetically in the text.

Send all the greaseballs back to where they came from ... Look around you. Hordes of coloured women. One baby pulling her saree, another in her arm and one in her belly (180-81).

The satire is also directed against the Quebec separatist movement, whose aims are compared to the partition of India and Pakistan. The play collates through the pointed statements of each character a series of viewpoints on racism and the immigrant experience. The didacticism is sometimes mitigated through humour, but because the focus shifts from one issue to another, the characters function primarily as mouthpieces.

No Man's Land was co-written with Ken McDonough, who also played the lead role of the father. Increasingly, Teesri Duniya productions use "colour-blind casting" in order to be as culturally inclusive as possible, and that, maintains Varma, includes the dominant culture: "We are guided by the principle of 'who will listen to what,' not 'who should speak for whom.'"[16] In response to questions of "authenticity" and "appropriation," McDonough relates a personal anecdote:

> After the play, several white Canadians approached me to explain that they could understand my predicament, even though they respected that my country was different. I am white, English-speaking, and from Scarborough, Ontario.[17]

Counter Offence, Varma's first full-length play, also offers a composite of different immigrant responses to Canadian society. It complicates the mosaic by pitting one social practice against the other, and raises the question as to whether imported customs that infringe on the rights and freedoms of others should be tolerated. There are no heroes here; everyone is compromised, and even the best of intentions goes tragically awry. Shapoor, an Iranian immigrant, is accused of abusing his South Asian Canadian wife, who has sponsored his immigration, and whom he wants to sponsor his parents. He argues for his defence that wife-beating is permitted in his native country. And when the majority culture in the form of a white policeman intervenes, the policeman is accused of racism by an anti-racist activist. To complicate matters further, a black social worker who advocates zero tolerance for violence against women, comes to the policeman's defence, even though she fully realises that the police record of violence against ethnic minorities is highly suspect. According to Soraya Peerbaye, "this complexity reflects South Asian Canadian audiences' reality, as the conflicts of cultures and values

---

[16] Rahul Varma, "Contributing to Canadian Theatre," *Canadian Theatre Review* 94 (Spring 1998): 25.

[17] Ken McDonough, "Cultural Appropriation or Cross-Cultural Dialogue?" <http:/www/aei.ca/~tduniya/alt.theatre/cultural_appropriation.htm>.

which are a part of [their] identity are expressed in the most private aspects of [their] lives."[18]

The play opens with a speech by Moolchand Misra, an Indo Canadian anti-racist activist, directed at the audience. He positions Canada as a multi-ethnic country in which social justice and equality should be possible—despite its racist history—but in his confrontations with the two policemen, he provokes defensive responses with his assumptions of racism. The test case for tolerance is that of a white policeman accused of murdering an Iranian immigrant, but everyone in the play is placed on trial at some point. Questions of guilt and innocence become increasingly problematic as individual motives are discovered in a series of flashbacks. The first is Shazia's discovery of Galliard, a white policeman, with the murdered Shapoor in a room at the YMCA, where the latter has returned following his extradition from the country. The next flashback focuses on the brutal interrogation of Shapoor by Galliard seven months previously when he was first accused of abusing Shazia. Shazia's point of view is provided in another flashback, in which she is speaking to Clarinda and Galliard about Shapoor's violence. She is supported by her parents, but their response to her failed marriage outside of her own community is critical. Moolchand attempts to assist Shapoor, but finds him to be poor material for a test case: he is indecisive, weak-willed, and unpredictable. In casting an Iranian in this negative light, Varma himself was accused of racism by some Iranians in the audience. The introduction to the published play includes a defence of Varma's use of a multi-racial cast by Shahrzud Mojab:

> It is not difficult to see, in this case, how nationalist feelings allows (*sic*) victims of racism to deny their own racist and sexist beliefs and practices. Indeed, to argue the Iranians are not racist or sexist is itself rooted in a belief in nationalist or racial superiority. Denial is easy; it comes naturally and it only leads to the constant reenactment of the tragedy. The real challenge is realising the problem, facing it, and going through the process of transformation.[19]

In his determination to win his case, Moolchand attempts to persuade Clarinda to align herself with him against the white majority, and to convince Shazia to drop her charges. Clarinda, however, constructs the case along gender rather than racist lines, for which she is accused of being disloyal to the coloured community. The only voice of compas-

---

[18] Soraya Peerbaye, "A Subtle Politic," *Canadian Theatre Review* 94 (Spring 1998): 8.

[19] Shahrzud Mojab, "Introduction: Anti-Racism and Anti-Sexism: from the Legislative Halls to Theatre Houses," in *Counter Offence* (Toronto: Playwrights Canada, 1995): 11-12.

sion and sanity is that of Shazia's mother, who defends her daughter against her father and her husband; her mordant views on marriage provide some comic relief in a play in which everyone is compromised and conflicted. Shapoor's murder is finally played out, and its motives revealed as entrenched in racism. In Moolchand's final speech to the audience, he unveils his own personal motivation for his politicised actions—his reception as "ethnic" in Montreal, and the systemic denial of opportunities:

> Some years ago, I was already a Canadian citizen, had a degree from McGill and one from New Delhi and an immigrant's discipline. But I was bumped out of a job. Why? "Mr. Moolchand belongs to a behind-the-desk job—at the census bureau, for example, where many of his countrymen are doing wonderful work ... He is not a suitable candidate for the classroom." I guess it was my Bombaywallah accent and my lack of humour. Do you think I lack humour? The reason was, they will let you get only so far ahead and then they will cut you down.[20]

For every "offence," there is a counter offence: retribution replaces justice, and personal injuries preclude communal resolutions.

The plays of Rana Bose, written for the collective theatre Montreal Serai, are characterised by fluidity and reciprocity of ideas and cultures; as exemplified in *The Death of Abbie Hoffman* (1991) and *Baba Jacques*, which is set in a cemetery and "draw[s] out the skeletons of cultural prejudices and political betrayal."[21] *Five or Six Characters in Search of Toronto* features a similar "endgame" configuration. Written for the Desh Pardish Festival (Country in a Foreign Country) in 1993, it portrays the aftermath of a bus crash en route from Montreal to Toronto. These urban polarities—postulated as the origins of Canadian culture and determinants of the official language—are interrogated in the spaceless, timeless zone in which the victims find themselves: perhaps the border between the "two solitudes" should be relocated to Gerrard Street, where the signs are only in Punjabi and Chinese. The six characters, who are travelling to Toronto for very different conferences all bearing the same acronym of H.U.M.P., embody a cross-section of Canadian society: Woman 1 is an intellectual and academic, whose discourse is heavily larded with politically-correct jargon, particularly in respect to "marginalised" minorities:

---

[20] Rahul Varma, *Counter Offence* (Toronto: Playwrights Canada, 1995): 102.
[21] Uma Parameswaran, *op. cit.*: 129.

If you are talking about representation, or rather the appropriation of Black consciousness, we all agree that one of the biggest problems in the discourse of post-modernism, is that it marginalises the black subject ...[22]

The Hockey Jock embodies a stereotypical racist and anti-intellectual. Woman 2 is a Quebec Gen-X activist, who rejects the hippy philosophy that she thinks is exhibited by Woman 1. Woman 3 is an arts council critic, "who has abandoned Canada's messy multiculturalism for the businesslike 'oneness' south of the border" (64). Man 1 represents a pan-fundamentalist, who is carrying a brick to Toronto that he will use to destroy and rebuild religious paradigms. His extremist diatribes sound wholly irrational. Man 2 is an aspiring, paranoid South Asian writer. The dead bus driver functions as a lunatic oracle and a choric musician figure.

The play begins with an introduction by the "Director," who sets the scene, drawing attention to the meta-theatrical nature of the play in which actors and lighting designer are identified as participants, and provoking the audience into an awareness that this is not "mainstream" theatre: "you are part of this alien journey, my friends. So, don't play audience, like you do in most anglo plays in this city, and you with the striped shirt ... yes, you ... sit up straight, there is a bomb under your seat ... this bus takes no slack, my friends ..."[23] Although each character embodies a mindset, the style of delivery and the content may shift to effect another satirical thrust: the play targets a broad range of social injustices and religious bigotries—from the smuggling of cigarettes to the 1994 Racial Minority Conference of the Writers' Union of Canada. Man 1, for example, switches from the accents of a Southern Preacher to those of a Hindu guru or a Muslim fundamentalist. In Scene Two, there is another dislocation: the decapitated bus driver appears as an oracle announcing Time Zero and interpreting Canadian history in terms of the American frontier myth now manifested in the empire of Bill Gates. In Scene Three, the passengers flag down another bus, while debating hitch-hiking techniques. Man 2 accosts Woman 2 with a lengthy diatribe against "established" mainstream Canadian authors, who are fully funded, while ethnic writers are not. He poses the question, "Now why on earth in the midst of all this English/French mess in the ancient ruins of Hochelaga, would a man from India, try to impose his post colonial heritage in a postmodern bus, headed for the west?" (94). The bus actually never reaches Toronto, and the passengers find themselves again in

---

[22] Rana Bose, *Five or Six Characters in Search of Toronto*, *Canadian Theatre Review* 94 (Spring 1998): 65.

[23] *Ibid.*: 65.

Quebec. The bus driver informs each of them that their goals are futile, and that there is no such thing as Toronto. He also wrote the script, and so they have no choice in the matter.

Although the title alludes to Pirandello's play, there is little in the way of philosophical speculation in this work. The characterisations are unstable, but only because they function as mouthpieces for a variety of grievances. As Uma Parameswaran suggests, this is "agitprop, agitational propaganda no holds barred."[24]

South Asian theatre is construed by practitioners such as Sheila James as a political act in a white-dominated profession—a deliberate attempt to fracture the mosaic as constructed by white liberalism. It represents an anti-racist movement, growing "in tandem with First Nations and People of Colour theatre communities,"[25] and embracing an anti-nationalist perspective critical of fundamentalism and communalism."[26] James argues against the commodification of "ethnicity" as exotic entertainment, or as limited polemic:

> Globalization seems to have made our communities and cultures more of a commodity as opposed to a living and changing reality. Multiculturalism swallows up anti-racism, and very often art produced by people of colour becomes a cultural display, rather than critical, complex expression.[27]

Her own play, *A Canadian Monsoon*, was produced by Cahoots Theatre Projects as part of the series "Lift Off!," a new play development series initiated in 1992. Cahoots' mandate is to develop, produce and promote new Canadian theatre, and to present theatrical works "reflective and representative of Canada's diverse cultural mosaic."[28] The company was founded in Toronto in 1986 by Beverly Yhap, a writer who remained its artistic director until 1992, and its productions have included *Big Buck City* (1991) by Native playwright Daniel David Moses, and *Mom, Dad, I'm Living with a White Girl* (1995) by Marty Chan. In 1999, Guillermo Verdecchia assumed the position of artistic director.

---

[24] Uma Parameswaran, *op. cit.*: 131.

[25] Sheila James, "South Asian Women: Creating Theatre of Resilience and Resistance," *Canadian Theatre Review* 94 (Spring 1998): 46.

[26] *Ibid.*

[27] *Ibid.*: 50.

[28] Company Brief.

Autobio-mythography

In his work and life, Verdecchia has continually negotiated "border zones." He was born in Argentina and immigrated to Canada when he was ten. In his monologue, *Fronteras Americanas*, first produced at the Tarragon Theatre, Toronto in 1993, he constructs for himself a dual *persona*: that of the stereotyped "Latino," as perceived in North American popular culture, and that of a "Canadian" trying to deconstruct the stereotype. The play stages an attempt to resist the objectification effected by naming in terms of race and place through the formation of an "oppositional consciousness" which "provide[s] repositories within which the subjugated citizens can either occupy or throw off subjectivities in a process that at once enacts and yet decolonizes the various relations to their real conditions of existence."[29] According to Ann Wilson, "*Fronteras Americanas* is a type of confession, but one which views the individual as a social being and so emphasises individual identity as produced within the context of ideologies."[30]

Verdecchia begins his play with naming. Through the persona of the "Latino" narrator, he aggressively deconstructs the North American stereotype of the "Hispanic":

> Des terms, Latino and Hispanic, are inaccurate because dey lump a whole lot of different people into one category. For example, a Mayan from Guatemala, an eSpaniard from eSpain and a Chicano who speaks no Spanish might all be described, in some circles as Hispanic.[31]

To demonstrate the offensive homogenising effect of stereotyping to his audience, the narrator applies the name "Saxon" to those whose ancestry is "European." Such stereotypes have been reified by a polarisation of "North" and "South" America through the imposition of a psychological and cultural border. The narrator posits a "border zone" in which differences can co-exist—a bridging of differences without denying them. The play opens with a slide on which the words of Simon Bolivar are projected:

> It is impossible to say to which human family we belong. We were all born of one mother America, though our fathers had different origins, and we all

---

[29] Chela Sandoval, "U.S. Third World Feminism: The Theory and Method of Oppositional Consciousness in the Postmodern World," *Genders* 10 (Spring 1991): 10.

[30] Ann Wilson, "Border Crossing: The Technologies of Identity in *Fronteras Americanas*", *Australasian Drama Studies* 29 (October 1996): 8.

[31] Guillermo Verdecchia, *Fronteras Americanas* (Toronto: Coach House, 1993): 27. Further references to this play appear parenthetically in the text.

have differently coloured skins. The dissimilarity is of the greatest significance (19).

It ends with the words of Guillermo Gomez-Pena:

> The West is no longer west. The old binary models have been replaced by a border dialectic of ongoing flux. We now inhabit a social universe in constant motion, a moving cartography with a floating culture and a fluctuating sense of self (70).

The border zone is imagined as a positive space, where the mosaic is acknowledged as unique fragments which resist the imposition of a pattern, but which can accommodate juxtaposition.

Fronteras Americanas also plays out a personal biography, and an imaginative return to the country of origin, patterns which typify "immigrant theatre," according to critic Jane Moss:

> Plot, structure, and linear chronology are often exploded by a traumatised memory of the country of origin that refuses to be forgotten and returns to disrupt the present. The dramatization of memory often displaces and disorients—transporting the spectator/reader towards the playwright's native country, toward the psychic space of memory, or toward the site of myth.[32]

The "Verdecchia" *persona* in the play provides a history lesson on the diaspora of "Latin" peoples in order to construct for himself an historical context, and then recounts his experiences when he went "home" to Argentina. He discovers that he travels as a tourist—an outsider looking in. Only in his dreams can he experience the landscape and the people, and he conjures up the Spanish names of his family's home like a mantra:

> I dream of Mount Aconcagua, of Iguacu, of Ushuaia and condors, of the sierras yellow and green, of bay, orange, quebracho and ombu trees, of running, sweating horses, of café con crema served with little glasses of soda water, of the smell of Particulares 30, of the vineyards of Mendoza, of barrels full of ruby-red vino tinto, of gardens as beautiful as Andalusia in spring (50).

In a dream he has in Argentina, while sleeping in his grandmother's bed in her home in Buenos Aires, the Verdecchia *persona* reclaims the disparate parts of himself which he has lost in the places through which he travelled, but in which he has never fully lived. The play establishes a sense of communal space in terms of the shared experience of the actor

---

[32] Jane Moss, "Multiculturalism and Postmodern Theatre: Staging Quebec's Otherness," in *Mosaic* 29:3 (September 1996): 77.

and the audience, initially extended as an invitation to participate: "Here we are. All together. At long last. Very exciting ... Here we are" (19).

In *Afrika Solo*, African-Canadian playwright Djanet Sears also constructs for herself a sense of self and of place in terms of a story in which she recounts a journey to a "homeland." As the "Afterward" to the published play suggests,

> The longing to tell one's story and the process of telling is symbolically a gesture of longing to recover the past in such a way that one experiences both a sense of reunion and a sense of release.[33]

Like *Fronteras Americanas*, *Afrika Solo* contains a form of "autobiomythography"—the imaginative construction of self through a reclamation of a history as story, memory, and dream. According to Sears, the form follows that of traditional West African theatre—called "Sundiata Form": "a story being told through narrative, music, and dance" (96). The "characters" are Janet/Djanet—"a woman in her mid-twenties, British by birth, Jamaican on her Mother's side, Guyanese on her fathers [sic], presently living in Canada, claiming Canadian citizenship"; Man One—a Missionary, a Priest, and various other characters, also a synthesiser player, singer, and percussionist; and Man Two—Djanet's African lover, also a percussionist. In the premiere production at the Factory Theatre in Toronto, 1987, Djanet performed herself—framing a human subject through representation.

The play opens with a Prologue: the compelling beat of tenor and bass West African drums is joined by voices invoking the country of Senegal, where Djanet is discovered writing a farewell letter to her lover Ben before she leaves Senegal to return "home." Then, in a sudden shift in delivery and style, she addresses the audience in a funky "hip-hop" rhythm, introducing a journey that dispelled stereotypes of Africans as "primitive" jungle-dwellers. As does "Verdecchia," she evokes the richness of the many diverse cultures through a litany of names. The play comprises a series of memories as she awaits her departure flight and resists the recurring summons to pick up the phone and return to Ben's space. Ironically, the airport replicates "Canadian" cultural experiences, with voices in English and French announcing flights and paging travellers, and a "Star Trek" movie playing on the pay television. There are no longer any culturally specific and isolated experiences: borders have become porous. The television images, however, remind her of the ways in which cultural products are constructed to reflect an idealised appearance, and the ways in which her appearance as a

---

[33] bell hooks, quoted in "Afterward," in *Afrika Solo* by Djanet Sears (Toronto: Sister Vision, 1990): 95. Further references to this play appear parenthetically in the text.

"coloured" child in England diverged from that ideal. She never saw herself reflected in the images of her first "homeland," and she is informed of her "aberrations" and then subjected to racist names by her best friend. The only "black people" whom she sees on television are the "savages" or "servants" in the Tarzan movies. When she is told to "go back to where she came from," she cannot determine exactly where that would be, since her mother is from Jamaica and her father from Guyana, and she was born in England. Ironically, in returning to her "roots," she determines that the home she is seeking is the place that she left—Canada. But in the various landscapes she visits, she discovers a rich, varied history that dispels the negative and limiting stereotypes. She even finds a more "authentic" version of her name: "Djanet" is an oasis town in the Sahara and means "paradise" in Arabic. It is also the gateway to the Tassili plateau, the location of ten thousand-year-old rock paintings. She adds a "D" to her name as an indicator of her African origins. When she tries to summon up an "authentic" Canadian song for the Ba Mbuti people in Zaire, all she can think of is "O Canada," which she sings like a gospel ballad to make it more accessible, and discovers the African heartbeat in a Canadian song: "African Canadian. Not coloured, or negro ... Maybe not even black. African Canadian" (88).

Djanet Sears uses no hyphen in her self-designation, perhaps intentionally, since in the last decade the concept of hyphenated identity has become a fractious one: in North America, it may represent a "linguistically neutral and politically correct short-hand for multiculturalism" and "a politics of cultural pluralism," or "the process and ideology of assimilation."[34] However, more recently, and particularly since the debate occasioned by Trinidadian/Canadian Neil Bissoondath's *Selling Illusions: The Cult of Multiculturalism in Canada*, hyphenated identity has been rejected by some members of ethnic minorities as an indicator of otherness and difference:

> Thus the weight of the multicultural hyphen, the pressure of the link to exoticism, can become onerous—and instead of its being an anchoring definition, it can easily become a handy form of estrangement.[35]

According to Jane Moss, "ethnic memory establishes links of continuity with the past—often by returning to the country of origin—without

---

[34] W. M. Verhoeven, "How Hyphenated Can You Get?: A Critique of Pure Ethnicity," in *Mosaic* 29:3 (September 1996): 97.

[35] Neil Bissoondath, *Selling Illusions: The Cult of Multiculturalism in Canada* (Toronto: Penguin, 1994): 116-17.

losing its main orientation toward the present."[36] In some plays this memory may simply be played out as nostalgia, as for example in Dirk McLean's radio play, *The House on Hermitage Road*, published in *Canadian Mosaic II*, a volume edited by Aviva Ravel. McLean, a Trinidadian/Canadian, adapted the play from his autobiographical novel of the same name, set during the time when Trinidad became independent of British control in the 1960s. In effect, the narrator tells a story that is illustrated with the voices from the past—the grandmother and aunt who raised him, his friends and teachers. This is an unconflicted play: the memories are left intact, without any adjustment in light of the narrator's relocation to Toronto. At the end of the play, his arrival is facilitated by the welcoming arms of his mother, and the date stamped as the first day of a happy new life.

In her introduction of *Canadian Mosaic II*, Ravel reifies the ideal of the cultural mosaic of shared experiences, aspirations, and concerns, each contributing to "our survival as a nation."[37] However, the "ethnic" voices in her anthology—Jewish, Irish, French, Ukrainian, Japanese, and Chinese—are not always *of* those communities; for example, "The Golden Door" by W. Ray Towle, which recounts the discrimination against the Japanese in Canada during the Second World War, originated in the friendship of the British/Canadian author with his Japanese neighbours in Alberta; likewise, the play which documents the immigration of the Irish in the nineteenth century, "Like the Sun" by Veralyn Warkentin, is based on the experiences of the playwright's ancestors, who with the English and the Scottish immigrants, have come to constitute the "majority culture" that has subsequently defined the "ethnic other." Similarly, "Beautiful Deeds/De beaux gestes" by Marie-Lynn Hammond examines the "two solitudes" in terms of a French and an English grandmother, and their influence on a granddaughter, who presumably, then, is the quintessential Canadian.

Intercultural Drama

The limitations of both the "two solitudes" and "multicultural" paradigms are evident in three "intercultural" plays—*The Tale of a Mask, Mom, Dad, I'm Living with a White Girl*, and *House of Sacred Cows*. The first takes an iconoclastic view of the mosaic, which is configured as disparate and isolated fragments. *Mom, Dad, I'm Living with a White*

---

[36] Jane Moss, "Multiculturalism and Postmodern Theatre: Staging Quebec's Otherness," in *Mosaic* 29.3 (September 1996):76.

[37] Aviva Ravel, "Editor's Note," in *Canadian Mosaic II: 6 Plays* (Toronto: Simon & Pierre, 1996): 8.

Girl enacts generational conflict in terms of a hybridisation of cultures—the overlaying of Western popular culture on traditional immigrant values. *House of Sacred Cows* dramatises the consequences of an infiltration of an Eastern consciousness into a Western microcosmic community. In these three plays, "interculturalism," as an interpenetration of distinct cultures that retain a deeply-rooted identity, is portrayed respectively as a failure, as a possibility, and as a realised ideal.

Terry Watada's *The Tale of a Mask*, included in *Canadian Mosaic: 6 Plays*, focuses on the cracks in the cultural mosaic, showing how isolation and alienation can result in madness. The play was commissioned by Workman Theatre Projects and premiered in Toronto in 1993.[38] The story of a Japanese woman forced to immigrate to Canada because of the ambition of her husband to be a *karaoke* star is interwoven with a Japanese folktale. The woman in effect assumes the devil-mask of Harumi, the peasant woman who murders a *Samurai* warrior during the time of the feudal wars, because men like him had taken away her husband and son to be killed, and driven her to a state of insanity. Similarly, Aiko expresses her desperate frustration and anger by slaying her husband, her son, and herself. A character in a folktale becomes the mask through which she can act.

Watada skilfully blends Eastern and Western dramatic traditions: the set is based on the *Noh* stage design: a bridge runs across the stage, at a ninety degree angle towards the audience. In the raked elbow of the bridge, a frame acts as an entrance way. The form of the play itself, like Varma's *Counter Offence*, is that of a murder-mystery: it opens from the point of view of the investigating detective, confounded by the tragedy of the deaths of three members of a Japanese family, who have come "all the way from Japan just to end up ... murdered,"[39] and then moves back in time to a happy New Year in Japan, when the family is finally able to spend time together. The play tracks the dissolution of the family once it arrives in Canada. The husband's values are heavily coloured by a Disneyland and Hollywood view of Western culture:

> America is the land of the free. All restrictions are off. Madonna! Star Trek! American Express! If I want to be the world's best *karaoke* singer, I can go for it! (50)

---

[38] In 1991, Watada received the City of Toronto's William Hubbard Race Relations Award, and in 1993, the Ministry of Multiculturalism and Citizenship's Citation for Citizenship for his community work.

[39] Terry Watada, *The Tale of a Mask*, in *Canadian Mosaic: 6 Plays*, ed. Aviva Ravel (Toronto: Simon & Pierre, 1995): 47. Further references to this play appear parenthetically in the text.

He spends his nights in *karaoke* bars hoping to be "discovered," while working days as a kitchen helper in a Japanese restaurant. His wife, Aiko, remains isolated at home because she does not know English, and feels alienated by the "multicultural" environment.

When she does venture out, she is appalled by the rudeness of Canadians and the numbers of *gaijin* in the buses:

> When I came home from Eaton, the bus was packed with foreigners. Chinese, Indian ... a negro sat beside me! Canada is full of dirty immigrants (64).

Even the *nikkei*—the Japanese outside of Japan—she finds unfriendly, like "white ghosts" (66). Her son, Kentaro, is bullied by the Chinese boys at his school, because his English is poor and he is the only Japanese in the school. The detective's assumption that "they're all in the same boat" proves incorrect. Kentaro's response is to fight back, and he then becomes a "discipline problem." As he learns English and forgets Japanese, he grows increasingly shut off from his mother. The Japanese/Canadian community distances itself from the tragedy, accusing other ethnic groups such as Chinese or Korean drug gangs with the crime, in order to save face. The tragedy, then, comes across as the avoidable consequence of Japanese denial of family problems and insanity, and of Canadian assumptions about Japanese self-sufficiency.

Edmonton playwright, Marty Chan, has also written extensively about the Asian/Canadian experience in a popular series for CBC Radio, *The Dim Sum Diary*, which exposes the racial skeletons in his own family closet in a comic way. One of his plays included in *Canadian Mosaic II—Mom, Dad, I'm Living with a White Girl*—satirises the integrative, beneficent Canadian self-concept by foregrounding implicit racism which can operate in both directions—against the white majority, as well as against a Chinese minority. Like *Tale of a Mask*, it works through a juxtaposition of fantasy and reality, the imaginative personas of the characters projected in terms of "masks." *Mom, Dad, I'm Living with a White Girl* was workshopped at Cahoots Theatre Project's new play development programme, "Lift-Off," in 1994, and produced by Cahoots in association with Theatre Passe Muraille in 1995. A revised version was produced in 1998 by Theatre Network at the Roxy Theatre in Edmonton, and published in *Ethnicities: Plays from the New West*.[40]

Issues of "otherness" are internalised in the play, as the protagonist, a young second-generation Chinese male, resists the traditional expecta-

---

[40] Marty Chan, *Mom, Dad, I'm Living with a White Girl*, in *Ethnicities: Plays from the New West*, ed. Anne Nothof (Edmonton: NeWest, 1999). Further references to this play appear parenthetically in the text.

tions of his parents and opts to live with his white girlfriend. His mother reacts strongly against his relationship with a "Gwai mui," whom she considers little better than a prostitute, and his father wants him to learn acupuncture so that he can take over the family business. Mark's psychological defence is to demonise his parents in terms of the B-movie characterisations of the "yellow peril" as a sinister dragon lady, "Yellow Claw," and her henchman who are seeking world domination. Through these Western constructions of personified evil are expressed the racist stereotypes of the majority culture, but also Mark's denial of his own heritage. The play works on two interacting planes, then—the literal and the imaginative—and the rapid changes from one to the other are punctuated by the sound of a gong. In the fabricated world of the B-movie, Mark plays a secret service agent named Agent Banana; his girlfriend, Sally, assumes the identity of his partner, Snow Princess. In these roles they enact the battle of "good versus evil" in the terms constructed by Western society, although in the play Sally also embodies the voice of liberalism shown to be misplaced in its response to perceived racism. For example, Mark's reaction to a filmscript of "The Wrath of the Yellow Claw" that Sally is reviewing as part of her job is that "it's got potential," whereas Sally believes that Asian caricatures and racist jokes are not funny because they "marginalise" the Chinese. Mark responds that Sally herself is guilty of appropriation of voice in speaking on behalf of the Chinese, and that "it's better to have everything in the open" (126). Through such "role reversals," Marty Chan turns the mirror on his audience, so that it will see clearly its own racist assumptions and the inadequacies of a "politically correct" response. But he also expresses his own right to make "ethnic" jokes in his plays and to explore complex issues of ownership. He satirises entrenched and unacknowledged racism and apathy, but also the tendency to exoticise difference. For example, Mark's quest for "independence" as "the right to speak [his] mind. And the apathy to say nothing" is recognised by Sally as being distinctively Canadian (99). On the other hand, Sally's fascination with Chinese culture is conveyed in terms of her knowledge of enough Cantonese to order Chinese food.

In *Mom, Dad, I'm Living with a White Girl*, the tensions between past and present, between a traditional culture that exacts obedience and a Western culture which assumes a freedom of choice, remain unresolved. Mark finally decides to leave his girlfriend, but for a variety of personal and cultural reasons. The *shurken* that he wields in his persona as Agent Banana doing battle with Li Fen, his mother, and Kim Gee, his father, is a double-edged sword, since in erasing them from his life, he also destroys something of himself. Although he resists adherence to his parents' expectations, he also withstands the assimilative pressures of

Canadian society. His final three statements, which have the formality of Chinese aphorisms, acknowledge his "rite of passage":

> MARK: The panda lets go of her cubs.
> *Mark looks to where Kim left.*
> MARK: The butterfly climbs out of its cocoon.
> *Mark finally notices his shadows on the back wall. He turns around and looks to Li Fen.*
> *Then he looks out.*
> MARK: The young tree has deep roots (167).

In *House of Sacred Cows* by Padma Viswanathan, the Indian protagonist, Anand, also finally acknowledges his "deep roots," and returns to visit his origins with his new partner from Canada, January, a young woman engaged in tracking her own paternity. Anand is a university student who comes to live in a co-op in a Western-Canadian city. This co-op functions as a microcosm for Canadian society, with its social and political struggles, its shared ideals and ongoing fractiousness, its conflicts between "haves" and "have-nots." January, the daughter of the founder of the co-op, attempts to reinstate the original ideals of democracy and equality, and learns that even democracy cannot be imposed. Leaf, the single mother who has absorbed the rhetoric of self-realisation, is wholly preoccupied with her own needs. Orwell, like his namesake, is concerned with social equality, but finds himself working for a right-wing Tory government and absorbing some of its business tenets. The twin brothers, Guy and Gui, both of whom claim to be the father of Leaf's child, manifest opposing philosophies of pacificism and aggression. Their French and English names also suggest the "two solitudes" paradigm of Canada, particularly in light of their obsessive and contentious relationship with Leaf, whose name evokes the maple leaf icon of Canadian identity.

This fraught society of individuals is further complicated by the arrival of a foreign element—Anand—accompanied by the ghosts of his dead parents. They refuse to abandon him to the idiosyncrasies of Canadian society, and try to induce him to return to his family obligations and traditions in India, most particularly to arrange for his sister's marriage—against her will—to a designated bridegroom. That Anand's attitudes and assumptions are very much informed by his culture and religion becomes evident in the stories which he tells from the *Mahabharata*—a Hindu epic that recounts the conflict between five brothers and their one hundred cousins—in response to the very Western conundrums he faces in the co-op. The traditions of one culture speak to the conditions of another.

The "sacred cows" in this house are shown to be both negative and positive values: the difficulty lies in distinguishing them. For Anand, they are both repressive and liberating: as embodied in the authority of his parents and their expectations of his behaviour, they are limiting; as embodied in the stories of the *Mahabharata*, they are strengthening and enlightening. Anand's stories and advice interact with the dynamics of the co-op. For the Canadian residents, Anand brings with him the wisdom of the East and an exotic otherness, even though he has very real human limitations, such as his indecisiveness, and prevarication in dealing with pressing family matters. The West infiltrates the East when he returns to India with January for his sister's marriage to the man of her own choosing and for his uncle's funeral. These social and cultural rituals symbolise an end and a beginning. The play concludes on a recasting of the *Mahabharata* in contemporary terms—as the hybridisation of two cultures: January and Anand are seen as characters from the epic as depicted on a postcard that they are sending back to the co-op:

> ANAND: The West holds our hopes but the East holds our inspiration.
> JANUARY: West and East should be seen for what they are now, not what they have been or will be.
> ANAND: We will meet again when we have overtaken the inevitable turning of the globe, if and when we are ever in the same place at the same time.[41]

House of Sacred Cows was workshopped at Teesri Duniya Theatre in Montreal and produced in Edmonton in 1997 by Northern Light Theatre. The intercultural associations across Canada continue to strengthen, as does the imaginative potential for intercultural theatre. The complex configurations of political conflict and social tension, as well as the conflicting desires and responses expressed in ethnic theatre mark it as a meeting ground for cultural differences, a "border zone" for self-assertion, negotiation, and invention.

Works Cited

Berry, J.W. and J.A. Lapone, eds. *Ethnicity and Culture in Canada: The Research Landscape* (Toronto: U of Toronto P, 1994).

Binning, Sadhu. "Vancouver Sath: South Asian Canadian Theatre in Vancouver," *Canadian Theatre Review* 94 (Spring 1998): 14-17.

Bissoondath, Neil. *Selling Illusions: The Cult of Multiculturalism in Canada* (Toronto: Penguin, 1994).

---

[41] Padma Viswanathan, *House of Sacred Cows*, in *Ethnicities: Plays from the New West*, ed. Anne Nothof (Edmonton: NeWest, 1999): 90.

Bose, Rana. *Five or Six Characters in Search of Toronto, Canadian Theatre Review* 94 (Spring 1998): 64-74.

Chan, Marty. *Mom, Dad, I'm Living with a White Girl*, in *Ethnicities: Plays from the New West*, ed. Anne Nothof (Edmonton: NeWest, 1999): 93-167.

Giroux, A. Henry. "Living Dangerously: Identity Politics and the New Cultural Racism: Towards a Critical Pedagogy of Representation," *Cultural Studies* 7.1 (1993): 1-17.

Granatstein, J.L. *Who Killed Canadian History?* (Toronto: HarperPerennial, 1998).

Hooks, Bell, quoted in "Afterward," *Afrika Solo* by Djanet Sears (Toronto: Sister Vision, 1990): 95.

James, Sheila. "South Asian Women: Creating Theatre of Resilience and Resistance," *Canadian Theatre Review* 94 (Spring 1998): 45-50.

Karpinski, Eva. "Multicultural 'Gift(s)': Immigrant Women's Life Writing and the Politics of Anthologised Difference," in *Literary Pluralities* (Peterborough: Broadview, 1998): 111-19.

McDonough, Ken. "Cultural Appropriation or Cross-Cultural Dialogue?" <http://www.aei.ca/~tduniya/alt.theatre/cultural_appropriation.htm>

McDonough, Ken. "In their own words," *alt.theatre* 1.3 (June 1999): 8-9.

McLean, Dirk. *The House on Hermitage Road*, in *Canadian Mosaic II. 6 Plays*, ed. Aviva Ravel (Toronto: Simon & Pierre, 1996).

Mojab, Shahrzud. "Introduction: Anti-Racism and Anti-Sexism: from the Legislative Halls to Theatre Houses," in *Counter Offence* (Toronto: Playwrights Canada 1995): 9-12.

Moss, Jane. "Multiculturalism and Postmodern Theatre: Staging Quebec's Otherness," *Mosaic* 29:3 (September 1996): 75-96.

Padolsky, Enoch. "Ethnicity and Race: Canadian Minority Writing at the Crossroads," in *Literary Pluralities*, ed. Christl Verduyn (Peterborough: Broadview, 1998): 19-31.

Parameswaran, Uma. "Protest for a Better Future: South Asian Canadian Theatre's March to the Centre," in *Contemporary Issues in Canadian Drama*, ed. Per Brask (Winnipeg: Blizzard, 1995): 116-35.

Peerbaye, Soraya. "A Subtle Politic," *Canadian Theatre Review* 94 (Spring 1998): 6-8.

Ravel, Aviva. "Editor's Note," in *Canadian Mosaic II: 6 Plays* (Toronto: Simon & Pierre, 1996): 7-8.

Sandoval, Chela. "U.S. Third World Feminism: The Theory and Method of Oppositional Consciousness in the Postmodern World," *Genders* 10 (Spring 1991): 2-11.

Sears, Djanet. *Afrika Solo* (Toronto: Sister Vision, 1990).

Siemerling, Winfried. "Writing Ethnicity: Introduction," *Essays in Canadian Writing* 57 (Winter 1995): 1-32.

Tepperman, Shelley. "At the Teesri Duniya," <http://www.aei.ca/~tduniya/alt.theatre/at_teesri_duniya.htm>.

Varma, Rahul. *No Man's Land*, in *Canadian Mosaic: 6 Plays*, ed. Aviva Ravel (Toronto: Simon & Pierre, 1995): 164-212.
—— *Counter Offence* (Toronto: Playwrights Canada, 1995).
—— "Contributing to Canadian Theatre," in *Canadian Theatre Review* 94 (Spring 1998): 25-7.
—— "Diversity: Its Promise and its Potential," <http://www.aei.ca/~tduniya/alt.theatre/diversity.htm>.
—— "Mission and History," <http://www.aei.ca/~tduniya/backstage.htm>.
Verdecchia, Guillermo. *Fronteras Americanas* (Toronto: Coach House, 1993).
Verhoeven, W.M. "How Hyphenated Can You Get?: A Critique of Pure Ethnicity," *Mosaic* 29:3 (Sept. 1996): 97-116.
Viswanathan, Padma. *House of Sacred Cows*, in *Ethnicities: Plays from the New West*, ed. Anne Nothof (Edmonton: NeWest, 1999): 11-91.
Watada, Terry. *The Tale of a Mask*, in *Canadian Mosaic: 6 Plays*, ed. Aviva Ravel (Toronto: Simon & Pierre, 1995): 44-85.
Wilson, Ann. "Border Crossing: The Technologies of Identity in *Fronteras Americanas*," *Australasian Drama Studies* 29 (October 1996): 7-15.

Drew Hayden Taylor's Dramatic Career

ALBERT-REINER GLAAP

Heinrich-Heine-Universität, Düsseldorf

The Author and His Work—An Overview

Drew Hayden Taylor was born in 1962 on what is now, politically correctly, called Curve Lake First Nations Reserve. His mother was Ojibway, his father white, but Drew never knew him. He was raised on the Reserve and lived there with his mother and his mother's family till the age of eighteen, when he went to college in Toronto. There everybody seemed to have "this preconceived idea of how every Indian looked and acted."[1] Drew Hayden Taylor has often been mistaken for someone of British descent—because of his blue eyes and light brown hair. In an article, first published in 1991, he comments on his outward appearance:

> I have both white and red blood in me, I guess that makes me pink. I am a "Pink" man ... My pinkness is constantly being pointed out to me over and over and over again ... "You *don't* look Indian?," "You are not Indian, are you?," "Really?!" I got questions like this from both white and Native people. For a while I debated having my status card tattooed on my forehead.[2]

The name "Taylor" comes from his mother's family, a Native family. Many people on Drew's reserve are named Taylor. He does not speak his Ojibway language, but understands the gist of it. Sometimes, he incorporates Ojibway words and expressions into his text, but ninety-five per cent of what he has written is in English.

Drew graduated from Seneca College with a diploma in Radio and Television Broadcasting. Thereafter, he worked as a Native Affairs reporter for CBC Radio and wrote articles on Native arts and culture for several Canadian periodicals. With his background in journalism, he

---

[1] Drew Hayden Taylor, "Pretty like a White Boy: The Adventures of a Blue-eyed Ojibway," in: *Toronto at Dreamer's Rock*, ed. Albert-Reiner Glaap (Berlin: Cornelsen, 1995): 53.

[2] *Ibid.*: 53-54.

seemed to be the right candidate when in 1988 Native Earth Performing Arts received a grant for a Playwright-In-Residence programme from the Ontario Government. In retrospect, this job paved the way for Drew Hayden Taylor's later career as a writer, as he himself points out:

> I am ashamed to say, I took the job for purely monetary reasons. The number of plays I had seen you could count on my fingers. Theatre held no attraction for me ... until I was bitten by the bug during rehearsals and opening night. I was then asked to write a play and I further discovered the wonders of live theatre. I *didn't* choose theatre. Theatre chose me.[3]

Drew has never been formally educated in a university literature and drama department. His playwriting is free of academic taint:

> When I write a play, all I want to do is create some interesting characters involved in an interesting plot line that takes the audience on a journey, either emotional or intellectual ... characters involved in what has been described as a theatrical discussion—characters involved with an issue, involving very little action.[4]

All his plays are concerned with the Native community. Taylor basically tells stories about what happened to him, to his mother, to his family, and how it affected these people. He explores what being "Native" means to different people. But he also wants to show that Native people, except for cultural and language differences, are the same as all people. Whereas other writers are very culture-specific, Drew Hayden Taylor is often referred to as a cross-cultural writer. "Being half Native and half white," he himself says, "I write for both Native and non-Native audiences," and "I believe good theatre and hopefully good writing should be cross-cultural and not dependent on ghettoising stories for particular audiences."[5]

Another distinctive feature of his plays and—as Taylor believes—of most Native theatre can be found in the "non-confrontational" nature of such works, in the sense that they do not necessarily move through conflict or aggressive behaviour. Taylor accounts for this by saying that "many Native tribes existed in small family groupings through most of the year" and that "any conflict or confrontation within that group would threaten, even endanger the harmony and existence of that community."[6]

---

[3] Albert-Reiner Glaap, "Margo Kane, Daniel David Moses, Yvette Nolan, Drew Hayden Taylor. Four Native Playwrights from Canada in Interview," in *Anglistik. Mitteilungen des Verbandes deutscher Anglisten* 7.1 (März 1996): 10.

[4] *Ibid.*: 11.

[5] *Ibid.*: 13.

[6] *Ibid.*: 15-16.

Native theatre can, to a great extent, be traced back to the oral culture of the First Nations Peoples, more specifically to the art of traditional story telling in Native communities. The stories told by an Elder function as tales on different levels. They may be of historical relevance, contain elements of comedy or relate to contemporary issues. They may educate and entertain. The narrative techniques used for such stories have had a great impact on Native authors who write for the theatre. Drew Hayden Taylor's work is steadily gaining in popularity because he chooses to tell his stories through the stage, and even more so because of the endemic humour which pervades his plays.

In the theatre, humour often allows for moments of levity in the audience, and as regards Native plays there exist hardly any without a dose of humour. In the past, more than in our day and age, humour was the only means of making life bearable or escaping the pain and the sorrow with which the Native people were constantly being confronted. A play in which Drew Hayden Taylor explores the concept of comedy is *Someday*, whereas *Toronto at Dreamer's Rock* comes across as a serious play with the odd funny point in it. Real comedy, to Taylor, is born of pain, and *Someday* provides a good example of the fine balance of tragedy-drama in comedy. In an interview Taylor tried to account for the function of humour in his plays:

> It's been my experience that the majority of Native plays deal with the hardships and tragedies inflicted on Native people in the last 500 years. As a cathartic process, most Native playwrights are working out these demons through theatre. I, on the other hand, like to celebrate the characteristic that made it possible to survive—our humour. I want to honour the Native sense of humour.[7]

What essentially characterises Native humour remains difficult to define. Native humour ranges from the biting and vicious to the gritty and the self-deprecating. One must turn to a particular play and discover the function of humour in a specific context, that of *The Bootlegger Blues*, for instance. Drew Hayden Taylor recalls a compliment received from an elderly Native who had seen this play, which is a comedy about a fifty-eight-year-old woman who "finds herself in possession of 143 cases of beer she has to bootleg to buy an organ for the church."

> He told me the play made him homesick. Meanwhile, at the same play, I overheard a white woman saying that she thought the play was funny and clever but if a white person had written it, he would have been killed.[8]

---

[7] *Ibid.*: 13.

[8] *Ibid.*: 19.

Since 1988, Drew Hayden Taylor has become a prolific and extremely popular Native playwright. His best known plays include the following:

Toronto at Dreamer's Rock (Fifth House, 1990)
   Premiered on the Sheshegwaning Reserve, Manitoulin Island, Ontario, 1989
Toronto@Dreamer'sRock.com (not published)
   Premiere: De-Ba-Jeh-Mu-Jig Theatre, Manitoulin, 1999
Education is Our Right (Fifth House, 1990)
   Premiered: East Main, Quebec, De-Ba-Jeh-Mu-Jig Theatre, Manitoulin, 1990
Someday (Fifth House, 1993)
   Premiere: De-Ba-Jeh-Mu-Jig Theatre, Manitoulin, 1991
Only Drunks and Children Tell the Truth (Talonbooks, 1998)
   Premiere: Native Earth Performing Arts, Toronto, 1996
400 Kilometers (not published)
   Premiere: Festival Theatre, Wolfville, 1999
The Bootlegger Blues (Fifth House, 1991)
   Premiere: De-Ba-Jeh-Mu-Jig Theatre, Manitoulin, Ontario, 1990
The Baby Blues (Talonbooks, 1999)
   Premiere: Arbour Theatre, Peterborough, 1995
The Bus'gem Blues (in the offing)
alterNatives (Talonbooks, 2000)
   Premiere: Port Dover's Lighthouse Theatre and Bluewater Theatre, 1999
The Boy in the Treehouse (Vancouver: Talonbooks, 2000)
   Premiere: Manitoba Theatre for Young Audiences, 1998

Running the gamut of these titles reveals that, when writing a new play, Drew Hayden Taylor often likes to continue from where he left off in a previous one. *Toronto@Dreamer'sRock.com* forms a sequel to his earlier play *Toronto at Dreamer's Rock*, written ten years before. The word "Blues" occurs in the titles of three of his plays. *The Bootlegger Blues* corresponds to part one in what is finally to be a four-part series, *The Blues Quartet*. The second instalment is called *The Baby Blues*. In the foreword to the edition of the play, the author writes:

> The next to make its way onto the stage will be *The Bus'gem Blues*. The fourth ... who knows? All four are designed as a way of applauding the humour and merriment that exists in today's Native community.[9]

Three other Taylor plays constitute a Native trilogy. The first two instalments—*Someday* and *Only Drunks and Children Tell the Truth*—took place primarily in the rural area of the Otter Lake First Nation. In *400 Kilometers*, the place of action has been moved to the white world

---

[9] Drew Hayden Taylor, *The Baby Blues* (Burnaby, B.C.: Talonbooks, 1999): 7 (Foreword).

Kilometers, the place of action has been moved to the white world of commerce and power.

The mere titles of some of the works listed above indicate that many of Taylor's plays centre around young people, adolescents or children. Other titles contain implicit meanings: Toronto is to be understood in the Indian sense of the word—meeting(-place); the ambiguity of *alterNatives* derives from the spelling. At the centre of this play, there are three Native people who act together in a group which they call the "alterNatives." They question current social, cultural and political issues, and suggest alternative solutions. *400 Kilometers* raises the question "away from where?," which is answered in the very play.

Most revealing are also the ideas that went into the making of some of Drew Hayden Taylor's plays. *Someday* was originally a short story that was expanded upon request by various artistic directors. The original idea came from meetings with adopted Indians who were trying to find out their identity and where they came from. The play deals with the so-called scoop-up operation of the 1960s, a government programme that planned to take Native children and give them up for adoption. *The Bootlegger Blues* came from a real incident on Taylor's Reserve, *The Baby Blues* from the author's idea to explore a minor character from an earlier play. In *Toronto at Dreamer's Rock*, he wanted to investigate the common ground of and the differences between three Ojibway adolescents of the same age: what does being Native mean to different people? *Education is Our Right* was written "less than a year after Pierre Cadieux, then the Federal Minister of Indian and Northern Affairs [at the end of the 1980s], announced a cap on post-secondary education for Native students ..."[10] All of the vignettes in Taylor's plays are based on real incidents.

With reference to interviews conducted with Drew Hayden Taylor during the past eight years, the following part of this chapter will focus on the author's development as a playwright. The fact that some of his plays form sequels to others which he previously wrote helps to account for the various stages in this development, i.e. to point out how specific topics and issues have been taken up, carried on, emphasised and modified, or replaced by new ones.

---

[10] Drew Hayden Taylor, *Toronto at Dreamer's Rock* and *Education is Our Right. Two One-Act Plays* (Saskatoon: Fifth House Publishers, 1990): 78 (Production Notes).

Toronto at Dreamer's Rock and Its Sequel *Toronto@Dreamer'sRock.com*

Toronto at Dreamer's Rock movingly portrays a teenage boy who oscillates between the traditions of his people and the lure and demands of a technological future. The play is set at the top of Dreamer's Rock, a sacred place where Native adolescents would go on vision quests. Sixteen-year-old Rusty, an Ojibway youth of our time, climbs to the top and meets two other young men—both also sixteen years old and of the Ojibway tribe. Keesic, however, is from four hundred years in the past and Michael from a hundred years in the future. The three experience a "toronto" on the Rock, a meeting in which they find a common language and discover more similarities than differences. The differences are due to their respective eras. Keesic lives in the time before the North American continent was settled by the Europeans. He cannot believe how the centuries have changed his people. He cannot cope with "man-made rock," i.e. the cement factory and the roads. Michael realises that many of the cultural events have been reduced to mere memories, that no Native language exists any more. Rusty's encounter with Keesic and Michael renders him aware of the fact that he does not really know what it means to be an Indian. The three young men, through their vision quest, finally gain insight into what binds them together, and understand that they must change their lifestyles. In the end, Rusty is not in possession of all the answers, but he has a path or direction to follow. The journey to Dreamer's Rock acts as a catalyst.

For nearly five years Drew had toyed with the idea of writing a sequel to *Toronto at Dreamer's Rock* by coming back to the characters a dozen or so years later:

> I was thinking of coming back to Keesic when he is a medicine man in his village, but everybody is dying of smallpox. And he has no way of fighting it. Rusty—I want him to have a relapse and be an alcoholic and the whole thing to take place while he's strapped to a bed. I don't know yet if I'm going to write the sequel. It's just an idea. I haven't found Michael's story yet.[11]

The main idea for writing the sequel consisted in examining the issues in the original version from a more adult perspective. Ten years after *Toronto at Dreamer's Rock*, the new play made its first appearance on stage, its title being *Toronto@Dreamer'sRock.com*. We encounter the characters twenty years later. Rusty is in a detox centre near Dreamer's

---

[11] Drew Hayden Taylor, *Toronto at Dreamer's Rock. Teacher's Book,* ed. Albert-Reiner Glaap (Berlin: Cornelsen, 1996): 10 (Foreword).

Rock. He has married, has a child, but has become addicted to alcohol. Michael and Keesic have changed too. Michael is confronted with a world in which the environment has been destroyed. He blames the previous generation for not having taken measures against the environmental deterioration. Keesic appears powerless in the face of the disease that befell his entire village. They are all suffering from great problems in life. But Michael and Keesic find themselves again in the position to think of ways and means of helping Rusty.

Toronto@Dreamer'sRock.com takes the audience on a time travel into a future in which things do not turn out to be as happy as the ending of the original may have suggested. Whereas *Toronto at Dreamer's Rock* is set on a high site, Dreamer's Rock, its sequel and a much darker play, takes place in the shadow of that rock and in a detox centre ward. Whereas, at the end of the original play, Rusty has found a path which may help him to preserve the values of his ancestors and at the same time be prepared for a technological future, *Toronto@Dreamer'sRock.com* depicts a possible outcome of our future, if we do not learn to be vigilant. The humour of the earlier play, however, has been retained. This applies particularly to Rusty, who even in his deplorable situation still resorts to humour as the best cure.

The sequel represents a self-contained play, but for those audiences who have seen the original version, the production of *Toronto@Dreamer'sRock.com* will, as an additional effect, make it easy for them to re-discover the three characters after their twenty-year journeys. They will find out that the second play does not just embody a continuation of the first. The similarities and differences of the two plays are reflected in their titles. When spoken, these sound similar; the written version, however, points to the implicit differences.

Someday, *Only Drunks and Children Tell the Truth* and *400 Kilometers*—A Trilogy

Someday

In the late 1950s, the eldest daughter of Anne Wabung, Grace, was taken from her mother at the age of seven months by the white *Children's Aid* and given for adoption. At the time, Grace's father had been working in the army—a fact that no one was allowed to find out. Barb, Grace's sister, is sceptical and a little jealous. Everyone, however, feels quite excited as Grace finally arrives—after thirty-five years of silence. She looks pretty, successful and well-groomed, but appears to be out of context, asks inappropriate questions and wants to know the real reasons for which she was taken into care. The unexplained whereabouts of her father do not seem to be a plausible reason. She senses that she no longer belongs here and she wants to leave immediately. Being asked when she will come back Grace—or Jane, as she is now known—replies "Oh, someday, I suppose."

Although *Someday* is not based on real people, it is a true story. "The Scoop Up," a policy instituted by the government in the 1950s and 1960s, urged people in Canada to adopt Native children. In Saskatchewan the programme was called AIM (Adopt Indian Metis); there was a backlog of Native children in the system. The central idea was to take children out of their culture so that they would become part and parcel of the white Canadian culture. The inspiration to thematise this part of Native history came from people whom Taylor met when he was travelling across the country—children of the 1960s who, in the meantime, had become adults trying to find out who they were and where they came from. In *Someday*, Taylor examines the conflicts between Native and Western values. The play reflects the frustration still felt by many Natives today, and it focuses on the anger of both the families that had their children kidnapped in the 1960s and the children who want to find out why they were taken away. The issue is not new, particularly for the Native community. *Someday* offers a sensitive, honest and humorous approach to the scoop-up programme and its impact on the whole family. It conveys emotions which—though presented here in a Native context—on another level have universal appeal and can be related to by all.

Only Drunks and Children Tell the Truth

> RODNEY: When do you think you'll be back?
> JANICE: Oh, someday, I suppose. Goodbye, Rodney. And Merry Christmas.
> *Janice exits, carefully picking her way along.*[12]

This ending will linger in the minds of those who have read *Someday* or seen a production of the play—an ambiguous ending open to various potential suppositions and conclusions. Following a suggestion made by Larry Lewis, the director of *Someday*, Drew Hayden Taylor wrote another play on this very topic, which he had never intended to do. But when Lewis asked him if he thought that Janice/Grace would ever return, Taylor began to wonder if Janice did not only walk out, but

---

[12] Drew Hayden Taylor, *Someday* (Saskatoon: Fifth House Publishers, 1993): 80.

Drew Hayden Taylor 225

actually walked out on the family.[13] The new play, *Only Drunks and Children Tell the Truth*, is more than just a sequel to the earlier piece. It constitutes a play in its own right, although a spin-off from *Someday*. A shift in focus has occurred, away from the mother and the family to Janice/Grace. "I felt Janice wasn't as sympathetic in *Someday* as she could have been. It was time for Janice to have her day and face her demons" (12), writes Taylor in his introduction to *Only Drunks and Children Tell the Truth*. Taylor started thinking about a new play on which to hang the story of the previous one: "What could or would bring Janice back after all she has gone through?" Then it dawned on him: "Maybe a funeral or something. Maybe the Mother dies" (11). And the new play begins with Barb coming to Toronto, where her sister is now living in an apartment, to tell Janice that her mother has died. Janice has become a successful lawyer. Barb, however, has stayed with close family ties; yet, in her heart of hearts, she has not fully been enjoying life, because their mother, Anne, never stopped being obsessed with her missing daughter. Barb forces Janice to face her mother's death: "She's your Mother. Our Mother ... Put some flowers down, say good-bye" (22). The other two in this four-character play, Tonto and Rodney, join in: "It's the proper thing to do," and "You really should, Grace" (23). Janice, however, thinks that she cannot go back: "I knew her for one hour, that was all" (23).

The play is centred around the juxtaposition of the two sisters: Janice/Grace, the successful lawyer, who somehow understands her little sister who grew up without her, and Barb, who stayed on the Reserve closely connected to her community. Taylor's humour, which also functions as an indispensable element in this play, is expressed by Rodney and Tonto, the sage. In the second act, the four go back to Otter Lake Reserve, to the old lived-in house, which sets Janice's mind going about the mother she never knew and about her leaving the Reserve on Christmas Day. Standing at the mother's grave in the final scene of the play Janice articulates her emotional pain. She addresses her mother:

> I'm sorry I left the way I did. It must have been a horrible Christmas for you. But you must understand I didn't walk out on you. I walked out on me. To everybody I was Grace, but to me I'm Janice. I don't know if I can ever be the Grace you wanted, or the Grace Barb wants (109).

Only Drunks and Children Tell the Truth deals with conflicts within a family which has disintegrated not through the fault of its members, but

---

[13] Drew Hayden Taylor, *Only Drunks and Children Tell the Truth,* (Burnaby, B.C.: Talonbooks, 1998): 11. Further references to this play appear parenthetically in the text.

under external pressures. But more than anything else, this play—in Lee Maracle's words—is about:

> The conflict between Western and Native values played out through the sisters, free of the usual didactic preaching [and] the conflict between Western ideology and Native wisdom, played out through the interaction between Tonto and Grace.[14]

400 Kilometers

The final play of the trilogy is concerned with building bridges between white and First Nations worlds, with reconciliation, which ultimately turns out to be indispensable. Together with her boyfriend Tonto, Janice is living on a reserve in Nova Scotia, 400 kilometres away from Halifax, where her white, adoptive parents live. When she finds out that she is pregnant, she retreats home to Halifax to let her parents know. These are middle-class people, originally from England. The audience is confronted with the chatter and banter of these well-meaning but misguided people. When Tonto butts into the conversation, he is the only one who does not yet know that Janice is pregnant. At once, there is a marked contrast between the formal middle-class people and the cheerful, but eccentric Tonto, whose different reactions to the question as to where the baby should be raised lead to the adoptive mother throwing him out because he has blamed her for denying Jane her heritage.

On another level, her dead biological mother is haunting Jane's dreams. She tells her what it was like to give birth to Grace. Every now and then, she reappears in dream sequences and drifts away. Where Tonto and Janice are actually going to live is left open.

The idea for this play came again from the outside, as it were. Two Planks and a Passion Theatre talked Drew Hayden Taylor into writing it. At stake in *400 Kilometers* is not only Jane's identity, but also the (future) identity of her yet unborn child. Jane is torn between Tonto, who has also become her spiritual guide, and her Native mother, Anne, on the one hand and the expectations of her adoptive parents on the other. The only solution, it seems, will be to try to build bridges, i.e. through confrontation gently aspire to reconciliation. But this cannot be achieved by programmes and speeches. There are hardly any speeches in Taylor's plays, but some very funny and pithy one-liners which reflect a quintessential element of Native life and storytelling humour.

---

[14] Lee Maracle, "Foreword," in *Only Drunks and Children Tell the Truth* by Drew Hayden Taylor (Burnaby, B.C.: Talonbooks, 1998): 7.

alterNatives

alterNatives, one of Drew Hayden Taylor's more recent plays, does, once again, not exclusively address Native issues. It also functions as a funny social satire on views, attitudes and trends that were popular in the 1990s. Taylor pokes fun at vegetarians, Natives, liberals in one fell swoop. As always with this author, the play has a story line, because—as he keeps emphasising—people relate to people, not to issues, and it contains a good dose of that multifaceted humour which constitutes a hallmark of his work. Rumour has it that when Taylor was asked if he was a vegetarian, his answer was "Never! I believe all vegetarians should be cooked and eaten."[15]

The story of *alterNatives* is quickly told. Twenty-four-year-old Angel, an Ojibway Indian, shares an apartment with Colleen, a thirty-five-year-old Jewish professor of Native Studies. They are preparing for their first dinner party. Two of their guests, Michelle and Dale—both non-Natives and friends of Colleen's—are to meet Angel. The other invited couple are Bobby and Yvonne, two of Angel's "pals" from his past on the Reserve. Somehow, they all embody "alternative" people. Colleen wants Angel to write the Great First Nations Novel, which he, however, takes a dim view of. A belligerent Bobby discloses Angel's earlier relationship with Yvonne and mocks Colleen's fascination for Native Studies. Michelle, the vegetarian veterinarian, has an aversion to meat, and Dale, the computer programmer and a reluctant vegetarian, cannot stay away from the moose Colleen is cooking.

Needless to say, all this yields material for controversy and disputes, which are, however, not resolved on stage. Rather, the audience is left to draw its own conclusions: the most general of these would be that human beings cannot just be subcategorised into "goodies and baddies," and another that they recognise themselves in this or that character on stage. At any rate, they will chuckle about what they see happening, be it because they can easily identify with what the characters are saying and doing, be it that they are happy about not being in the character's shoes, or be it that they just have fun. Here Taylor's affinity with playwrights like Alan Ayckbourn or Neil Simon—often maintained by theatre critics—seems a valid observation.

The play, moreover, raises Native issues too. The history of First Nations People and the "appropriation of voice" are both under discussion. Yvonne, who objects to Colleen trying to talk Angel into writing the Great First Nations Novel, argues:

---

[15] In an interview with Patricia Black in September 1998.

> So you, as a white University Native Lit professor, want our Angel, a Native writer, to write specifically about Native people and the Native community. Sounds a bit like ghettoising ... Do you think Jewish people should only write about Jewish things?[16]

And Bobby, later on, points out what he thinks makes a Native a Native.

> Just because someone had a great-great-grand-mother that was boffed by some Indian a century ago, doesn't give them the right to call themselves Native or share our experiences, or claim heritage. According to your scientists, we, the Indigenous of this land, have been roaming this continent for 15,000 to 100,000 years. And that experience, those origins, make a Native a Native (118).

The Boy in the Treehouse

This is another play about a vision quest. In *Toronto at Dreamer's Rock*, Rusty goes up to a rock; in this play, Simon climbs into his treehouse. A treehouse refers to a wooden structure built in the branches of a tree for children to play in. But in this instance, it symbolises a refuge, a retreat from the adult world. Simon wants to be alone and go on a vision quest up there. Yet, this twelve-year-old boy is not just waiting for a vision to come that might show him the way into his future. Through a fasting ritual, which he read about, he wants to find his identity. His late mother having been Ojibway and his father being white, he meanders aimlessly in between and wants to reconnect with his deceased mother to find out about the Native branch of his family. Three characters in the play represent different attitudes towards the vision quest. Simon's father takes it for a video game, calls it "a Native thing, huh"[17] and does not understand why his son should be starving himself up in a tree. Reports about unusual noises in the tree make a cop come over to investigate if any monkeys have escaped from the zoo. He warns Simon that he could get dizzy and "fall out of that thing" and "they'll blame your father. Maybe take him to court" (40). There is also the neighbour who tells the father that this is "just a phase that [Simon] is going through" (28).

To the father the vision quest is something beyond comprehension, the cop merely discharges the duties of his office and the neighbour takes it for what it is to him—part of a transitory phase in the boy's life. It is a girl, new to the neighbourhood, by the name of Patty, who comes

---

[16] Drew Hayden Taylor, *alterNatives* (Burnaby, B.C.: Talonbooks, 2000): 104. Further references to this play appear parenthetically in the text.

[17] Drew Hayden Taylor, *The Boy in the Treehouse* and *Girl Who Loved Her Horses* (Vancouver: Talonbooks, 2000): 11. Further references to this play appear parenthetically in the text.

to his treehouse, borrows his book and asks him numerous questions. Simon thinks that the book will answer them all.

The quintessence of *The Boy in the Treehouse*, however, is that sitting at the top of the tree and starving oneself does not equate a vision quest, it has nothing to do with one's Native identity. When Simon hums a few bars of the song that his mother used to sing when it was time for him to go to bed, Patty joins in and finishes it. It is not a "Native" song, as Simon believed it was, but a hymn that everybody knows—"Amazing Grace." This releases Simon's pent up frustration. He comes down from the tree and is then ready for future quests.

Simon's concept of the vision quest as an Indian ritual is based on book-learning. Patty tells him that he must "find somebody who knows what they [the books]'re talking about. It says that white people have even been known to go on these Vision Quests" (75). Patty kept pestering Simon for answers to her many questions. But he was not Native enough to be able to answer them. In the end, when he asks his father for his Native mom's middle name and hears that it was Patricia, this meaningful name makes him conclude the play with the sentence. "That's what I thought" (81). Finally, he seems to realise that he, and Natives in general, do have the tradition of the deceased and the guidance of the living ones to turn to when they are uncertain about which route to take.

Simon's process of learning what "being Native" means can give insights into the fabric of Native rituals, habits and life-styles—to young audiences, but also generally to all those, wherever they may live, who still hang on to old *clichéd* images of Indians. *The Boy in the Treehouse* can help to break the—all too often—romanticised stereotypes of the First Nations Peoples.

Bootlegger, *Baby Blues* and *Bus'gem Blues*

Two of the plays in what Taylor calls *The Blues Quartet* have so far not been released. *Bus'gem Blues*—Bus'gem being an Ojibway word for boyfriend/girlfriend—is in the offing, details about the fourth play remain unknown. But the end product will be a four-part comedy series. In the aforementioned introduction to the edition of *The Baby Blues*, Drew Hayden Taylor summarises what he had in mind when planning this series.

> After many decades of seeing the media highlight the image of the "tragic" or "stoic" Indian, I felt Native people, and consequently non-Native People, were being given a raw deal. I know far more laughing first Nations people

than depressed ones. I felt this disproportionate representation had to be addressed.[18]

Elements of humour are part and parcel of all Taylor comedies. *The Blues Quartet*, however, is as a whole designed to applaud "the humour ... that exists in today's Native community" (7). Each of the plays stands alone, but all of them contain strong farcical elements. If farce deals with everyday characters in unusual situations, if—in other words—the laughter triggered off by farce is rooted in a particular situation that the characters find themselves in, *The Bootlegger Blues* and *The Baby Blues* can be called Native versions of British farces in the Ayckbourn line.

The Bootlegger Blues

The Bootlegger Blues is set on a Reserve. Martha, a fifty-eight-year-old woman, finds herself stuck with one hundred and forty-three cases of beer which she must bootleg for an organ in the church. Her son Andrew, nicknamed Blue, takes a dim view of all this. He is learning to be a constable on the Reserve. On another level, she must face the romantic love affairs of her two children. Andrew has fallen for a young woman he thinks is his cousin, and his sister Marianne, David's wife, has taken a liking to Noble, a fancy dancer at the pow-wow. The play is a typical example of a situation comedy with a lot of movement, a set divided into three areas—Martha's kitchen, the pow-wow grounds and Blue's bedroom, where the beer cases were located. The areas—in the original production—were painted yellow, green and blue, respectively.

The Baby Blues

Here the setting is a typical pow-wow including a campground and food court. In the centre of this stands Noble (aged 38) who refuses to grow up. At the pow-wow the sins of his youth force him to re-evaluate his life. The characters in the play belong to three different generations. The men, all careless vagrants, are juxtaposed with their former women partners. Values like heritage, family and identity are not thought of as being important in life anymore, they have lost their meanings and have given way to cultural relativism. Under the veneer of a sex farce, *The Baby Blues* is a sharp satirical discussion of universal problems in everyday life "whether it be a mother dealing with a rebellious daughter, or a good-looking young man on the hustle, or a man who refuses to acknowledge the passing years" (8).

---

[18] Drew Hayden Taylor, *The Baby Blues* (Burnaby, B.C.: Talonbooks, 1999): 7 (Foreword). Further references to this play appear parenthetically in the text.

The first two plays of *The Blues Quartet* feature many of the characteristic elements of Drew Hayden Taylor's stage plays; first and foremost, however, both works encapsulate his specific kind of humour, which is rooted in the original sense of humour endemic to Native story-telling.

Instead of a Summary: Drew Hayden Taylor's Credo

In Native communities, history and education were usually passed down through story-telling. Drew Hayden Taylor's plays are, at heart, stories about life and people on the Reserve. But they are written in such a way that people, regardless of their heritage, can relate to the characters they see on stage. One component of this playwright's work lies in the "common ground" that human beings, Native and non-Native people, share. Taylor finds it interesting to watch a mixed audience watch one of his comedies, because some of the jokes are specifically aimed at a Native audience. Humour which used to be almost the only way of making life bearable, is now, in Taylor's eyes, indicative of the merriment in today's Native community. He writes two types of plays: "heavily plotted ones where the characters revolve around what is happening in the stories," and on the other hand "pieces that have the characters involved in what has been described as a theatrical discussion—a group of characters involved with an issue involving very little action."[19]

In his introduction to the annotated edition of *Toronto at Dreamer's Rock*, Drew Hayden Taylor writes about himself as a playwright:

> It's always difficult to separate oneself from one's work and one's life, since for an artist, they are usually intertwined on many levels. I am a product of my community and my work is a product of me ... if nothing else. Perhaps I can, through my work, open a window or door into that community for the rest of the world."[20]

Works Cited

Glaap, Albert-Reiner. "Margo Kane, Daniel David Moses, Yvette Nolan, Drew Hayden Taylor. Four Native Playwrights from Canada in Interview," *Anglistik. Mitteilungen des Verbandes deutscher Anglisten* 7.1 (März 1996): 5-25.

Maracle, Lee. "Foreword," in *Only Drunks and Children Tell the Truth* by Drew Hayden Taylor (Burnaby, B.C.: Talonbooks, 1998): 5–9.

---

[19] Glaap, *op. cit.*: 11.
[20] Drew Hayden Taylor, *Toronto at Dreamer's Rock*, ed. Albert-Reiner Glaap (Berlin: Cornelsen, 1995): 5.

Taylor, Drew Hayden. *Toronto at Dreamer's Rock* and *Education is Our Right. Two One-Act Plays* (Saskatoon: Fifth House Publishers, 1990).

——— *The Bootlegger Blues* (Saskatoon: Fifth House Publishers, 1991).

——— *Someday* (Saskatoon: Fifth House Publishers, 1993).

——— "Pretty like a White Boy: The Adventures of a Blue-eyed Ojibway," in *Toronto at Dreamer's Rock*, ed. Albert-Reiner Glaap (Berlin: Cornelsen, 1995): 53-57.

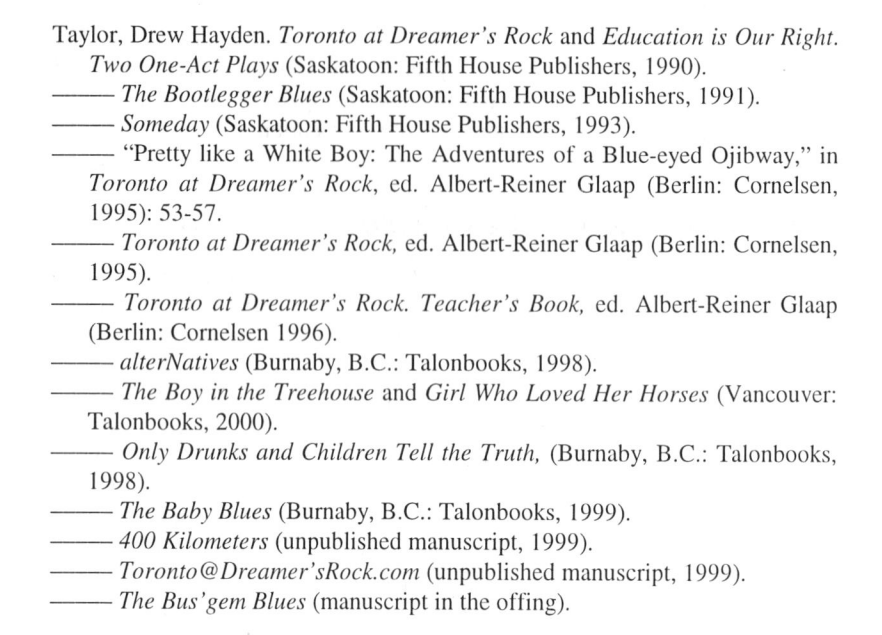

——— *Toronto at Dreamer's Rock,* ed. Albert-Reiner Glaap (Berlin: Cornelsen, 1995).

——— *Toronto at Dreamer's Rock. Teacher's Book,* ed. Albert-Reiner Glaap (Berlin: Cornelsen 1996).

——— *alterNatives* (Burnaby, B.C.: Talonbooks, 1998).

——— *The Boy in the Treehouse* and *Girl Who Loved Her Horses* (Vancouver: Talonbooks, 2000).

——— *Only Drunks and Children Tell the Truth,* (Burnaby, B.C.: Talonbooks, 1998).

——— *The Baby Blues* (Burnaby, B.C.: Talonbooks, 1999).

——— *400 Kilometers* (unpublished manuscript, 1999).

——— *Toronto@Dreamer'sRock.com* (unpublished manuscript, 1999).

——— *The Bus'gem Blues* (manuscript in the offing).

Making Relations Visible in Native Canadian Performance

Robert Appleford

University of Alberta, Edmonton

> What is seen by the mainstream is only the tip of the cultural iceberg, its totality submerged in a cloak of silence. The surface reflection is your deception, and it is we who are watching you.[1]

Native Canadian performance[2]—whether it resembles Western-style theatre, an indigenous oral tradition or performance art—serves to keep audiences, regardless of ethnicity, off-balance. It often mingles stereotype and parody with earnestness and recognisably "traditional" content, thus challenging non-Native audience members—many of whom, one suspects, have bought their tickets expecting "real" stories told by "real" Natives on stage—to confront their own expectations of what Native theatre can encompass. One way to view this impasse is to accept the failure of non-Native audiences to understand what is being performed. The non-Native spectator may always feel that the authentic story of Native experience is somehow consciously withheld from view. The failure to communicate, in this context, can be seen as the inevitable consequence of intercultural communication. While this failure is persistent, it also masks an idealism which presupposes a perfect relationship between the Native performer and his or her "natural" audience. This idealism is not just perpetuated by non-Native audiences. Many Native artists see the very concept of a non-Native audience as an inherent impossibility given the oppositional nature of Native discourse. Native American performance artist Jimmie Durham writes:

---

[1] Edward Poitras, quoted in *Indian Territory*, ed. Matthew Teitelbaum (Saskatoon: Mendel Art Gallery, 1989): 24.

[2] The term "aboriginal" is more accurate here, since it encompasses performance by all peoples with First Nations ancestry. But since this collection includes discussion of Australian Aboriginal performance, I shall use the more restrictive term "Native" to avoid confusion.

> ... all those [Indian artists] who do remember and see cannot effectively say what they see because there is no podium, and no audience except a designated audience. The motive for the designation is cancellation; designated, the audience becomes passive, a nonaudience.[3]

From this perspective, the desire on the part of Native playwrights to replace stereotype with more heterogeneous and responsible images is met by the audience's desire—equally ardent—to reify these fresh constructs and thereby rob them of their oppositional power.

However, I think that this acceptance of intercultural miscommunication is non-productive. Instead, it proves more useful to explore the ways in which Native performance is a contingent construction, one which foregrounds its own premises, the better to subject them to scrutiny. In her illuminating article on N. Scott Momaday, Elaine Jahner argues that it is the very breakdown of understanding between Native North American artists and their non-Native audiences that can yield valuable insight into how the act of intercultural communication operates:

> The stage has been set so that characters from different traditions can speak to each other, asking questions that made no sense in earlier philosophical settings. The characters may still talk past each other, but such failures to communicate can now become the focus of the exchange as scholars address why the failures occur and what such failures may tell us about how to refine our means of intercultural communication.[4]

What Native performance does, I shall argue, is to make relations within this exchange visible rather than obscure. By relations, I mean the relations between Native images, their manipulation, and their reception. Native theatrical performance—as represented by the work of artists such as Daniel David Moses, Margo Kane and Floyd Favel Starr—seeks to denaturalise Native images on stage, and it is useful to realise that Native theatre does not simply introduce "new and improved" images and tropes for consumption by non-Native audiences. Rather, Native theatre challenges non-Native audiences to understand how images of Natives circulate within cultural discourse. By making the relations between performer, story and audience visible, Native playwrights and performance artists articulate a sense of self that is at once multivalent

---

[3] Jimmie Durham & Jean Fisher, "The Ground Has Been Covered," *Artforum International* (Summer 1988): 101-2.

[4] Elaine Jahner, "Metalanguages," in *Narrative Chance: Postmodern Discourse on Native American Indian Literatures*, ed. Gerald Vizenor (Alberquerque: U New Mexico P, 1989): 167.

and grounded, both destabilising passive definitions of identity and championing active subjectivity.

The problem that presents itself to Native artists is how to construct workable identities without their being rendered into inflexible templates through the act of spectatorship. Many so-called marginal groups (feminist, gay, non-Eurocentric etc.) have been confronted with this same problem, and one recurrent strategy of oppositional discourse has been to adopt anti-realistic modes of representation. However, in the case of Native performance, it is clear that the use of anti-realistic elements does sometimes not suffice to counteract the reifying power of the spectator's gaze. For example, the tendency to treat Native drama as a kind of docudrama occurs frequently in the critical responses to the work of Tomson Highway, considered by many to be the first breakthrough Native playwright in Canada. Despite Highway's use of self-consciously theatrical devices like gigantic rubberised female body parts in *Dry Lips Oughta Move to Kapuskasing*, critics sometimes choose to read the work as reflecting a verisimilar world. Roberta Imboden affirms that "what appears as wild exaggeration on the printed page [of *Dry Lips*] is a faithful representation of the tragedy of reservation life."[5] Similarly, Ray Conlogue, in a 1989 review of the premiere performance of *Dry Lips*, claims that Highway's use of the "medicines" (Conlogue's term) of laughter and dreams "are part of Native thought."[6] While I would not seek to prove that Highway's—or any other Native playwright's—work is somehow *un*-Native, I would question the process through which fictive constructs are automatically championed as "faithful representations" of Native "life" and "thought." I believe—following critics like Susan Bennett and Alan Filewod—[7] that any study of Native artistic expression must begin at the sites of reception, in this case, with the desires and ideologies that influence how non-Natives perceive Native theatre. By foregrounding these desires, it becomes impossible to reify the constructs of theatre as self-authenticating truth and to immerse oneself uncritically in the enacted worlds.

---

[5] Roberta Imboden, "On the Road with Tomson Highway's Blues Harmonica in 'Dry Lips Oughta Move to Kapuskasing,'" *Canadian Literature* 144 (Spring 1995): 117.

[6] Ray Conlogue, "An Emotionally Riveting Dry Lips," *The Globe and Mail* (24 April 1989): A17. I am indebted to Alan Filewod for his emphasis on the problematic nature of Conlogue's review; see his article "Receiving Aboriginality: Tomson Highway and the Crisis of Cultural Authenticity," *Theatre Journal* 46.3 (Oct 1994): 368.

[7] See Alan Filewod, *op. cit.*: 365-374; Susan Bennett, "Who Speaks?: Representations of Native Women in Some Canadian Plays," *Canadian Journal of Drama and Theatre* 1.2 (1991): 13-25.

Many Native artists seek to champion the hybridity of Native discourse as a source of discursive power, eluding the essentialising tendencies of the cultural marketplace. The play *Moonlodge*, by Saulteaux/Cree playwright Margo Kane, explores the complex role of stereotype in the construction of a hybrid Native self.[8] The play dramatises the life story of Agnes, a young Native woman removed at a young age from her family and brought up in a series of white foster homes, who seeks to know her Native heritage. Because of her alienation from her cultural origins, she cannot simply adopt a ready-made authentic ethnicity, but must investigate and reject several different mainstream conceptions of "Indianness," conceptions that would be seen by the sympathetic spectator as patently ridiculous. As a Brownie, Agnes learns her "first Indian song"—E. Pauline Johnson's "Land Of The Silver Birch"—which she enacts with great comic effect. Agnes's parody of Hollywood *clichés* is relatively gentle in its satire, in that Kane does not emphasise the implication of the mainstream audience in the process of stereotyping. Agnes's performance of the song "Running Bear" invites the audience to laugh along with her*:*

AGNES: Little White Dove was her name
such a lovely sight to see
All the women were either subservient or sexy. I preferred sexy! [Is dancing seductively flaunting and pouting.] All the women always followed their men ten paces behind.
But their tribes fought with each other
so their love could never be
Hollywood version. Lots of leg. [Chorus line kicks.]
Running Bear loved Little White Dove
with a love as big as the sky
Fringed mini-skirts. Lots of skin. [More chorus line kicks.]
Running Bear loved Little White Dove
with a love that couldn't die
Savage tragedy! [Melodramatic pose. Dives onto floor and does frog stroke.]
He couldn't swim the raging river
'Cause the river was too wide
[*Continues swimming various strokes.*] Because his name was Running Bear and not Swimming Bear!
He couldn't reach Little White Dove
waiting on the other side
[*She shades her eyes.*] And Indians always looked like this because if they looked like this [*Covers them*] they couldn't see anything.

---

[8] Premiered 1990, Native Earth Performing Arts, Toronto.

> In the moonlight he could see her
> blowing kisses across the waves
> her heart was beating faster
> waiting there for her brave

[*Much shimmy with breasts and shoulders.*] Primitive, primal, savage, supernatural love.[9]

While the glimpses of a Native subjectivity are fleeting in this play, there are attempts made to challenge the unreal with the real. In *Moonlodge*, Agnes is threatened both physically and spiritually by the dominant cultural systems, but her ultimate reward lies in an identity grounded in the concept of Native community. The Native elder Millie tells Agnes that "your medicine will come from your own people" (290), a suggestion that while Agnes's personality is composed of many parts, the site of ethnicity becomes not the individual but the Native community, and more specifically the community of Native women. This provides Agnes with an actual soil in which to grow her own sense of self. Kane maps the struggle of the Native subject to excavate the site of ethnicity. What the Native subject must contend with are the persistent signs of the "Indian" which fix themselves at the expense of the bodies which are forced to enact them.

While Native playwrights invite the audience to participate in the exorcism of stereotype and cheer on the struggle towards Native selfhood, they also—often simultaneously—demonstrate for the audience that there are experiences that cannot be apprehended, that not every story can or should be told. This reminder serves to confront the audience with its own desire for an authenticity sanctioned by the Native subject. When Agnes stumbles upon Native dancers performing traditional dances at a powwow, her representation of the dances is clumsy and ends up "becoming quite comic" in an earlier draft of the play.[10] While the audience is included in the process of ridiculing stereotype, it is denied a mimetic enactment of Agnes's engagement with authentic Native culture. Similarly, when Agnes is taken away from her natural parents in the Social Services car at the start of the play, she mimes a silent scream which the audience is not permitted to hear (279). We as audience members are outside observers of the car and her suffering; her pain eludes the scene/seen. In some cases, the conspicuous and therefore frustrating absence of the authentic Native self in Native art is not due to

---

[9] Margo Kane, *Moonlodge*, in *An Anthology of Canadian Native Literature Written in English*. ed. Daniel David Moses and Terry Goldie (Toronto: Oxford UP, 1992): 283. Further references to this play appear parenthetically in the text.

[10] Margo Kane, *Moonlodge. Performance File.* (U of Guelph Native Earth Performing Arts Archives, 1990): 21.

the artist's masterly control. Anishnaabe performance artist Rebecca Belmore's piece *For My Kokum* consists of a wooden box wrapped in furs and decorated with floral beadwork, containing a tape machine playing a recording of Belmore's grandmother speaking Anishnaabe. At the time of completing the piece, the artist could not understand this language.[11] Belmore's highly personal tribute to her grandmother also expresses the artist's feeling of unwitting distance from her own roots. Unable to interpret this sign of difference, she chooses to represent her cultural heritage as both cherished birthright and untranslatable absence.

While Kane's play deftly combines invitation and interdiction, other playwrights are more aggressive in their interrogation of formal constraints on subjectivity. One playwright who challenges the limiting definitions of Native identity is Daniel David Moses, a Toronto-based writer of Delaware heritage who grew up on the Six Nations lands near Brantford, Ontario. Concerned with exploring the shifting signifiers of Native identity, he rejects the notion of an authentic core of Native discourse:

> The idea of presenting something that someone will decide is authentically "Native" seems absurd to me. I can remember asking an interviewer, because I wanted to try and understand what they meant by authentic and Native, "Does that mean that Margaret Atwood is authentically Caucasian?"[12]

Moses also sees Native identity as existing in a definitional space created by desires both internal and external to Native consciousness. For example, he describes why he feels Native peoples have a heightened ecological awareness:

> I think Native people have a sense of larger responsibility to the planet, whether we come at it just from the idea that Native traditions honour the environment as a mother, or whether we come at it from the idea that *we are looked at as people who should have those ideas and therefore we're allowed to have them*.[13]

There is a heightened awareness in his work of the gaze of the mainstream culture, and how this gaze often desires a "real" Native presence

---

[11] Charlotte Townsend-Gault, "Having Voices and Using Them: First Nations Artists and 'Native Art,'" *Arts Magazine* (February 1991): 67.

[12] Robert Appleford, "The Desire to Crunch Bone: Daniel David Moses and the 'True-Real' Indian," *Canadian Theatre Review* 77 (Winter 1993): 21.

[13] Daniel David Moses and Terry Goldie, "Introduction," in *An Anthology of Canadian Native Literature Written in English*. eds. Daniel David Moses and Terry Goldie (Toronto: Oxford UP, 1992): xii. Emphasis added.

to be represented for its view. In his play *Almighty Voice and His Wife*,[14] Moses tells the story of the nineteenth-century Saskatchewan Cree folk hero Almighty Voice, whose initial poaching of a settler's cow leads to the killing of a Mountie and an eventual stand-off involving Almighty Voice, two of his companions, and one hundred officers and civilian volunteers.

The first act of the play focuses on the relationship between the Cree man and his young wife White Girl, retelling their courtship on the One Arrow Reserve and their subsequent flight from the law after the killing of the Mountie. It ends with Almighty Voice's grim vision of his wife and his child as he lies dying, cornered in a poplar grove:

> *The drum heartbeats in the night. The moon is low in the sky, pulsing. Almighty Voice lies by the dead fire, leg badly wounded. The spectral tipi appears and the drum goes silent. Inside the tipi are White Girl and her baby, mother and child, a destination. Almighty Voice rises and uses his Winchester as a crutch to come to the tipi. White Girl comes out and shows him the baby and the baby cries. The moon turns white. Almighty Voice dies.*[15]

Moses has called this first act "a poetic but straightforward narrative"[16] in terms of representation; the audience is able to lose itself in the tragic-romantic martyrdom narrative with little reminder of its own presence or of the narrative's fictionality. However, the playwright has indicated that the direction of the second act was determined by his need to shift the narrative away from Almighty Voice in order to see "who the people who were pursuing him were."[17] The play's second act makes it clear that Almighty Voice is not simply being tracked by angry Mounties and vigilantes: he is also being tracked by the non-Native spectator, and for very different reasons. The pursuit of Almighty Voice by his audience symbolises the pursuit of the "almighty Native voice," the authentic Native self, and Moses' play emphasises the destructive nature of such a pursuit.

---

[14] Premiered 1991, Great Canadian Theatre Company, Ottawa. Portions of this commentary on *Almighty Voice and His Wife* first appeared in my article "The Desire to Crunch Bone: Daniel David Moses and the 'True-Real' Indian," *Canadian Theatre Review* 77 (Winter 1993): 21-26.

[15] Daniel David Moses, *Almighty Voice and His Wife: A Play in Two Acts* (Stratford, Ont.: Williams-Wallace Publishers, 1992): 52. Further references to this play appear parenthetically in the text.

[16] Daniel David Moses, "How My Ghosts Got Pale Faces," in *Speaking for the Generations: Native Writers on Native Writing*, ed. Simon Ortiz (Tucson: U Arizona P, 1998): 141.

[17] Robert Appleford, *op. cit.*: 24.

Moses presents us in the second act with a grotesque mixture of vaudeville and minstrel show, with both White Girl (now playing the part of the Interlocutor) and Almighty Voice (now Almighty *Ghost*) wearing whiteface and performing a bizarre mixture of racial slurs, melodramatic *clichés*, and never-ending puns. The juxtaposition of Almighty Ghost/Voice's confused but earnest description of his own death (enacted in its "pure" form in Act I) with the wisecracking commentary of the Interlocutor/White Girl re-presents the tragic event as black comedy:

Ghost: All I remember—
Interlocutor: Come on Ghost, this won't make you the toast of the town.
Ghost: My leg was gone.
Interlocutor: Come on, Chief, be a friend.
Ghost: It was! I used a branch from a sapling.
Interlocutor: Be a pal, Chief.
Ghost: No, it was my gun for a crutch.
Interlocutor: This is a bit much for this early in the proceedings.
...
Ghost: My legs were gone.
Interlocutor: Are we talking vacation?
Ghost: Like they were already dead. I must have screamed.
Interlocutor: Maybe we're talking shopping.
Ghost: But my throat was too dry.
Interlocutor: Can I get you something?
Ghost: There was no sound in my mouth.
Interlocutor: Quite the come down for Almighty Vocal Cords.
Ghost: I couldn't sing my song.
Interlocutor: Oh lord, talented, too!
Ghost: My death song. I crawled out of the pit.
Interlocutor: And we're not talking orchestra pits out here in the sticks (58-60).

The device of the minstrel/vaudeville show—with its racist agenda and its self-consciousness of playing to an audience—serves to emphasise the means of cultural production of Native images. Ironies abound here. The minstrel show, historically allowing white performers strategically to enact the African American as object of fear and ridicule, becomes a spectacle of Native performers enacting their own objectification. And while they are hidden behind the masks of "white-face," the characters of Almighty Voice and his wife White Girl are in fact painfully exposed as what they are: Native subjects struggling to subvert the voyeurism of the audience in a spectacle of knowledge withheld. The savvy Interlocutor lets her rookie "end man" Almighty Ghost know exactly what commodity the voyeuristic marketplace demands:

These fine, kind folks want to know the truth, the amazing details and circumstance behind your savagely beautiful appearance. They also want to be entertained and enlightened and maybe a tiny bit thrilled, just a goose of frightened. They want to laugh and cry. They want to know the facts. And it's up to you and me to try and lie that convincingly (57).

Moses appears highly cognisant of the fact that every signifying act the Native actor performs for an audience runs the danger of being perceived as natural rather than acts of theatrical representation. Terry Goldie reminds us of this risk: "If in the theatre, the voice, the human sound actually heard, is from an indigene throat, how much more difficult for the audience to recognize the distance between 'voice' and referent voice."[18] By injecting an historical narrative with self-conscious and anti-illusionistic elements, Moses prevents the audience from fixing its gaze. He is able to create what Terry Eagleton (in his discussion of Barthes) calls a "'healthy' sign, one which does not try to palm itself off as 'natural' but which, in the very moment of conveying a meaning, communicates something of its own relative status as well."[19]

Part of Moses' design is to throw the audience off-balance by juxtaposing supposedly pure and authentic Native tropes with clearly parodic inversions of these tropes. In this way, he denies both Native and non-Native spectators the comfort of the real. For example, when Almighty Ghost ironically repeats the phrase most associated with Chief Dan George, "My heart soars!" (69), the issue of textual purity becomes truly complex: the audience's perception that Moses is parodying George's authentic poetic mysticism must be tempered with the observation that the phrase "My heart soars like a hawk" (while adopted and developed by George in his writing) was, as Goldie points out, first spoken by the actor in the film *Little Big Man*, whose text and direction were determined almost entirely by white artists.[20] Moses lampoons not George's sentiment but the ignorance of the realities of cultural hegemony, a hegemony that helped to produce the text and make it famous.

Like Moses' work, Saskatchewan Cree playwright Floyd Favel Starr's play *Lady of Silence*[21] also attempts to make the relation between audience and performance visible. In this play, the standard counters brought to play in detective stories are present: a murder, four likely suspects, and a tireless detective. A white woman, Jane, is found beaten

---

[18] Terry Goldie, *Fear and Temptation: Images of the Indigene in Canadian, Australian, and New Zealand Literatures* (Kingston: McGill-Queen's UP, 1989): 138.

[19] Terry Eagleton, *Literary Theory* (Minneapolis: U of Minneapolis P, 1983): 135.

[20] Terry Goldie, *op. cit.*: 189.

[21] Premiered 1993, Native Earth Performing Arts, Toronto.

and stabbed to death outside a seedy "Indian" bar. The four suspects—Village, Sheila, Ruth and Lisa—each possess ample motive for the crime. Village is the jilted Native lover of Jane, while the three Native women each have been used and betrayed by Village in his pursuit of her. Clues, such as a charm bracelet with the engraved name "Nestor" left at the scene of the crime and traces of blood on Village, suggest that a speedy solution to the puzzle is possible through the piecing-together of material and circumstantial evidence by the Native detective Belmondo. However, from its opening scene, the play flouts logical causality. Two of the characters (Lisa and Sheila) confess to the murder with mutually exclusive retellings of the event, and the charm bracelet bears the name of an imaginary lover of Sheila. While the play parodies the standard signs of detective narrative, there are both real crimes and equally real culprits, not in bourgeois drawing rooms or seedy flophouses, but in the realm of identity politics.

Lady of Silence focuses primarily on the self-hatred suffered by Native peoples living in an environment where the ideals of beauty and worth are determined by non-Native dominant culture. Village, the jilted lover, is masterful in his manipulation of dominant tropes of aboriginality, in turn strutting the stage, mouthing the animalistic similes of Native male potency, and begging victim status due to his genetic inferiority.[22] He incarnates the image of Other-directed Native identity, constantly pursuing the non-Native perfection that the murdered Jane comes to represent. For the three Native women, Jane, too, embodies a symbol of the promised land, but one which serves to remind them of their perpetual exile:

> SHEILA: She was born among the marble ruins of a dead civilisation, chalk white and slender as a yew tree. Her blue eyes sparkled mediterranean blue, azure. Lips blew kisses soft as pussy willows. Against her whiteness our hate pounded its teeth and nails, until there was only blood and shreds of skin. Our screams died to hoarse whispers in our dazed oppression (24).

Just as the narrative in traditional detective form profluently reveals the hidden relationship between cause and effect in a positivist sense, Belmondo's investigation in the play mirrors a racial/cultural search for cause and effect in the sphere of identity. In this case, the crime under investigation, the murder of Jane, is of secondary interest to the audience, who needs to "know" the causes of Native violence and self-

---

[22] Floyd Favel Starr, *Lady of Silence* (unpublished playscript, U of Guelph: Native Earth Performing Arts Archives, 1993): 7-8. Further references to this play appear parenthetically in the text.

Native Canadian Performance 243

abuse which have resulted in the effect of murder. And because the crime was interracial, a white woman murdered by Natives, the discovery of guilt and motive proves, from a non-Native perspective, vital to either the reestablishment of good intercultural relations or the reintrenchment of cultural hegemony. Thus, there is an explicit awareness in this play of the human need to witness the process through which order emerges out of chaos. Impatient with the slowness of his investigation, Belmondo reminds his suspects that "the clock is ticking, and our audience waits. It's a confession they want, it's a confession we must find" (36).

The play is framed as a particular performance of a ceremony which all the characters are doomed to repeat nightly, as Belmondo warns Village: "until this cancerous crime is burned from the cells of your body you will remain here under the harsh light where no secret stays hidden for long, the curtain will not drop" (6). This ceremonial frame is reinforced by the play's staging, where Belmondo, as detective/priest, officiates over the proceedings from a raised altar on which are placed ritual objects such as roses, a silver chalice and a silver bell. By presenting the investigation story in the heightened style of ritualised action and speech, Favel accomplishes two very important things. First, he reveals the submerged identity of the standard detective form *as ceremony*, in that in the detective story group solidarity and communal health are restored by the expiation of both the sacrificial victim and the scapegoat murderer. But perhaps in a more important sense, the representation of the investigation in ritual terms illuminates the goal of the performance, namely a reorientation of how identity is constructed. Ritual, in its basic sense, involves not the narration of fact, but rather the narration of recombination, where the reordering of cultural elements effects a change in the subject's consciousness, thereby restoring harmony on both an individual and communal level. Despite the confessions of both Sheila and Lisa to the murder of Jane, it is Village, as the principal actor in this ceremony, who must "confess his crime" of racial self-hatred using the death of Jane as a catalyst (Belmondo admonishes him that he will be incapable of love until he does [7]).

What becomes apparent throughout the play is the role Jane plays as a signifier of Native longing and self-loathing. Her corpse is never shown on stage, only signified by a white dress and a bouquet of red roses. She is eulogised in a hymn sung during a procession of the characters who bear her relics at the start of the play:

Lady of silences/Calm and distressed
Torn and most whole/rose of memory
rose of forgetfulness/exhausted and lifegiving

worried reposeful/the single rose is now the garden
where all loves end/where all loves end (5).

This union of opposites reflects Jane's symbolic importance in the minds of the characters, but also reinforces her unreality as a murder victim. She is not a body murdered but a body desired, and her murder is a kind of "blessed fall" which holds the promise of Native redemption. Between the standard trope of detective fiction and its subversion, absolute order versus absolute disorder, Favel constructs a morality tale about Native self-image that partakes of both, but legitimates neither.

Such narratives of absence/presence reveal the inherent slipperiness of the Native subject. The interplay between interdiction and invitation, between self and non-self, remains vital to the project of cultural rehabilitation. No simple authenticity which can be reconstituted as public—and therefore subject to the dominant's hegemony—is represented unproblematically. What becomes important is the positionality of the Native subject rather than the cultural elements that the subject chooses to embrace. In the cat-and-mouse game enacted perpetually between performer and audience, the Native subject invites identification while demonstrating its often fraught consequences.

The performer's confrontation with the audience on this score can be quite unequivocal. In Moses' play *Kyotopolis*,[23] the central focus revolves around the search by a non-Native character for a reified Native identity. The character called Ricky Raccoon describes in a taunting monologue directed at the audience this desire for presence by using the metaphor of cannibalism:

> And you don't want to know how how how we feel now, do you? You don't want to know what we think, do you? We aren't Indian enough, are we? Or are we, like, too Indian for you to chew? Are you hungry enough now finally to eat anything? Are you? Are you?[24]

Similarly, the Native American troupe Spiderwoman Theater's collective work *Winnetou's Snake Oil Show From Wigwam City*[25] attacks the mainstream's voracious hunger for easily digestible Native values and images by using the medicine show form to foreground the commercialism of cultural and spiritual theft. However, this play also articulates the paradox of Native discourse, where the survival of Native cultural expression is in part predicated upon its suitability for co-option. It is with great irony, anger and frustration that the actress Gloria Miguel

---

[23] Premiered 1992, The Drama Centre, Toronto.

[24] Daniel David Moses, *Kyotopolis* (Unpublished playscript, 1992): 63.

[25] Premiered 1989, Theater for the New City, New York.

turns to the audience and says "for only through your eyes am I remembered."[26] Although the audience's gaze can be reflected back upon itself, it can never be permanently evaded.

Jean Fisher argues that this strategy in Native art of foregrounding the audience's gaze and reflecting it back onto itself is more inherently radical than returning the gaze, which she believes simply reaffirms the non-Native audience's dominant status:

> If the purpose of the undead Indian of colonialism is to secure the self-identity of the onlooker, the shock of his real presence and the possibility that he may indeed be watching and listening disarms the voyeuristic gaze and denies it its structuring power.[27]

This gaze and the desire that determines what it apprehends seems far from uniform. There exist a myriad ways of constructing any audience's point(s) of view. There is no stable position in this field of perception, neither in the audience nor on stage. The Native performer moves discursively between shadow and substance, constantly on the verge of disappearing from view, while the audience shifts from insider to outsider according to the ideological moment. This instability, far from being lamented by the Native self-performer, is used as a source of strength. "For me," writes Gayatri Spivak, "the question 'who should speak?' is less crucial than 'who will listen?'"[28] By investigating "who will listen," Native artists ensure that their multivalence as speaking subjects is both protected and valued.

Works Cited

Appleford, Robert. "The Desire to Crunch Bone: Daniel David Moses and the 'True-Real' Indian," *Canadian Theatre Review* 77 (Winter 1993): 21-26.

Bennett, Susan. "Who Speaks?: Representations of Native Women in Some Canadian Plays," *Canadian Journal of Drama and Theatre* 1.2 (1991): 13-25.

Conlogue, Ray. "An Emotionally Riveting Dry Lips," *Globe and Mail* (24 April 1989): A17.

Durham, Jimmie & Jean Fisher. "The Ground Has Been Covered," *Artforum International* (Summer 1988): 101-2.

---

[26] Spiderwoman Theater, *Winnetou's Snake Oil Show From Wigwam City*, *Canadian Theatre Review* 68 (Fall 1991): 63.

[27] Jean Fisher, "In Search of the 'Inauthentic': Disturbing Signs in Contemporary Native American Art," *Art Journal* (Fall 1992): 48-49.

[28] Gayatri Chakravorty Spivak and Sneja Gunew, "Questions of Multi-Culturalism," in *The Post-Colonial Critic*, ed. Sarah Harasym (New York: Routledge, Chapman and Hall, 1990): 60.

Eagleton, Terry. *Literary Theory* (Minneapolis: U of Minneapolis P, 1983).
Filewod, Alan. "Receiving Aboriginality: Tomson Highway and the Crisis of Cultural Authenticity," *Theatre Journal* 46.3 (October 1994): 365-74.
Fisher, Jean. "In Search of the 'Inauthentic': Disturbing Signs in Contemporary Native American Art," *Art Journal* (Fall 1992): 44-50.
Goldie, Terry. *Fear and Temptation: Images of the Indigene in Canadian, Australian, and New Zealand Literatures* (Kingston: McGill-Queen's UP, 1989).
Imboden, Roberta. "On the Road with Tomson Highway's Blues Harmonica in 'Dry Lips Oughta Move to Kapuskasing,'" *Canadian Literature* 144 (Spring 1995): 113-25.
Jahner, Elaine. "Metalanguages," in *Narrative Chance: Postmodern Discourse on Native American Indian Literatures*, ed. Gerald Vizenor (Alberquerque: U New Mexico P, 1989): 155-85.
Kane, Margo. *Moonlodge*, in *Moses and Goldie* (1998): 326-40.
―――― *Moonlodge. Performance File* (U of Guelph: Native Earth Performing Arts Archives, 1990).
Moses, Daniel David and Terry Goldie, eds. *An Anthology of Canadian Native Literature Written in English* (Toronto: Oxford UP, 1998).
Moses, Daniel David. "How My Ghosts Got Pale Faces," in *Speaking for the Generations: Native Writers on Native Writing*, ed. Simon Ortiz (Tucson: U Arizona P, 1998): 119-47.
―――― *Almighty Voice and His Wife: A Play in Two Acts* (Stratford, Ont.: Williams-Wallace Publishers, 1992).
―――― *Kyotopolis* (Unpublished playscript, 1992).
Poitras, Edward. Quoted in *Indian Territory*, ed. Matthew Teitelbaum (Saskatoon: Mendel Art Gallery, 1989): 24.
Spiderwoman Theater. *Winnetou's Snake Oil Show From Wigwam City*, *Canadian Theatre Review* 68 (Fall 1991): 56-63.
Spivak, Gayatri Chakravorty & Sneja Gunew. "Questions of Multi-Culturalism," in *The Post-Colonial Critic*, ed. Sarah Harasym (New York: Routledge, Chapman and Hall, 1990).
Starr, Floyd Favel. *Lady of Silence*, (unpublished playscript, U of Guelph: Native Earth Performings Arts Archives, 1993).

Translators, Traitors, Mistresses, and Whores: Monique Mojica and the Mothers of the Métis Nations[1]

RIC KNOWLES

University of Guelph

Monique Mojica's play *Princess Pocahontas and the Blue Spots* has been well and widely discussed in criticism, though rarely at very great length. The play has been variously cited and analysed in parts of articles and chapters in which it is dealt with as one among several examples of postcolonial metatheatre or hybridity, cultural cross dressing, canonical revisionism, dialogic monologue, the use of the trickster/clown figure, or transformational performative dramaturgy.[2] What has

---

[1] I would like to thank Patricia Tersigni for gathering an immense body of research material for me, without which I could not have written this essay; my thanks also go to Christine Bold for reading and making her typically perceptive and helpful comments on an earlier draft.

[2] For discussions of the play as postcolonial metatheatre, see Joanne Tompkins, "'Spectacular Resistance'": Metatheatre in Postcolonial Drama," *Modern Drama* 38 (1995): 48, and "'The Story of Rehearsal Never Ends': Rehearsal, Performance, Identity in Settler Culture Drama," *Canadian Literature* 144 (Spring 1995): 150-53. For an examination of the play's postcolonial hybridity, see Robert Nunn, "'They Kinda Wanta Play it Their Own Way.' Hybridity and Mimicry in Play by Three Native Canadian Playwrights," paper presented at the conference on "Compr(om)ising Post-Colonialism(s)," University of Wollongong, Wollongong, Australia, 10-13 February 1999: 4-5. For interpretations of the play as cultural cross-dresssing, see Diana Brydon, "'Empire Bloomers': Cross-Dressing's Double Cross," *Essays on Canadian Writing* 54 (1994): 33-35. For readings of the play in terms of canonical revisioning, see Diana Brydon, "No (Wo)man is an Island: Rewriting Cross-Cultural Encounters with the Canadian Context," *Kunapipi* 15.2 (1993): 54-55. For studies of the play as dialogic monologue, see Jennifer Harvie and Ric Knowles, "Dialogical Monologue: A Dialogue," *The Theatre of Form and the Production of Meaning: Contemporary Canadian Dramaturgies* by Ric Knowles (Toronto: ECW, 1999): 207-08. For analyses focusing on the use of the figure of the trickster/clown, see Cheryl Cashman, "Toronto's Zanies," *Canadian Theatre Review* 67 (1991): 22-31. For interpretations of the play as resistant performative dramaturgy, see Ric Knowles, *The Theatre of Form and the Production of Meaning: Contemporary Canadian Dramaturgies* (Toronto: ECW, 1999): 148-50, and Helen Gilbert and Joanne

been less thoroughly considered—though it is usually acknowledged—has been the revisioning performed by both *Princess Pocahontas and the Blue Spots* and Mojica's radio play published with it, *Birdwoman and the Suffragettes,* of the representation of a very specific group of Native women throughout the Americas across several centuries: the mothers of Métis and Mestizo nations, who have been both celebrated and cursed for their roles as the translators, guides, mediators, and mistresses of early European explorers, settlers, traders, and conquistadors.

The omission is not accidental or incidental, since what is at issue for Mojica in these plays, among other things, is a contestation of ownership over the representation of Native women by those who have exploited those representations for political purposes ranging from the colonialist and the nationalist through to the feminist and the academic. And for a not unrelated series of historical reasons rooted in colonialism,[3] most academics writing about these plays, myself included, have been non-Native women or men whose potential complicity with that exploitation—for academic advancement, if nothing else—represents a very real danger. Indeed, the very analytical tools used in the academic analysis of Native plays are seen by many to be grounded in European theorising and thinking which themselves marginalise or colonise indigenous ways of knowing, and remain in any case rooted in the lived, material realities of the colonising cultures. Mojica makes clear in *Princess Pocahontas* her own struggles, as "Contemporary Woman #1," with Western "feminist shoes" that fail to fit her "wide, square, brown feet."[4] Moreover, like many women and men of colonised cultures, she rejects with considerable derision the very term "postcolonial" and its implications[5]—however much academic discourse may define the postcolonial moment as beginning with first contact and continuing uninterrupted into the present. And of course, the history and practice of cultural analysis, literary and dramatic criticism, ethnography, and anthropology have naturalised the positions of the knowing academic subject versus the passive and static object of his/her knowl-

---

Tompkins, *Post-colonial Drama: Theory, Practice, Politics* (London: Routledge, 1996): 208-9.

[3] There continue to be few First Nations people in the academy, particularly in drama and literature departments.

[4] Monique Mojica, *Princess Pocahontas and the Blue Spots: Two Plays* (Toronto: Women's Press, 1991): 58. Further references to these plays appear parenthetically in the text.

[5] She did so in public presentations at the "Gender/Colonialism/Postcolonialism" conference at the University of Guelph (5-8 November 1992) and at the annual conference of the Association for Canadian Theatre Studies in Ottawa (June 1998).

edge, and those of (European) master discourses versus those of "native informants"—positions that reinscribe colonial relations within the academy, as well as between the academy and its "objects of study."

This cultural gap applies to my own analysis here. In attempting to write about the work of a playwright who aims to "return the [imperial] gaze,"[6] and to write from the cultural position of the (white, male) imperialist, I run the risk of reinscribing the colonial and gender relationships and power differentials that Mojica's work interrogates and exposes, since I am in danger of appropriating—in the styles of Cortés, John Smith, or Lewis and Clark—the work of Monique Mojica as (unlikely) "Indian Princess and guide" for my own advancement and sense of "discovery." Not to undertake this type of analysis, however—to retreat into more comfortable (and structurally continuous) analyses of plays and dramaturgies from the Western canon, without opening spaces within the academy for alternative modes of both creation and analysis (and for the consideration of alternative dramaturgies)—would simply amount to "disappearing" the cultural work that plays such as Mojica's can do in shifting power relationships in society, in the theatre, and in the academy. Such an attitude would also entail participation by omission in the colonial project. The following analysis, then, is offered less as an attempt to determine what these plays essentially *are*—to formulate definitive truth claims about them, to "place" them within a Canadian dramatic canon, or to police aesthetic (and therefore political) standards—than as a consideration, made with respect and without claims of cultural authority, of the cultural work which they might perform in shifting power relationships within contemporary Canadian and "American" (in its broadest senses) societies.[7] My analysis, therefore, begins with and focuses on sources, inspirations, genealogies and intertexts identified and enacted by Mojica herself in the published and performed versions of the plays. Moreover, this study tries to take into account the caution delivered by Paula Gunn Allen, the Native American woman whose work, *The Sacred Hoop*, contributed significantly to the writing of *Princess Pocahontas and the Blue Spots*:

> I would caution readers and students of American Indian life and culture to remember that Indian America does not in any sense function in the same

---

[6] Himani Bannerji, ed., *Returning the Gaze: Essays on Racism, Feminism and Politics* (Toronto: Sister Vision, 1993): xxii-xxiii.

[7] Like many First Nations writers and activists, Mojica resists the geopolitical boundaries established by late-coming colonialist Nation States, and prefers to discuss the first peoples of either the Americas (including South America), or of "Turtle Island" (North and Central America). See Monique Mojica, "Theatricial Diversity on Turtle Island: A Tool Towards Healing," Editorial, *Canadian Theatre Review* 68 (1991): 3.

ways or from the same assumptions that western systems do. Unless that fact is clearly acknowledged, it is virtually impossible to make much sense out of the voluminous materials available concerning American Indians.[8]

***

My essay begins by attempting to place and contextualise the cultural moment of the plays' production. *Princess Pocahontas and the Blue Spots* and *Birdwoman and the Suffragettes* emerged in the late 1980s and early 1990s, at the intersection of several historical forces.[9] These years marked the beginning of a First Nations *political* resurgence in Canada, as registered in the staking of Native land claims across the country, the mounting of protests and blockades over the ownership or exploitation of sacred Native sites and old-growth forests from Temagami, Ontario, to Clayoquot Sound on the coast of British Columbia, and, most obviously, the so-called "Oka Crisis" in 1990 over the expropriation of sacred Mohawk land near the Quebec-Ontario border for a golf course—a standoff between Mohawk warriors and the Quebec police and Canadian army that attracted international attention. In the arts, and most notably in drama and theatre, as Barbara Godard noted in 1990 citing examples primarily from the theatre, "Native Canadian Culture had never before received such public attention as it did in Toronto in the spring of 1989."[10] In 1990, Penny Petrone published her book *Native Literature in Canada: From the Oral Tradition to the Present*, in which she noted that "the most exciting development in the 1980s has take place in Drama,"[11] providing a nine-page survey as

---

[8] Paula Gunn Allen, *The Sacred Hoop: Recovering the Feminine in American Indian Traditions* (Boston: Beacon, 1986): 7.

[9] *Princess Pocahontas* was first workshopped in Toronto in the Spring of 1988, received a second workshop by Nightwood Theatre in co-production with Native Earth Performing Arts in May 1989, and was given a work-in-progress presentation in November of that year. It received its first full production at the Theatre Passe Muraille Backspace in co-production with Nightwood in February-March of 1990. It was first published in *Canadian Theatre Review* 64 in Fall 1990 and republished by Women's Press, together with *Birdwoman and the Suffragettes*, in 1991. *Birdwoman and the Suffragettes* was first broadcast in 1991 for CBC Radio Drama's *Vanishing Point* series, *Adventures Stories for Big Girls*.

[10] Barbara Godard, "The Politics of Representation: Some Native Canadian Women Writers," in *Native Writers and Canadian Writing: Canadian Literature Special Issue*, ed. N. H. New (Vancouver: UBC Press, 1990): 183.

[11] Penny Petrone, ed., *Native Literature in Canada: From the Oral Tradition to the Present* (Toronto: Oxford UP, 1990): 170.

evidence.[12] And Monique Mojica was a central figure in much of this activity: as a writer, she contributed to TV Ontario's *Many Voices* anti-racism series; as an actress, she played the title role in the Maria Campbell/Linda Griffiths collaboration, *Jessica*, as performed at Theatre Passe Muraille in February 1996, created the role of Marie-Adele Starblanket in Tomson Highway's *The Rez Sisters* in 1986, and played Ariel in the Lewis Baumander/Skylight Theatre postcolonial production of *The Tempest* in 1987 and 1989.

A large percentage of this activity in Native culture, and in Native drama and theatre in particular, was nevertheless undertaken by, or acknowledged as the work of, Native men. In fact, its most prominent "mainstream" manifestation—a 1989 production of Tomson Highway's *Dry Lips Oughta Move to Kapuskasing* at the venerable Royal Alexandria theatre and the National Arts Centre, and a subsequent production at the Manitoba Theatre Centre—came under attack from Native and non-Native women as misogynistic.[13] Marie Annharte Baker, in a special issue of *Canadian Theatre Review* on Native Theatre edited by Mojica in 1991, confessed to being made "Angry enough to Spit" by the representation of Native women in the Manitoba Theatre Centre production.[14] This gendered division in the Native community in the late 1980s and early 1990s is not necessarily new. Race and gender in Native and other communities have long been split, divisive, or overlapping issues, and the division at the moment of production of Mojica's plays echoes what some—mostly non-Native—writers have seen as gendered division in response to first contact among many of the Native communities that Mojica was researching at the time when she was writing *Princess Pocahontas* and *Birdwoman and the Suffragettes*. According to many of her identified sources, the arrival of Europeans in

---

[12] *Ibid.*: 170-79. It is also worth noting that in 1984 The Women's Press published Beth Brant's *A Gathering of Spirit: A Collection by North American Women* (reprinted in 1988); in 1987 ECW Press published the Thomas King, Cheryl Calver, and Helen Hoy collection, *The Native in Literature*; and in 1990 *Canadian Literature* published a special issue on *Native Writers and Canadian Writing* edited by N. H. New, in which the Godard article appeared.

[13] See, in particular, Marion Botsford Fraser, "'Contempt for Women Overshadows Powerful Play.' Review of *Dry Lips Oughta Move to Kapuskasing* by Tomson Highway. Royal Alexandria Theatre, Toronto," *Globe and Mail* (Toronto: 17 April 1991): C1; and see my discussion of the controversy in Richard Paul Knowles, "Reading Material: Transfers, Remounts, and the Production of Meaning in Contemporary Canadian Drama and Theatre," *Essays on Canadian Writing* 51/52 (1993-94): 279-86.

[14] Marie Anneharte Baker, "Angry Enough to Spit, but with *Dry Lips* it Hurst More than you Know," *Canadian Theatre Review* 68 (1991): 88-90.

the Americas, and in particular the arrival of European technologies that introduced such things as "kettles, knives, awls and woollen cloth," was more welcome, at least at first, among Native women than men, insofar as it made their lives easier—even as European expectations of the gendering of strength and endurance quite literally lessened the burden of women who, in their own cultures, were often expected unceasingly to haul, toil, and carry to an extent that far exceeded that of their male partners.[15] Sylvia Van Kirk argues of the fur trade society in Canada—and the argument to some extent applies to the *other* central subjects of Mojica's plays and research—Pocahontas in colonial Virginia, Sacagawea on the Lewis and Clark expedition in the American West, and Doña Marina/La Malinche, the translator and mistress of Cortéz in sixteenth-century Mexico[16]—that "the notable instances that can be cited of the Indian woman acting as ally or peacemaker to advance the cause of the trader [or coloniser] suggests that it was in the woman's interest to do so."[17] "To become the wife of a fur trader," Van Kirk argues, "offered the Indian Woman the prospect of an alternative way of life that was easier physically and richer in material ways."[18] This to some extent explains the willingness of the Native women who are the subjects of Mojica's plays—and who are celebrated within the myths of the colonisers, as "trusty little Indian guides" or "faithful interpreters"—to *act* as translators and guides, and to become the sexual partners (wives "*à la façon du pays*" in the Canadian context of the fur trade, or mistresses and apparent objects of exchange in Mexico and elsewhere) of European colonisers. It also perhaps explains why these women have so often been demonised in the mythologies of their own cultures as traitors and whores.[19]

---

[15] Sylvia Van Kirk, *"Many Tender Ties": Women in Fur-Trade Society in Western Canada, 1670-1870* (Winnipeg, Manitoba: Watson & Dwyer, [1980]): 6.

[16] The best accounts of these women, all of which (except Cypess) are cited as "recommended" in the published versions of Mojica's plays, are Barbour's *Pocahontas and Her World* (which should, however, be read with the articles by Green and Young); Clark and Edmonds's *Sacagawea of the Lewis and Clark Expedition* (which Mojica spells as "Sacajawea," and which, though she recommends it, she suggests should be read "with a historical grain of salt" [85]); and Cypess's *La Malinche in Mexican Literature*.

[17] Sylvia Van Kirk, *op. cit.*: 6.

[18] *Ibid.*

[19] It is startling how vehemently this demonisation continues, even in websites that are clearly attempting to reclaim pride among what Anzaldúa calls "the new Mestiza." One site, for example, "a tribute to my native culture" by a self-identified "Mexica (NOT HISPANIC, NOT LATINO)," which sets out to celebrate "a beautiful history" and culture, nevertheless feels obligated to preface its comments on La Malinche by

Mojica's research also reveals, however, that the cultural difference that promised technological advancement and decreased subjection to Native women also ultimately restricted their freedom (particularly their sexual freedom), and finally eroded or destroyed their positions of power in tribal and other societies. Paula Gunn Allen, in a 1986 book upon which Mojica draws extensively,[20] traces the "chaos" caused by the European introduction of patriarchal philosophies and cultures into Native colonial societies, and the direct and specific destruction of matriarchal and gynocratic structures that had flourished in many pre-contact cultures. She points the way both in spirit and specific wording for Mojica's rallying "call to arms" (60) to Native women "Word Warriors" in *Princess Pocahontas and the Blue Spots* (Mojica 59)[21] to reverse that history, and to claim for Native and mixed-blood women, in a passage quoted from Gloria Anzaldua, "the freedom to carve and chisel my own face, to staunch the bleeding with ashes, to fashion my own gods out of my entrails" (Mojica 59).[22]

At the same time as the resurgence of First Nations political, cultural, and theatrical activity of the late 1980s and early 1990s was taking place, and at the same time as concerns were being voiced about the gendering of that resurgence, feminist criticism and theory were under attack from a range of locations for purported biological (and other) essentialisms, and for their own elisions of racial and cultural difference.

---

saying, "as horrible as a traitor as she was, she didn't do this alone" (see "Nimexihcat!!!," <http://www.hooked.net/~mictlan/mexica.html>). Sites by non-Natives, -Mexicans or -Mestizas, on the other hand—especially men—tend to defend or celebrate "Doña Marina" (see, for example, Lenchek, "Harlot" and "Unrecognised," <http://www.mexconnect.com/mex_travel/slenchek/slmalinche.html>), picking up on the "standard" non-Native representation of her (and of "her own race") in Fehrenbach's 1973 history of Mexico, which in some ways echoes Van Kirk's account of the Canadian "fur-trade wives":

> If there is one villainess in Mexican history, she is Malintzin. She was to become the ethnic traitoress supreme. The modern Mexican view, however, is totally emotional rather than accurate. Malintzin was not a symbolic traitress, but an unfortunate and intelligent Amerindian girl, who made the best of the situations life handed her. She was made a slave by her own race and presented to the Spaniards as a concubine, and as Doña Marina, Cortés' mistress, she enjoyed more prestige and consideration than almost any woman of Mexico had ever had. (T.R. Fehrenbach, *Fire and Blood: A History of Mexico* [New York: Macmillan, 1973]: 131)

[20] Paula Gunn Allen, *op. cit.*: 31-42.
[21] *Ibid.*: 51-183.
[22] Gloria Anzaldúa, *Borderlands/La Frontera: The New Mestiza* (San Francisco: Aunt Lute, 1987): 22.

Just as 1960s and 1970s movements from the political left had reinscribed patriarchal privilege in "universalist" fights for social justice according to class,[23] so concern was being expressed by the mid-to-late 1980s that the contemporary feminist movement had reinscribed white privilege in its fights for gender equality and what in *Birdwoman and the Suffragettes* is called "the eternal womanly" (Mojica 83). The phrase is used by Mojica to parody and critique contemporary transcultural and universalising feminism, but it is drawn directly from a speech, quoted at length in the play, that was originally delivered in 1905 by Dr. Anna Howard Shaw to the National American Women's Suffrage Association at the unveiling in Portland, Oregon, of the first of dozens of statues dedicated to Sacagawea (Mojica 83).[24] It is not incidental or accidental that in 1989, between the first work shopping of *Princess Pocahontas and the Blue Spots* and its first production, and in response to contemporary debates, Toronto's feminist Nightwood Theatre, the show's co-producer, inaugurated its new, corrective mandate to focus on work by women of colour.

Many of the acknowledged sources for Mojica's plays are selected from among the writings by Mestiza women and women of colour (which she calls "Poetry, Narratives, Testimonies," as opposed to other entries by non-Native authors on "Biography and History") to which Nightwood and other feminist groups were attempting to respond. Throughout the 1980s, while Mojica was researching and writing her plays, women such Gloria Anzaldúa, Chrystos, and Cherríe Moraga explicitly contested, on the basis of race, culture, and sexuality, the transcultural claims of contemporary feminisms.[25] It is the cultural work

---

[23] See Amanda Hale, "A Dialectical Drama of Facts and Fiction on the Feminist Fringe," in *Work in Progress: Building Feminist Culture*, ed. Rhea Trebegov (Toronto: The Women's Press, 1987): 77-99.

[24] According to *Colliers Encyclopedia*, as quoted by Clark and Edmonds, "there are more statues dedicated to her [Sacagawea] than to any other American Woman." The authors provide an appendix listing these "Sacagawea Memorials" which in itself is almost comic, and on which Mojica draws extensively. See Ella E. Clark and Margot Edmonds, *Sacagawea of the Lewis and Clark Expedition* (Berkeley: U of California P, 1979): 1, 95-96, 155-59.

[25] Chief among these are Anzaldúa's (significantly) bilingual book, *Borderlands/La Frontera* (which includes on pp. 22-3 Anzaldúa's rejection of the Chicana's internalisation of the role of betrayer, quoted below, in which she compares herself to La Malinche); Chrystos's *Not Vanishing* (which includes her poem, "I am Not Your Princess" [66-67]), which Mojica cites in *Princess Pocahontas and the Blue Spots*, and which would seem to have been inspirational); Moraga's *Loving in the War Years* (which includes the important essay "A Long Line of Vendidas" [90-144], in which Moraga presents herself as a "traitor" to her people, and compares herself to La Malinche); Anzaldúa and Moraga's important edited collection, *This Bridge*

performed by the writings of these women, largely, like Mojica, of mixed race,[26] in which Mojica's plays most directly participate, and they do so—to an extent largely unremarked upon in the critical writing about the plays by non-Native academics—by linking together in a kind of oppositional transnationalism—also very much a product of the late 1980s cultural climate—the stories of legendary women *across* the Americas: Pocahontas, Sacagawea, La Malinche, and Mojica's "Marie/Margaret/Madeleine," representative of "the hordes of Cree and Métis women who portaged across Canada with white men on their backs" (15)—not to mention the alternative stories of the separatist Peruvian Women of the Puña, the murdered Nova Scotian AIM (American Indian Movement) activist Anna Mae Aquash, and other stories that *Princess Pocahontas* also tells.[27] The plays' transnationalism is important, at a time when Native political struggles were increasingly against the governments, legislative bodies and armies of Nation States, together with their constructions of national histories, identities, and (often coercive or exclusive) "imagined communities" (Benedict Anderson). This was also a time when, on the one hand, political gains were increasingly made either through international courts or appeals to international (bad) press, and, on the other, resistance was proving effective through the creation of transnational Native communities through the

---

Called My Back (which includes a major section on "Racism in the Women's Movement" [59-101]); Beth Brant's edited collection *A Gathering of Spirit* (which is dedicated to murdered Native Nova Scotian Anna Mae Aquash, whose story comes at the end of *Princess Pocahontas and the Blue Spots*, and which includes Paula Gunn Allen's poem to Sacagawea, "The One Who Skins Cats" [19-24]); Diane Burns's *Riding the one-eyed Ford*, and Paula Gunn Allen's *The Sacred Hoop*, already cited as both essential and inspirational.

[26] As the published script of the plays indicates (86), "Monique Mojica is a Kuna-Rappahonnock half-breed," the daughter of a Native mother and Jewish father born in New York City, of which more below.

[27] Because my focus is on the mothers of mixed-race nations and their descendants, I am not considering in detail here the important role in history or in Mojica's play of the (bleakly) alternative stories of the Women of the Puña or of Anna Mae Aquash. For historical accounts of the former, see Irene Silverblatt, *Moon, Sun, and Witches: Gender Ideologies and Class in Inca and Colonial Peru* (Princeton: Princeton UP, 1987): 197-210; for historical accounts of the latter, see Johanna Brand, *The Life and Death of Anna Mae Aquash* (Toronto: J. Lorimer, 1978). The Women of the Puña appear in *Princess Pocahontas and the Blue Spots* in Transformation 7 (35-38), "betrayed by our own fathers brothers uncles/husbands," but refusing to weep, and setting up their own separatist society. The murder of Anna Mae Aquash is treated near the end of the play, in Transformation 11, which also deals with the interrogation of Chilean women through the insertion of live rats, wired for electric shocks, into their vaginas.

256   *Siting the Other*

Internet. The instant international circulation of information through email, for example, saved at least one Native community—the Chiapas peoples of Mexico in 1995—from extinction by armies under the command of national governments.[28] And it is worth noting that Mojica's partner is Chiapas, and with her, an active activist networker through e-mail and the Internet with Native communities throughout the Americas.

Interestingly in this regard, the similarities *across* settler/invader cultures in the Americas of the symbolic significance of the various "Indian Princesses" who are Monique Mojica's subjects are rarely acknowledged in writings by non-Natives, for whom National identity is forged through the supposed uniqueness of each of these women, both as *different from* and *naturally superior to* their tribespeople, *and* as "National heroines" at the foundational moment in historical narratives that are framed as the teleological histories of distinct (colonising) nations.[29] Thus, for example, one children's version of the Pocahontas story from 1946, which treats her as the saviour of the fledgling Nation, presents her as being "as sweet and pretty as he[r father] was ugly and cruel,"[30] confirming the natural superiority of the colonisers, their culture, and their values; and George Washington Parke Custis's 1830 play, *Pocahontas or The Settlers of Virginia* is subtitled "*A National Drama.*" A popular 1979 biography/historical romance of epic proportions (1359 pages), Anna Lee Waldo's *Sacajawea*, is described on its front cover as "THE HEROIC STORY OF A GREAT WOMAN WHOSE LIFE TELLS THE STORY OF A NATION." The back cover blurb is even more explicit in its construction of the heroine's solitary

---

[28] The best account and analysis of the Chiapas' use of technology in their struggles is Cleaver's article "The Zapatistas and the Electronic Fabric of Struggle," published on the web as listed in the Works Cited. A shorter version appeared as a chapter in John Holloway and Eloína Peláez, eds., *Zapatista! Reinventing Revolution in Mexico* (London: Pluto, 1998). In (only) apparent contradistinction to this internationalist thrust, Native peoples in Canada achieved much of their success in these years through the tactic of calling themselves "First Nations." This title implicitly denied the nineteenth-century retroactive authority of the Canadian Nation State and its right to legislate on their behalf, and also constructed "Nations" that crossed later-day political and geographical boundaries. This is most noticeably the case in the instance of reserves/reservations that straddle the U.S./Canada border and cause perennial headaches for legislators and politicians concerned with everything from tariffs and taxes to smuggling.

[29] Barbour is to some extent an exception to this rule, pointing out as he does parallels between the colonisation of Virginia and Mexico (6, 23). In spite of the fact that his book is called *Pocahontas and Her World*, however, Barbour presents these as general cultural parallels or lines of historical influence without mentioning links between the stories of Pocahontas and La Malinche.

[30] Ingri d'Aulaire and Edgar Parin, *Pocahontas* (New York: Doubleday, 1946): 11.

uniqueness and mythic National significance: "Clad in a doeskin, alone and unafraid, she stood straight and proud before the onrushing forces of America's destiny." And La Malinche is similarly celebrated in non-Native accounts of the conquest of Mexico, notably those of the prolific web-apologist Shep Lenchek in articles with titles such as "La Malinche, Unrecognised Heroine," or "La Malinche—Harlot or Heroine?"[31] More scholarly non-Native sources—particularly Clark and Edmonds, Hebard, Howard, and Fehrenbach—differ from these popular accounts only in degree of subtlety: each treats its particular heroine as at once unique among her race, exemplary, heroic, and foundational for her respective (colonial) National narrative.

All of these sources, of course, come under Mojica's withering satirical gaze in such sequences as her parodic 1950s doo-wop song, accompanied by the back-up group, "The Blue Spots" ("If I'm savage don't despise me,/'cause I'll let you civilise me./Oh Captain Whiteman, I'm your buckskin clad dessert") (26-7), and her Troubadour ballad of Pocahontas (28-32), with its refrain of "Heigh-ho wiggle-waggle/ wigwam wampum,/roly-poly papoose tom-tom/tomohawk squaw" (32). But in many ways the play's real subversions come less from direct parody than from linking together the histories of these women, presenting those histories *as* representations, and implicitly or explicitly noticing the similarities among them as constructs, ideologically coded through the discourses of colonisation. For, of course, these similarities do not emerge from considering or contesting the "actual" histories or biographies of these women. The (*written* and therefore *authoritative*) materials that might serve as the bases for such revisionism, considered by Western history to be "primary sources," are exclusively European: Captain John Smith's dubious accounts of his "adventures" (dubious because they were written long after the fact, and long after his early accounts, in which Pocahontas did not appear); Bernal Diaz's "eyewitness" account of *The Conquest of New Spain*; the clearly interested "discovery" journals of Cortés and of Lewis and Clark; and so on. The *linkages* emerge, for Mojica as for other Native writers, from considering these women less as "actual" figures in history than as subjects of Western colonialist historical *representation*. The similarities among their stories emerge, that is, through resistant transliteration that foregrounds and denaturalises the ways in which the stories have been *mobilised* as agents in the subjectification of Native women through colonialist historical discourses.[32]

---

[31] See <http://www.mexconnect.com/mex_travel/slenchek/slmalinche.html>.

[32] There are also, however, various websites mounted by Natives that do offer contestatory accounts of the Western histories of all of these women, but attacks on dis-

Unlike non-Native authors, Native, Métis, and Mestizo writers, particularly women, frequently group Pocahontas, La Malinche, Sacagawea, and the fur-trade women together.[33] They treat their stories as ideologically coded representations; and they do so more or less explicitly, as Mojica does, by considering those figures to have been variously constructed in history as archetypal princesses, "squaws," translators, traitors, mistresses, and whores. Finally, they foreground the cultural role that is played by so representing the women who ultimately became the mothers, actual or symbolic, of Métis and Mestizo nations—women whose roles and reputations, internalised by their descendants, need to be rehabilitated for the sake of the psychic health of those descendants and those nations. As Gloria Anzaldúa argues, in a passage from which Mojica quotes,

> Not me sold out my people but they me. *Malinali Tenepat*, or *Malintzin*, has become known as *La Chingada*—the fucked one. She has become the bad word that passes a dozen times a day from the lips of Chicanos. Whore, prostitute, the woman who sold out her people to the Spaniards are epithets Chicanos spit out with contempt.
>
> The worst kind of betrayal lies in making us believe that the Indian woman in us is the betrayer. We, *indias y mestizas*, police the Indian in us, brutalise and condemn her. Male culture has done a good job on us.[34]

And she calls for "an accounting with all three cultures—white, Mexican, Indian"[35]—as she calls for the dormant spirit of the *mestiza* to "fight for her own skin and her own piece of ground to stand on, a ground from which to view the world."[36]

It might be useful, in understanding the double-bind of Native women caught between cultures—as it plays itself out in Mojica's performative history of their representation from Pocahontas, La Malinche, Sacagawea, the Women of the Puña, and the women of the fur trade in Canada through to tortured Chilean women, Anna Mae Aquash, and

---

torted "facts" in Western representations have been as ineffectual, it seems to me, as were offers from the Powhatan Confederacy to "assist Disney with cultural and historical accuracy" in the making of their 1995 film, *Pocahontas* (see "Pocahontas Myth").

[33] See, for example, Paula Gunn Allen, *op. cit.*: 282. She notes the reputation of traitress shared by these women within their own cultures, and the fact that they all bore sons to their imperialist partners—both things crucial to Mojica's interrogations, and to the subsequent histories and lives of their descendants.

[34] Gloria Anzaldúa, *op. cit.*: 22.

[35] *Ibid.*

[36] *Ibid.*: 23.

Contemporary Women #s 1 and 2 in *Princess Pocahontas and the Blue Spots*—to invoke some of the insights of recent feminist and post-colonialist translation theory, where the traditional Italian proverb, "to translate is to betray," is at issue—together with the traditional *gendering* of translation as a service role. In almost all of Mojica's recommended historical sources—together with those sources which she lists as "not recommended" except as "good source material for satire" (85)—the images of her Indian Princesses circulate around a cluster of associations involving translation and faithfulness (or lack of it), associations that link cultural mediation with variations on linguistic, representational, racial, and sexual impurity—including, of course, *métissage* and hybridity—and conflating, more or less explicitly, translation, miscegenation, and cultural betrayal. As Tejaswini Niranjana phrases it, in traditional discourses of colonialist humanist translation the dilemma has generally been whether a translator should be "literal or licentious, faithful or unfaithful?,"[37] which raises the crucial question for women caught between cultures, of, in Suzanne de Lotbinière-Harwood's phrasing, "who are you going to be faithful to?"[38]

In the introduction to *Siting Translation: History, Post-Structuralism, and the Colonial Context,* Niranjana points to the political value, in undoing hegemonic representations of colonial subjects, of Derrida's insight that translation, like other representations, "does not re-present an 'original'; rather, it re-presents that which is always already re-presented."[39] She also points to the post-structuralist critique of historicism, "which shows the genetic (searching for an origin) and teleological (positing a certain end) nature of traditional historiography":

> [O]f immediate relevance to our concern with colonial practices of subjectification is the fact that "historicism" really presents as *natural* that which is *historical* (and therefore neither inevitable nor unchangeable). A critique of historicism might show us a way of deconstructing [in her example] the "pusillanimous" and "deceitful" Hindus of Mill and Hegel.[40]

It might also show us a way of deconstructing the "warlike," "primitive," and equally deceitful "savages" of colonial Virginia, of sixteenth-century Mexico, and of the nineteenth-century North Ameri-

---

[37] Tejaswini Niranjana, *Siting Translation: History, Post-Structuralism, and the Colonial Context* (Berkeley: U of California P, 1992): 54.

[38] Susanne de Lotbinière-Harwood, *Re-Belle et Infidèle: La traduction comme pratique de réécriture au féminin/The Body Bilingual: Translation as Rewriting in the Feminine* (Montréal: Les éditions du remue-ménage/Toronto: Women's Press, 1991): 101.

[39] Tejaswini Niranjana, *op. cit.*: 9.

[40] *Ibid.*: 10.

can West. What Western legal and epistemological systems construct as deceitful—such as the shifting use of multiple names (and therefore *identities*—or multiplicities?) that notably characterise all of the women about whom Mojica writes, versus the "capturing" through definitive naming that her character Sacagawea (or Grasswoman, Birdwoman, Phoenaïf, or Porivo [Chief Woman])[41] eloquently resists—Native cultures might consider to be natural, evocative and liberatory.

In any case, what Niranjana ultimately proposes, drawing on the work of Gayatri Spivack and Homi Bhabha, is a Subaltern transliterative historiography that resonates with Monique Mojica's project, in that it is "concerned with revealing the discursivity of [Western] history,"[42] and in that it "tries to show how ... [h]istory and translation function, ... creating coherent and transparent texts through the repression of difference, and participating thereby in the process of colonial domination".[43] Set against this in Niranjana are Walter Benjamin's critical strategies of citation, quotation, or montage (which pre-echoes Derrida's double inscription), Homi Bhabha's notion of hybridity ("the revaluation of the assumption of colonial identity through the repetition of discriminatory identity effects"[44]), and Nirnanjana's own attempt to initiate "a practice of translation that is speculative, provisional, and interventionist."[45]

All of this motivates theorists of resistant translation to veer away from gendered conceptions of faithful *re*-production toward genuinely *productive* theorisations that involve, on the one hand, "'enabling' discursive failure" and "affirmative deconstruction,"[46] and on the other hand, a taking advantage of the *liberatory* possibilities of *multiplication* and *choice*—what Lotbinière-Harwood calls "deux mots pour chaque chose".[47] In these configurations, translation, transliteration, and the slippages in meaning they involve, do not suggest *du*plicity but *multi*plicity; they do not suggest *lack*—of purity, of faithfulness, or of unitary

---

[41] There is a considerable literature on the naming of Sacagawea, which Mojica capitalises on by stressing the non-Native obsession with naming (understood as pinning down, entrapping, and limiting). See, for example, Irving W. Anderson's representative web article "Sacajawea?–Sakakawea?–Scagawea?: Spelling–Pronunciation–Meaning," <http://www.lewisandclark.org/pages/sactext.html>.

[42] Tejaswini Niranjana, *op. cit.*: 43.

[43] *Ibid.*

[44] Homi Bhabha, "Signs Taken for Wonders: Questions of Ambivalence and Authority under a Tree outside Delhi," *Critical Inquiry* 12.1 (Fall 1985): 154.

[45] Tejaswini Niranjana, *op. cit.*: 173.

[46] *Ibid.*: 24-42 (citing Spivak).

[47] Susanne de Lotbinière-Harwood, *op. cit.*: 75.

meaning (or epistemological authority)—but *abundance*, fecundity, endurance, and sustenance.

One task of the women Word Warriors that Mojica invokes, then, consists in replacing the harmful, internalised representations of their roles as translators and mediators with more positive translations, metaphors and material practices. And central to this task, in the work of Mojica and that of her Chicana, Mestiza, and Métis sisters, it seems, is corn. When I first began thinking seriously about Mojica's work, I was puzzled by what seemed to be the pervasiveness, and flexibility, of images of and references to *corn* in *Princess Pocahontas and the Blue Spots*—many of which are, well, *corny*: corn adorns the cover of the published text, where "The Blue Spots" are represented as cartoon images of dancing cobs of corn, and in performance the winning by Princess Buttered-on-Both-Sides of the "Miss Congeniality" prize at "the 498th annual Miss North American Indian Beauty Pageant" is marked by the awarding of a *"tablita-style corn 'crown' and ear of corn 'bouquet'"*(52):

> *Screaming; jumping up and down flat footed as the Host presents her with her "bouquet" and "crowns" her with a headdress covered with small ears of corn which light up. She begins her triumphant walk down the runway, weeping and blowing kisses, while HOST throws popcorn at her feet singing "You Light Up My Life," in true lounge lizard tradition. When PRINCESS BUTTERED-ON-BOTH-SIDES reaches upstage centre she strikes the pose of the Statue of Liberty, and the ears of corn on her headdress are fully illuminated* (52).

And more seriously, early in the play, CONTEMPORARY WOMAN #1 provides a commentary on Mojica's riff on "Redskin Princess, calendar girl,/Redskin temptress, Indian Pearl," by quoting Cherríe Moraga: "... the concept of betraying one's race through sex and sexual politics is as common as corn" (21).[48]

It is interesting to note, in this context, the centrality of corn in Native stories as reported in Paula Gunn Allen's chapter on "the ways of our Grandmothers." For the Keres people of the American Southwest, for example, corn "holds the essence of earth and conveys the power of earth to the people."[49] And corn—as metaphor, but also as a *material* and *nurturing* fact of life and sustenance, both mundane and magical, "common" (as the quotation from Moraga indicates), but also transformative—might usefully replace the less savory images of hybridity and

---

[48] Cherríe Moraga, *Loving in the War Years: lo que nunca pasó por sus labios* (Boston: South End, 1983): 103.
[49] Paula Gunn Allen, *op. cit.*: 22.

métissage in ways articulated most clearly by Gloria Anzaldúa, who describes herself and other *mestizas* as

> Indigenous like corn, like corn, the *mestiza* is a product of crossbreeding, designed for preservation under a variety of conditions. Like an ear of corn—a female seed-bearing organ—the *mestiza* is tenacious, tightly wrapped in the husks of her culture. Like kernels she clings to the cob; with thick stalks and strong brace roots she holds tight to the earth—she will survive the crossroads.[50]

It is, then, the *mestiza*, Métis, or half-breed woman herself who is the lived, *material* embodiment—as opposed to the metaphoric representation, no matter how suggestive—of what often represents in postcolonial theorisings a purely *formalist métissage*, or purely *discursive* hybridity, most of which draw upon Homi Bhabha—and more importantly upon Gayatri Spivak and the emerging field of Subaltern studies—but which nevertheless tend to shift discursive analysis away from the material to the (purely) textual.[51]

In the brief biography that concludes the published text of her plays, Monique Mojica aligns herself directly with the women who are the historical subjects of her theatrical works *and* with the women of the 1980s—Anzaldúa, Chrystos, Moraga, and others—who provide her with her poetic, narrative, and testimonial source material—her lived theoretical frame. Identifying herself as "a Kuna-Rappahonnok [the Nation of Pocahontas, a] half-breed, a woman word-warrior [like Anzaldúa, Chrystos, Gunn Allen, and Moraga], a mother [like Pocahontas, La Malinche, Sacagawea, and the fur-trade women] and an actor" (86), Mojica constructs for herself and other women (as did the women of the Puña) a living lineage: a nation, an alternative "imagined community." And as a mixed-race woman who in *Princess Pocahontas* performs her *own* rewritings of the revisionist histories of that lineage, she quite literally and visibly embodies it, even as she embodies, as an actor, the characters whom she performs. These women and their histo-

---

[50] Gloria Anzaldúa, *op. cit*: 81. Even the Disney film version of *Pocahontas* nods in the right direction, when Pocahontas responds to John Smith's description of gold—"you know, it's, it's yellow. Comes out of the ground. It's really valuable"—by showing him a fat and glistening cob of corn. Ironically, of course, what she shows him is clearly sweet corn, not what is now known as "Indian corn."

[51] See Bhabha on hybridity. The canonical progenitor of subaltern studies is Gayatri Chakravorty Spivak; see her "Can the Subaltern Speak?," in *Marxism and the Interpretation of Culture*, eds. Cary Nelson and Lawrence Grossberg (Urbana: U of Illinois P., 1988): 271-313; and her earlier "Subaltern Studies: Deconstructing Historiography," in *Subaltern Studies IV: Writings on South Asian History and Society*, ed. Ranajit Guha (Delhi: Oxford UP, 1986): 330-63.

ries *are, in fact*, embodied in her. Her acting, then, becomes genuinely *performative*. She is, in Niranjana's terms, "*living* in translation,"[52] inhabiting what Susanne de Lotbinière-Harwood calls (in reference to *her* own position between Canada's founding cultures as signalled by her double-barrelled, bicultural name) "the *body* bilingual" (my emphasis),[53] when she moves, at the end of *Princess Pocahontas*, towards the *actual* bilingualism (in this case Spanish and English) that also characterises the work of Anzaldúa, Moraga, and others. In *Princess Pocahontas*, then, Mojica *enacts* a move from Western teleological historiography, with its claims to represent originary realities and to translate the past "faithfully," to a *performative, embodied* genealogy that might be considered to be less Western history's cataloguing and controlling of the dead and their meanings than a First Nations project of keeping the ancestors alive and granting them agency in the present. Thus, Mojica takes part—as actor, activist, and mother—in the (ongoing) *creation* of the nation of women Word Warriors for which she literally "stands in," for which her plays are constitutive, and for the members of which they function as a call to arms.

Works Cited

Acosta, Juvenal, ed. *Light from a Nearby Window: Contemporary Mexican Poetry* (San Francisco: City Lights, 1993).

Allen, Paula Gunn. *The Sacred Hoop: Recovering the Feminine in American Indian Traditions* (Boston: Beacon, 1986).

Anderson, Benedict. *Imagined Communities: Reflections on the Origin and Spread of Nationalism* (London: Verso, 1991).

Anderson, Irving W. "Sacagawea?–Sakakawea?–Sacagawea": Spelling–Pronunciation–Meaning,"<http://www.lewisandclark.org/pages/sactext.html>.

"Anna Mae Aquash Time Line," <http://www.journalism.wisc.edu/nfic/aquash.html>.

Anzaldúa, Gloria. *Borderlands/La Frontera: The New Mestiza* (San Francisco: Aunt Lute, 1987).

Baker, Marie Annaharte. "Angry Enough to Spit, but with *Dry Lips* it Hurst More than you Know," *Canadian Theatre Review* 68 (1991): 88-90.

Bannerji, Himani, ed. *Returning the Gaze: Essays on Racism, Feminism and Politics* (Toronto: Sister Vision, 1993).

Barbour, Philip L. *Pocahontas and her World* (Boston: Houghton Mifflin, 1969).

---

[52] Tejaswini Niranjana, *op. cit.*: 46 (my emphasis).
[53] Lotbinière-Harwood begins her chapter entitled "Deux mots pour chaque chose" by saying "Je suis une traduction. Dans mon corps bilingue habitent au moins deux mots pour chaque chose" (*op. cit.*: 75).

Benjamin, Walter. "The Task of the Translator," in *Walter Benjamin: Selected Writings Volume 1: 1913-1926*, eds. Marcus Bullock and Michael W. Jennings (Cambridge, Mass: Belknap, Harvard UP, 1996): 253-63.

Bhabha, Homi. "Signs Taken for Wonders: Questions of Ambivalence and Authority under a Tree outside Delhi," *Critical Inquiry* 12.1 (Fall 1985): 144-65.

"A Biography of Anna Mae," <http://ww.dickshovel.com/bio.html>.

Brand, Johanna. *The Life and Death of Anna Mae Aquash* (Toronto: J. Lorimer, 1978).

Brant, Beth (Degonwadonti), ed. *A Gathering of Spirit: A Collection by North American Indian Women* (Toronto: The Women's Press, 1984).

Brobribb, Somer. "The Traditional Roles of Native Women in Canada and the Impact of Colonisation," *The Canadian Journal of Native Studies* 4.1 (1984): 85-103.

Brydon, Diana. "'Empire Bloomers': Cross-Dressing's Double Cross," *Essays on Canadian Writing* 54 (1994): 23-45.

———. "No (Wo)man is an Island: Rewriting Cross-Cultural Encounters within the Canadian Context," *Kunapipi* 15.2 (1993): 48-56.

Burns, Diane. *Riding the One-Eyed Ford* (New York: Contact II, 1981).

Cashman, Cheryl. "Toronto's Zanies," *Canadian Theatre Review* 67 (1991): 22-31.

Clark, Ella E. and Margot Edmonds. *Sacagawea of the Lewis and Clark Expedition* (Berkeley: U of California P, 1979).

Cleaver, Harry. "The Zapatistas and the Electronic Fabric of Struggle," <http://www.eco.utexas.edu/faculty/Cleaver/zaps.html>; repr. (shorter version) in *Zapatista! Reinventing Revolution in Mexico*, eds. John Holloway and Eloína Peláez(London: Pluto, 1998).

Custis, George Washington Parke. *Pocahontas or the Settlers of Virginia*, in *Representative American Plays from 1767 to the Present Day*, ed. Arthur Hobson Quinn (Century Company, 1917; New York: Appleton-Century Crofts, 1953, 7th ed. revised): 165-92.

Crystos. *Not Vanishing* (Vancouver: Press Gang, 1988).

Cypess, Sandra Messinger. *La Malinche in Mexican Literature: From History to Myth* (Austin: U of Texas P, 1991).

d'Aulaire, Ingri and Edgar Parin. *Pocahontas* (New York: Doubleday, 1946).

Fehrenbach, T.R. *Fire and Blood: A History of Mexico* (New York: Macmillan, 1973).

Fiske, Jo-Anne. "Pocahontas's Granddaughters: Spiritual Transition and Tradition of Carrier Women of British Columbia," *Ethnohistory* 43 (1996): 663-81.

Fraser, Marion Botsford. "'Contempt for Women Overshadows Powerful Play.' Review of *Dry Lips Oughta Move to Kapuskasing* by Tomson Highway. Royal Alexandria Theatre, Toronto," *Globe and Mail* (Toronto: 17 April 1991): C1.

Gilbert, Helen and Joanne Tompkins. *Post-colonial Drama: Theory, Practice, Politics* (London: Routledge, 1996).
Godard, Barbara. "The Politics of Representation: Some Native Canadian Women Writers," in *Native Writers and Canadian Writing: Canadian Literature Special Issue*, ed. N. H. New (Vancouver: UBC Press, 1990): 183-225.
Green, Rayna. "The Pocahontas Perplex: The Image of Indian Women in American Culture," *Canadian Journal of Native Studies* 4 (1984): 698-714.
Hale, Amanda. "A Dialectical Drama of Facts and Fiction on the Feminist Fringe," in *Work in Progress: Building Feminist Culture*, ed. Rhea Trebegov (Toronto: The Women's Press, 1987): 77-99.
Harvie, Jennifer and Ric Knowles. "Dialogical Monologue: A Dialogue," in *The Theatre of Form and the Production of Meaning: Contemporary Canadian Dramaturgies* by Ric Knowles (Toronto: ECW, 1999): 193-210.
Hebard, Grace Raymond. *Sacajawea: A Guide and Interpreter of the Lewis and Clark expedition, with an Account of the Travels of Toussaint Charbonneau, and of Jean Baptiste, the Expedition Papoose* (1932; Glendale, California: Arthur H. Clark, 1967).
Howard, Harold P. *Sacajawea* (Norman, Oklahoma: U of Oklahoma P, 1971).
King, Thomas, Cheryl Calver, and Helen Hoy, eds. *The Native in Literature* (Toronto: ECW Press, 1987).
Knowles, Richard Paul. "Reading Material: Transfers, Remounts, and the Production of Meaning in Contemporary Canadian Drama and Theatre," *Essays on Canadian Writing* 51/52 (1993-94): 258-95.
Knowles, Ric. *The Theatre of Form and the Production of Meaning: Contemporary Canadian Dramaturgies* (Toronto: ECW, 1999).
Lenchek, Shep. "'La Malinche'–Harlot or Heroine?" <http://www.mexconnect.com/mex_travel/slenchek/slmalinche.html>.
——— "La Malinche, Unrecognised Heroine," <http://www.mexconnect.com/mex_travel/slenchek/slmalinche.html>.
Lionnet, Françoise. *Postcolonial Representations: Women, Literature, Identity* (Ithaca: Cornell UP, 1995).
Lotbinière-Harwood, Susanne de. *Re-Belle et Infidèle: La traduction comme pratique de réécriture au féminin/The Body Bilingual: Translation as Rewriting in the Feminine* (Montréal: Les éditions du remue-ménage/Toronto: Women's Press, 1991).
McDonald, Christie V., ed. *The Ear of the Other: Otobiography, Transference, Translation: Texts and Discussions with Jacques Derrida* (New York: Schocken, 1985).
Mojica, Monique. *Princess Pocahontas and the Blue Spots: Two Plays* (Toronto: Women's Press, 1991).
——— "Theatrical Diversity on Turtle Island: A Tool Towards the Healing," Editorial, *Canadian Theatre Review* 68 (1991): 3.

Moraga, Cherríe. *Loving in the War Years: lo que nunca pasó por sus labios* (Boston: South End, 1983).
Moraga, Cherríe and Gloria Anzaldúa, eds. *This Bridge Called My Back: Writings by Radical Women of Color* (Watertown, Mass.: Persephone, 1981).
New, W.H., ed. *Native Writers and Canadian Writing: Canadian Literature Special Issue* (Vancouver: UBC Press, 1990).
"Nimexihcat!!!," <http://www.hooked.net/~mictlan/mexica.html>.
Niranjana, Tejaswini. *Siting Translation: History, Post-Structuralism, and the Colonial Context* (Berkeley: U of California P, 1992).
Nunn, Robert. "'They Kinda Wanna Play it Their Own Way.' Hybridity and Mimicry in Plays by Three Native Canadian Playwrights," paper presented at the conference on "Compr(om)ising Post-Colonialism(s)," University of Wollongong, Wollongong, Australia, 10-13 February 1999.
Parin D'Aulaire, Ingri and Edgar. *Pocahontas* (Garden City, NY: Doubleday, 1946).
Petrone, Penny, ed. *Native Literature in Canada: From the Oral Tradition to the Present* (Toronto: Oxford UP, 1990).
Pocahontas, directed by Mike Gabriel and Eric Goldberg (Disney, 1995).
"Pocahontas Myth," <http://www.powhatan.org/poce.html>.
Robinson, Douglas. *The Translator's Turn* (Baltimore: Johns Hopkins, 1991).
Silverblatt, Irene. *Moon, Sun, and Witches: Gender Ideologies and Class in Inca and Colonial Peru* (Princeton: Princeton UP, 1987).
Spivak, Gayatri Chakravorty. "Can the Subaltern Speak?," in *Marxism and the Interpretation of Culture*, eds. Cary Nelson and Lawrence Grossberg (Urbana: U of Illinois P., 1988): 271-313.
—— "Subaltern Studies: Deconstructing Historiography," in *Subaltern Studies IV: Writings on South Asian History and Society*, ed. Ranajit Guha (Delhi: Oxford UP, 1986): 330-63.
Tompkins, Joanne. "'Spectacular Resistance': Metatheatre in Post-Colonial Drama," *Modern Drama* 38 (1995): 42-51.
—— "'The Story of Rehearsal Never Ends': Rehearsal, Performance, Identity in Settler Culture Drama," *Canadian Literature* 144 (Spring 1995): 142-61.
Van Kirk, Sylvia. *"Many Tender Ties": Women in Fur-Trade Society in Western Canada, 1670-1870* (Winnipeg, Manitoba: Watson & Dwyer, [1980]).
Waldo, Anna Lee. *Sacajawea* (New York: Avon, 1979).
Young, Philip. "The Mother of Us All: Pocahontas Reconsidered," *Kenyon Review* 24 (1962): 391-441.

Beatrice Chancy: Slavery, Martyrdom and the Female Body

ANN WILSON

University of Guelph

As a work of imagination, *Beatrice Chancy*,[1] a verse drama by Afri-Canadian writer George Elliott Clarke, takes as its topic a neglected aspect of Canadian history: slavery. In his introduction, "On Slavery in Nova Scotia," Clarke states that "Essentially, African slavery was a hemisphere-long practice, from Quebec to Argentina ..."[2] He continues by saying that, while slavery in what is now Canada only represented a minor aspect of the colonies' economic activity, it nevertheless constitutes a part of the country's history which demands attention.

Clarke's consideration of slavery focuses on Beatrice Chancy, the offspring of a slave raped by her owner, Francis Chancy. Raised in Chancy's household, Beatrice is—as described on the jacket of the published version of the play—"beautiful, clever, kind and cultured—her father's prize possession." The play opens with the return of Beatrice after several years of absence during which she was educated in a convent in Halifax. When she announces that she is in love with another slave, she incurs the ire of her father, who wants her to himself. He claims her by raping her, which triggers a sequence of violent events that will lead to Beatrice killing her father, an offence for which she will later be tried, convicted and hanged.

The narrative of the play makes clear the violence inherent in the condition of men, women and children who were—and, indeed, in some parts of the world still are—taken and sold into slavery. As the mere

---

[1] Clarke has worked *Beatrice Chancy* in a number of forms. Initially, it was an opera that was workshopped at the Canadian Opera Company in Toronto on 7 June 1996. The complete opera premiered at the Music Gallery in Toronto on 18 June 1998. The libretto was published in *Canadian Theatre Review* 96 (Fall 1998). The verse drama which is the subject of this essay expands and rewrites the libretto. Published in 1999, it was given a reading at Theatre Passe Muraille on 10 and 11 July 1997. It has never received a full production.

[2] George Elliott Clarke, *Beatrice Chancy* (Victoria: Polestar Book Publishers, 1999): 7. Further references to this work will appear parenthetically in the text.

property of another human being, a slave becomes a human machine whose labour forms the basis of the slave owner's economic enterprise. The status of the slave as the labouring-body-who-is-property has particular implications for the enslaved woman. Her value not simply derives from her work, but also from her body which can bear children, who in turn become the property of the slave owner and increase his assets at little cost to himself. Because of their reproductive capacity which sexualised them as property, female slaves were often sexually exploited by slave owners. As a consequence, children were frequently born to female slaves and male masters, which created a situation in which the master/slave relationship took on the familial dimension of father/mother and child. This connection between slavery and family generates a fundamental contradiction, as the violent inscription of relations of power characteristic of the institution of slavery clashes with the nurturing usually associated with that of the family.

In *Beatrice Chancy*, Clarke establishes this crucial contradiction by focusing on the daughter of a slave raped by her master. As the dramatic narrative unfolds, however, the playwright's engagement with this contradiction seems increasingly problematic. The cue is offered by the epigraph from Bourne which opens the first act: "The abolition of slavery ... is emphatically the duty and privilege of women"(9). Through paternal rape, Beatrice's condition evolves from that of a young woman whose social identity is hybridised as both slave and daughter to that of a daughter effectively renounced by her father. Clarke's depiction of the transformation of her identity includes her vow to avenge the rape and her refusal to be a passive victim. As described in the *Dramatis Personae*, Beatrice becomes "a martyr-liberator" (10) who sacrifices herself in order to eradicate the evil of slavery metonymically embodied by Chancy. Given that the rape occurs at Easter, Beatrice's sacrifice appears analogous to that of Christ's death on the cross. While the analogy is rhetorically powerful, its effect nevertheless detracts from issues of gender and slavery by rendering Beatrice more masculine than feminine. *Beatrice Chancy* seems to depend on the martyr-liberator developing into a phallic avenger.

The importance of Christianity strikes one from the opening moment of the play when the

> *enslaved Africans gather and circle counter-clockwise, leapshouting ...*
> Massa Winter
> Be dyin now—
> Our icy chains
> Will be no mo.
> O sweet Jesus,
> Won't we be free?

> O King Jesus,
> Slay slavery! (12)

For some of the slaves, the promise of Christianity entails the redemption from evil and, therefore, their liberation: "Ma Lawd's gonna hurl down fire," says Moses, adding later that having played the "foolhardy, happy banjo/Negroes, then pick up knives, and cut and stab" (16). For others, the belief that God's plan includes their liberation amounts to a ruse. As stated by Lead, Beatrice's lover, "If prayer could bust iron, we'd be free" (13). In this context, one should note that none of the slaves behaves like Uncle Tom who, in Harriet Beecher Stowe's novel, passively accepts slavery as the will of God. In Clarke's work, all slaves yearn intensely to be liberated. Slavery does not make part of God's plan, but represents a manifestation of evil personified by Francis Chancy, who is associated with "*Sade, Machiavelli*" and, more broadly, "*deceit*" (23).

In a curious moment, however, Chancy is also associated with God. Says Dice to Chancy, "Look, you's white—the colour of God himself" (23). This marks the beginning of Clarke's complex deployment of Christianity in the play, suggesting that even though some of the slaves profess belief in God, He remains inscribed within the economy of race: understood as white, the slaves see Him as implicated in the power enjoyed by the white masters, inasmuch as "white" comes to be associated with "purity" and "goodness." God symbolises the Father, but Chancy also embodies a father who perverts all that God supposedly stands for within Christian theology. He claims that "My power isn't violation, it's love" (27); but clearly, it is violation which poses as love.

The relation which Clarke forges between God and Chancy, the Father and the other who perverts His image, is linked to colour and, in turn, to race and morality. Chancy, as a figure of evil, may be white racially, but given that Clarke describes his biography as *"an encyclopedia of sin,"* his moral hue is black (58). In a conversation with the Reverend Ezra Love Peacock, Chancy articulates the relation between race and purity in what amounts to a self-serving apology for his power and privilege:

> What is whiteness without blackness?
> How can we be beautiful, free,
> Virtuous, holy, pure, *chosen*
> If slaves be not our opposites (26).

Replies Peacock, "Slavery shackles whites to the blackest crimes" (26). Throughout *Beatrice Chancy,* Clarke insistently positions black and white in relation to each other, as if one anticipated or resulted from the other. "Whiteness" appears defined not simply on its own terms, but needs the antithetical "otherness" of "blackness" to establish what "whiteness" is not. For example, "whiteness" stands for beauty and freedom and hence, "blackness" for ugliness and slavery.

As the child of a woman slave and the master who owned her, Beatrice literally embodies the sign of a hybridity which, in the context of the performance, threatens the stability of slavery by positioning her as both daughter and slave. The play heavily stresses the alternation and negotiation of her identity between these two categories which stand for black and white. After the death of her biological mother, Beatrice is taken into Chancy's household, where she is recognised as the daughter of the family, because Chancy and his wife Lustra have no children of their own. Lustra assumes the role of Beatrice's surrogate mother. Indeed, Beatrice is "dispatched" by her father to Lustra's old convent in Halifax, where, in Chancy's words, she is to receive instruction that will make her become "more like us—white, modern, beautiful" (52). Thus, "whiteness" exceeds the function of a mere descriptor of race and serves as the sign of "modernity" and "beauty," implying that "blackness" is "primitive" and "ugly."

Ostensibly, Chancy considers that Beatrice's convent education will make her "white"; he idealises her as well-schooled and pure when he refers to his "... daughter's chaste-like unstanched steel" (52). As Beatrice herself realises, idealising her purity also sexualises her: "Father, only your wife deserves such worship" (52). Seeing Beatrice as chaste and white sets the scene for the rape, because within the logic of the play, "chaste" and "white" invoke their antithesis of "sexual" and "black," with the additional associated meanings that Chancy assigns to them: ugliness, amorality, and the primitive. Within this economy of substitution in which whiteness functions as the sign of various values—beauty, purity, modernity—rape does not simply, or even primarily, amount to an act of incest; rather, Chancy "manages" his daughter by finally treating her as a mere female slave sexually available to him (3).

Chancy's discovery of his daughter's love for Lead, another slave, triggers off the process that will end in rape. Enraged by the fact that he is not the object of his daughter's erotic interest, Chancy provokingly asserts "My daughter can't love some bull-thighed nigger!/It's April 1st, but this is no glad joke. Confess now, Beatrice, whom you really love" (55). Without hesitation, she replies that "To live without Lead would wither my life" (55). In retaliation, Chancy instructs to "Lock up this heated bitch, this mutiny./Let her chill—like new wine—in the basement./Since she craves a slave, teach her slavery" (56). Chancy's identification of Beatrice as black—which, from his perspective, becomes synonymous with being a slave—culminates into her rape. As he explains, "My hands will speak horror to her body./She'll learn what it means to be property" (82).

Initially, Beatrice's whiteness is marked by her piety, including her love for her father and her desire that he be redeemed: "Oh Father, Who art in Heaven,/Lead's steady love is a blessing./But may I steal one more blessing?/Heal my father's sin-cankered soul" (37). Chancy, enraged that Beatrice loves Lead, approaches his daughter before he rapes her and says "Beatrice, you've satisfied my prayers" (83). As the exchange evolves, Beatrice assures Chancy that "God loves us, father. God adores sinners" (83). In answer to which, Chancy perverts the assurance of pardon by asking "Come, kiss your father Christian-like" (83). To Beatrice's "On the cheek, sir," Chancy replies "On the lips, lamb ... A Christian kiss beatifies us, Beatrice" (84).

The terms of this exchange, which occurs over Easter, are worth noting. Throughout its history, Catholicism has insisted on forging the relation between the believer and God/Christ in sexualised terms: nuns are referred to as the "brides of Christ"; in some instances, the terms used to convey the ecstasy of pious belief verge on the orgasmic. The erotic of piety casts the sexual abuse in a particular light. In the scene prior to the rape, Chancy—agitated—expresses his attraction to Beatrice:

> At sex, dumping blood—swank, nervous—like Christ's
>   Wantonly I'll discover her verse—
> Wet, shining, under a black bush, a language
> That is flesh webbing us, the mouth feel of poetry
> The Word in her mouth—like salt water ... (81)

Because she holds The Word—Christ—in her mouth, Beatrice is portrayed by her father as a means to his salvation. When later in the chapel he calls her "the lamb," he invokes the notion of Christ as the sacrificial "lamb of God" whose crucifixion redeems the world of sin. He adds that the kiss will make them saints. Seeing Beatrice as a Christ-like figure perverts the crucifixion as rehearsed in the Catholic communion, in which the wine and bread are transformed into the blood and body of Christ. The rape, by contrast, produces no trans-substantiation, since Chancy takes his daughter's body by assaulting her physically, which consumes and destroys her spirit. This perversion of the communion ritual initiates the re-gendering of Beatrice—likening her to Christ associates her with the masculine.

In the play's deployment of opposites as effects of each other—one element of the pair anticipating its antithesis—Beatrice's purity and potential to be a saviour is nevertheless countered by her evocation as Eve: "Your chastity, Eve, has a fault" (86). Interpretations of the story of creation read Eve as introducing sin into the world, when she invites Adam to eat the fruit from the tree, even though forbidden by God to do so. Eve symbolises treacherous female sexuality which is irresistibly alluring to men and over which they have no control, even if it leads to their destruction. The image of Eve provides a link with Clarke's earlier representation of female slaves as amoral and sexually available property. When Chancy addresses Beatrice as "Half-black Negress, scented slave of *Nature,*"(86) of whom" Easter demands such small sacrifices," he identifies her as his slave and denies her relationship to him as his daughter. Furthermore, assimilating her to a "slave of *Nature*" naturalises slavery and places her outside the social, as if her identity were not directly shaped by the institution of slavery and its relations of power.

Through Clarke's representation of her as an emblem of salvation and destruction, Beatrice's identity is rendered figurative to the point of verging on the allegorical. Clearly, the same might be said of Chancy, who predominantly incarnates a figure of evil contrasting with Beatrice's goodness. In the context of a verse drama which features richly concise, densely allusive language, the allegory between good and evil seems consistent with the play's form. Because it defiles her, Beatrice's rape becomes the first step in a self-sacrifice that will lead to the liberation of the slaves. The move to turn Beatrice into a martyr depends on the annihilation of her identity and on a recasting of her gender, so that, while she occupies the body of a woman, her slave status subsumes her social identity as female and makes her stand metonymically for all the slaves on the estate.

In the aftermath of the rape, Beatrice stumbles in shock to Lustra, to whom she describes herself as both dead and infected by Chancy—and by extension his evil:

> I was black, but comely. Don't glance
> Upon me: This flesh is crumbling
> Like proved lies, I'm perfumed, ruddied
> Carrion. Assassinated (90).

When she emerges from shock, alluded to in the stage direction as an "*awakening,*" the heroin says "Beatrice? What is she? Oh, Beatrice is dead" (92). In the course of pronouncing herself dead, she also translates herself into an object, not asking "who is she?" but "what?" The moment perverts the resurrection, because Beatrice is reborn not into ever-lasting life, but into a living death which destroys her female identity and places her into a process of reconfigured identities as she prepares for her self-sacrifice.

Besides the reference to Easter, Clarke includes a rich pattern of allusions which help to forge an association between Beatrice and Christ.

The terms of ritual and sacrifice laid out by René Girard in *Violence and the Sacred* serve as a useful reminder that sacrifice, even in a Christian context, involves ritualistic contamination. Girard, writing of royal incest within African societies, suggests that the king must perform transgressions before he takes office:

> For example he must eat certain forbidden foods, and commit certain acts of violence. In some instances, he is literally bathed in blood and fed concoctions whose ingredients (bloody offal and refuse of all kinds) indicate their evil character. In some societies the whole enthronement ceremony takes place in an atmosphere of blood-stained confusion.[3]

Later, Girard warns that

> Rather than welcome the powers of evil with open arms, the rites seek to exorcise them. The king must show himself "worthy" of his punishment—fully as worthy as the original outcast from whom the ceremony derives. It is important to cultivate the future victim's supposed potential for evil, to transform him into a monster of iniquity—not for esthetic reasons, but to enable him to polarize, to literally draw from himself, all infectious strains of the community and transform them into sources of peace and fecundity.[4]

As intimated in this lengthy citation of Girard, the rape episode allows Clarke to show Beatrice absorbing part of Chancy's evil into her own body. Says Beatrice, "womb's a fractured vase,/Teeming, itching, with cockroaches" (94), and later, "My womb's a stew of vinegar and blood,/Some Easter pollution" (95). The representation of her body—and particularly of the female biological marker of the womb—as enduring "some Easter pollution" heightens and extends the abjection inherent in the martyrdom of Christ, who on Palm Sunday rode intoJerusalem as the King of the Jews, only to be tried and crucified with criminals on Golgotha.

As an act of violent, destructive contamination which leads Beatrice to describe herself as "dead" (92), the rape also symbolises her father's defilement of the purity which forms the core of her sense of identity:

I knelt and prayed. He pried out my heart. I fell.
He jeered. I feared God. He feared nothing. I wept.
He jeered. I hurt. He enjoyed. I choked. He chafed.
I groaned. He grinned. I was pure. He was powerful (94).

As well as the physical violence of sexual assault, the play makes clear that the penetration destroys Beatrice's spirituality and the associations

---

[3] René Girard, *Violence and the Sacred,* tr. Patrick Gregory (Baltimore: The Johns Hopkins UP, 1972): 105.

[4] *Ibid.*: 107.

of "whiteness" which it carries as a set of beliefs learned at the convent which Lustra attended. Raped by her father, Beatrice feels betrayed by God; when Lustra calls out "God God God...," Beatrice replies "Ha! Don't utter that name./I want nothing more to do with Him" (94). Her faith shattered, she says "I've died here in just four days,/But won't be resurrected," and then declares herself "impure" and "unclean" (97).

Clarke portrays the rape as absolute destruction without any possibility of healing. Betrayed by her white father, who violently exerts his power over her, she pronounces herself as "black blackened blacker" (95). She is dehumanised to such a degree that one of the slaves, Deal, describes the rape as Chancy sticking "his ramrod down her clean muzzle" (98). Besides emphasising the violence of rape, Clarke's metaphor of the gun also forcedly shifts the act into the terrain of the military, thereby implicitly masculinising it and negating issues of gender. At that moment, the rape—clearly a consequence of having to live in bondage—becomes a metonym for slavery and the violence inherent in a person's ownership of another. Within the logic of the play, Beatrice—already metaphorically dead—must don the mantle of the sacrificial victim, since by reason of its very magnitude, the evil of slavery can only be addressed if met on its own terms of masculine violence. As Girard writes of the kings, it is as if Beatrice had absorbed "all infectious strains of the community and [will] transform them into sources of peace and fecundity."[5] The crucial difference remains gender: because "she" is not "he," she has no access to power within the masculinist logic of the play; she will therefore never become king or queen, but be relegated to the rank of sacrificial martyr. Put bluntly, the release from bondage depends on the martyrdom of a woman whose body is in the end quite literally sacrificed to secure the freedom of the other slaves.

The order of the estate being overturned marks the beginning of the actual freeing of the slaves. To borrow Lead's words, "everything that is white must be murdered" (124), including the belief in God. As Beatrice says when she throws the Bible into the fireplace following her rape: "No more white lies, no more black pain" (110). Later, having murdered Chancy, she announces

> I'd rubbed raw the New Testament, weeping,
> The Old Testament, praying. I cut him.
> Two gashes, and he bled like a butcher.
>   White men, you took away my freedom
> And gave me religion.
> So be it: I became a devout killer (140).

---

[5] *Ibid.*: 107.

Annihilating all that is white generates a radical instability on the estate. In this process, links are forged between unlikely characters, creating the sense of a world in a state of rapid disintegration. For example, Lustra identifies herself as a slave, telling Beatrice "My chains are invisible, silent;/But they weigh me down, they press me down" (74). Thereby, Lustra aligns herself not only with Beatrice, but also with the latter's biological mother. Similarly, after discovering Beatrice's love for Lead, Chancy has her lover lashed so that his body gets scarred, as if to brand it with the violence of slavery (118); when raped by her father, Beatrice scratches his face, leaving "five scarlet lines" on his cheek (86). Rhetorically, these exchanges involve similes which suggest that in certain respects some characters become "like" others: Chancy is like Lead; Lustra is like Beatrice. The latter recognises the inaccuracy of these correspondences—at least of the one established between herself and Lustra, who has only endured metaphorical slavery as opposed to her actual one: "I'm still a slave; you've not suffered like me" (74). The gap between the elements of a simile—which parallels the slippage between the signified and signifier—suggests that instability is a property of language itself. This moment in the script acts as a forceful reminder of the fact that in the economy of language the relation between signifier and signified is not direct and unmediated. As hypothesised by Lacan in "Agency of the Letter in the Unconscious," this amounts to "the sliding of the signified under the signifier, which is always active in discourse."[6] This slippage is brought to the fore through rhetorical figures of metaphor and metonymy. It is as a consequence of this instability that Beatrice's identity—which like all identities is forged through language and thereby inscribed within the social—shifts from that of a young slave woman raped by her father to that of the "martyr-liberator."

Announcing "Slave days is over!," Beatrice *"seizes the dagger from Lead's fingers"* (126). The extent of her contamination becomes clear when Lead grabs Beatrice and she *"slams him in the face with the knife handle"* (126). Her fury turns on her lover, and so even her love for him has been contaminated, which prompts Lustra to comment that "His blood gluts your veins, but you crave it on your hands" (126). The moment rehearses another slippage between characters. Whereas the initially Christ-like Beatrice had offered the possibility of Chancy's redemption, her father's rape of her made her ingest his blood in a perversion of the salvation from death and sin promised through the crucifixion of Christ. The blood of Chancy, the anti-Christ, destroys her. The

---

[6] Jacques Lacan, "The Agency of the Letter in the Unconscious or Reason since Freud," in *Ecrits: A Selection*, tr. Alan Sheridan (New York: Norton, 1977): 160.

second part of Lustra's comment marks the height of Beatrice's transition from passivity to action, from being the object of her father's desire to becoming the agent of his destruction: *"Beatrice leads Lead towards the door. She can no longer distinguish desire from disease"* (127). Beatrice's full contamination completes the preparatory phase of the sacrifice, the action thereby reaching its climax.

The play does not actually culminate in the killing of Chancy. As the stage directions record, *"Unseen Chancy's body sprawls, shocked—like the subject of David's* Marat assassiné" (128). Displaced to the wings, the actual climax of the play coincides with the liberation of the slaves, which occurs in the context of the arrival of the colony's military. The slave rebellion ends with Beatrice killing Dice, one of Chancy's overseers, and with the death of Beatrice's lover, Lead (137-38). The final moments of the play are described in highly theatrical terms:

> *Drumrolls. A cannon peals. Light wails, bruised, peeling. A meringue storm pitches the Atlantic.*
> *Liberated: (Singing)* Oh freedom, oh freedom,
> O freedom over me.
> And before I'd be a slave,
> I'd be buried in my grave,
> And go home to my Lord and be free (148).

This song of liberation is followed by the hanging of Lustra and of Beatrice (148). Although the action of the play closes with the two hangings, Clarke includes several paragraphs of stage directions which describe the women preparing Beatrice's body for burial near the marshlands of the Minas Delta on the Bay of Fundy, a site that clearly links the suppressed history of slavery in Nova Scotia with that of another community which suffered at the hands of the British coloniser, the Acadians.[7]

Clarke's association of Beatrice with the Acadians also establishes significant parallels with the legendary figure of Evangeline: just as Beatrice Chancy represents a construct of the imagination of a male

---

[7] In 1755, these were exiled from the agriculturally rich marshlands of the Bay of Fundy, where the action of *Beatrice Chancy* is set. This expulsion—called by the Acadians "*Le Grand Dérangement*"—marked the high point of the vying of England and France for control over the territories known today as Nova Scotia and New Brunswick. By the middle of the eighteenth-century, these colonies were increasingly resisting British imperial rule and its concomitant economic exploitation. Because of the Acadians' total lack of loyalty to the British Crown, it became a military necessity for the English to control the area around the Bay of Fundy in order to contain the impending insurrection and the threat which the Acadians posed to British interests.

author, so too does Evangeline, who is known through Longfellow's poem *Evangeline: A Tale of Acadie* written in 1847. The poem purports to be based on a historical incident in which Evangeline, after being separated from her betrothed, wandered throughout the Midwestern territories and the Eastern seaboard of the United States, finally finding him as he is near death.[8] He dies in her arms, with Evangeline dying soon after, "released from a life of exile and steadfast loyalty that has received no reward on earth."[9] Both Clarke's play and Longfellow's poem present narratives of women from Acadia whose identities are shaped by the violent force of colonisation. Both women die having lived lives of sacrifice. Both emblematically embody modes of female virtue involving voluntary self-destruction, as if within the parameters of the maculinist imagination, femininity must be contained through death. Through the parallels with Evangeline, Beatrice and "*her sepia cadaver, lapped in ivory muslin*" (148) are eventually returned to the feminine, beyond the play and unseen by the audience. In so doing, Clarke re-hearses conventional depictions of femininity as idealised within patriarchal culture. When raped, Beatrice was regendered as the phallic avenger who had agency. Restored in death to the feminine, she recovers her purity, but is deprived of agency.

Historically, the basis of slavery was (and remains) the ownership of human beings by others. The reality of this economic arrangement meant that slaves had no rights to family and its affective ties. Slaves were chattel, and as such their bodies represented their value. In this context, the value of women slaves not only derived from their labour, but also from their sexual subjugation and reproductive capacity, since their children would automatically be the property of the slave owner. In its charting of the liberation of the slaves through the sacrifice of the heroine, *Beatrice Chancy* certainly explores this notion of property. But the story becomes an allegory of liberation in which Beatrice, as a woman, is elided through Clarke's deployment of figurative verse language. In the slippage, what is lost is a crucial element of slavery: its

---

[8] Nathaniel Hawthorne's *American Notebooks* record that his friend H.L.C. [the Reverend H. L. Conolly] heard the story of Evangeline from a member of his congregation. Conolly recounted the story to Hawthorne, because he thought that his friend might like to base one of his pieces of writing on it. Hawthorne was not so inclined, but when the pair happened to dine with Longfellow, the story was recounted to him. There is no historical evidence to support the veracity of the story. See Nathaniel Hawthorne, *The American Notebooks*, ed. Claude M. Simpson (1932; Chicago: Ohio State UP, 1972): 182.

[9] Francis Zichy, "*Evangeline: A Tale of Acadie*," in *The Oxford Companion to Canadian Literature*, eds. Eugene Benson and William Toye (Toronto: Oxford UP, 1997, 2nd ed.): 370.

particular impact on the labouring bodies of women, both as workers and sexual beings.[10] In Clarke's play, the force of the modifier "female" remains within conventional notions of the woman as virtuous, moral and self-sacrificing. The liberation of the slaves does indeed entail the sacrifice of a woman, of her body and identity. Despite her reconfiguration as the phallic avenger, the heroine is nevertheless in the end returned to femininity and its association with virtue. In short, the play's epigraph—"Men write history; Women are history"—constitutes an apt conclusion to the drama. Confined to silence, the stories of women are written by men, which casts them within the male imaginary of femininity.

Works Cited

Clarke, George Elliott. *Beatrice Chancy* (Victoria: Polestar Book Publishers, 1999).

Girard, René. *Violence and the Sacred*, tr. Patrick Gregory (Baltimore: The Johns Hopkins UP, 1972).

Hawthorne, Nathaniel. *The American Notebooks*, ed. Claude M. Simpson (1932; Chicago: Ohio State UP, 1972).

Lacan, Jacques. "The Agency of the Letter in the Unconscious or Reason since Freud," in *Ecrits: A Selection*, tr. Alan Sheridan (New York: Norton, 1977): 145-78.

Sussman, Charlotte. "The Other Problem with Women: Reproduction and Slave Culture in Aphra Behn's *Oroonoko*," in *Rereading Aphra Behn: History, Theory, and Criticism*, ed. Heidi Hutner (Charlottesville: UP of Virginia, 1993): 212-33.

Zichy, Francis. "*Evangeline: A Tale of Acadie*," in *The Oxford Companion to Canadian Literature*, eds. Eugene Benson and William Toye (Toronto: Oxford UP, 1997, 2nd ed.): 370-71.

---

[10] For a further discussion of the implications for slaves of family, and particularly of female sexuality and reproduction, see: Charlotte Sussman's "The Other Problem with Women: Reproduction and Slave Culture in Aphra Behn's *Oroonoko*."

"From Twisted History":
Reading *Angélique*

ALAN FILEWOOD

University of Guelph

In the introduction to her anthology, *Testifyin': Contemporary African Canadian Drama*, Djanet Sears makes the important point that "any informal examination into Canadian Theatre will likely reveal an absence of African Canadians as contributors altogether."[1] Taking this point a step further, the absence of African Canadian artists in the narrative of theatre history signals a more profound absence in the national imaginary. Historically, the notion of "Canadian Theatre," which conjoins two unstable terms, has always meant an imagined theatre projected within (and often inhibited by) the material theatre of the day. This idea of the imagined theatre brings into play the entire realm of theatre culture that is quoted, implied and legitimised by the theatre as it is understood at any given historical moment. At the same time, the imagined theatre brings into play the theatre that it rejects. If the theatre enacts the national imaginary, the absences which it frames—historically and materially—are equally constitutive of theatre culture. "Canadian theatre" can in this way be understood as a history of absences: the actual theatre culture of the moment always refers to an imagined theatre that defers realisation.

I make this point to introduce Lorena Gale's *Angélique*, because in both its narrative performance strategies and its production history, the play exposes the crises of contemporary Canadian theatre as it seeks to re-imagine the nation that it enacts. *Angélique* represents to my mind the most remarkable and important play staged in Canada in the late 1990s. Its vision of Canadian history is unsettling to those raised in the dominant myth of liberal multiculturalism, and its theatrical history signals alarms about the inability of Canadian theatre culture to accept radical revisioning.

---

[1] Djanet Sears, ed., *Testifyin': Contemporary African Canadian Drama: Vol. 1* (Toronto: Playwrights Canada Press, 2000): i.

Angélique is a product of the theatre enterprise that developed in Canada to model the liberal pluralist nation. Lorena Gale, herself a theatre worker, has for over twenty years pursued a career as an actor, director and now playwright in a theatre enterprise that affords few possibilities for African Canadian women. Since an early draft of her play won a national playwriting award in 1995, it has moved through the entire realm of possibilities offered by the informal network of play development programmes that function as the dramaturgical crucible—the research and development laboratory—of Canadian theatre. *Angélique* has evolved through a long sequence of seven different workshop productions, leading to a culminating fully staged production in Alberta Theatre Projects' renowned PlayRites programme. The whole pre-history of *Angélique* is worth restating here, because it clearly shows on the one hand the systemisation of play development, and on the other the somewhat disconcerting end result. Here follows the production pre-history, as compiled by the playwright:

1995   Excerpt published in *Canadian Theatre Review*.
Monologue published in *Another Perfect Piece: Monologues From Canadian Plays* (Playwrights Canada Press 1995)
Winner, Du Maurier National Playwriting Competition.
Workshop/staged reading, Women in View Festival, Vancouver.
Workshop/reading, Nightwood Theatre Company, Groundswell Festival, Toronto.

1996   Workshop/staged reading, Spring Writes Festival, Vancouver.
Excerpt published in *Beyond the Pale: Dramatic Writings by First Nations and Writers of Color* (Playwrights Canada Press).

1997   Workshop production, On the Verge Festival, National Arts Centre, Ottawa.
Presentation, 4th International Women Playwrights Conference, Galway, Ireland.
Workshop production, Celafi Festival/First Afri-Canadian Playwrights Conference, Canadian Stage, Toronto.
Production draft development, Banff Centre for the Arts, Playwrights Colony.

1998   Staged reading, Calypso Productions, Dublin, Ireland.
Professional premiere, Pan Canadian playRites Festival, Alberta Theatre Projects, Calgary.
Nomination, Outstanding New Play, Betty Mitchell Awards, Calgary.

2000   Journal publication, *Canadian Theatre Review* (CTR 100).
Book publication, Playwrights Canada Press.

This seems, by any account, a distinguished pedigree for a new play, with prestigious publications, workshops at the National Arts Centre and

Canadian Stage Company, and a premiere at the most respected new play showcase in Canada. But there are two ways to read this history. The first is as an accumulation of distinction, the second as a tier of absences. Few plays "arrive" on the canonising stage with this degree of distinction. This represents the kind of history that would seem to record the efforts and investments (of time, of labour, of creativity, and of money) of a great number of people, all of whom appear committed to putting *Angélique* on the stage. But since its Alberta premiere, *Angélique* has not appeared on a stage in Canada. It has, however, appeared twice in the United States, with productions in Detroit and New York, where, in both cases, African American theatre is an established fact. This might seem to suggest that *Angélique* "speaks" to audiences drawn from the African diaspora, but the fact that the play appears to have better chances of production in the United States than in Canada suggests as well that it summons an *imagined* audience in Canada, that the productions that *it does not receive* are as important to an understanding of the play as those that actually take place.

Why, after such a long workshop history, has *Angélique* not been programmed on the main stage of a major theatre in Canada? We can only guess, but the expected answer would be that artistic directors are too cautious, that *Angélique*'s enactment of nation and history is too "risky." From there, it is not too far a step to surmise—perhaps cynically—that Lorena Gale has written a play that satisfies the needs of play development bodies, but not of institutional theatres. By hosting a workshop of the play, Canadian Stage receives the credit for sponsoring it without actually having to produce it or invest financial risk in it. This cynical reading implies that *Angélique* functions as a value-producing commodity in an economy of reputation.

There may be some truth in this, but I tend to another interpretation, which gives the play and the author more agency. *Angélique* is a genuinely radical statement that uses the moment of performance to destabilise the narratives that have historically secured Canadian nationhood. And in the same way, it destabilises structures of critical authority: it forces the critic, the "I" that authorises value, into a personal response. There is a moment in the first scene of the play, in which the character of François Poulin de Francheville, speaking from Gale's imagined New France in 1730, describes his first sight of Angélique, the African (descended) slave whom he has been invited to buy:

So I said I'd take a look. What does it cost to look?

ANGÉLIQUE in shadows.

The figure of this fine creature could not but attract my particular notice. She was standing off to the side with some others. Perfectly straight ... with the most elegant shapes that can be viewed in nature. Her chestnut skin shone with double lustre. Her large ebony eyes with their inward gaze. Her proud face ... immobile ... I don't know ... (7).[2]

In a similar complex of fascinated desire, the play itself attracts the "particular notice" of the critical eye that presumes to survey and value theatrical commodities. And just as François' capturing "notice" of Angélique's blackness takes him to the point where language fails, so too does the blackness of the play paralyse critical discourse. One of the lessons of *Angélique*, a lesson that runs through much African Canadian drama, is that the Canadian imaginary marks its limitations with the notion of the black other. Blackness may be a shifting, plural and historically contingent category, but it always functions as the border. Angélique is one of several slaves in the play, each captured by a different system of servitude—Claude, the French indentured servant, has traded freedom for opportunity; Manon, the aboriginal slave, thinks of herself as free because she is in her own land. But Angélique comes to believe that neither she nor her children will ever negotiate a place in this new country: there will always exist a blackness that borders the map of the cultural imagination.

Critical authority ruptures when reading *Angélique*, because Lorena Gale exposes the structures of power and desire which have erased African presence from the Canadian imaginary, and in the performative structures of the play she implicates the audience in that erasure. The fact of imagining the play in that sense verifies the story it tells, and if we accept the story, then we must also accept that we are produced by the structures that have denied the story, that we are part of it, that, as Gale tells us in her stage directions, "Then is now. Now is then" (6). Other "thens" cross through the play, awakened by the politics of reception; the one that frames my own reception is a dimly remembered Halifax school yard in the late 1950s, where white and black kids looked at each other across a playground that was in practice segregated. In a very real sense, *Angélique* plays in the space between those gazes.

Lorena Gale juggles boldly with a complex of uncomfortable and disconcerting subjects, beginning with the fact of slavery in the pre-Canadian colonies. The dominant narratives of Canadian history condemn slavery as an American institution, preferring instead to construct Canada as a haven of liberty and justice. *Angélique* indicts the past as much more complex and contradictory. Perhaps the most harrowing aspect of the play's historical vision is the complexity of the slave

---

[2] All quotations from *Angélique* are taken from the following edition: Lorena Gale, *Angélique*, *Canadian Theatre Review* 100 (Fall 1999): 5-27. Further citations appear parenthetically in the text.

system which it exposes—a system where aboriginal First Peoples and Africans are caught in a web of slavery, where commodity slavery and indentured servitude intertwine, where slavery is systematically enforced through rape. In a stylistic frame that offsets cool distance with intense emotion, the play exposes the psychology of a slavery so abject that a mother cannot bear to see her children grow into it, and ensures they do not. The historical episode recalled (and reclaimed) by the play concerns the execution by hanging of a young woman in Montreal in 1734, on charges of setting a fire that ripped through the city. In a community where slavery fulfills no economic purpose—except in an economy of status and distinction—Angélique is a "gift" from François to his embittered wife Thérèse (who, as Angélique will do, mourns a dead child). But as Thérèse well knows, Angélique is in fact François' gift to himself.

The substructure of the play exposes a complex world in which Angélique is a diasporic voice who is ironically more European than many of the proto-Québécois amongst whom she lives. She is an African who has never seen Africa; instead, she has been "imported" from Madeira, taken from a context of slavery that at the very least offered the comfort of family. As she tells César, an American-born slave with whom she is expected to produce children for the slave market,

> We toiled for them. Yes! But it was work. Just work. Hard work is a part of life. And at least we were together ... I cannot understand this coldness and this cruelty. I may have always been a slave. But I did not feel like one until I came to this land ... (15).

From the island of Madeira, Angélique could "imagine I could see the land of my ancestors." In the middle of the North American continent, she cannot: all that she can envision is a future of rape and brutality, for herself and her children. This loss of any sense of a future (which corresponds in fact to the erasure from the social imaginary) is the condition which separates the African slaves from the indentured French servants and aboriginal slaves who share their toil. In the span of the play, Angélique brings five children into the world. None lives very long. In one of the most harrowing moments of the play, Angélique sits alone with her first infant—whose fair complexion excites gossip and speculation among the townsfolk. To the accompaniment of a "new heart beating," she tells the baby a long, lyrical and mythic story about the origin of the world and the separation of the originary, "seamless" and profound darkness, and about the light it birthed:

> Light
> was now everywhere.
> Cutting through the darkness

with the sharpness of an axe.
Cruelly
severing
the umbilicus between them.

Darkness
was so blinded by the light
she could no longer
see.
And so
retreated.
To where she could have some sense of
herself.
Though light still
pierced
her.
As a reminder that
It
now
ruled
every
thing.

Light and darkness.
That
is how the two became separate
forces.
In constant
opposition.
Light
in the forefront
and darkness ...
waiting ...
on the edge
of everything (13).

At the end of the story, with a tenderness that is hard to witness—the more so because we see it coming—Angélique does what we know she must do, and gently smothers the baby, with the words, "Fly home and greet the darkness. There are others waiting there. Mama loves you and will join you there" (13). Perhaps the most disconcerting thing about this moment is that it occurs fairly early on in the play, not as the tragic climax of a sentimentalised plot, but as an almost routine incident of daily life.

But routine as it may seem, the birth and death of this first child transforms Angélique. When she first arrives in New France, she is still able to envision futurity. She is introduced to her new slavery as a worker—and the stage directions remind us that "Unless otherwise stated, in every scene in which the slaves are present they are working"

(6). Angélique meets her new mistress on this ground of work and duty (with the play of anachronism that is so crucial to Gale's argument):

> THÉRÈSE   Beds each morning, change the linen every other day or so. Bathrooms every other morning. Vacuum the main living spaces, bedroom, living room, stairs daily ... Don't worry, we have a deluxe machine. I hear it makes vacuuming a breeze ... Floors swept and washed every day. Waxing every third week. Are you getting all this ...?
>
> ANGÉLIQUE (*Eager to please*)   Oui, Madame.
>
> THÉRÈSE   I am very sensitive to dust. You'll have to dust each day. Metal and wood surfaces polished. Mirrors and windows clear. Without streaks ...
>
> ANGÉLIQUE Oui, Madame.
>
> THÉRÈSE   Let's see. What else is there? Laundry, including dry cleaning, is Tuesday and Friday. Hand washing daily. Mending as necessary. Marketing is Saturday.
>
> ANGÉLIQUE Oui, Madame (7).

The depersonalised nature of this work deceives Angélique. It promises a secure structure of duty which can be separated from the self and in effect disguises slavery as a "job." Thus in the next scene, we witness Angélique "moving through space in an abstracted dervish of cleaning" to the sound of urban club "jungle" music on a boom box. "This time," she tells herself, "will be different":

> This time,
> I will be treated with loving kindness and understanding.
> I will work hard.
> From sun to sun.
> Do exactly as I'm told .
> I will perform each duty with pride and obedience.
> I will maintain their order.
> Everything will go smoothly.
> I'll know my place.
> I will give freely of myself.
> Repaying their humanity with loyalty.
> Earning their protection
> and their care.
> They'll wonder how they ever lived without me (8).

This promise of a humanised life that enables private subjectivity is almost immediately extinguished by rape, which makes explicit the fact that Angélique's "job" is to be a commodity and an actor in François' private theatre of desire. Gale shows this suppression of self in a theatricalised demonstration of the way in which rape eradicates the illusions of autonomy. In this gestic demonstration, the instrument of sexual torture is the corset in which François dresses Angélique. François masks his sexual ownership in his erotic fantasy of seduction, and in this dramaturgy of desire and power, Angélique experiences a deceptive illusion of freedom:

> From behind, François reaches around and removes Angélique's uniform, revealing period undergarments beneath her modern clothing. He then commences to dress her up again, only this time, in period clothing. Angélique does not resist.
>
> ANGÉLIQUE A dog barking ... A baby crying ... Footsteps ... The wind whistling low and breathy ...
>
> Thérèse enters and watches in the shadows
>
> ANGÉLIQUE The faint creek of wood giving way
> to weight ...
> Someone stepping stealthily on the fourth floorboard
> before the doorway to my room.
> There is no sneaking in this house where every sound
> betrays ...
> A cat scrowling ...
> Perhaps the dog has caught the cat.
> Or maybe
> the cat has caught the dog.
>
> *François places a corset on Angélique.*
>
> I could leave here. Right now ...
>
> She takes a step away from him. Then another and another. Which has the effect of tightening the corset.
>
> I am walking towards the door ... I open it ... I step outside and ...
>
> *She falls forward. Her arms spread like a bird. She is kept aloft by the laces of the corset which François holds like reins on a wild horse. But he doesn't notice anything happening with her. He pumps her, like he is fucking her from behind.*
>
> I'm freeeeeeee! I'm free! I'm free! I'm free! Look at meeee ... ! I'm running through the gates of the city. I'm racing across the land. I'm floating across the big river. I am washed up on the shores of my beloved Madeire ...
>
> *He pulls her back to him and ties the corset.*
>
> But I am not really out there ... (16).

The birth of her child projects this dehumanisation into a future of erasure and despair, and it leads Angélique to her own understanding of radicalism as an existential choice. Lorena Gale never shows us whether Angélique actually starts the fire that begins and ends the play, but she shows how she might have, and replays the voices that condemn her. Before the fire, Angélique seeks escape. When François dies (after drinking water that may have been deliberately contaminated by the

Reading Angélique

slaves), Thérèse make plans to sell Angélique, and the need to escape becomes urgent. Angélique has fallen in love with Claude, who fuels her hopes of escape by telling her of the free Blacks whom he has seen in New England. He promises to escape with her, but defers until the night of the fire. For Claude, escape is about opportunity:

> In New France, I'll never be more than peasant scum who signed five years of his life away for some new clothes, a few sacks of grain and a stony piece of land that may never bear fruit. But in New England, or farther south, there's no telling what a man could make of himself (23).

What Angélique does not see is that Claude dreams of becoming another François, that his dream of power and wealth reiterates the conditions that have enslaved her.

The consuming fire that offers Angélique escape, but leads to her execution, starts with a pail of hot coals which we see Angélique take from Claude:

> ANGÉLIQUE Love ... I had almost forgotten it felt like ... freedom.
>
> CLAUDE   Soon. *(he exits leaving the pail with Angélique)*
>
> ANGÉLIQUE How long can I wait? Each minute brings me closer to a living death. And I'm alive. I am alive!
>
>   His touches burn, sear, scorch, igniting fire deep inside where pain and ice had been. And I feel ... heat, life, force, power, black and strong.
>
> She envies that. Cold, passionless bitch. Just like her bastard husband. Both sucking. Sucking life. Denying life.
>
> No! I am not a chair, a sack of grain or a calf to be fattened and sold for slaughter. I am alive. And loved. And I can't wait ... any longer.
>
> *Smoke begins to fill the stage.*
>
> THÉRÈSE   Fire!
>
> ANGÉLIQUE Fire!
>
> IGNACE   Fire!
>
> CÉSAR   Fire!
>
> *Pandemonium breaks out. Church bells ringing, people shouting, panicking. The actors run around and organize themselves into a line in which buckets pass from person to person. Angélique is at the end of the line. Buckets pass swiftly and desperately from person to person. Claude enters picking his teeth and watches silently for a moment. Angélique turns to grab another bucket, sees Claude and instead grabs Claude's hand.*
>
> ANGÉLIQUE Now?
>
> CLAUDE   Now! (23-24)

As they make their bid for freedom, we observe the testimony of witnesses, all of whom implicate Angélique. In alternating scenes, Angélique and Claude find themselves lost in the winter bush; they celebrate their freedom by making love, but as Angélique sleeps, Claude deserts her because "with you, I will always be running" (26). When she awakes, she is arrested, tortured (this we hear from the voices of witnesses) and the play ends with its beginning: then is now, and Angélique is hanged.

In its subject matter and its theatrical technique alike, *Angélique* works a ruthlessly effective critique of the naturalised fictions that historical narrative so often conceals. The conventional mode of historical narrative in the theatre—at least on Canadian stages—is one in which revelations of past crime speak to present injustice. The mapping of past and present tends to result in a "living history" form of dramatic realism that dehistoricises the past. Lorena Gale deliberately dismantles this convention with a strategic play of spectatorial politics in which every moment of the drama is constructed through frames of testimony and witnessing. In her introductory directions, Gale writes that "Although the specifics are not written into the text, what can be explored is the concept of witnessing. As servants and slaves are essentially invisible, experiment with who sees what, knows what etc"(6). This notion of witnessing, of observation and testimony, is built into the performance text of the play. It destabilises the receptive experience of the audience through anachronism, ambiguity and contradiction. Not knowing whom to believe, we depend on visual evidence. But the visual evidence of *Angélique* functions as deliberately unsettling.

In *Angélique* the past crime is not only slavery—humanised and perhaps in danger of being sentimentalised in the tragic history of one woman—but the erasure of it from dominant historical narratives. To address this, Gale intervenes in the structures of historical representation, to turn history on its head. In her cast list, she pointedly describes Angélique as "a slave in a history book"(6), and throughout the play we are confronted with the construction of history as a textual frame that can be manipulated to reveal or suppress. Characters move from period to contemporary dress; language shifts from conventionalised "historical" realism to contemporary idiom, and our points of historical reference are destabilised by the intrusion of artifacts of modernity (a computer, a bic lighter, a boom box) into the imagined past. Angélique herself begins and ends the play with a book in hand—the book in which she has been reduced to a minor note and, through the agency of the play, restored.

Reading Angélique

To this end, Gale plays with the technologies of authentification that verify representations in popular culture, but at the same time construct the "twisted history" that Angélique, in her closing speech, condemns, and which condemns her. By taking to its logical next step the common trope of historical melodrama, in which the past is always a costumed present, the intrusion of the world of the audience into the action of the play through the tactical planting of anachronisms naturalises the representation of the past. But at the same time, this play of anachronism *de*naturalises the past by exposing the limits and erasures of historical narration.

As audiences imagined in the theatre by the play, we witness Lorena Gale's interventions in what we take to be our shared history; as participants in the drama, we are the constructed witnesses to the monologues, addresses and testimonies of her characters. In this duality, the foundational concept of witnessing itself shifts, as what begins as an act of resistance becomes a medium of oppression. The act of witnessing that is so instrumental to the survival of enslaved peoples is also the act that legitimises the oppressive power of the slave-owners. To this end, video screens on the stage reinforce what Gale herself refers to as "documentary" evidence, when the characters testify to Angélique's (alleged) guilt. That such mediatised authenticity is as much a part of the "twisted history" as the records themselves, Gale makes clear by her passing allusion to the hyperbolic media coverage of the O.J. Simpson case:

> *On all screens.*
>
> REPORTER   In dramatic new developments in the O.J. ... I mean Marie Joseph Angélique case ... four year old Amable Le Moine was brought before the court. Amable, daughter of Alexis Le Moine Monière and brother in law of Madame de Francheville, who swore under oath to tell the truth, testified that on the day of the fire she saw the negress, Marie Joseph Angélique, carrying a coal shuttle up to the attic (25).

In the structure of complicity fixed by the returned gaze of the testifying characters and the audience, Angélique must be condemned, as she recognises at the end of the play. She exists only to be systematically erased. This is in fact the opening moment of the play which the rest of the action restores. The play begins with Angélique dancing, book in hand, as a depersonalised, authentifying voice-over gradually removes her from the historical record:

> SFX   And in seventeen thirty four a Negro slave set fire to the City of Montreal and was hanged.
> in seventeen thirty four a Negro slave set fire to the City of Montreal and was hanged.

> seventeen thirty four a Negro slave set fire to the City of Montreal and was hanged.
> a Negro slave set fire to the City of Montreal and was hanged
> slave set fire to the City of Montreal and was hanged
> set fire to the City of Montreal and was hanged
> fire to the City of Montreal and was hanged
> to the City of Montreal and was hanged
> City of Montreal and was hanged
> Montreal and was hanged
> and was hanged
> was hanged
> hanged (6).

In the play, Lorena Gale restores Angélique in the historical narratives that supply the national imaginary with evidence of its origins; *with* the play, she challenges the theatre profession—and its authorising structures of value and critical reception—to recognize that "we" are invested in the erasure of African Canadian experience, and that like François, we take "particular notice" of blackness for reasons we seldom choose to examine. *Angélique* activates a crisis in critical response, because it calls on us to confront the sliding glances of racism, the twisted and unspoken histories, the boundaries that we do not admit because they have been erased, the lost Angéliques in our shared history. No play in recent years has so deeply affected my sense of self as *Angélique*, a play of lost futures enacted on the stages of imagined theatres.

Works Cited

Gale, Lorena. *Angélique*, in *Canadian Theatre Review* 100 (Fall 1999): 5-27.
——— *Angélique* (Toronto: Playwrights Canada Press, 2000).
Sears, Djanet (ed.). *Testifyin': Contemporary African Canadian Drama: Vol. 1* (Toronto: Playwrights Canada Press, 2000).

Defying Category: Re/viewing John Herbert's *Fortune and Men's Eyes*

ROBERT WALLACE

Glendon College, York University

In the second edition of *The Oxford Companion to Canadian Literature*, Peter Dickinson introduces the drama section of the "Gay Literature" entry with the following assertion: "One could argue that gay drama in Canada actually began elsewhere." He substantiates his claim by stating that "John Herbert's *Fortune and Men's Eyes* (1967) opened to great acclaim off-Broadway in 1967 and was subsequently performed around the world, but did not receive a full-scale Canadian production until 1975." In his ensuing commentary, Dickinson implies one reason why Herbert's play failed to achieve production once he completed it in 1964: "Set in a prison, [it] questions the rigid gender roles imposed on men in our society, demonstrating how sex becomes an instrument of power ..." Dickinson's brief plot summary indicates the physical and psychological violence that Herbert's play depicts: "new inmate Smitty learns from Rocky what it means to rape, from Mona what it means to be raped." All three inmates are adolescents; together with Queenie, the fourth juvenile incarcerated in the play's reformatory setting, and a Guard that Herbert uses to represent Canadian penal authority, the characters dramatise "the brutal lessons of masculine identity formation" that the reform system perpetuates.[1] These "lessons" trouble not only catego-

---

[1] Peter Dickinson, "Gay Literature, 2: Drama," in *The Oxford Companion to Canadian Literature*, ed. Eugene Benson & William Toye (Toronto: Oxford UP, 1997, 2nd ed.): 451. The production history of Herbert's play is more complicated than Dickinson suggests. While the play premiered in New York on 23 February 1967 at the Actors' Playhouse off-Broadway and had received hundreds of productions around the world by 1975 (see Fulford for corroboration of this assertion), it was also produced in Canada well before the mid-1970s. Although its first Canadian production was a small non-professional "preview" at Toronto's Central Library Theatre on 19 October 1967, the New York production toured to Montreal in November that same year, where it played at Le Centre before proceeding to Toronto's Central Library Theatre for a short run as well. In 1968, the French translation of the play that was published in 1971 premiered at Montreal's Théâtre de Quatre Sous. In 1969, Montreal's Centaur Theatre presented the original

ries of gender but of sex as well. Further, they challenge the stability of genres such as "gay drama" so as to precipitate a crisis of category itself.

Eugene Benson, in his entry on *Fortune and Men's Eyes* in *The Oxford Companion to Canadian Theatre*, illustrates the resistance of Canada's theatrical establishment during the 1960s to questions posed by the play. Benson reports that the Stratford Festival workshopped Herbert's drama in October 1965, then denied it a full production, "because [the play's] subject and language were judged to be unsuitable for Stratford audiences."[2] In 1967, Nathan Cohen, then theatre critic for the *Toronto Star*, suggested that such resistance was typical of "the entertainment departments of the press and other media" of the time— institutions that, according to Cohen, demonstrated not only "indifference but active hostility" to Herbert's play. Trying to account for this attitude, Cohen foreshadows Dickinson's summation of the drama: "*Fortune and Men's Eyes* poses a truly critical challenge. It asks deeply disturbing questions about long-established personal and social assumptions."[3]

A quick review of academic commentary on the play reveals that resistance to *Fortune and Men's Eyes* was not restricted to mainstream Canadian institutions during the 1960s. In 1972, Neil Carson observed that Herbert's drama had suffered "astonishing neglect" in scholarly journals despite its widespread commercial success.[4] Unfortunately, his observation remains pertinent today. While many plays suffer such neglect, some achieve and maintain recognition as "established" texts through the processes of canonisation. Although "*Fortune and Men's Eyes* quickly became internationally famous—in its first ten years it was

---

English version, which was followed by other professional productions in Ottawa, Winnipeg and Vancouver that same year. In all likelihood, the 1975 production to which Dickinson refers is the first professional Canadian production that the play received in Toronto, a production which, under the direction of Graham Harley, opened at the Phoenix Theatre in November 1975. This production won Herbert the Chalmer's Award for Best New Canadian Play produced in Toronto. See Richard Plant, ed., *Modern Canadian Drama, Vol. 1* (Markham: Penguin, 1984): 175; and Eugene Benson, "*Fortune and Men's Eyes*," in *The Oxford Companion to Canadian Theatre*, eds. Eugene Benson and L.W. Conolly (Toronto: Oxford UP, 1989): 212-13.

[2] Eugene Benson, *op. cit.*: 212.

[3] Nathan Cohen, *Toronto Daily Star* (17 April 1967) quoted in Neil Carson, "Sexuality and Identity in *Fortune and Men's Eyes*," *Twentieth Century Literature* 18 (January-October 1972): 207.

[4] *Ibid.*

performed in more than hundred countries in some forty languages,"[5] it failed to generate the scholarly discussion necessary to establish it as an "important" text. The play led to the founding of the Fortune Society in the United States, was published by Grove Press in 1967 and was adapted into a film by MGM in 1970. Its continuing occlusion from academic study, however, led Brian F. Tyson to begin an article in 1978 with the following comment:

> It is now a decade since John Herbert's *Fortune and Men's Eyes* achieved a *succès de scandale* in New York, Toronto and London; but apart from one sensitive article by Ann Messenger, little serious attention has been given this study of corruption and brutality in a boys' reformatory, although its theme is as timely today as when it was written.[6]

In 1984, *Fortune and Men's Eyes* was the only play chosen by the editors of three anthologies of Canadian drama for inclusion in each, which seemingly would ensure its status in the Canadian canon if not consolidate Herbert's reputation as a prominent Canadian playwright.[7] A review of these anthologies by Michael Scholar for *Canadian Drama/ L'Art dramatique canadien* suggests some of the reasons why this has not happened. Scholar writes: "All of the plays [in these anthologies] are 'main stream' [*sic*] efforts; all are cautiously chosen, and controversial works are avoided; ... all are recognized pieces, or are written by 'recognized' playwrights."[8] Scholar's judgement—typical of other reviews of these anthologies (including my own)[9]—erases the difficulties that inhibited the premiere of Herbert's play and ignores the controversy that attended its early productions. Moreover, his evaluation misrepresents the position of both Herbert and the play in the mid-1980s. While *Fortune and Men's Eyes* possibly remained a "recognised piece" at this

---

[5] Benson, *op. cit.*: 213.

[6] Brian F. Tyson, "This Man's Art and That Man's Scope: Language and the Critics in *Fortune and Men's Eyes*," *Canadian Drama/L'Art dramatique canadien* 4:1 (Spring 1978): 34.

[7] Richard Plant, ed., *Modern Canadian Drama, Vol. 1* (Markham: Penguin, 1984); Richard Perkyns, ed., *Major Plays of the Canadian Theatre 1934-1984* (Toronto: Irwin, 1984); Jerry Wasserman, ed., *Modern Canadian Plays, Vol. 1* (Vancouver: Talonbooks, 1993). While the play's inclusion in these anthologies can indicate its canonical significance, its *availability* for anthologisation also indicates its decline in popularity. Seemingly, Grove Press, the original publisher of the play, was ready to relinquish its publication rights.

[8] Michael Scholar, "A Plethora of Plays: Three New Anthologies of Canadian Drama," *Canadian Drama/L'Art dramatique canadien* 11:1 (Spring 1985): 280.

[9] See Robert Wallace, "Constructing a Canon: A Review Essay," *Theatre History in Canada/Histoire du théâtre au Canada* 10:2 (Fall 1989): 218-22.

time, it is unlikely that John Herbert continued to be "recognised" by Canada's theatre-going public. The international success of *Fortune and Men's Eyes* did little for Herbert's career in Canada. As Jerry Wasserman points out, "Between 1972 and 1974 [Herbert] staged two ambitious new plays, *Born of Medusa's Blood* and *Omphale and the Hero*, and four one-acts under the title *Some Angry Summer Songs*, but no one seemed to be listening."[10] Since then, the playwright, along with his work, has sunk into obscurity.[11]

To redress this situation, this essay "re/views" not only *Fortune and Men's Eyes* but, in addition, academic commentary on the play. Besides examining the techniques by which Herbert problematises gender and sexuality, it considers how critical misreadings of his play substantiate its challenge to genre. In both its content and form, Herbert's play represents "the crisis of category"—a phrase that Marjorie Garber uses in *Vested Interests: Cross-dressing and Cultural Anxiety* to describe "a failure of definitional distinction, a borderline that becomes permeable, that permits of border crossings from one (apparently distinct) category to another."[12] Richard Perkyns alludes to the aspect of this crisis that has attracted the most attention in scholarly discussions of *Fortune and Men's Eyes* when he notes that "some of the greatest confusion arises from the nature of the play's homosexuality." Perkyns quotes the playwright from an interview in 1978 to suggest that "Herbert makes it clear that audiences have come to realize that the play is not specifically about homosexuality nor prison life, but rather about the reality of life and its great forces: 'envy, destruction, masochism and sadism'."[13] In fact, Herbert does not deny in this interview that his play focuses on homosexuality and imprisonment; rather, he confirms that these are "some of the basic realities of life." More relevant to my ensuing remarks, he also states that "My play's appeal has not been, as many of my detractors

---

[10] Wasserman, *op. cit.*: 63. In his entry on Herbert included in *Contemporary Dramatists*, ed. K.A. Berney (London: St. James, 1993, 5th ed.), D.D.C. Chambers lists twelve plays by Herbert (293).

[11] Besides the entries and papers already mentioned, I have been unable to locate any critical discussions of either John Herbert or *Fortune and Men's Eyes* published since 1984, with the exception of Chris Johnson's article on Herbert included in the *Dictionary of Literary Biography Vol. 53. Canadian Writers Since 1960, First Series*, ed. W. H. New (Detroit: Gale Research,1986), and D.D.C. Chambers' entry on Herbert included in the fifth edition of *Contemporary Dramatists* mentioned above, a shortened version of his original entry published in 1973.

[12] Marjorie Garber, *Vested Interests: Cross-dressing & Cultural Anxiety* (New York: Harper Perennial, 1993): 16.

[13] Richard Perkyns, ed., *Major Plays of the Canadian Theatre 1934-1984* (Toronto: Irwin, 1984): 77.

would have it, to a predominantly homosexual audience. If I'd had to depend on that for survival the play wouldn't have made its way to the extent that it did, in New York and elsewhere. It has lasted because it deals with perennial problems ..."[14]

Peter Dickinson is one of few critics to recognise that sex and power constitute the perennial problems that Herbert addresses in *Fortune and Men's Eyes* and that, to return to his comment that introduces this essay, Herbert represents these problems by creating a drama that "questions the rigid gender roles imposed on men in our society."[15] Not coincidentally, Dickinson is the only Canadian scholar to discuss the drama as a gay play. Other Canadian critics who have considered Herbert's text have either ignored or dismissed its gay content for reasons similar to those that Michael Scholar supplies in his review. Richard Paul Knowles, for example, in a discussion of the three 1984 anthologies, characterises Herbert's play as a "social realist" text that positions the audience either as voyeurs or as "self-congratulatory liberal 'concerned spectators.'"[16] Presumably, Knowles considers that audiences see something other than a gay play in *Fortune and Men's Eyes* for, elsewhere in his essay, he answers his own question "What is left out?" [in these anthologies] with the statement "virtually all regional, 'ethnic,' native, feminist, lesbian, gay, non-literary, or explicitly political drama that is subversive or 'ex-centric' on a formal or structural level, and that therefore cannot be readily absorbed into the canon."[17]

Knowles does not appear to be alone in his occlusion of *Fortune and Men's Eyes* from the category of gay drama. Inadvertently or not, John M. Clum omits the play from *Acting Gay: Male Homosexuality in Modern Drama*. This seems especially egregious given that Clum's roaming study of gay drama in Canada, the United States and Britain accords extensive coverage to "pre-Stonewall gay plays" in New York city, being particularly concerned to delineate them from gay plays written after the Stonewall riots of June 1969—insurrections in Greenwich Village that historians generally credit as galvanising the movements for lesbian and gay liberation in western cultures during the late twentieth-century. Clum carefully points out that "gay drama refers

---

[14] Rota Lister, "Interview with John Herbert," *Canadian Drama/L'Art dramatique canadien* 4:2 (Fall 1978): 176.

[15] Dickinson, *op. cit.*: 451.

[16] Richard Paul Knowles, "Voices (off): Deconstructing the Modern English-Canadian Dramatic Canon," in *Canadian Canons: Essays in Literary Value*, ed. Robert Lecker (Toronto: U of Toronto P, 1991): 99.

[17] *Ibid.*: 101.

to two kinds of plays written for two kinds of audiences."[18] The "post-Stonewall gay play" is one "written for gay audiences and which speaks to their shared experience."[19] In contrast, the "pre-Stonewall gay play" is "written primarily for the mainstream theater by a homosexual playwright."[20] While Herbert's play would seem to fit the latter category by virtue of its date of writing, production premiere and the author's characterisation of its audience cited above, it defies the category by resisting Clum's primary criteria for such a work—namely, that homosexuality be "the 'problem' that must be solved or eliminated by the final curtain."[21] Clum elaborates that the history of "homosexuals and homosexual desire is one of integration into, compromises with, and extension of this dramatic form ..."[22] Herbert's depiction of homosexual behaviour in *Fortune and Men's Eyes* rejects this paradigm by making the politics of incarceration—not homosexuality—the problem. As Vito Russo, another gay American scholar, explains, "The play made the point that in this kind of situation [prison] the system seized upon and used sex as a weapon against everyone, that all became victims of the institution."[23]

Although Herbert's focus on incarceration as "the problem" in *Fortune and Men's Eyes* might account for Clum's exclusion of the play from his study of "pre-Stonewall gay plays," the playwright's open identification of the play's relation to his own homosexuality certainly qualifies it for the category "post-Stonewall gay drama" that Clum and other critics attempt to define. In his introduction to *Out Front*, an anthology of gay and lesbian American plays published in 1988, Don Shewey writes: "To present homosexuality in the theater, someone (an author, speaking through an actor) has to stand up and say, 'This is me. I am gay.'"[24] Shewey accounts for "the strange, strained nature of most gay characters" in plays written and produced prior to 1968 by suggesting that during this time "playwrights and performers tended to view

---

[18] John M. Clum, *Acting Gay: Male Homosexuality in Modern Drama* (New York: Columbia UP, 1992: xii.

[19] *Ibid.*: xii.

[20] *Ibid.*: xiii.

[21] *Ibid.*

[22] *Ibid.*

[23] Vito Russo, *The Celluloid Closet: Homosexuality in the Movies* (New York: Harper and Row, 1987, rev. ed.): 198.

[24] Don Shewey, "Introduction. Pride in the Name of Love: Notes on Contemporary Gay Theatre," in *Out Front: Contemporary Gay & Lesbian Plays*, ed. Don Shewey (New York: Grove, 1988): xiii.

homosexuals as 'other,' as 'them' ..."[25] Clum makes a similar claim by proposing that "pre-Stonewall gay drama" "may seem to capitulate to the prejudices of its audience but actually reflects the internalized homophobia of the playwright."[26] Such suggestions become understandable when one remembers that in North America during the 1960s, homosexuality remained illegal and that "depictions of homosexuality were limited, if not eliminated, by legal sanctions against representing [it] onstage."[27] The situation in Great Britain was the same: until 1968, when its power was revoked, the Lord Chamberlain's office "was expected to keep homosexual characters and relationships off the British stage."[28]

In the 1978 interview quoted above, John Herbert reveals that *Fortune and Men's Eyes* is autobiographical, "based on a morals charge and had to do with my sexual nature. Laws were applied which have since been changed, but I was then sent to Guelph Reformatory, charged with homosexuality and convicted, in 1948."[29] Excerpts from a memoir published that same year in *Stage Voices*, a collection of statements by Canadian playwrights, clarify that Herbert's "sexual nature" was an issue early in his life. In one excerpt, the playwright details how, as a "very feminine looking"[30] young man working in Toronto, he was beaten "into complete unconsciousness" by homophobic police officers in 1944.[31] In another excerpt, he recounts the events that saw him "convicted of having impersonated a woman for immoral purposes"[32] in 1946. Throughout this excerpt, Herbert employs third person narration to distance himself from memories of "the most traumatic event of my early life."[33] He recalls that, wearing feminine attire, he exited a restau-

---

[25] *Ibid*. Despite the fact that *Fortune and Men's Eyes* ran for eleven months off Broadway in 1967, Shewey, like Clum, fails to mention it in his introductory history of gay American theatre. For Shewey, "the turning point" in the history of gay representation that marks the appearance of what Clum sees as "post-Stonewall" gay drama is the production of Mart Crowley's *The Boys in the Band* in 1968.

[26] Clum, *op. cit*.: viii.

[27] *Ibid*.: 89.

[28] *Ibid*.: 90.

[29] Lister, *op. cit*.: 173. While Herbert here cites his incarceration as occurring in 1948, he elsewhere documents it as occurring in 1946, the date that Dickinson uses.

[30] John Herbert, "The Sissy," in *Stage Voices*, ed. Geraldine Anthony (Toronto: Doubleday, 1978): 186-87.

[31] John Herbert, "The Good City," in *Stage Voices*, ed. Geraldine Anthony (Toronto: Doubleday, 1978): 186.

[32] Herbert, "The Sissy": 186.

[33] *Ibid*.

rant near the corner of Church and Wellesley Streets in downtown Toronto—now the epicentre of Toronto's thriving Queer Village—whereupon he accepted a ride from a married man "who thought [he] was a prostitute."[34] Herbert explains what ensued:

> When the police stopped the car and took the driver and passenger from it, the man was so frightened that he agreed to anything and everything the police said or advised. Subsequently, the police charged the boy with the homosexual equivalent of prostitution, "gross indecency," and he was convicted, on the spoken evidence of the two policemen and the "victim." The boy says that he did not tell them that he was not a woman until they all reached the police station, on the chance that he might be treated more carefully as a woman and perhaps let go before arrest was completed.[35]

Herbert was not released, but incarcerated for six months in the reformatory that he characterises in *Fortune and Men's Eyes* as a *"prep school for the penitentiary."*[36] Moreover, if one can accept his play as a valid representation of his experience inside Canada's penal system, he was subjected to harsher treatment for impersonating "feminine" qualities and female sexuality than if he had not. This impersonation did not end with his arrest, but continued while he served his sentence. In his memoir, Herbert explains that, inside the reformatory,

> He got cold cream from the hospital, supposedly for chapped skin, and made eye mascara from a mixture of soot off the window sill of his cell and the cold cream. He used a carpenter's pencil to accent his eyebrows, made up his cheeks and lips with a lipstick given to him by a boy who had begged it from his own sister on visiting day. He cut the toes and heels out of his shoes to make them look like sandals ... He rolled up his trousers to show his foot gear to advantage and rolled the sleeves of his shirt to below the elbow. If the guard forced him to roll them down, then the next day he cut them off at the same place, so that there was nothing to roll down. He set his hair in curlers made of toilet paper and achieved fantastic hair styles that finally resulted in the order to shave his head.[37]

In *Fortune and Men's Eyes*, the character Queenie uses many of these techniques to construct a feminine persona that is *"big, showy and*

---

[34] *Ibid.* In 1997, at a public reminiscence celebrating the twenty-fifth anniversary of the Canadian Lesbian and Gay Archives, Herbert returned to this event, citing the Devon Restaurant—which still exists—as the establishment near the place where he was arrested. He also suggested that, at the time, his performance of drag was considered indictable under the charge "disguised by night."

[35] *Ibid.*

[36] John Herbert, *Fortune and Men's Eyes* (New York: Grove, 1967): 9. Further references to this play appear parenthetically in the text.

[37] Herbert, "The Sissy": 189-90.

extravagant" (7). In Act One, Scene Two, for example, Queenie enters the claustrophobic dormitory that is the play's only setting carrying "*a small, white, cone-shaped Dixie cup*" (40). When the Guard asks him what he does "with all those gobs of goo from the dispensary," Queenie replies "I mix the cold cream with coal dust off the window sills, an' sell it to the screws for mascara ..." (41). The performance of femininity that Queenie enacts with such techniques achieves its apotheosis near the beginning of Act Two, when he rehearses a drag act for the reformatory's annual Christmas Concert. Herbert describes Queenie's appearance in this scene as "*a combination of Gorgeous George, Sophie Tucker and Mae West. He wears a platinum-blond wig, spangled sequin dress, long black gloves, large rhinestone jewellery on ears, neck and wrists, heavy make-up and is carrying a large feather fan*" (70). Here, as elsewhere in the play, Queenie's appearance accounts for his name: together, they establish him as a quintessential "drag queen," which "in homosexual terminology, [designates] a homosexual male who often, or habitually, dresses in female attire."[38] Although scholars such as Marjorie Garber and Judith Butler would be able during the 1990s to theorise drag queens and cross-dressing as progressive, in 1972 Esther Newton still could observe that during the 1960s "the drag queen symbolizes all that homosexuals say they fear the most in themselves, all that they say they feel guilty about; he symbolizes, in fact, *the* stigma."[39] As Andrew Ross explains, prior to its recuperation by "queer theorists" such as Garber and Butler, drag and other "camp" techniques "fell out of step and even into disrepute (as a kind of blackface) with the dominant ethos of the women's and gay liberation movements," primarily because "in its commitment to the mimicry of existing cultural forms," it was seen as "prepolitical, even reactionary."[40]

Ross contends that the survival and "crossover presence" of drag in "straight, masculine culture has been directly responsible for the most radical changes in the constantly shifting, or hegemonic, definition of masculinity in the last two decades"[41] of the 20th century. In *Fortune and Men's Eyes*, Queenie's performance of drag illustrates the challenge that cross-dressing poses to masculinity by demonstrating how it "plays

---

[38] Esther Newton, *Mother Camp: Female Impersonators in America* (Chicago: U of Chicago P, 1979, rev. ed.): 100; repr. (excerpt) in *Camp Grounds: Style and Homosexuality*, ed. David Bergman (Amherst: U of Massachusetts P, 1993): 39-53.

[39] *Ibid.*: 103.

[40] Andrew Ross, "Uses of Camp," *Yale Journal of Criticism* 2:1 (Fall 1988): 1-24; repr. in *Camp Grounds: Style and Homosexuality*, ed. David Bergman (Amherst: U of Massachusetts P, 1993): 54-78.

[41] *Ibid.*: 73.

upon the distinction between the anatomy of the performer and the gender that is being performed."[42] In this scene, Queenie coordinates his movements, which Herbert describes as *"bold [and] sex-conscious,"* to an ironic choice of music: "A Good Man is Hard to Find" (70). Herbert's characterisation of Queenie's performance as a *"parody"* of *"an old night-club favorite"* (70) illustrates the theory of drag that Judith Butler develops three decades later:

> Although the gender meanings taken up in these parodic styles are clearly part of hegemonic, misogynist culture, they are nevertheless denaturalized and mobilized through their parodic recontextualization. As imitations which effectively displace the meaning of the original, they imitate the myth of originality itself.[43]

Queenie not only parodies femininity in his performance, but also imitates other performers who exaggerate the signifiers of gender in similar acts of excess—entertainers that Herbert identifies as male and female. In effect, his performance of "A Good Man is Hard to Find" emphasises the irony of the "femininity" which he enacts throughout the play by parodying acts of parody, thereby buttressing Butler's assertion that *"in imitating gender, drag implicitly reveals the imitative structure of gender itself—as well as its contingency."*[44] Not coincidentally, Queenie's act also emphasises the contingency of the "masculinity" that other characters, chiefly Rocky and Smitty, affect. While neither of these characters professes to be "good," each performs himself as a stereotypical "man." Indeed, most scholarly interpretations of the play propose that Smitty functions as an "everyman" who illustrates the corruptive influence of institutionalised "reform" by usurping Rocky's position as "topman" of the dormitory at the play's end. To substantiate this view, for example, Neil Carson notes that Herbert initially describes Smitty's face as *"strong and masculine with enough sensitivity in feature and expression to soften the sharp outline"* (7), only to require near the end of the play that *"his face now seems to be carved of stone, the mouth narrow, cruel and grim, the eyes corresponding slits of hatred"* (96). As for Rocky, the other "man" in the group of inmates, Carson views him as "a caricature male. He prides himself on his aggressiveness and toughness. He is the Jungle King who rules by force, is suspicious of soft or gentle feelings, and is incapable of anything but stereotype [sic]

---

[42] Judith Butler, *Gender Trouble: Feminism and the Subversion of Identity* (New York: Routledge, 1990): 137.

[43] *Ibid.*: 138.

[44] *Ibid.*: 137, original italics.

thinking."[45] According to Carson, Queenie is merely Rocky's counterpart, "the caricature female [... who] has come to think of himself almost exclusively as a sexual object (or sexual manipulator)."[46]

Like the few other scholars who discuss *Fortune and Men's Eyes*, Carson argues that Mona, the fourth of Herbert's adolescent characters, is the most interesting by virtue of his ability "to retain a sense of his own identity and a reasonable control over his own destiny."[47] Unfortunately, this requires that Mona repeatedly endure gang rape—which Carson interprets philosophically rather than politically. Valorising Mona's separation of mental activity from physical abuse, Carson contends that the character represents an existential condition, not a social reality. Ann Messenger regards the character similarly, proposing that the play "would stand or fall on the character of Mona ... [who] must be played as profoundly different from the others yet [be] believable in their milieu."[48] Messenger goes so far as to propose that Mona be considered a Christ figure who "is not of this prison world," but who rather "is an ascetic, separating body and soul in so far as possible."[49]

Messenger's opinion that "crucified in body, raped and beaten, Mona's spirit remains clear"[50] casts the character as a Christian martyr, which seems at odds with the condemnation of religion that Herbert implies throughout the play. Repeatedly, he has his inmates denigrate the Guard as "Holy Face," for example. Other terms that the youths use to ridicule this representative of social authority attribute both religious and imperialist connotations to his power. Early in Act One, for example, Queenie calls the Guard "our Cockney cunt" after observing "he's always goin' on about the 'Days of Empire' and 'God and Country' and all suchlike Bronco Bullcrap" (13). This is significant in that the Guard, who Herbert describes as a man "*of about forty-five to fifty who looks like an ex-army officer*" (8), is himself corrupt—an example of a "P.I." or "political influence" (12) that the inmates manipulate through coercive methods such as blackmail. Herbert's construction of the Guard subtly reveals the influence that religious, military and imperial structures exercised over Canadian penal institutions during the 1960s. By

---

[45] Carson, *op. cit.*: 214.
[46] *Ibid.*
[47] *Ibid.*: 215.
[48] Ann P. Messenger, "Damnation at Christmas: John Herbert's *Fortune and Men's Eyes*," *Dramatists in Canada: Selected Essays*, ed. William H. New (Vancouver: U of BC P, 1972): 173.
[49] *Ibid.*: 176-77.
[50] *Ibid.*: 178.

overtly identifying him as a "political influence," however, it also indicates the vulnerability of these institutions to the manipulation of their own "moral" instruction—an ironic exposure of penal corruption that castigates the hypocrisy of "criminal reform" and, in the process, impugns the legal system it enforces.

"Canadian 'justice' is only one of the 'long-established personal and social assumptions'"[51] that Herbert challenges with his play; in all likelihood, however, his challenge to this, more than to other assumptions, caused such state-funded institutions as the Stratford Festival to pass on a production. The full force of Herbert's challenge to Canada's justice system becomes most clear near the end of Act Two, when Smitty and Mona reveal the reasons for their incarceration. Smitty tells Mona that "I stole a car—to get my mother out of town, away from my drunken slob of a father. [...] I slugged a cop when they were arresting me" (87). To explain how his father successfully condemned him in court despite evidence of his own abusive behaviour, Smitty sarcastically points out, "After all, he was the respectable married man, a substantial citizen with his own business" (87). Smitty's comment indicates Herbert's recognition that political influence works similarly inside and out of the reformatory: in each instance, it privileges economies of heterosexuality and ownership—although, ironically, inside the reformatory, the currency of both is homosexual behaviour. Earlier in this scene, Mona, who can claim neither heterosexuality nor property and who is dressed in "rags" throughout the play—the Guard eventually calls him "Raggedy Ann"(77)—indicts Canada's legal system with another narrative of political influence:

> Magistrate's court is like trial in a police station—all pals, lawyers and cops together! Threw me on the mercy of the court. Oh, Christ—that judge with his hurry-up face, heard the neat police evidence and my lawyer's silly sugar-sweet plea. So half-hearted—I wanted to shout, "Let me speak; leave me some damn dignity!"(85-86)

Ann Messenger suggests that Mona's desire to speak and be accorded some dignity resembles Herbert's own. To substantiate her claim, Messenger cites a *Maclean's* review of *Fortune and Men's Eyes* that quotes Herbert as saying of Mona, "C'est moi."[52] Indeed, Mona's description of the "crime" that led to his imprisonment resembles

---

[51] Cohen in Carson, *op. cit.*: 207.
[52] Messenger, *op. cit.*: 176. *Maclean's* is a Canadian newsmagazine published weekly. The article that Messenger does not reference is John Hofsess, "*Fortune and Men's Eyes*—A Report from the Set in a Quebec City Prison," *Maclean's* 83 (December 1990): 81.

Herbert's narrative of his incarceration quoted above. Mona tells Smitty that

> A gang—of guys—in the neighbourhood—that night—pushed me around. My payday—had it on me—they knew. Next thing—I'm on the ground—kicking me—kicking. I look up—all those legs, but there's a big cop ... Then—he looked at me, and I saw his sympathy shift—to the gang (85).

The gang, Mona continues, "laid charges—said I made passes. Four gave witness in court" (85). Mona's "crime," in other words, is being different or, rather, is being *seen* as different by a gang of boys, being viewed as "other" in "men's eyes." Ultimately, Mona's "fortune" is fated not just by the way he looks but also by the way he is seen—a distinction that Herbert clearly draws in his initial description of the character:

> *[Mona is a] youth of eighteen or nineteen years, of a physical appearance that arouses resentment at once in many people, men and women. He seems to hang suspended between the sexes, neither boy nor woman. ... His nature seems almost more feminine than effeminate because it is not mannerism that calls attention to an absence of masculinity so much as the sum of his appearance, lightness of movement, gentleness of action. His effeminacy is not aggressive ... just exists* (8).

In *Vested Interests*, Marjorie Garber theorises that "*transvestism is a space of possibility structuring and confounding culture*"; for her, it represents "the disruptive element that intervenes, not just a category crisis of male and female, but the crisis of category itself."[53] Queenie, in his drag act, enacts the most obvious example of transvestism in *Fortune and Men's Eyes*. Mona disrupts gender categories more subtly, however, by consistently blurring the line between the sexes—by appearing "*neither boy nor woman*" (8). Consequently, he also poses the most effective challenge to the binary of sex. More to Garber's point, when Mona appears cross-dressed early in Act Two, he figures "the crisis of category" more thoroughly than Queenie does earlier, a difference in effect that Herbert registers by having his characters react less positively to his appearance than they do to Queenie's. While all respond enthusiastically to Queenie's burlesque, only Smitty shows interest in Mona's presentation of Portia's court scene from Shakespeare's *The Merchant of Venice*. This difference foreshadows the play's conclusion, in which Herbert creates an alignment between Mona and Smitty that separates the two from everyone else.

---

[53] Garber, *op. cit.*: 17 (original italics).

Although the irony of Mona's choice of Portia's speech appears to elude the characters, Smitty professes to "know the scene" from high-school English class (75). If this is true, he will recall that Portia disguises herself as a man in order to plead for mercy from the court on behalf of her lover. By having Mona choose Portia's speech, Herbert allows the theatre audience to witness a double instantiation of drag: a male character plays a female character pretending to be male. Besides compounding the challenge to gender that Mona consistently poses, this layering of performance calls into question the "naturalism" of the play that most critics presume embodies Herbert's stylistic goal. Messenger is especially interesting to read in this regard. Criticising the argot that Herbert creates for his characters, she writes:

> Some of the terms are obviously made-up, two of the most universal four-letter words are conspicuous by their absence, and a general air of self-consciousness pervades the specialized vocabulary, plaguing the whole verbal texture in a way that not only defeats the intended naturalness and realism, but also undermines the mythic potentiality.[54]

Messenger's assumption of authorial intent proves useful inasmuch as it leads her to comment on the "general air of self-consciousness" that the play creates. This "air" need not be problematic if the play is viewed as a "self-conscious" manipulation of the elements of performance in the service of high theatricality. The drag performances imbedded in the play signal Herbert's interest in this effect as much as his psychological portraiture indexes any attempt at realism. Along with his "made-up" argot and stylised use of song,[55] Herbert uses drag to establish role-playing as a major focus of the play. Mona's drag performance, while less stereotypical than Queenie's, is more sophisticated in its technique. Replacing the obvious parody of Queenie's act with complex intertextual ironies, Mona's performance politicises role-playing by eliciting negative reactions. Viewed together, these two instances of drag illustrate how role-playing can be both expedient and dangerous. This links *Fortune and Men's Eyes* with "post-Stonewall gay plays," which, according to John Clum, "[revel] in their own theatricality" in order to emphasise "that acting has been, to some extent, an essential part of the gay man's life."[56]

While Clum foregoes consideration of Herbert's play in his study, Peter Dickinson foregrounds Herbert's use of drag to explain its inclu-

---

[54] Messenger, *op. cit.*: 177.
[55] The play begins with an "*Overture ... sung by Group of Boys' Voices*" (*Fortune*, 9); all the inmates sing at various other points.
[56] Clum, *op. cit.*: 200.

sion in his "gay drama" entry. Dickinson considers that Queenie's drag act not only provides the play with its "climactic" scene, but also allows the character to circumvent the social norms prescribed by the reformatory and thus become the only character to escape victimisation.[57] Although Messenger and Carson propose that Mona also survives victimisation, they efface the violence that attends his survival by invoking psychological and philosophical arguments. Choosing to ignore the political implications of Mona's repeated abuse, they ironically substantiate Garber's theory of the "transvestite effect" in which discomfort over an "irresolvable conflict or epistemological crux" is displaced "onto a figure that already inhabits, indeed incarnates, the margin."[58]

Garber posits that the "transvestite effect" focuses cultural anxiety and challenges vested interests. For her, the presence of a cross-dressed character in a play or a film signals a crisis of category that opens to question not only the sex/gender system, but other norms of social regulation and cultural signification as well. While a cross-dressed figure most obviously signifies gender disruption, Garber locates its power—and therefore its threat—in its challenge to category itself. In stylistic terms, representations of transvestism frequently disturb notions of genre as well as interrupt verisimilitude. By foregrounding artifice, transvestism potentially endistances the audience for whom the coherence of realism—like the cohesion of gender—depends on its unconscious display. Arguably, academic confusion about the "nature" of *Fortune and Men's Eyes* illustrates Garber's theory. Metonymically, the performance of Mona, like Queenie's performance, initiates a crisis of category that more than subverts stable classifications of Herbert's play: indeed, it confounds them.

To present Portia's speech, Mona dons *"a converted red velvet curtain"* whose *"graceful, almost classic"* appearance Herbert calls *"incongruous"* in comparison to *"Queenie's glittering ensemble"* (73). Despite his cellmates' ridicule, Mona *"remains as enigmatic in expression as the painting he is named for,"* (74) until he *"begins very hesitantly, stuttering (with comic pathos and badly spoken)"* (75) to speak Portia's words. Although all the characters but Smitty deride his performance, the Guard hustles Mona and Queenie to the Christmas Concert where they are due to appear; quickly, however, he returns Mona to the dormitory, explaining that "Whenever that one gets into an assembly, there's trouble. Last time it was at church-up ... somebody split its pants down the back with a razor blade" (82).

---

[57] Dickinson, *op. cit.*: 451.
[58] Garber, *op. cit.*: 17.

In this and subsequent speeches, the Guard's use of the pronoun "it" to refer to Mona signifies the radical disruption that the character effects in the play. While, on an obvious level, the Guard's language provides yet another example of the extreme homophobia that the play depicts, it also invites a more complex reading of Mona's function. To employ Garber's terminology, Mona evolves throughout the play to represent a space outside the binary of heterosexuality: neither male nor female, Mona represents the subject who defies gendered terms. The "third" position that Mona can be seen to occupy is, as Garber asserts with emphasis, "*not* a *term*. Much less is it a *sex*, certainly not an instantiated 'blurred' sex as signified by a term like 'androgyne' or 'hermaphrodite' ... The 'third' is a mode of articulation, a way of describing a space of possibility."[59]

The final scene of *Fortune and Men's Eyes* dramatises the potential of the "'third' mode of articulation" to rupture the power relations of sex and gender at play in the boys' dormitory, as well as the ability of such a mode to figure the play's defiance of category itself. In this scene, Mona rejects Smitty's sexual advances. Trying to explain his reasons for this, Mona tells Smitty that "You're looking for a girl—not for me" (88). After Smitty dismisses such reasoning as "crazy," Mona continues with a speech beginning "It's to the world I dream in you belong. It endures better." (89). Subsequently, Smitty admits that "I was afraid of everyone—everything—except you—until now" (89). Moments later, desperate to escape Mona's continued explanations, he "*bangs wildly on the bars [of the cell] with his fists.*"(90). At this point, Herbert provides Mona with contradictory movements that indicate the complexity of the "space of possibility" that this "*enigmatic*" character has come to occupy: "*Mona follows to stand behind Smitty, puts out a hand gently, but not touching him, then with difficulty, punches him on the shoulder.*"(90). Smitty turns violently to Mona who immediately offers him a book of Shakespeare's sonnets. Together, the characters sit on a bed where they "*laugh, embarrassed*"(90) and read aloud from Sonnet XXIX. Herbert now directs that the characters "*continue to read until they are in a slight hysteria of laughter that causes them to break up and fall against each other*" (90). Within moments, Rocky and Queenie return to the cell, whereupon Queenie "*Smashes his fist into Mona's cheek*"(91). Subsequently, Rocky "*throws Mona to the floor,*" but is prevented from continuing his attack by Smitty, then by the Guard who enters with his "*gun drawn*" (91).

---

[59] Garber, *op. cit.*: 11.

This scene presents difficulties for many critics. Carson, for example, characterises it as "rather ambiguous,"[60] finding that "it is not at all clear what [the characters] are amused by. Is it Smitty's reading? the sonnet itself? or is their laughter simply the result of released tension?"[61] Others wonder at the nature of Smitty's fear. Garber's comments in *Vested Interests* provide a way of interpreting the scene that accommodates the fear of Mona that the characters register with their shock and violence, as well as explains the slightly hysterical intimacy that Smitty and Mona share. Writing about drama, Garber suggests that "the binary, often rivalrous structure of protagonist/antagonist, hero/villain, or even husband/wife ... could be disrupted by the manifestation of a 'third'." This disruption is also an "interruption"

> of things that "exist" in a theatrically conceived space and time but were not present onstage as agents before, [one that] reconfigures the relationships between the original pair, and puts in question identities previously conceived as stable, unchallengeable, grounded, and "known."[62]

Using Garber's theory, it is possible to read Mona's rejection of Smitty as an interruption of the binary structure that previously appeared stable, at least to Smitty. His overture to Mona, combined with Mona's rejection of him and their subsequent argument, now require him to consider that the sexuality which he previously perceived as "known" is not fixed but, rather, challengeable—is, as Mona would have it, a sexuality that exists in the world that one can only dream about. As an agent of interruption throughout the play, Mona disrupts not only the categories of gender but of sex as well, simultaneously defying the binaries of masculine/feminine and heterosexual/homosexual—a frightening prospect for all of the characters in the play, especially Smitty. Although the violent intervention of Queenie and Rocky in this scene can be viewed as a function of their rivalry with Mona given that each of them seeks to use Smitty as sexual currency, it can also be read as their homophobic reaction to the intimacy that Smitty and Mona perform on the bed. This intimacy is ambiguous not because it is unreasonable, but, rather, because it pulls into question Smitty's sexuality as well as Mona's, opening a space of possibility that causes confusion, if not alarm, for Queenie, Rocky and, perhaps, members of the audience. Mona's choice of Shakespeare's sonnet to facilitate the interruptions of this scene is as important as his choice of Portia's speech earlier in the act. The poem links the two scenes linguistically and provides Herbert with the title of

---

[60] Carson, *op. cit.*: 216.
[61] *Ibid.*: 213.
[62] Garber, *op. cit.*: 12-13.

his play. Moreover, as Messenger points out, it uses "thoughts of the Friend, with whom some critics believe Shakespeare had a homosexual relationship"[63] to help Smitty and Mona escape the "outcast state" that attends their "disgrace with fortune and men's eyes." The intimacy that the poem celebrates eludes historical qualification at the same time that it defies categorical definition, which is especially important in the context of this scene. Mona and Smitty *"fall against each other"*(90) in a display of intimacy that defies the limits of category they previously had occupied. Their actions are as ineffable as the love that Shakespeare's poem articulates as an ideal possibility.

Mona and Smitty escape their outcast state for only a few moments in *Fortune and Men's Eyes*, which Herbert emphasises with potent, political effect. After the Guard takes Mona from the dormitory at the end of the play, Mona is beaten violently (off-stage) while Smitty remains alone in the cell, having sent Queenie and Rocky to the latrine after asserting full control of the dormitory by invoking his political influence as "a wheel in the office" (95). Smitty's actions during these final minutes signify not only the anguish of the character as he listens to Mona's screams in the distance—screams that only he can hear—but, more importantly, the degree to which Herbert directs the play away from realism. Before Smitty utters the play's final line, he

> *contorts in pain as Mona had done before, but there is no sound from his distorted mouth. He seems to be whipped by unseen strokes of a lash, until he is spread-eagled across the upstage bars. When it seems he can bear no more he covers his ears with both hands, stumbling blindly downstage. Standing thus, head and shoulders down, he rises slowly out of the hunched position to full height, hands lowering* (96).

Smitty's contortions signify Herbert's movement into imagistic representation, a complete break with naturalism that Smitty's final line punctuates like an exclamation mark. After regarding the audience with "*a slight, twisted smile that is somehow cold, sadistic and menacing,*" Smitty speaks to them directly, issuing the warning "I'll pay you all back" (96).

Smitty's direct address to the audience provides a fitting end to a play that Perkyns recognises is "well ahead of its time,"[64] but only if it is heard, seen and discussed more often than is currently the case. The society that Smitty threatens with his final words is the same one that first sent Herbert to a reformatory for the "crime" of being "other," then relegated to relative obscurity his dramatic representation of that same

---

[63] Messenger, *op. cit.*: 174.
[64] Perkyns, *op. cit.*: 277.

"otherness" by condemning it to neglect. Or is it? I leave it to others to determine whether and to what degree Canadian society has improved the reform system that Herbert's play depicts. With this essay, however, I hope to have stimulated new interest in his play. Only when they are read and produced will Smitty's last words, like the rest of *Fortune and Men's Eyes*, achieve the impact which they promise. And only then will they become unnecessary.

Works Cited

Benson, Eugene. "*Fortune and Men's Eyes*," in *The Oxford Companion to Canadian Theatre*, eds. Eugene Benson and L. W. Conolly (Toronto: Oxford UP, 1989): 212-13.

Butler, Judith. *Gender Trouble: Feminism and the Subversion of Identity* (New York: Routledge, 1990).

Carson, Neil. "Sexuality and Identity in *Fortune and Men's Eyes*," *Twentieth Century Literature* 18 (January-October 1972): 207-18.

Chambers, D.D.C. "John Herbert," in *Contemporary Dramatists*, ed. K.A. Berney (London: St. James, 1993, 5th ed.): 293-94.

Clum, John M. *Acting Gay: Male Homosexuality in Modern Drama* (New York: Columbia UP, 1992).

Dickinson, Peter. "Gay Literature, 2: Drama," in *The Oxford Companion to Canadian Literature*, eds. Eugene Benson & William Toye (Toronto: Oxford UP, 1997, 2nd ed.): 451-52.

Fulford, Robert. "Notebook: A Canadian Play Makes Its Way Around the World," *Saturday Night* 90 (October 1975): 8, 12.

Garber, Marjorie. *Vested Interests: Cross-dressing & Cultural Anxiety* (New York: Harper Perennial, 1993).

Herbert, John. *Fortune and Men's Eyes* (New York: Grove, 1967).

—— "The Good City," in *Stage Voices*, ed. Geraldine Anthony (Toronto: Doubleday, 1978): 180-86.

—— "The Sissy," in *Stage Voices*, ed. Geraldine Anthony (Toronto: Doubleday, 1978): 186-92.

Hofsess, John. "*Fortune and Men's Eyes*—A Report from the Set in a Quebec City Prison," *Maclean's* 83 (December 1990): 81, 83.

Johnson, Chris. "John Herbert," in *Dictionary of Literary Biography Vol. 53. Canadian Writers Since 1960, First Series*, ed. W.H. New (Detroit: Gale Research, 1986): 222-25.

Knowles, Richard Paul. "Voices (off): Deconstructing the Modern English-Canadian Dramatic Canon," in *Canadian Canons: Essays in Literary Value*, ed. Robert Lecker (Toronto: U of Toronto P, 1991): 91-111.

Lister, Rota. "Interview with John Herbert," *Canadian Drama/L'Art dramatique canadien* 4:2 (February 1978): 173-76; repr. (excerpt) in

Canadian Drama and the Critics, ed. L.W. Conolly (Vancouver: Talonbooks, 1995, rev. ed;): 51-53.

Messenger, Ann P. "Damnation at Christmas: John Herbert's *Fortune and Men's Eyes*," in *Dramatists in Canada: Selected Essays*, ed. William H. New (Vancouver: U of BC P, 1972): 173-78; repr. (excerpt) in *Canadian Drama and the Critics*, ed. L. W. Conolly (Vancouver: Talonbooks, 1995, rev. ed.): 48-50.

Newton, Esther. *Mother Camp: Female Impersonators in America* (Chicago: U of Chicago P, 1979, rev. ed.); repr. (excerpt) in *Camp Grounds: Style and Homosexuality*, ed. David Bergman (Amherst: U of Massachusetts P, 1993): 39-53.

Perkyns, Richard, ed. *Major Plays of the Canadian Theatre 1934-1984* (Toronto: Irwin, 1984).

Plant, Richard, ed. *Modern Canadian Drama, Vol. 1* (Markham: Penguin, 1984).

Ross, Andrew. "Uses of Camp," *Yale Journal of Criticism* 2:1 (Fall 1988): 1–24; repr. (excerpt) in *Camp Grounds: Style and Homosexuality*, ed. David Bergman (Amherst: U of Massachusetts P, 1993): 54-77.

Russo, Vito. *The Celluloid Closet: Homosexuality in the Movies* (New York: Harper and Row, 1987, rev. ed.).

Scholar, Michael. "A Plethora of Plays: Three New Anthologies of Canadian Drama," *Canadian Drama/L'Art dramatique canadien* 11:1 (Spring 1985): 280-85.

Shewey, Don. "Introduction. Pride in the Name of Love: Notes on Contemporary Gay Theatre." in *Out Front: Contemporary Gay & Lesbian Plays*, ed. Don Shewey (New York: Grove, 1988): xi-xxvii.

Tyson, Brian F. "This Man's Art and That Man's Scope: Language and the Critics in *Fortune and Men's Eyes*," *Canadian Drama/L'Art dramatique canadien* 4:1 (Spring 1978): 34-39.

Wallace, Robert. "Constructing a Canon: A Review Essay," *Theatre History in Canada/Histoire du theatre au Canada* 10:2 (Fall 1989): 218-22.

Wasserman, Jerry, ed. *Modern Canadian Plays Vol. 1* (Vancouver: Talonbooks, 1993).

Crackwalking: Judith Thompson's Marginal Characters

ROBERT NUNN

Brock University

While Judith Thompson's first play, *The Crackwalker*, concerned characters on the margins of society, its intention was not primarily sociological, that is, its purpose was not to expose the lives of the underprivileged; indeed, in subsequent plays, she has expanded her range to include characters who are clearly mainstream. But all her central characters represent people situated on the margin in Victor Turner's sense:

> Turner, looking to van Gennep's rites of passage, emphasizes not so much the "set-apartness" of performance, but its "in-betweenness," its function as transition between two states of more settled or more conventional cultural activity. This image of performance as a border, a margin, a site of negotiation, has become extremely important in subsequent thinking about such activity ...[1]

Margins in Judith Thompson's plays are situated between conscious and unconscious, dream and waking, sanity and madness, life and death. These margins are permeable, like the "screen door swinging between the unconscious and conscious mind" to which Thompson once compared her psyche.[2] If they are described as walls, these walls are betwixt-and-between spaces, uncannily alive, like the wall described in *I Am Yours*. If they are described as borders, they are the turbulent borders between weather systems, filled with violent disturbances, "major heavy weather" (*I Am Yours*), tornadoes (*Tornado*), and "twisters" (*Lion in the Streets*).

The social dimension of Thompson's plays, the concern for characters on the margins of the dominant order—the physically and mentally challenged, the mentally ill, the *lumpenproletariat*, the working class, racial and sexual minorities—is mapped on top of those other margins, the psychic and the theatrical. Together they constitute an intricate sys-

---

[1] Marvin Carlson, *Performance: A Critical Introduction* (London: Routledge, 1996): 20.
[2] Nigel Hunt, "In Contact with the Dark," *Books in Canada* 17.2 (March 1988): 12.

tem in which the borders between social groups is metaphorically expressed in terms of psychic borders and margins, and vice versa, while both borders are located in the liminal space of the theatre.

"Pink," a brief monologue first performed for an Arts Against Apartheid Benefit in Toronto in the spring of 1986, permits us to see certain patterns in bold outline.[3] Lucy, a ten-year-old white girl, speaks to Nellie, her dead black nurse, in her coffin after the latter was shot in a march. In the course of the monologue, Lucy goes through a shattering political awakening as it dawns on her that her own complicity in apartheid makes her responsible for the train of events that culminated in Nellie's death: "Even though I'm ten years old I made you die. I made you go in that march and I made you die" (77). The political awakening comes about through a psychological process that compresses the formation of subjectivity into a few minutes. In the beginning, Lucy's subjectivity is almost entirely constituted through the psycho-political process which Louis Althusser called *interpellation*, or hailing. She has been hailed by various "Ideological State Apparatuses," both named (her mother) and unnamed (school, judicial system, etc.), as a subject in and of the ideology of apartheid. Althusser writes:

> ... the "obviousness" that you and I are subjects—and that that does not cause any problems—is an ideological effect, the elementary ideological effect. It is indeed a peculiarity of ideology that it imposes (without appearing to do so, since these are "obviousnesses") obviousnesses as obviousnesses, which we cannot *fail to recognize* and before which we have the inevitable and natural reaction of crying out (aloud or in the "still small voice of conscience"): "That's obvious! That's right! That's true!"[4]

At the beginning of her monologue it seems "obvious" to Lucy that apartheid is good for black people. It is obvious for example that there should be "separate movies, cause you like to talk back to movie stars and say 'amen' and 'that's the way' and stuff and that drives us crazy so we might tell you to shut up and then you might cry" (75), and she is mystified by her awareness of Nellie's unhappiness. This, and the fact that Nellie was paid so little, troubles her, and represents a fracture in her subjectivity. This fracture has been widened to the point where it has become acutely painful for Lucy to maintain her faith in the obviousness of apartheid. She is aware of a contrast between the unconditional love

---

[3] Judith Thompson, "Pink," in *The Other Side of the Dark* (Toronto: Coach House Press, 1989): 73-77. Further references to this play appear parenthetically in the text.

[4] Louis Althusser, "Ideology and Ideological State Apparatuses (Notes towards an Investigation)," in *Lenin and Philosophy and Other Essays*, tr. Ben Brewster (London: NLB, 1971): 161.

which she received from Nellie when she was small, and the withdrawal of that love as she grew older: "when I asked you why that day, you were cleaning the stove and I said Nellie why ... don't you like me anymore, and you said, 'you're not a child anymore, Lucy, you're a white person now' ..."(77).

But Lucy can only see apartheid as ideology through the recapitulation of another stage in the formation of the subject. Lucy as a child has been in a state of utter infantile dependence on her black nurse, who has proved far more of a mother to her than her own—"Mummy" only figures in the monologue as the voice of apartheid, the Family as an Ideological State Apparatus—and has indeed been pre-Oedipal, as neither her mother nor her father exist as objects of her love, while Nellie's own husband barely registers as a presence, since he only occasionally defies the law forbidding visitation. Lucy has had no identity separate from that of her nurse. When Nellie severs that unity—or rather reveals it to have been an illusion all along—Lucy screams:

> SLAVE, SLAVE, DO WHAT YOU'RE TOLD, SLAVE OR I SLAP YOUR BLACK FACE, I SLAP YOUR BLACK FACE AND I KICK YOUR BLACK BELLY I KICK YOUR BLACK BELLY AND KICK IT TILL IT CAVES RIGHT IN AND IT CAN'T HOLD MORE BABIES EVER AGAIN. NO MORE UGLY BLACK BABIES THAT YOU'LL ... that you'll like more than me (77).

This transformation of desire for unity with Nellie into an utter rejection of her recapitulates what Julia Kristeva terms "abjection": "The abject ... represents the first effort of the future subject to separate itself from the pre-Oedipal mother. Nausea, distaste, horror: these are the signs of a radical revulsion (or *expulsion*) which serves to situate the 'I', or more accurately to *create* a first, fragile sense of 'I' in a space where before there was only emptiness."[5] Lucy's new fragile subjectivity, the space remaining after she has expelled Nellie—and with her the ideology of apartheid that had made her infantile dependence seem obvious, right and true—brings her face to face with her complicity in Nellie's death. From this new, intolerable subject-position, she yearns for a return to the unity which she knows now to be impossible:

> ... I want you to come back, and sing those songs, and roll mealie pap and be washing the floor in your nice uniform so I can come in and ask you to make a pink cake and your eyes will tickle me.

---

[5] Toril Moi, introductory note to "Freud and Love: Treatment and Its Discontents," tr. Leon S. Roudiez, in *The Kristeva Reader*, ed. Toril Moi (New York: Columbia UP, 1986): 238.

And you will say 'yes.'
'Yes, I'll make a pink cake ....' (77)

Her impossible wish to return to the imaginary unity with the pre-Oedipal mother recalls Jacques Lacan's theorising of the workings of desire for the Other.[6] Lucy, swinging violently back and forth between desire and horror for her dead nurse, embodies the subjectivity constructed in South African whites by the ideology of apartheid, in the very process of such subjectivity coming apart. This liminal space into which she has been thrown by the death of her nurse is, as Carlson argues, inherently theatrical. Lucy *must* speak, her liminality *must* be proclaimed aloud in language that pours unstoppably out of her.

A number of motifs in this monologue appear again and again throughout Judith Thompson's works. First, the social is viewed through the lens of the psychoanalytic, and vice versa. As Terry Eagleton observes, "one point of Freud's work is that it makes it possible for us to think of the development of the human individual in social and historical terms. What Freud produces, indeed, is nothing less than a materialist theory of the making of the human subject."[7] Freud's insights into the formation of the human subject—especially as elaborated by Lacan, Kristeva, and Althusser—provide essential tools for analysing Judith Thompson's plays. Second, there is always an Other, viewed from the subject position of a figure immersed within dominant ideology —the bourgeois ideology of the Canadian social formation, with the exception of this monologue. The relation between "I" and "Other" throws "I" into a dangerous liminal space in which subjectivity comes violently apart and is just as violently reshaped. The relation of "I" to "Other" is marked by the presence of powerful currents of desire and repulsion. Finally, the liminal space in which Thompson's characters are thrown is urgently and inherently theatrical.

In the remarks that follow, I would like to sketch out these motifs in a selection of Judith Thompson's writings for the theatre (for reasons of space I will not consider her extensive work in radio and television

---

[6] Malcolm Bowie writes: "More consistently than any other of Lacan's terms 'the Other' refuses to yield a single sense; in each of its incarnations it is that which introduces 'lack' and 'gap' into the operations of the subject and which, in doing so, incapacitates the subject for selfhood, or inwardness, or apperception, or plenitude; it guarantees the indestructibility of desire by keeping the goals of desire in perpetual flight." See "Jacques Lacan," in *Structuralism and Since*, ed. John Sturrock (Oxford: Oxford UP, 1979): 134.

[7] Terry Eagleton, *Literary Theory: An Introduction* (Minneapolis: Minnesota UP, 1996, 2nd ed.): 141.

drama). Her first play, *The Crackwalker* (1980),[8] presents characters who are all on the underside of the boundary between the poor and the middle-class audience watching the play.[9] The middle class exists inside the world of the play only in the person of the social worker whom we hear about frequently, but never see. But there are graduated steps. To put it simply, people in the audience watch—with compassion fighting against disgust—a working-class couple, Joe and Sandy, quarrel and make up. Through Joe and Sandy's eyes, they watch—this time, with compassion fighting against disgust and horror—the doomed relationship between two truly wretched members of the underclass, Theresa, mentally retarded, and Alan, psychotic. Through Alan's eyes, finally, the spectators watch—now with horror, pity and revulsion—The Man, a Native street person, who is bleeding, drunk, and hallucinating. These receding social depths, from proletarian to the lowest of the low, register in language which suggests a parallel between class difference on the one hand and the difference between (in Julia Kristeva's terms) the symbolic and the semiotic.[10] Joe and Sandy speak in standard English with working-class grammatical inflections and obscenities. Theresa and Alan speak a language in which the censorship of unconscious impulses is very weak, and which is therefore constantly registering the presence of another language erupting through—a language both shocking and poetic. The Man speaks in a completely uncensored dreamlike babble of unconnected images.[11] Thompson's strategy in this play consists in confronting a middle-class audience with theatre that at one and the same time fascinates and disgusts. For this reason, each character (except The Man) speaks directly to the audience in an extended monologue—even, in Alan's case, appealing directly to them for help as he takes them deeper and deeper into the terrible poetry of his psychosis.

---

[8] Judith Thompson, *The Crackwalker*, in *The Other Side of the Dark* (Toronto: Coach House Press, 1989): 15-71. Further references to this play appear parenthetically in the text.

[9] This is a safe assertion to make regarding the audience of any not-for-profit subscription theatre in Canada.

[10] Julia Kristeva terms the linguistic system with all its rules and codes the *symbolic*, while the *semiotic disposition* is "this 'space' prior to the sign, this archaic disposition of primary narcissism that a poet brings to light in order to challenge the closure of meaning." *Desire in Language: A Semiotic Approach to Literature and Art*, ed. Leon S. Roudiez, tr. Thomas Gora, Alice Jardine, and Leon S. Roudiez (New York: Columbia UP): 281.

[11] This argument is developed in my essay "Spatial Metaphor in the Plays of Judith Thompson," *Theatre History in Canada/Histoire du théâtre au Canada* 10 (1989): 3-29.

Dee, the central character of *I Am Yours* (1988),[12] shifts abruptly back and forth between desire and horror, between the endlessly deferred search for the lost object theorised by Lacan, and the abjection of the loathed object theorised by Kristeva. Since the common thread linking these two theories of subject formation runs through the mother, it is not surprising that the key to Dee's shocking behaviour is her terrible relationship with her mother, now dead. In an astonishing scene early in the play, she has an encounter with her husband from whom she has separated. She drives him away, begs him to stay, drives him away. At the climax of the scene, the two impulses collide head-on:

> DEE I said get out of my life, and I mean it, don't believe the mewling pisshead, in the hall, believe me, I hate you, I hate you, I hate you!!!
>
> [MACK *leaves*]
>
> No, stay! Please stay, please stay! Go! Get out, get out! Stay! Go! [*she puts her head back and wails*]
>
> MAAAAACKIEEEEE MACKKKKKIEEEEE MAAACKIEE (127).

In compressed form, this is the pattern that is played out on several different levels. Shortly after, Dee has a passionate one-night stand with the superintendent of her apartment building, Toi, who has fallen in love with her, and the next day drives him away. She conceives a child. As the foetus grows in her womb, she alternates between desiring it and picturing it as a monster. Through all this, she struggles more and more vainly to keep what she calls an "animal" from breaking through the psychological wall that she has maintained for so long. She confides to her sister Mercy: "It's like it got out of the wall. Like a shark banging at the shark cage and sliding out. Out of the wall and inside me" (140).

There occur thus several metonymic substitutions for the lost object that Dee both desires and rejects with loathing. First, there is her husband. In the case of Toi, class difference overshadows Dee's inner psychic struggle. Dee is middle-class, and initially is tremendously aroused by Toi's desire for her—partly, it is suggested, by the erotic attraction for a man way below her socially, who for that reason can release the "animal" in her—but then does everything in her power to use her status as a middle-class person to put him—and the "animal"—back in their place. However, Toi, with his formidable mother Pegs at his side, can break through the wall just as his child will. The metaphorical connection with animals is stressed by Pegs: "we're not animals," she says to Mercy after she and Toi fail in their attempt to use the courts to prevent

---

[12] Judith Thompson, *I Am Yours*, in *The Other Side of the Dark* (Toronto: Coach House Press, 1989): 115-76. Further references to this play appear parenthetically in the text.

Dee from giving the child up for adoption (164). Dee goes into labour while Toi and Pegs are with her. Pegs delivers the baby, and she and her son abduct it. Dee experiences childbirth as "a lion, breaking through the wall a lion roaring all the stones breaking, flying, roaring" (165). When she comes to in hospital, she is "purified" of her conflicted feelings for her mother and finally able to love her baby—who of course is miles away. Dee's resolution of her interior struggle between desire and abjection is thus left hanging.

Lion in the Streets (1990)[13] further plays out the motifs observed in *Pink* in a series of variations on a theme. The theme is the turbulent border between subjectivities located towards the centre of society and those located on the edges. The play begins with a group of children in a playground attacking another child who appears strange to them, because of her Portuguese accent and strange behaviour—which they characterise in whatever words are available to them to expel someone (nutty, crazy, ugly, witch, faggot)—and because of the fact, which even she does not recognise yet, that she is a ghost of a nine-year-old girl who was raped and murdered seventeen years ago. She follows the scent of ugly scenes between people in search of the "lion" who killed her. She sees a man reject his wife and publicly humiliate her by revealing that the "other woman" has accompanied him to the dinner party that she herself has had to crash. She sees a mother (Laura) attack a day-care worker (Rhonda) for feeding jelly doughnuts to her twins. As her attack escalates, it becomes clear that what is at stake is not the introduction of sugar into her children's diet, but the threat of a blurring of the boundary between social classes. Middle-class mothers feed their children a healthy diet, working-class mothers like Rhonda give them sweet things to eat as treats, thus putting them on the road to cocaine addiction. Rhonda's vigorous defence identifies clearly what lies behind Laura's attack. It simply boils down to the most extreme version of the tactics that all the middle-class parents of her charges use to police the boundary between their class identity and hers, a boundary which she insists is not at all secure:

> You think the books you read are deeper more ... higher, well it's the same story, don't you see that? What's makin me cry in my book is, when ya come right down to it, is exactly the same thing that's makin you cry in your book ... (31)

We see the same pattern in other scenes in the play. Christine, a journalist, interviews Scarlett, who is severely disabled with cerebral palsy.

---

[13] Judith Thompson, *Lion in the Streets* (Toronto: Coach House Press, 1992). Further references to this play appear parenthetically in the text.

Scarlett breaches the barrier between the "normal" and the "handicapped," dwelling on her sexual encounters with the mysterious intruder, her "midnight man" who only comes when there is no moon. Christine is determined to print this story over Scarlett's objections, and the conflict between them escalates. Christine beats and kicks Scarlett, and when Scarlett comes on to her sexually, kills her. What drives her to kill Scarlett is this: "The way you, you, you talked to me like that. Like, like, like you belong. In the world. As if you belong. Where did you get that feeling? I want it. I need it" (49). The difference between them is accentuated by class difference, revealed in their speech patterns. Scarlett feels the way Christine, a non-handicapped member of the dominant class, is supposed to feel. The breach of the boundaries of Christine's subjectivity therefore appears threatening on many fronts and must be sealed off at all costs. Later scenes feature other forms of rejection of the Other who threatens the boundaries of the self.

There is, in brief, a pattern of various subject positions desperately rejecting the threatening Abject in order to safeguard their boundaries—between classes, between ingroup and outcast, between the able and the disabled, between the "normal" and the "deviant." As Julia Kristeva explains, "It is ... not lack of cleanliness or health that causes abjection but what disturbs identity, system, order. What does not respect borders, positions, rules."[14] This especially applies to the borders of the self: "from its place of banishment, the abject does not cease challenging its master."[15] The final encounters in the play set the pattern up only to reverse it. The first of these happens in a scene which appeared in the original radio version of the play, which Thompson cut from the 1990 stage version, and which she restored for a student production at the University of Guelph in April 2000.[16] In this scene, Isobel's killer reveals to his adoptive mother that his adoptive father sexually abused him. The mother, who has believed in his innocence for years, realises that her son did indeed commit the crime, and that it was her blindly trusting nature—which he saw reflected in the eyes of Isobel—that drove him to kill her. She "backs off in horror."[17] In the next moment Isobel approaches for her showdown with the "lion," and as she is about to have her revenge, forgives him instead, telling him that she loves him.

---

[14] Julia Kristeva, *The Powers of Horror: An Essay on Abjection*, tr. Leon S. Roudiez (*Pouvoirs de l'horreur*, 1980; tr. New York: Columbia UP, 1982): 4.

[15] *Ibid.*: 2.

[16] This scene was published for the first time in Richard Paul Knowles, "Great Lines Are a Dime a Dozen: Judith Thompson's Greatest Cuts," *Canadian Theatre Review* 89 (Winter 1996): 8-11.

[17] *Ibid.*: 11.

Having let go of her loathing and hatred, she is released and "ascends, in her mind, into heaven" (63). Many people—myself included—have found this ending problematic. However, given the pattern I have been outlining, of scene after scene of characters doing terrible things to others in order to force the abject outside their own threatened boundaries, Isobel's act of forgiveness is a challenge thrown directly at the audience, whom she addresses in the last lines of the play: "I want you to take your life. I want you to have your life" (63).

Judith Thompson's most recent play, *Perfect Pie*,[18] takes the theme of abjection in a new direction. Throughout her body of plays, Thompson has written numerous scenes of abject humiliation and expulsion. In none of these scenes can an ally or helper be found. *Perfect Pie* changes the pattern radically. There is still the abjected one, a girl (Marie Begg) who moves to the small rural Ontario community of Marmora at the age of eight. She is an outsider from Chicago—not even Canadian. She has head lice. She has scabs and running sores. She has a drunken mother who beats her. She is a Catholic in a community of Protestants. She has *grand mal* seizures. Her schoolmates throw stones at her, cough whenever she is present, and call her ugly names.[19] At the crux of the story of her girlhood, at age fifteen, she suffers the humiliation of being taken to her first school dance by a boy from another school, who when he realises that he is holding hands with "the school dog" ditches her. As she tries to walk home, she is set upon by a gang of boys, who tear her clothes, masturbate and urinate on her. But Marie has had a friend since her arrival in town, a farm girl (Patsy Willet) whose parents are pillars of the community. Their friendship seems a profound mystery which Patsy herself cannot explain. The play interweaves the story of the two girls from age eight to fifteen with the meeting of the two friends, years later in their late thirties. Patsy is now a farm wife with a family. Marie has transformed herself into Francesca, a successful actress. Over the course of the visit, they relive their past, circling around and around the train accident that had separated them for so many years. We finally learn what happened as the two women relive

---

[18] Judith Thompson, *Perfect Pie* (Toronto: Playwrights Union of Canada, 2000). Further references to this play appear parenthetically in the text. An earlier monologue version of *Perfect Pie* was published in *Solo*, ed. Jason Sherman (Toronto: Coach House Press, 1994): 161-71.

[19] In a talk which she gave at the Stratford Festival in 1996, Judith Thompson speaks frankly about aspects of her own life which would find their way into *Perfect Pie*. She talks about her epilepsy and its relation to her creativity, and also recounts her year of torment at age fifteen, when she "was the one they threw rocks at and made animal noises at, called lewd and vicious names." Cited in "Epilepsy and the Snake: Fear in the Creative Process," *Canadian Theatre Review* 89 (Winter 1996): 6.

the accident at the climax of the play: Marie came straight to Patsy after the assault. Patsy was running a high temperature from the flu. Marie, desperate to get away from Marmora, dragged her friend to the railway track that runs past her house, intending either to jump on the train or in front of it. Patsy tried to pull her off the track as the train approached, then, mesmerised and feverish, clung to Marie as the train bore down on them. Patsy recalls Marie pulling her away as the train struck. She was in a coma for two months, and when she recovered, she learned that Marie had recovered from her injuries and had run away. This whole episode triggered off a strange alchemy: having crossed the border between her own subjectivity and that of the outcast, Patsy emerged from the coma afflicted with the epileptic seizures of which Marie has been free since the accident. This alchemy leads to the moving conclusion of the play. Prior to the visit, Francesca has lived in terror that the *persona* she has created still carries the stain of the hated outcast:

> FRANCESCA On my bad days I think it was something in me. Something they detected? Something that is ... (*She chuckles*) still there. There was a reason they picked on me, and not, say, Darlene Rowan, who was also poor.
> PATSY Because Darlene, she knew her place, right? (33)

Something about Marie—the potential artist, perhaps—made all the things that set her apart from the others threaten them. Not knowing her place, disturbing "identity, system, order," not respecting "borders, positions, rules." Years later, at the end of the visit, something happens to Francesca. Her terror of returning to Marmora and losing "Francesca" has been met and overcome—by losing *both* Francesca *and* Marie Begg, and welcoming a new undefined subjectivity. Patsy for her part confesses that Marie did not merely save her life the night of the accident:

> You saved my life ... but you always had ... saved my life, Marie. Ever since we were little girls ... Ever since you looked at me. With those crazy eyes ... And spoke, with your mouth, all those ... those thoughts ... You will never ... know (89).

Patsy has lived on two planes at once: the utterly conventional life of a farm wife, and the outlaw life of the imagination; and the latter, Marie's gift, has saved her. To put it another way, Patsy has always known that her subjectivity is not simply and straightforwardly answerable to the interpellation of the social formation in which she lives. The transfer of epilepsy from Marie to Patsy symbolises the otherness that has also been transferred and whose marks Patsy cherishes: "I will not forget you. 'You are carved in the palm of my hand'" (91).[20] Indeed the narrative line is ambiguous enough for the whole play to be read in retrospect as a

---

[20] The passage paraphrases Isaiah 49.16.

story about Patsy keeping the precious gift of her dead friend alive in memory:[21]

> ... I'll be lookin' at the snow and I will feel the pastry dough in my hands and I knead it and knead it until my hands they are achin' and I think I'm like making you. I like ... form you; right in front of my eyes, right here at my kitchen table into flesh. Lookin' at me, talking soft (91).

This constitutes a self-reflexive moment, for what else is Patsy describing but the "kneading" whereby the playwright, actor and audience give material existence to an imaginary character? The two possible narratives—both by themselves following recognisable conventions of enigma and resolution, yet both containing enough disturbances and gaps to ensure that neither is clearly privileged—enrich the play, since in the final analysis it is about the turbulent and unsettled boundaries between two subjectivities, that of a perfectly ordinary person and that of a hated abjected outcast. In this relationship, both characters recognise and accept the contradictory and unsettled nature of their subjectivity, a recognition which each receives as a gift from the other. The play also invites the audience to construct provisional—unsettled—meanings rather than take a definitive one on offer.[22] The play itself can be seen as Judith Thompson's gift to her audience, a gift of the very things that both made her an outcast and were her salvation. Thompson's open use of her own epilepsy,[23] an affliction that even today carries with it a stigma, represents an act of courage and an invitation to her audience to live a life that transcends systems, rules and boundaries.[24]

Borders and margins, then, in Judith Thompson's plays, do not mark out impermeable boundaries around the self. They do not establish a "no thoroughfare" between conscious and unconscious, or immutable divisions between social classes, between the ingroup and the outcast, between the sane and the insane. Her plays often refuse narrative clo-

---

[21] The play begins with Patsy taping a message to her long-lost friend, whom she has recognised on a television ad. In the middle of the message, she recalls the accident and says, "I know you did not survive. I know in my heart you did not survive, Marie. So how is it? How is it that I see you there, out there, in the world?" (5)

[22] See Richard Paul Knowles, "The Dramaturgy of the Perverse," *Theatre Research International* 17 (1992): 228. He writes of a scene from *Lion in the Streets* that it has "a structure that employs familiar signposts, but is unsettlingly *dis*continuous because it refuses to resolve into a single dominant fiction."

[23] This open use features in this play and in the earlier radio play *Tornado* (1987), published in *The Other Side of the Dark*: 79-114. A later stage version, produced as a work in progress at the University of Guelph in 1992, is published in *Canadian Theatre Review* 89 (Winter 1996): 45-64.

[24] My thanks to my wife Janet Nunn for this insight.

sure, instead provoking audiences into maintaining multiple and contradictory realities which bleed into each other. Judith Thompson's work thus invites the spectator to approximate the unsettled subjectivities of her characters—subjectivities whose borders and margins are within as well as without.[25]

Works Cited

Althusser, Louis. "Ideology and Ideological State Apparatuses (Notes towards an Investigation)," in *Lenin and Philosophy and Other Essays*, tr. Ben Brewster (London: NLB, 1971): 121-73.

Bowie, Malcolm. "Jacques Lacan," in *Structuralism and Since*, ed. John Sturrock (Oxford: Oxford UP, 1979): 116-53.

Carlson, Marvin. *Performance: A Critical Introduction* (London: Routledge, 1996).

Eagleton, Terry. *Literary Theory: An Introduction*, (Minneapolis: Minnesota UP, 1996, 2nd ed.).

Harvie, Jennifer. "Constructing Fictions of an Essential Reality or 'This Pickshur is Niiiice': Judith Thompson's *Lion in the Streets*," *Theatre Research in Canada / Recherches théâtrales au Canada* 13 (1992): 81-93.

Hunt, Nigel. "In contact with the Dark," *Books in Canada* 17.2 (March 1988): 10-12.

Knowles, Richard Paul. "The Dramaturgy of the Perverse," *Theatre Research International* 17 (1992): 226-35.

——— "Great Lines are a Dime a Dozen: Judith Thompson's Greatest Cuts," *Canadian Theatre Review* 89 (Winter 1996): 8-18.

——— "Introduction: The Fractured Subject of Judith Thompson," in *Lion in the Streets* (Toronto: Coach House Press, 1992): 7-10.

Kristeva, Julia. *Desire in Language: A Semiotic Approach to Literature and Art*, ed. Leon S. Roudiez, tr. Thomas Gora, Alice Jardine, and Leon S. Roudiez (New York: Columbia UP, 1980).

——— *The Powers of Horror: An Essay on Abjection*, tr. Leon S. Roudiez (*Pouvoirs de l'horreur*, 1980; tr. New York: Columbia UP, 1982).

Moi, Toril. Introductory note to "Freud and Love: Treatment and Its Discontents," tr. Leon S. Roudiez, in *The Kristeva Reader*, ed. Toril Moi (New York: Columbia UP, 1986): 238-39.

Nunn, Robert. "Spatial Metaphor in the Plays of Judith Thompson," *Theatre History in Canada/Histoire du théâtre au Canada* 10 (1989): 3-29.

---

[25] My thinking about subjectivity in Judith Thompson's plays is indebted to the following: Richard Paul Knowles, "Introduction: The Fractured Subject of Judith Thompson," *Lion in the Streets* (Toronto, Coach House Press, 1992): 7-10, and Jennifer Harvie, "Constructing Fictions of an Essential Reality or 'This Pickshur is Niiiice': Judith Thompson's *Lion in the Streets*," *Theatre Research in Canada/ Recherches théâtrales au Canada* 13 (1992): 81-93.

Thompson, Judith. *The Other Side of the Dark* (Toronto: Coach House Press, 1989).
——— *Lion in the Streets* (Toronto: Coach House Press, 1992).
——— "Perfect Pie," in *Solo*, ed. Jason Sherman (Toronto: Coach House Press, 1994): 161-71.
——— "Epilepsy and the Snake: Fear in the Creative Process," *Canadian Theatre Review* 89 (Winter 1996): 4-7.
——— *Tornado*, *Canadian Theatre Review* 89 (Winter 1996): 45-64.
——— *Perfect Pie* (Toronto: Playwrights Union of Canada, 2000).

Escaping the "Savage Slot": Interpellation and Transgression in George F. Walker's *Suburban Motel*

REID GILBERT

Capilano College

As the Postcolonial critique moves from ethnographic projects based in settler culture and Imperialist influence to a wider conjecture that, as Edward Said puts it, reflects a "contrapuntal" discourse between centre and margins,[1] examinations of who is colonised and by whom also broaden. At the same time, such investigation demands that attention be paid to the receiving subject (as, indeed, the critiquing subject) and the intricate web of colonising forces (including and most especially language) that enwrap the object(s) of study.

In theatre, these notions are particularly concrete: the *dramatis personae* are clearly specular objects though they operate in a fictional world in which they are apparent subjects. Playwrights manipulate these fictions according to various criteria of their own positions, but always as colonising subjects; and spectators constitute themselves as viewing subjects, but are also determined by the playwright's design and the greater metanarratives in which they live. Such a matrix of positionality illustrates the Poststructural assumption, by now widely held, that identity is non-essential, negotiated and contingent.[2] It also illustrates the

---

[1] Edward Said, *Culture and Imperialism* (New York: Knopf, 1993): 259, 336.

[2] This assumption is, however, not held universally or without qualification. See Diane J. Austin-Broos, "Falling through the 'Savage Slot': Postcolonial Critique and the Ethnographic Task (N1)," *Australian Journal of Anthropology* 9 (1998): 295-310. As she points out, Postcolonial thought "reflects an important conjunction [which] involves ... the repudiation of the holism and the autonomy of the 'culture' concept. Also rejected is the essentialism of much cultural analysis, based on notions of cognitive structure or binary opposition. On the other hand, the conjuncture involves casting aside those varieties of Marxist thought that propose a generalised theory of history, economistic in its intent" (295). Since this essay will assume Althusserian neo-Marxist ideas as part of its collateral, Austin-Broos's caution against a simplistic Marxist historicity is salutary advice. Trouillot had previously alerted anthropologists to the danger of easy binary thinking.

contemporary notion that "The 'us and all of them' binary is an ideological construct."[3] However false, this binary is implicit in the symbolic order that creates the West, a fact reflected in many of George F. Walker's plays. Walker repeatedly examines the control of created subjects, and he regularly explodes his audience's complacent assumption that colonial control remains stable. Walker, then, is representative of a Postcolonial drama in Canada which recognises the manoeuvres of power but subverts, or perverts[4] them. In doing so, and in creating both colonised and resistant characters and themes, Walker orchestrates a contrapuntal design. As Said warns, to think and to write this way is "more rewarding—and more difficult" than to think only about "us,"[5] but this is the task Walker sets his audience.

Although much of Walker's success can be attributed to the commercial viability of his plays—partly because of the contemporaneity of his cynical sense of humour, partly because of the fast-paced action within urban settings—his plays primarily engage contemporary audiences, because they interrogate the largely unconscious fears of bourgeois theatre spectators about the tenuous control they maintain on their own subjectivity and about that of subjects over whom they hold imperial sway. As always, it would be dangerous and wrong-headed to generalise across audiences. Reception is a function of individual spectators in particular venues at particular performances. Yet common in many contemporary spectators is the growing realisation of the instability of all classifications and a congruent urgency on the part of some spectators to reformulate categories that can still contain identity, or a desire among other spectators to escape any such fixity, to "queer" the pitch.[6] Walker's plays urge spectators to do either or both, often simultaneously, layering contradictory desires of the audience into a polyphonic pattern, "making up a set of ... intertwined and overlapping histories."[7] The plays, then, open up audience subjectivity, though, at first glance, they appear to support the determination of many Western viewers to

---

[3] M.-R. Trouillot, "Anthropology and the Savage Slot: The Poetics and Politics of Otherness," in *Recapturing Anthropology: Working in the Present*, ed. R. G. Fox (Santa Fe, NM: School of American Research P, 1991): 39.

[4] See Richard Paul Knowles, *The Theatre of Form and the Production of Meaning: Contemporary Canadian Dramaturgies* (Montreal: ECW P, 1999).

[5] Edward Said, *op. cit.*: 336.

[6] Walker's dramaturgy, which I have called "perverse," using Knowles's term, is a prime example of a current notion that the 'queer" and the "perverse" need not have directly to do with sexuality, but often arise at the junction of the sexual and non-sexual.

[7] Edward Said, *op. cit.*: 18.

maintain the anthropological myth of a "savage" (as an "exotic") slot, the eagerness to fabricate an Other against whom to measure. In Walker's work, such others are drawn from a palette of urban types (of different ages and socio-economic groupings), whose variety and consistent subjugation to (varying) ideologies pose problems for reception and containment. Walker's dramaturgy relentlessly plays with reception, refusing easy identification even as he paints characters who appear, on the surface, to fulfil expectation as "savage" or—at least—as failed.

The group of one-act plays collectively called *Suburban Motel*, especially the companion plays *Problem Child* and *Risk Everything*, reflect these theoretical notions.[8] An analysis of these plays, then, may stand to illustrate a post-modern and post-colonial dramaturgy increasingly evident in Canada.

The two plays—first produced by Rattlestick Productions at Theatre Off Park in New York on 13 May 1997 and 15 June 1997 respectively, and first produced in revised versions by Factory Lab Theatre in Toronto on 25 October 1997 and 17 June 1998, present characters who, as the original director, Daniel De Raey remarks, "are usually presented ... marginally, if at all ... On the fringes, these characters are barely visible, never audible, seem vaguely cloddish and are certainly easy to miss. In Walker's center [*sic*] stage light, however, they are seen to be vivid, articulate, perceptive and never to be forgotten."[9] In the same motel room in the two plays, the protagonists, Denise and her husband, R.J., engage in highly verbal and generally frantic action with a social worker, a chronic alcoholic, Denise's gambling-addicted mother, and the latter's lover, a pornographic film director.

Walker first contemporises the colonial Other in *Problem Child* by presenting representatives of the Canadian underclass as victim of the totalising narratives of capital, class, and government. In this play, the protagonists seem figures from the "savage" slot and partly complicit in their own victimisation. Walker, however, reveals the fragility of any construction of reality and the danger in allowing the negative half of any binary to be seen. Diane J. Austin-Broos points out the split that accompanies any identification by summing up Trouillot's notion of European identity as "a double image of the Reason that it was, and the

---

[8] George F. Walker, *Problem Child* and *Risk Everything* in *Suburban Motel* (Vancouver: Talonbooks, 1999, rev. ed.). Further references to these plays appear parenthetically in the text.

[9] Daniel De Raey, "Chords: Lost and Vocal, An Introduction," in *Suburban Motel* by George F. Walker (Vancouver: Talonbooks, 1999, rev. ed.): n.p. This comment is on the first page.

unreason that it might encompass."[10] Denise is read as an unreasonable Other who must be contained, but the very acts of conjuring her (R.J. and the alcoholic Phillie) within the specular field and of controlling these characters, allows the category of the unreasonable to exist—indeed, requires it in the action of *Problem Child*, and opens the door for its subsequent personification in Carol in *Risk Everything*. Kathryn Woodword has suggested that "discourses create what it is possible to think by articulating different elements into a discursive formation at particular times"[11]; Walker routinely gathers diverse elements (characters, themes, moral attitudes) together to create a discourse which at once amuses and challenges his audiences. Once the unreasonable is conceived in a Walker play, it threatens quickly to take over. An intertext of television-as-substitute-reality underscores these themes while also foregrounding the more intriguing question of the role of all theatricality (including the plays themselves) in the delicate matrix of reality and performativity, voyeurism and participation.

In *Risk Everything*, Walker first seems to validate the very normative system he has just repudiated by presupposing a "savage slot" to which his protagonists can return, and by having them transfer the same false binaries into this under-world of petty crime and pornography. The world of *Risk Everything* is established on a moral hierarchy parallel to that of the social worker in *Problem Child*, though "black," affirming Alan Sinfield's contention that "Subcultures should not be envisaged ... as having clearly defined boundaries."[12] The unreasonable becomes reasonable, though inverted. In this apparent imitation, Walker shows the seductive power of those regimes of mainstream society and of etiquette that he has previously depicted as cruel and constricting; in doing so, however, he reveals them as contextual, shifting, and subject to rupture. In this second play, Walker also extends the trope of television, continually questioning layers of reality. And, finally, he does show, in Ric Knowles's use of the term, a contingent escape though "perversity." Significantly, he gestures to this possible hegira through the character of Carol who is a mother.

Problem Child concerns the plight of Denise and R.J., a couple who have lost their baby to the state, ostensibly because Denise's mother has

---

[10] Diane J. Austin-Bross, *op. cit.*: 297. See also M-R. Trouillot, "Culture, Color and Politics in Haiti," in *Race*, eds. S. Gregory and R. Sanjek (New Brunswick: Rutgers UP, 1994): 146-74.

[11] Kathryn Woodward, ed., *Identity and Difference* (London: Sage/Open University, 1997): 255.

[12] Alan Sinfield, *Cultural Politics: Queer Readings* (Philadelphia: U of Philadelphia P, 1994): 68.

reported alleged child neglect to "the government" (20). Living in the city, Denise became "a drug addict ... when [the social workers] took my child away"(26), and has "turned a few tricks" (24) to pay her rent while R.J. was in prison. While incarcerated, R.J. has also become addicted— to television, especially to daytime talk shows that present "Mothers who confront their cross-dressing sons" (8) and similar aberrations in a bourgeois world. The set indexes their life as the play opens: in the dingy motel room, "R.J. Reynolds is watching TV ... There are two old suitcases on the floor and a small baby crib against the wall ..."(8). The cramped space is important not only to Walker's characterisations and tone, but within the colonial critique. As Said reminds us, "In too small a space, you cannot see clearly, you cannot think clearly, you cannot have regulation or attention of the proper sort. [Such limited space] renders very precisely the dangers of unsociability, of lonely insularity, of diminished awareness that are rectified in larger and better administered spaces."[13] Agents of The Law in *Problem Child* and of the criminal boss in *Risk Everything* are free to roam, and to speak from the larger world: it is the colonised protagonists in both plays who are trapped in an isolated environment that is controlled from afar and by the voice of the absent Father/Law. The resemblance to the history of imperialism seems clear.

The farcical plot is too complicated to summarise, but involves the attempts of the two protagonists to convince a social worker, Helen, to return their child, Denise's outrageous decision after "thinking it through" to "bury" Helen "alive" (41) when the latter cuts herself and swoons, Denise's subsequent decision to engage the motel employee (who is literally falling down drunk) to steal back her child from its foster parents, a confrontation with the revivified social worker, and the capitulation of the pair to authority as Denise slides into a deep depression "trapped in a sadness and an anger so deep I know I'll never get out" (47).

Denise is driven by nervous desperation in her efforts to reclaim her child; she is "in hell" (47). R.J., who "is disgusted," who feels "Life is disgusting" (10), has opted out to watch television, and has consented to "make the effort to impress [the social workers]" (27) by moving the family to a small town, getting a menial job and joining a church "to make points with you people" (43).

In falsifying himself, R.J. accepts the practical power of The Law, but Walker makes clear the active cynicism and self-defeat with which he views this new self-inscription. That "Life is the place that fucks

---

[13] Edward Said, *op. cit.*: 89.

people like you and me up" (10) is the pivot of R.J.'s self-image. He suffers a deeply embedded sense that " ... I can't do anything about life" (10), despite the fact that he is striving to pass as a member of mainstream society and has obtained the necessary documents to testify to his submission to Foucault's "strategic unities"[14] and their attendant agencies of control: "we've got doctor's papers. We've got a social worker's letter. We've got a letter from our landlord" and "from my boss" from whom he is learning "a trade" (14). His attempts to satisfy the social workers affirm Jonathon Dollimore's observation that "the subculture, even as it imitates, reproducing itself in terms of its own exclusion, also demystifies, producing a knowledge of the dominant which excludes it."[15] Althusser warns that there is always "a reproduction of submission to the ruling ideology"[16] and R.J.'s attempts to reinvent himself in the image of the social worker (and of, and against television characters) represent examples of such repetition. To view such transparently hollow self-construction, however, assails the spectators' own careful masquerades. This "reproduction of submission" on stage may trigger either the distasteful realisation that we all act out our abjection and that any stability of self requires that we continually repeat such performance, or the unsettling recognition that those who submit to us are not only playacting, but are thereby also constructing us mimetically. Denise understands the necessity to act out "reality" within known conventions and media in order to win acceptance:

> I don't know, maybe I should go on TV and sit on one of those stupid chairs. Cry. And then you'll see me and hear my story and your heart will go out to me and you'll understand. But if I just tell you how it happened and I'm just me and you're just you ... I don't know, I don't know .... (31).

Giving up any attempt to fabricate an identity outside a normative citational chain, R.J. has traded any attempt to interact with "real" life with a passionate engagement with television. In this world, he not only escapes persecution, but can take what *feels like* positive action, attempting to redress the abuse of guests by talk show hosts, aiming to "write that show a letter" (10), and telephoning the producer to complain. The hopelessness of his actually changing the TV world, however, throws into high relief his inability to change his "real" life. That R.J. is actually

---

[14] Michel Foucault, *The History of Sexuality, Volume One: An Introduction*, tr. Robert Hurley (New York: Pantheon, 1978): 103.

[15] Jonathan Dollimore, S*exual Dissidence: Augustine to Wilde* (New York and London: Routledge, 1990): 287.

[16] Louis Althusser, "Ideology and Ideological State Apparatuses (Notes Towards an Investigation), in *Lenin and Philosophy and Other Essays*, tr. Ben Brewster (New York: Monthly Review Press, 1971): 127.

a fictional character trapped between the "real" and the make-believe reminds the audience again of the instability of categories: all that might finally be possible is to take what *feels like* action, to become what *feels like* an independent subject. Lacan has pointed out that "feeling like" an ideal who is a creature of the symbolic is, in fact, an identification with the *moi* (in the famous mirror) and a loss forever of the *je*.[17] It means to become a character in a drama; it entails an escape into language that assumes its own degradation.

As Helen points out, however, R.J.'s "letters" contain "no reference" to Denise "at all" (26). They attest to his male adherence to a normative world, but say nothing about the central issue of Denise's fitness to be a mother. Foucault argues that the female body and its reproductive capacity is the primary target of control, that the "hysterisation" of the Mother constitutes a key mechanism for the bringing of human sexuality into consciousness and under control.[18] In these two plays, Denise, her mother, and even her grandmother are presented as women whose bodies are sexualised but maverick. In Foucault's view, the regulation of parental sexuality by various regimes of power is fundamental to corporate regulation of the body politic, to the "homeostasis of the social body."[19] R.J. and Denise have failed the test of acceptable parenthood ultimately, it seems, because Denise has exactly failed Foucault's rubric for socially acceptable womanhood and motherhood. As Helen outlines her shortcomings, Denise does not cook for her husband, does not clean the house adequately, does not seek religious values, and wants her child only because she is "mine" and as a "friend" (27), not so that she can educate the child or complete herself as woman. On R.J.'s talk shows, examples of Foucault's "perverse pleasures" (105) and failed families abound, each of them being brought to ridicule and justice by a studio audience. While the theatre audience sees through the circus of these shows—Walker makes sure no spectator can take them seriously and differentiates them from the "real" world of his protagonists—it also sits in judgement of Denise and her mother. Helen uses Carol's testimony against Denise who insists that "We've got to investigate my mother's part in this" (25). Whether any given spectator believes Denise is a fit mother or not, each is part of the web of regulations and binaries that ultimately control each spectator as surely as they do Denise. And, again, the stage world also comes across as a fiction, which causes a

---

[17] Jacques Lacan, *Écrits: A Selection*, tr. Alan Sheridan (London: Tavistock, 1977): 304. For an illustration of my comments, see the graph which Lacan creates on p. 315 (*Le Graphe Complet*).

[18] Michel Foucault, *op. cit.*: 104-07.

[19] *Ibid.*: 107.

doubling of audience reaction. If TV is false, but the stage is "real," what epistemological foothold remains available to the spectator in daily life?

Cast by the legal gaze as an unfit mother, and delivered to the law by her own mother, Denise is pushed into the role of the "hysterical woman" by the medical gaze of the social worker. (It is a wonderfully retributive touch, and typical of Walker's wry humour, that her "hysteria" should reach its peak when she overreacts to Helen's faint and "buries her alive.") Yet the play makes clear that her excitable actions are a necessary response to a subjectivity that interpellates "people like us" (48) for whom "things don't work out" (47) and her own articulation of self. Austin suggests that conversation not only carries fact, but also functions as speech act to hail both speaker and auditor.[20] Denise reads herself backwards from her own pronouncements of self: to R.J.'s claim that they "could have gotten a lawyer," and in response to his Foucaultian certificates of respectability, Denise replies, "No. No lawyers. No law ... It's not our route ... We're doing it our way. The only way we've got" (34). Denise's speech is excitable, partly because, as Butler suggests, "speech is always in some ways out of control,"[21] but mainly because of the psychic tension which she inflicts upon herself by the circular path of her discourse. She defines herself by a statement which presupposes itself—the Lacanian "effect of retroversion."[22]

While R.J. is becoming one of many constituting subjects who, as Althusser puts it, "work by themselves,"[23] Denise is a "bad subject"; indeed, Helen tells her, "You're a bad girl, Denise. That's all you are. Someone should have told you this a long time ago. You're a very bad girl." With her "smart-ass mouth" (26), Denise replies, "Ah, shut up" (41), railing against The Law, attempting to resist its power while also rejecting R.J.'s substitute reality: "That wasn't life, R.J. It was a TV talk show" (10). Beneath it all, however, the Denise of *Problem Child* operates out of the conviction that a "bad girl" is, indeed, *all* she is. However revolutionary she may at times fancy herself, Denise knows that any supposedly anterior self (the "old" Denise [15]) was always already "scum," already figured in the negative and, again, read back-

---

[20] See J. L. Austin, *How to Do Things with Words* (Cambridge, MA: Harvard UP, 1962).

[21] Judith Butler, *Excitable Speech: A Politics of the Performative* (New York: Routledge, 1997): 15.

[22] See Slavoj Žižek, *The Sublime Object of Ideology* (London and New York: Verso, 1989): 102-05. This notion is discussed in more detail later.

[23] Louis Althusser, *op. cit.*: 169.

wards from the "Denise" she now speaks into being. (This self-identity in the future anterior is a central Lacanian principle.[24]) In the end, she has nothing left but language—the play ends with a forty-three-line soliloquy in which she admits, "I'm not really there" (47). She knows that if "I" could speak out how "I" "really felt and what I really wanted to do ... maybe they'd just cancel the fucking show" (47). The elaborate performativity of human life, however, depends upon a mute *je* and a vocal *moi* to prevent its cancellation.

Denise and R.J. "speak" themselves, then, but only within an interpellation as beings in the objective case "suspected of being inadequate" (24). Their bitterness reflects their sense that they cannot escape a fate that is in the hands of others—"Listen it was over before [Helen] fell. We were finished as parents. Our life. Our future. Everything we wanted to do was over" (33)—but it also raises the question of whether they were somehow destined to such a fate even before they took independent action. An audience might well dismiss their plight as the inevitable predicament preordained by their family background, breeding, and what Helen calls their "senseless self-indulgent life style" (41), but Walker prohibits any such essentialist assumptions. In *Risk Everything*, Carol knows the newly docile Denise is merely acting and that a "real you, Denise, the dangerous adventurous Denise, not the scared suspicious Denise" also exists (299). She insists "there are a few Denises" (278). She attempts to hail her daughter anew, to alter the powerful interpellation which has almost destroyed her in *Problem Child*. R.J. replies that "None of the Denises are going to listen to a word [Carol] says" (299): the power of the state (which holds her child) is stronger than her Mother's call, but both act upon her. In the tug of war for Denise's subjectivity, Walker requires of his audience a "contrapuntal" reading which, Said cautions "must take account of both processes, that of imperialism and that of resistance to it."[25] The characters of *Problem Child* are not simply colonial subjects to whom the dominant culture speaks in fixed language. They are part of a complex hegemony which reproduces itself through constant adjustment and assimilation and which speaks out its own subjectivity in "excitable" language that continuously struggles to maintain control. As "excitable" speech cannot be admitted into evidence, the human subject must learn to speak in a regulated manner:

---

[24] See Jacques Lacan, *op. cit.*: 86.
[25] Edward Said, *op. cit.*: 66.

Helen: It's important to be polite ... Politeness is a cornerstone of civilised behaviour ... Politeness. Moderation ... Reasonable behaviour. I don't think people know these things intuitively. They have to be taught (40).

Even Helen, however, loses verbal control when she is forced into a near-death experience. As a result, when she realises that she is no longer "all right," she must reiterate her sense of self within a reproduction of The Law. By screaming at Denise, she stabilises herself within the chain:

I was buried alive! I had to claw my way up through garbage and leafy smelly muddy things ... I won't shut up! ... I have a job here. I'm a representative of our government. And what government represents to me is the people's will to have a civilized society. And what that means is dealing with people like you and getting you back in line. You're out of line, Denise. Way out of line!" (42)

It is the *voice* of The Law that stabilises, both as its message is recited and as it is heard. In *Problem Child,* this voice is electronically mediated through the television and the telephone.

At the outset, Denise and R.J. are waiting for a telephone call that they erroneously believe will announce a decision regarding custody. In typical fashion, they have taken Helen's words to "stay put" (13) literally and haven't left the room for a week. They assume that the utterance when it finally comes will be "illocutionary"—a speech act that constitutes reality in the moment of its utterance—when in fact it will, at best, be "perlocutionary"—a speech act that ushers in effects.[26] By misdefining the call, Denise and R.J. reveal their eagerness to hear a voice that will bring them into being even though the same voice will abject them.[27] The actual illocutionary utterance(s) in this play are, in fact, Denise and R.J.'s own. The merely perlocutionary utterances of the social worker will have effects, but none as devastating as the fact of their own entry into a learned system of iteration. Alan Sinfield concludes from Althusser's comment that "ideology does not deceive us, we discover our selves through it."[28]

The audience, too, first mistakes the power of the telephone call, hearing it described only by Denise and R.J. Spectators appear quite

---

[26] J. L. Austin, *op. cit.*: 105-09.

[27] Consider Austin's famous example of a policeman who hails a pedestrian, "hey, you there." Many on the street turn in response and each, in that moment, recognises him/herself as now called into being. None, or only one, previously existed as the "you" the policeman sought. Since it is a representative of the law who beckons, each respondent, by turning, accepts guilt as the price of entry into representation.

[28] Alan Sinfield, *op. cit.*: 24.

willing—like the couple—to accept that they must await an important message (from the playwright, if not the "real" Law) in order to understand and to participate in the drama. When spectators learn that the couple has been overly obedient, and also that the phone has been out of order all along, they either laugh at R.J.'s ingenuousness, feeling superior, or experience a terrible pathos for this hapless couple. Either way, they ignore their own previous anticipation of exactly the same regimes and their own naïve belief in the "well-made" play. In a manner precisely analogous to Denise's surrender to the state's definition of appropriate behaviour, the audience has been tricked by the playwright, using well-established Aristotelian conventions. They are subject to manipulation only because they have previously learned appropriate responses to these very literary forms. Richard Knowles argues that "as structural principles that function to affirm 'unifying social ideologies' in the realms of literature ... reversal and recognition ... are linear and dialectical concepts that invoke social containment and dramatic closure."[29]

Modernist and Pre-modernist playwrights have depended upon such audience expectation. But, as Judith Butler asks, can they—should they—assume that the social structure which controls them, is in fact "static"?[30] Does an audience have any reason other than convention to anticipate closure? Walker certainly denies it. Denise's self-loathing "performs its deed at the moment of its utterance," but as Butler points out, "The 'moment' ... is a condensed historicity: it exceeds itself in past and future directions, an effect of prior and future invocations that constitute and escape the instance of utterance" (3). Walker's plays reveal the power, but also the fragility of such a historicity, and its essentially theatrical nature. Like the television world in which R.J. hides, the "real" world stands revealed as a linguistic and performative construct by Walker's refusal to cement his characterisations or to allow the audience any surety. Neither play is closed. Even the humour is so "black" as to cause sensitive spectators to feel guilty at their own enjoyment.

As Knowles points out in reference to other plays, the "Walker twist"[31] "replaces reversal as a structural principle; in which recognition is at the very least a more complex and less comfortable concept ... Indeed, if Walker follows any tradition it is that of dramaturgical perver-

---

[29] Richard Paul Knowles, *The Theatre of Form and the Production of Meaning: Contemporary Canadian Dramaturgies* (Montreal: ECW Press, 1999): 44. Knowles is quoting Northrop Frye, *The Myth of Deliverance* (Toronto: U of Toronto P, 1983): 13. The latter calls for "active and creative perversion" of such shaping structures.

[30] Judith Butler, *op. cit.*: 19.

[31] Walker's own term; see Knowles, *op. cit.*: .234, n.23.

sity ..."³² Knowles directs our attention to "intertexts that operate on the level of structure and semiotics without conjuring any conscious reflection of specific texts" (234.n24). It is also on these levels, Knowles points out, that audience self-identity is interrogated by Walker's "unreversed rising action ... in which expectations ... are aroused and together with all sense of poetic justice and dramatic containment, disappointed."³³ In *Problem Child*, events sweep along to a conclusion which promises the death of the social worker, or the abduction of the child, or the arrest of Denise. Audience reaction cannot be unitary: some will want Helen to die (she is a shallow, insensitive bully); others will agree with her attitude and her formula Christianity. Some will want Denise to regain her child; others will consider her an unfit mother. No one, however, will be ready for the "twist" when Helen returns from the dead. Once she is back on stage, however, the audience will anticipate the reversal such a farcical resurrection promises; none will be forthcoming. Instead, a further "twist" deflates the play in Denise's quiet, anguished monologue and then hints at new action in her understated mention that she might "come up with a way of letting [Helen] know" just how "angry" she is (48).

Knowles suggests that the "dramaturgy of the perverse ... foregrounds the expectations of its audience in order to disappoint, disrupt, or fracture them."³⁴ Audience response is dislodged: the tone is concurrently hilarious and almost Greek in its pathos, yet the audience must hold both responses without any clue as to which will finally be appropriate. The set and props are easy to read, but fail to fulfil their promise: the gun is not used; the broken telephone does not cause any outcome; likewise, the explosives in *Risk Everything* do not detonate. Indeed, the action does not conclude, but moves from the heavily indexed set to the apron where the audience is left, alone, with Denise's synopsis of inconclusive events and the inescapable evidence that her speech is all that gives her life—as abjected subject, as fictional character and as actor on the stage. The reality of the play becomes only words, but the power of these words to constitute subjectivity is starkly revealed, intensified by the earlier busy action.

In *Risk Everything*, Walker takes a lighter, less emotionally gripping, but even more stridently disruptive stance. Kate Taylor notes that "despite its title" this play "actually takes the least amount of risk of all

---

[32] *Ibid.*: 45.
[33] *Ibid.*
[34] *Ibid.*: 46.

the plays in the series,"[35] but *Risk Everything* is more complex than it may at first appear. It importantly repositions the serious discussions of *Problem Child*, and it plays with audience reception even as it seems to cater to a desire for easy comedy. (Although the plays need not be presented together, the action of *Risk Everything* flows from and comments upon that of *Problem Child*; I shall therefore take the second play as a sequel to the first.)

The play concerns Denise's mother, Carol, who has cheated on an underworld boss during a gambling deal, has been beaten, calls her daughter to the hospital, and plots to escape the retribution of the angry mobster and to increase her gains. Again, the plot races through farcical business: Carol attempts to con everyone; R.J. is taken by the mob and returns to the motel with explosives strapped to his body; Carol seduces the next door neighbour, Michael, who is directing a pornographic film and involves him in the action; Michael is also taken by the gangster and he too returns rigged with explosives; R.J. and Denise conceive a reckless plan in which R.J. will go the boss's place and "explode all over him" (310); Denise discovers Carol has lied and has retained the missing money "to make a fucking bet on a fucking horse" (298); Denise forces Carol to return the money; the men are freed from the explosives; Michael returns to the motel room and to Carol's sexual reward.

This action drives forward at breakneck speed, and the dialogue is often very funny, but under its plot-based action, the play reveals interpellation every bit as strong as that which governs the characters in *Problem Child*: a class of people in Canadian society live outside the mainstream, but, within this class, a hierarchy exists driven by economic power, controlled by punishment and supported by an ideological apparatus. The space between these two societies is more fluid than a simple ethnographic reading might suggest. The difference in *Risk Everything* is that the protagonist, Carol, accepts her interpellation but repudiates normative consequence.

This play brings together the Althusserian notions and colonial critique so obvious in *Problem Child*, but centres on Carol's maternal body. As Judith Butler has remarked, this body is "an effect or consequence of a system of sexuality in which the female body is required to assume maternity as the essence of itself and the law of its desire."[36] Carol simultaneously views herself as "mother," knows such an inscrip-

---

[35] Kate Taylor, "Suburban Motel Finale Is More Raucous than Risky," *Globe and Mail* (Toronto: 19 June 1998): C10.

[36] Judith Butler, *Gender Trouble: Feminism and the Subversion of Identity* (New York: Routledge, 1990): 92.

tion is illocutionary within the symbolic order, and pierces the act of interpellation with her own desire. In *Problem Child*, the audience learns that Denise agrees with R.J.'s characterisation of Carol as "the biggest screw-up in the universe" (21), and has "sent her in my mind to hell" (21) (where she will later describe herself as residing). In *Risk Everything*, however, we see a much more complex relationship between the two women. Denise, no longer "bad," but speaking from a morality which she is adopting in order "to impress" the authorities, asks, "Jesus, Mom. What's wrong with you?" (293) and calls her a "fucking liar" (313). Carol's responses are important. To the question of why she acts as she does, she reveals the same cynical self-awareness that hailed the young parents before they capitulated: "You can't leave the shit behind. It's a world made of shit. It's everywhere" (272), and describes herself and her children as "beyond blame" (293). To the question of her (dis)honesty, she replies, "Who are you calling a fucking liar, Denise? I'm your fucking mother" (270). As we shall see, this answer is central.

Carol attracts various signifiers of the categories *mother* and *woman*: she tells affectionate stories of rearing Denise, but she would not satisfy Helen's definition of a fit mother; she reports Denise for child neglect, but quite gleefully recalls similar abuse; she calls her daughter pet names, but also rails at her in obscene language; she wears a skirt, but appears in front of her son-in-law with it "around [her] fucking ankles" (270); she turns to her daughter when she is beaten up, but lies about the perpetrator in order to con the daughter; she insists on family loyalty, but responds to her daughter's depression by saying "Ah, who cares. You should just leave" (284). She cries, but is probably only acting to further her plan. She sees herself as a sexualised woman, but rejects any obligation to limit herself to "regulated fecundity."[37] In "a blast from the past," she has sex with "a total stranger" (286) in front of her daughter, who rages against her promiscuity, but the ending of the play turns on her unabashed sexual *jouissance*, both in Lacan's sense of desire in loss and in Nietzsche's sense of *affirmation*. She casts herself and Denise as a strong woman, preferring Denise when she is aggressive and outside The Law (and undermining R.J.'s self-confidence about his masculinity), but she also relishes a potent male sex partner and centres her interest directly on his phallus, an action to which I shall return. She does not, however, simply embody a set of self-contradictions; she is the product of a "quilting" of signifiers which temporarily fixes a shifting variety of *Mother* far outside Helen's ken.

---

[37] Michel Foucault, *op. cit.*: 104.

Carol is a rather special example of what Laclau and Mouffe have called a "nodal point."[38] As Slavoj Žižek sums up Laclau, Mouffe and Lacan:

> ... the multitude of "floating signifiers," of proto-ideological elements, is structured into a unified field through the intervention of a certain "nodal point" (the Lacanian *point de capiton*) which "quilts" them, stops their sliding and fixes their meaning.[39]

Of course, to apply Lacan's theory strictly, this *capitonnage* must reveal the "effect of retroversion" in that the hail as *Mother* that is momentarily fixed can only be a reading backwards onto Carol of normative signifiers of a category already situated within the Lacanian "Big Other (O)." In other words, her actions can be interpreted as rebellion only because such a possibility is already accepted by those who deal in symbolic identifications—namely, everyone in the play except her, as well as the bourgeois humanist audience: hence, the frustration Denise feels. Carol embodies an element of alterity, but only because the audience collectively pretends the Big Other is normative and has an existence other than as structure. Carol's triumph is that she appears to be able to see her identifications as merely performative. Unlike Denise, who slips into an imaginary identification which she acts out for the benefit of the Law (as Žižek reminds us, "imaginary identification is always identification on behalf of a certain gaze in the Other"[40]), Carol is aware that her position as nodal point is simply a quilting sought by the others, is by definition unsound, and means nothing to her. While the audience is actively engaged in misrecognition of Carol as an autonomous agent (who makes bad choices), Carol herself breaks through this illusion, knowing herself to be the product of an inauthentic structure, a structure whose symbol is the phallus (of which she makes sport). Žižek alerts us to the paradox in which "capitonnage is successful only in so far as it effaces its own traces."[41] Carol, however, refuses to efface the residual effects produced in her moments of quilting—they stream behind her, performing themselves as disruptions of the symbolic order. Carol offers to fix a rebellious meaning of *Mother* that disowns normalising conceptions of that elemental sign, but also refuses to reconstitute the category in the opposite pole of the binary. She is not simply moving to "the place" from which she would feel happier with herself, Lacan's symbolic identifica-

---

[38] See Ernesto Laclau and Chantal Mouffe, *Hegemony and Socialist Strategy* (London: Verso, 1985): 112.
[39] Slavoj Žižek, *op. cit.*: 87.
[40] *Ibid.* 105.
[41] *Ibid.*: 102.

tion;[42] she is living (sometimes happily) in a maelstrom of fluid signifiers and shifting subject-positions. She contributes to "a radically contingent process of retroactive production of meaning"[43] by her wilful acts of deceit. She "lies," and in doing so she exploits "the open temporality of the speech act ... Such a loosening of the link between act and injury, however, opens up the possibility for a counter-speech, a kind of talking back, that would be foreclosed by the tightening of that link."[44] While Denise has integrated her lifelong interpellation as "scum" with her current designation as "unfit Mother," Carol recognises her own hailing, but fashions a life for herself within it by running with the consequences of her actions, in full knowledge that these actions are already determined by an anterior illocution. Again, she knows that this illocution comes from a place within the Big Other and reads itself back onto her own rebellion so that whatever action she takes turns out to be ultimately pointless. The two women embody on stage the Hegelian couple, "for-the-other"/"for-itself." Denise is hysterical because she unhappily enacts roles for the other;[45] Carol is in control because she knows that she is, already, the other for whom "[she] is enacting a role ... [her] being-for-the-other is [her] being-for- [her]self."[46] She also accepts that she can never escape her symbolic identification within the Other (as none of us can, short of madness) and yet that she is powerless within it. Carol acknowledges the serious consequences of such a revolutionary attitude: she is beaten by men, she is censored by her daughter.

While Carol dodges the attempts of conventional signifiers to adhere to her name as Mother, but accepts her position as perverse and unstable nodal point, she does not accept that her body itself is unstable, or that it must, as Shuttleworth warns, be taken "metonymically" to represent the chaos of her class.[47] She stands in opposition to the social assumptions that an impulsive feminine body "is an element in, productive of and produced by, a disciplinary society deploying various regulatory prac-

---

[42] *Ibid.*: 105.

[43] *Ibid.* : 102.

[44] Judith Butler, *Excitable*: 15.

[45] Lacan says the hysteric asks of the Big Other, of the symbolic order, "Why am I what you're telling me that I am?—that is, which is that surplus-object in me that caused the Other to interpellate me, to 'hail' me as [scum; failed mother]?" Lacan, *Le Séminaire III—Les psychoses* (Paris, 1981); quoted in in Žižek, *op. cit.*: 112.

[46] Slavoj Žižek, *op. cit.*: 106.

[47] Sally Shuttleworth, "Female Circulation; Medical Discourse and Popular Advertising in the Mid-Victorian Era," in *Body/Politics: Women and the Discourses of Science*, eds. Mary Jacobus, Evelyn Fox Keller, and Sally Shuttleworth (New York and London: Routledge, 1990): 54-55.

tices to achieve a desired docility,"[48] and "that the construction of women ... helplessly subject to the tyranny of their bodies and in need of medical supervision has functioned as a necessary support for the idea of its opposite: autonomous man."[49] In this play, the men are far from autonomous and the threat to their bodies is to explode entirely. Carol, on the other hand, presents a punished body still eager for lovemaking (despite the pain of her bruises) and still very much in possession of itself.

Walker plays with the audience's reception of Carol, just as he twists his plot and spurns closure. The TV subplot is intensified to question each of the "strategies" by which the state constructs its reality and each is revealed as theatrical contrivance. Sexuality is linked to television by the fact that Michael directs pornographic films, and is revealed as both a pleasure that is not necessarily reproductive (Carol offers to fellate Michael), nor domestic, nor loving ("the sexual climate I'm used to isn't always happy and spontaneous"[303]). The final image of the play shows Michael returning to the motel room "*One hand casually over his crotch ... He has a massive erection. Carol looks at his crotch. Smiles*" and says, "Nice going" (319). In traditional usage, then, Walker perverts his world, but he also "perverts" it in Knowles's sense.

The audience's attention, like that of Denise, is drawn to the erection and to Carol's glee that "scum" like this family and—more important, perhaps—women of this class have managed, in the face of The Law (and its inverse, the criminal boss), to escape control, still to be active, to be sexually alive, to reject decorum, to have fun. The sexual irregularity echoes the *exposés* on R.J.'s television talk shows, and like the TV audience, this audience (while it likely laughs at the impropriety) also shares something of Denise's embarrassment in the final line of the play, "Ah ... Jesus ..." This powerful image, however, works to destabilise sets of conventional icons resonant for the spectators: a Mother pointing "proudly" to a penis which she has caused to become erect and which she intends unabashedly to use for her own pleasure, in front of her son-in-law who is wearing her panties, while her daughter (also a mother) blasphemously invokes the name of Helen's chaste God, the Son of the

---

[48] C. Smart, "Disruptive Bodies and Unruly Sex: The Regulation of Reproduction and Sexuality in the Nineteenth Century," in *Regulating Womanhood: Historical Essays on Marriage, Motherhood and Sexuality*, ed. C. Smart (London and New York: Routledge, 1992): 31; quoted in Jennifer Harding, *Sex Acts: Practices of Femininity and Masculinity* (London: Sage, 1998): 27.

[49] Jennifer Harding, *op. cit.*: 28. Harding paraphrases Sally Shuttleworth, *op. cit.*: 64. Note that the play begins with Carol's departure from the hospital in the care of her daughter and note her refusal to return to that medical institution.

absent Father/Law and His Ever-Virgin Mother. Indeed, as Žižek observes, "If the Name-of-the-Father functions as the agency of interpellation, of symbolic identification, the mother's desire, with its fathomless 'Che vuoi?'[50] marks a certain limit at which every interpellation necessarily fails."[51]

Carol reads herself backwards—as Lacan says we must—from the gaze of the spectators, writing alterity onto her sexually charged female body, but simultaneously and perversely teases the audience with its own potent Sign-of-the-Father. She knows she is other to the bourgeois and imperial gaze, but she also seems to know that the spectators' subjectivities (however diverse) are collectively grounded in what Butler has termed the call of the other,[52] Her playful actions are not simply "free play nor theatrical self-presentation,"[53] but formative[54] of the colonial masters who observe her and dismiss her as irresponsible, or vulgar, or even courageous.

That the spectators misrecognise their own formulation within Carol's (and, even Denise's, R.J.'s and Phillie's) alterities represents the final irony of Walker's seemingly simple farce. And it is fitting that this crucial misunderstanding should be contained in that powerful figure of imperialist misreading, the phallus. As Lacan argues, but as is often forgotten, the phallus is the sign of the ultimate failure of the Big Other. Carol's playfulness refuses a Freudian castration; it refuses to be mortified. It signals enjoyment and, as Žižek reminds us, reading Lacan's graph of *jouissance*, "as soon as the field of the signifier is penetrated by enjoyment it becomes inconsistent, porous, perforated—the enjoyment is what cannot be symbolised, [it] ... can be detected only through the holes and inconsistencies of this field, so that the only possible signifier of enjoyment is the signifier of the lack in the Other, the signifier of its inconsistency."[55] Walker, then, gathers bourgeois propriety, theatre

---

[50] Lacan's question in the third Graph. A gap always remains in desire and in the residue of any quilting. In this gap persists the question, "What do you want; what are you trying to receive back from the Big Other by naming yourself in this way?" In speech act theory, a similar gap develops between locution and the illocutionary power of any utterance. It is a pivotal concept in the analysis of Carol's role in these plays where locution, illocution and desire ricochet off one another to fuel transgression.

[51] Slavoj Žižek, *op. cit.*: 121.

[52] Judith Butler, *Bodies that Matter: On the Discursive Limits of "Sex"* (New York and London: Routledge, 1993): 94-95.

[53] Butler, *Bodies*, p. 94.

[54] *Ibid.*: 90-95.

[55] Slavoj Žižek, *op. cit.*: 122.

etiquette, theatrical convention and a much more complex psychological performativity together in his final stage image, and literally points it out to an imperialist audience predisposed to miscomprehend.

Walker presents a world that is alien to the experience of most of his ticket-buying audience, and offers his spectators a variety of possible responses. In the end, however, Carol offers "a blow for our side" that is "a victory over all the negative mingy shit that goes on in this world" (313). Her victory may well suggest to spectators a way out of the interpellations which configure them, a way to ignore the voice of The Law, a way to read the performative as simply that and to admit that "the Real is the writing itself as opposed to the signifier,"[56] and finally a way to displace psychic construction without pretending such a system does not exist. Walker insists that the spectators notice the implications of such visible theatricality in their own "real" lives. Equally important, however, Walker's dramaturgy disallows what Said calls a "'return' to culture and tradition"[57] as "protective enclosure."[58] Such retreats to a comfortable "source of identity ... accompany rigorous codes of intellectual and moral behaviour that are opposed to the permissiveness associated with ... hybridity"(xiii). *Problem Child* shows the grinding power of the call for such returns; *Risk Everything* declines the call, celebrating "hybridity" even in the chthonic icon of the Mother, and disclosing failure even in the apparently potent success of the Father.

As the colonial critique in Canadian drama moves in "counterpoint" with established social regulation and postmodern refiguration, plays like these of George F. Walker engage their audiences in important new ways, disrupting reception to open a liminal space which allows "new alignments made across borders, types, nations and essences ... that [have] been the core of cultural thought during the era of imperialism."[59] In Denise's words at the end of *Problem Child*, these plays "come up with a way of letting [authorities like Helen] know" (48) that this era has ended.

---

[56] Slavoj Žižek: 171.
[57] Edward Said, *op. cit.*: xiii.
[58] *Ibid.*: xiv.
[59] *Ibid.*: xxv.

Works Cited

Althusser, Louis. "Ideology and Ideological State Apparatuses (Notes Towards an Investigation)," in *Lenin and Philosophy and Other Essays*, tr. Ben Brewster (New York: Monthly Review Press, 1971): 127-86.

Austin. J. L. *How to Do Things with Words* (Cambridge, MA: Harvard UP, 1962).

Austin-Broos, Diane J. "Falling through the 'Savage Slot': Postcolonial Critique and the Ethnographic Task (N1)," *Australian Journal of Anthropology* 9 (1998): 295-310.

Butler, Judith. *Bodies That Matter: On the Discursive Limits of "Sex"* (New York and London: Routledge, 1993).

────── *Excitable Speech: A Politics of the Performative* (New York and London: Routledge, 1997).

────── *Gender Trouble: Feminism and the Subversion of Identity* (New York and London: Routledge, 1990).

De Rae, Daniel. "Chords: Lost and Vocal, An Introduction," in *Suburban Motel* by George F. Walker (Vancouver: Talonbooks, 1999, rev. ed.): n.p.

Dollimore, Jonathan. *Sexual Dissidence: Augustine to Wilde, Freud to Foucault* (Oxford: Clarendon, 1991).

Foucault, Michel. *The History of Sexuality. Volume One: An Introduction*, tr. Robert Hurley (New York: Pantheon, 1978).

Harding, Jennifer. *Sex Acts: Practices of Femininity and Masculinity* (London: Sage, 1998).

Knowles, Richard Paul. *The Theatre of Form and the Production of Meaning: Contemporary Canadian Dramaturgies* (Montreal: ECW Press, 1999).

Lacan, Jacques. *Écrits: A Selection*, tr. Alan Sheridan (London: Tavistock, 1977).

Laclau, Ernesto and Chantal Mouffe. *Hegemony and Socialist Strategy* (London: Verso, 1985).

Said, Edward. *Culture and Imperialism* (New York: Knopf, 1993).

Sinfield, Alan. *Cultural Politics: Queer Readings* (Philadelphia: U of Philadelphia P, 1994).

Shuttleworth, Sally. "Female Circulation; Medical Discourse and Popular Advertising in the Mid-Victorian Era," in *Body/Politics: Women and the Discourses of Science*, eds. Mary Jacobus, Evelyn Fox Keller, and Sally Shuttleworth (New York and London: Routledge, 1990): 47-68.

Taylor, Kate. "Suburban Motel Finale Is More Raucous than Risky," *Globe and Mail* (Toronto, 19 June 1998): C10.

Trouillot, M.-R. "Anthropology and the Savage Slot: The Poetics and Politics of Otherness," *Recapturing Anthropology: Working in the Present*. ed. R.G. Fox (Santa Fe: NM: School of American Research Press, 1991): 17-44.

────── "Culture, Color and Politics in Haiti," in *Race*, eds. S. Gregory and R. Sanjek (New Brunswick: Rutgers UP, 1994): 146-74.

Walker, George F. *Problem Child* and *Risk Everything* in *Suburban Motel* (Vancouver: Talonbooks, 1999, rev. ed.): 7-48; 261-319.

Woodward, Kathryn, ed. *Identity and Difference* (London: Sage/Open University, 1997).

Žižek, Slavoj. *The Sublime Object of Ideology* (London and New York: Verso, 1989).

"Fatherlands and Mother-tongues": Family Histories and Futures in Recent Australian and Canadian Multicultural Theatre

JOANNE TOMPKINS

University of Queensland

This paper has two points of origin. The first comes from Ghassan Hage's *White Nation*, a study of the failure of multiculturalism and of the persistence of the discourse of Anglo decline in Australia, in which Hage maintains that the lessons of psychoanalysis have been insufficiently applied to the nation and nationalism.[1] While I would hesitate to deploy psychoanalytic criticism on a concept like the nation,[2] I take up Hage's challenge: I use aspects of psychoanalytic criticism to explore multicultural theatre texts that, in my reading, provide an alternative,

---

[1] Ghassan Hage, *White Nation: Fantasies of White Supremacy in a Multicultural Society* (Sydney: Pluto, 1998): 73. He argues that Australian nationalists (such as Pauline Hanson, among others) are striving to maintain an enclosed, Lacanian fantasy space. Hage explains that *"the affective dimension of nationalism ... has been far too often neglected by analysts and that theories of nationalism that do not take on board psychoanalytic theory will always be less than complete"* (Hage, *op. cit.*: 73; original emphasis). He uses affect in particular to explain the rise of Hansonism (Hage, *op.cit.*: 182-231). Hage refers briefly to Canadian multiculturalism (Hage, *op. cit.*: 84), suggesting that Canada has the same problems with multiculturalism as Australia does. The arguments in Hage's book are much less inflammatory and much more grounded in experience and academic argument than those in Neil Bissoondath, *Selling Illusions: The Cult of Multiculturalism in Canada* (Toronto: Penguin, 1994). I have used Hage, then, as a text to cover both experiences, since I read Australian and Canadian multiculturalism—and multicultural theatre in particular—as comparable.

[2] Psychoanalytic criticism is appropriate to humans, to human subjects, and to characters, whereas its use in analysing objects such as nations is open to a misunderstanding of both the theoretical method and the objects in question. Attempts to psychoanalyse a country could result in parodied notions of nation, as is the case in Marty Chan's play discussed in this paper. Hage takes Žižek's lead (Hage, *op.cit.*: 73), but I intend to limit my application to the second-generation subjects in the plays examined here.

recombinative Lacanian fantasy space for Canadians and Australians. To demonstrate that the situation is less bleak than Hage depicts, I consider four plays—Janis Balodis's *The Ghosts Trilogy*,[3] and Noëlle Janaczewska's *Cold Harvest*[4] (both from Australia), Betty Quan's *Mother Tongue*[5] and Marty Chan's *Mom, Dad, I'm Living with a White Girl*[6] (from Canada)—which map the intersections of multiple cultural identities and fragmentary personal and social subjectivities for second-generation subjects among the cultural communities of Latvian, Polish, Korean and Chinese migrants.

My second starting point, which might facilitate psychoanalytic exploration, comes from *My Father's Father*, the third play in Janis Balodis's *The Ghosts Trilogy*, in which Armand considers the derivation of the expressions "fatherland" and "mother-tongue." Land, he reasons, is generally passed on through fathers, while language is frequently taught to children by mothers (186). That this does not happen in *The Ghosts Trilogy* is significant: Armand's father learns that there is no patrimony in Latvia to pass on, while Armand's imperfect Latvian, his mother's mother-tongue, creates comedy for the play's Latvian speakers and for the audience. Armand's mother proved also unable to teach him English, because hers remained only rudimentary when he was a child. Armand's contemplation offers the opportunity to discuss the strategic function of family, fatherlands and mother-tongues in contemporary Australian and Canadian multicultural theatre.

Armand's parents came to Australia as "displaced persons" following World War II. The arrival in Australia and Canada of thousands of post-war migrants like Ilse and Karl represented one of the factors that led to the development of multiculturalism as an official government policy in both countries. Originally hailed as a social experiment to integrate many different cultures under one umbrella nation, multiculturalism as a term sounds less august today, as the problems associated with its implementation[7] and the backlash against a perceived privi-

---

[3] Janis Balodis, *My Father's Father* in *The Ghosts Trilogy* (Sydney: Currency, 1997). Further references to this play appear parenthetically in the text.

[4] NoNlle Janaczewska, *Cold Harvest* (unpublished ms, 1997). Further references to this play appear parenthetically in the text.

[5] Betty Quan, *Mother Tongue* (Victoria: Scirocco, 1997). Further references to this play appear parenthetically in the text.

[6] Marty Chan, *Mom, Dad, I'm Living with a White Girl*, in *Ethnicities: Plays from the New West*, ed. Anne Nothof (Edmonton: NeWest, 1999): 99-167. Further references to this play appear parenthetically in the text.

[7] The potential shortfalls of multiculturalism also include homogenising cultures by failing to recognise numerous subgroups within a culture, or fixing cultures to one

leging of parts of the national community[8] continue to circulate in public discourse. In its current official and public form, multiculturalism is too often reduced to food, folkdance and national costume, placing value on these signifiers of "culture" at the expense of a more interactive dialogue between cultural groups. These signifiers of culture are also highly performative in the public sphere (especially for politicians), but conventional performance—such as theatre productions—tends to deploy multiculturalism and cultural signs less superficially.

In theatre generally, the concept of the "family" is well-known for the situation-recognition which it registers in audiences, and the opportunity to expose the inevitable internal conflicts where family resemblances can hide ideological differences of opinion. The potential to exploit the emotive identification for audiences seems obvious: families generate their own emotional problems, but they also provide a place to express emotions kept hidden by one's public face.[9]

Besides these conventional associations, the family in multicultural theatre has tended to adopt the additional role of cultural ambassador or even cultural gatekeeper. Connections between family and patrimony usually carry more weight for migrant cultures than for the dominant culture that boasts generations of settlement, if only because even second-generation subjects are burdened by cultural baggage from the fatherland, baggage that they did not pack, but for which they are nevertheless responsible. Part of the function of fictional families involved in acts of cultural gatekeeping has characteristically been writing cultures into the national imaginary, adding them to already-logged

---

substantial social/historical moment, forgetting that all cultures must necessarily evolve or die. While essentialising culture is one of the possible problems, diluting culture is another: mishandled, multiculturalism has the potential to impose a form of assimilation rather than to enable a more organic mix of cultures.

[8] Right-wing political groups including One Nation in Australia and the Alliance Party (formerly the Reform Party) in Canada have used multiculturalism as a provocation for mainly disempowered Anglo-Celtic supporters who feel the need to blame someone or something for their failures. Ghassan Hage notes in his analysis of multiculturalism in Australia, "[m]ulticulturalism constitutes a field of struggle for its definition and construction by the various interests of those who are positioned within it" (Hage, *op. cit.*: 164).

[9] This trope is also attractive in its provision of the option of either a comic reconciliation or a tragic destruction, and the chance of a homecoming, often with a prodigal child. Families have also long been used as metaphors for/of communities: the houses of Atreus and Laius provide a basis for Greek tragedy, while *King Lear* epitomises family dysfunction as politically-charged. Twentieth century American drama in particular (for example O'Neill, Williams, Miller, and Shepard) has played with the family as representative of the American Dream.

cultures in order to assemble a fuller multicultural register of each country. Such "witnessing" enacts an important pedagogical function in addition to the aesthetic and theatrical achievements of any examples of the model.[10]

Multicultural plays now incline towards staging culture in a more complex manner: they problematise an undifferentiated sense of belonging to work towards an interaction between cultures, families, and histories, in an effort to bridge—but not smooth over—the full range of different cultural communities that comprise Australia and Canada. Specifically, the plays discussed here figure a second-generation subject desire for a form of figurative "parental culture" in terms of Lacan's Oedipal structure.[11] The characters explore the idea of the self and the location of the self in a "homeland"—whether literal or figurative—in relation to a "mother" and "father" schema. These relationships play themselves out in cultural terms—rather than in strictly gendered and sexualised Oedipal ones—as fatherland and mother-tongue,[12] tropes which facilitate the tasks of self-definition and communication, in addition to gesturing towards the individuals' fantasies[13] and their repercussions for the families and the culture.

---

[10] The tendency to "exhibit" culture as difference can form a part of this representation, but the risk is that the culture will remain marked as "different." Later multicultural plays—like those of Tes Lyssiotis in Australia, which establish the Greek community in Melbourne and country Victoria, and Vince Rossi's plays, which detail the Italian community in Montreal, to name just two playwrights from the 1980s and early 1990s—have attempted to remove the purely exhibitionary function from their plays.

[11] Janelle Reinelt explains why Lacan is more useful than Freud in this context: "For Lacan, transcending Freud, the oedipal crisis is not just a crisis of the body; it is refigured as a social crisis of language acquisition ... Thus, the biological and familial relations of the child to its world become intimately tied to the sociality of which he or she is an inevitable effect. The conflation of physical and familial with social and juridical produces the intimate geography of the self, a geography of inner splintering and outer alienation." See Janelle G. Reinelt, "Psychoanalysis Introduction," in *Critical Theory and Performance*, ed. Janelle G. Reinelt and Joseph R. Roach (Ann Arbor: U of Michigan P, 1992): 385.

[12] I do not read the plays or the cultures depicted here in psychoanalytical terms. I am using the motif of the Oedipal parents in order to understand a larger cultural context. Connecting psychoanalysis to culture is, however, not new: for a detailed analysis of how Lacan has been used to explain culture, see Juliet Flower MacCannell, *Figuring Lacan: Criticism and the Cultural Unconscious* (London & Sydney: Croom Helm, 1986): 39-73.

[13] Fantasy for Lacan represents the ideal place that the subject tries to reach, where all aspects of the self will be integrated, even though such a place is impossible, since the attainment of this integration means death. Hage explains that Lacan's fantasy encompasses more than this, though. It is also "an ideal image of the self as a

"Fatherlands and Mother-tongues"

In perhaps the most straightforward of the four plays, all three members of the Chinese-Canadian family in Betty Quan's *Mother Tongue* experience crises of self-representation as a result of misidentifications of language and patrimony. The unnamed mother left China as a teenager to work in Vancouver and married a man who has since died. Steve, her son, becomes deaf following a childhood illness. Her trilingual daughter, Mimi, embodies her link to the outside world, but Mimi plans to accept a scholarship for postgraduate study in far-away Ontario.

Mother Tongue's title indicates the importance of language in this play, but each of the three characters speaks a different dominant language, complicating the notion of family. The mother cannot even communicate in the same language as her son: she has a command of Cantonese and only a few words of English—relying on her daughter to interpret for her)—but Steve uses American Sign Language. He lipreads English and some Cantonese, but his mother seems unwilling to learn to sign. In his monologues, Steve speaks fluent English, but he is disinclined to talk out loud in it with other people. Mimi masters all three languages and her father's voice—a memory—also intervenes to speak to her in yet another "language." In fact, despite the many languages that permeate the play, language fails altogether in the beginning, when the audience must follow the narrative from the characters' inner voices, which actually offer more contextual information than the interactions between the characters themselves.

Language is more than just a medium for (mis)communication in this play: it represents a state of being for the characters. At the beginning of the play, the mother exclaims with resignation, "I am my language" (14), meaning that her ability to speak Chinese and her inability to master English define where she has come from, where she is likely to work, and how she is likely to live her life. If the mother were able to communicate with her son, she would realise that he shares this awkward situation: people treat Steve as if his language defined him as simply "deaf." This dramatisation of Lacan's symbolic is a state that Mimi in particular attempts to overcome: this symbolic isolation predicated by "language"—the very structure necessary to existence—imprisons her mother and brother. While Mimi recognises this on one level, it is not until she reconciles herself with the notion of "fatherland" that she fully grasps its significance.

'meaningful' subject. That is, fantasy gives meaning and purpose to the subject's life, and the meaning and purpose which makes life worth living is itself part of the fantasy" (Hage, *op.cit.*: 70).

The most important representation of the fatherland transpires in the story of the jingwei bird. At the beginning of the play, the family's only means of communication with each other is the retelling of this fragmented, framing story: when their father was still alive, he frequently told the children the story of the jingwei bird, in which the beloved daughter of an emperor was drowned by an angry sea god. The girl's soul transformed into the bird, who was determined to build a bridge over the ocean to be reunited with her father. Every day the bird dropped a stone or twig into the ocean to build the bridge that would one day cross the ocean that separated them, even if it took millions of years. The play reveals the story slowly, with some of it narrated by the voice-over that represents Mimi's father; however, Mimi remembers a different version than the bare-bones one told by her mother, one that does not emphasise death. Whichever story is recounted, the bridge across the ocean represents the possibility of a reconciliation, despite the geographical distance, migration and death.

Yet, if the jingwei bird connects Mimi's mother regretfully to her dead ancestors, the bird acts for Mimi as an empowering tool for this life. It links Ontario with Vancouver, and "China" with "Canada." At the end, Mimi releases a bird from a cage as if to facilitate the bird's bridge-construction, a form of personal architecture as vital as the conventional theories of architecture which she studies; this action releases her grief over her father's death and her guilt regarding her responsibility for Steve's illness. Steve also renegotiates a renewed relationship with his mother as he learns how not to drown in the sea of isolation; his mother in turn learns a new "mother-tongue" that will enable her to "mother" again. The jingwei bird pursues her mission to bridge the ocean, using whatever tools are at her disposal. The reconstitution of mother-tongue as a multiple linguistic entity and the recognition of the continued possibility of a form of relationship with the father/land free Mimi and Steve to construct individuated ways to build bridges between their various subject positions. They have rediscovered the value of attempting to attain a fantasy space, knowing that they, like the jingwei bird, will not be able to fill the ocean with enough stones.

In Janis Balodis's *The Ghosts Trilogy*, the symbolic operates not via language but via patrimony, more specifically the memory invested in the fatherland that enables the male characters to construct the self. The trilogy begins at the end of World War II with a group of Latvian migrants arriving in Australia. The story of the Latvians unfolds amidst the journeys of Ludwig Leichhardt, the eccentric German explorer who travelled through Queensland in the 1840s. The two narratives occur on stage simultaneously as the Latvians inhabit the same land that Leichhardt explored and which his ghost continues to haunt. Aborigines

"Fatherlands and Mother-tongues" 353

whose presence predates Leichhardt also occupy the land.[14] The Latvians are figured as the latest intruders on the landscape. My analysis primarily considers *My Father's Father*, the third in the trilogy, which reassesses patrimony and language for the second-generation figure, Armand.[15]

My Father's Father finds Karl and Ilse visiting Latvia for the first time in fifty years, accompanied by Armand, their son. Karl's discovery that he does not have the right to claim his family estate devastates him, partly because this anticipated patrimony has been the foundation of his life. It confirms in him the decision to remain in Australia to end his days: "I won't go back to Latvia again ... My family is here [in Queensland]. There's nowhere to go. Right here is where I'll die. Right here is where I'll go on living" (276).[16]

While the journey back to Latvia is difficult for Karl,[17] it proves ultimately most instructive for Armand, who comes to understand his father and himself. A younger Armand, embarrassed by his father and determined to substitute Edvards, a family friend, in the role, had maintained that he would never be like his real father. Yet, the play demonstrates theatrically that he cannot escape the resemblance: in several short passages, Karl remembers his father, who appears on stage, performed by

---

[14] The two Australian eras (the 1990s and 1840s) and the return to Latvia that is the premise of *My Father's Father* are tied together theatrically: in 1990s Queensland, Ilse prepares a spirit evening for their dying friend, Edvards, by placing a trail of sand and pine boughs around the feast table. Her Latvian relatives prepare a similar ritual-like celebratory welcome home, while the Aboriginal guide, Brown, explains to Leichhardt that the sand and boughs which he spreads will look enough like white man's "magic" to protect them from attack by the "bad blackfellas" (197) who have killed the rest of the exploration party. The three narratives (augmented by several other ghostly and memory sequences) thus occupy the same stage space.

[15] This analysis of *My Father's Father* is, however, informed by an understanding of *Too Young for Ghosts* and *No Going Back*.

[16] Brown's situation is slightly different. While he sings the Latvian song with the ghosts of Ruth and Leonids, he comments "My Latvia is here. My people came and lived here. We were born here. We died here. We look to our own. There's nowhere to go. Right here is where I die. Right here is where I go on living" (247). Karl echoes this statement at the end of the play when he pronounces that he is also at home in Queensland, reinforcing the interconnections between Australia's various inhabitants.

[17] Ilse's re-evaluation is different: she has lost touch with her family to a much greater extent, having been separated from them during and after the war. The trip back also awakens memories of a war-thwarted engagement. Ilse laments leaving Latvia with nothing (232), whereas Karl assumes that he has something to return to/for. Leaving with nothing seems like a failure to Ilse, one which she has accepted and transcended.

the actor who plays Armand, his son. Armand collects his patrimony when he reassesses his relationship with his father and with his birth country (Australia), which is far more important to him than any land title might be. He adds Karl's legacy to the one that Edvards leaves for him, also incorporating the role of "Australia" in his personal and cultural definition of self.

The connection between "Australia" and Armand is demonstrated through Leichhardt, Gilbert (the naturalist who died on Leichhardt's first journey), and Brown (Leichhardt's last Aboriginal guide), who also explore memories and legacies. Leichhardt's legacy is not land or memory, but a distinguished place in history, although the loss of his journals interrupts the triumphant narrative which he was attempting to create for himself. The eventual discovery of Gilbert's journal, which contradicts Leichhardt's letters, further disrupts Leichhardt's narrative, the latter being thus memorialised as a tyrannical and unpredictable madman. Patrick White's *Voss*—one of many narratives loosely based on Leichhardt, and a segment of the *Voss* opera which is performed during the play—further skew the "facts" that Leichhardt wishes to be told: his ghost is disturbed, because he is not remembered as reverently as he yearns to be. The ghosts illustrate the complexities of the constructedness of belonging and subject positioning for both themselves and for the living.[18] More specifically, the ghosts also extend the realm of the fatherland for Armand, whose own construction of belonging and subject positioning must accommodate the layers of history and "unrest" that these ghostly figures represent.

While language embodies the location of the symbolic in *Mother Tongue*, its function in the other plays is often less central. In *The Ghosts Trilogy*, language bridges communication with theatre, since the characters' incomprehension of language (whether Latvian, English, German, or Aboriginal languages) is communicated by the actors' accents. The Latvian characters speak "English" with a heavy accent, complete with mistakes in word choice and word order. When they communicate in Latvian, their mother tongue, they speak flawless

---

[18] Spirits and ghosts in this play do not merely connect past and present. On one level, the spirits represent memories of the past, the powerful connections that the living want to retain with the dead. Yet, when the ghosts speak in the play, they reveal that they are actually trapped by these memories. The ghosts of Leonids and Ruth (who drowned at the end of the first play) appear anxious for Edvards's death so that they will be released. Leonids explains, "When we're forgotten we'll find peace" (230), and Edvards is the only person who continues to remember them. While the living are determined to remember, most of the dead wish only to be forgotten so that they may rest.

English—generally the language of the audience and the actors themselves.[19] This method complicates the notion of mother-tongue—or which languages are dominant—in order to renew the act of transmitting language. It also makes room for visual channels of communicating meaning that are appropriate to theatre texts. Language represents only one means of communication in theatre, since action, or a form of "visual language," is crucial on stage. For Ilse, the mother tongue also equates an unvoiced language of tears, the tears that her mother cries for her because Ilse does not come home during the war, does not return after the war, and eventually even stops writing (221, 223). Armand's own "language" of painting can be seen as yet another variation on language: it has become his dominant means of communication, if not a new mother-tongue by which he defines himself.

The Ghosts Trilogy uses fatherlands and mother-tongues to reconfigure subject positions for characters like Armand within an Australian context that turns out to be neither assimilative nor essentialist. Perhaps one of the most important achievements of the trilogy is that it extends the range of possible subject positions for Armand. Edvards, Armand's alternative father figure whose own idea of patrimony seems much less tangible than Karl's, gives Armand the freedom to indulge his own ideas, while reminding Armand that however he decides to reshape himself, he has to incorporate the layers of history and disruption into place.[20] The ghosts of Leichhardt and his colleagues perform several roles in the play, but for Armand, they help draw a more extensive map of/for subjectivity.

In *Cold Harvest*, two families are about to be united through the marriage of their children. In the course of preparing for the wedding, the two main characters, Kasia and Yong-su, learn about their respective relatives, their secrets, the difficulties that their parents encountered in migrating from Poland and Korea, and the process of becoming "Australian." The play at first appears to be a conventional generational-conflict narrative, but in the second-generation's demand for answers from their parents to identity-determining questions, the play shifts to

---

[19] Some characters like Armand, whose mother tongue is English and whose Latvian is elementary, invert the system.

[20] Using Ibsen's *Hedda Gabler* as her text, Elin Diamond discusses specifics of "history" as a significant absence in much psychoanalytic criticism, which tends to generate a homogenised audience or readership. See Elin Diamond, "The Violence of 'We': Politicizing Identification," in Critical Theory and Performance, ed. Janelle G. Reinelt and Joseph R. Roach (Ann Arbor: U of Michigan P, 1992): 390-98. Crucial to *The Ghosts Trilogy* is the function of the ghost-filled stage which emphasises the importance of the layers of history that formulate an Australian subject, even one who, like Armand, has connections to other lands.

question the boundaries of self-definition and thereby differs from *The Ghosts Trilogy*. The children know that their parents experienced hardships, but they ignore the details as to what precisely brought their parents to Australia. In the sharing of family recipes for baking wedding cakes, the families reveal secrets relating to their respective migrations to Australia, providing Kasia and Yong-su with the freedom to abandon the recipe-book and experiment with combining their own ingredients. The play frames seven characters—five of whom play multiple roles, whether in voice-over or in corporeal form—in a setting that includes an escalator or staircase, and a food storehouse with sliding glass doors in which two couples share a meal. The storehouse contains preserves in large glass jars, lit with coloured lights; it also functions as the figurative location of memory and culture for the play. The bride and groom are initially excluded from the meal which features a ritualised element. Eventually, the table is moved half way out of the storehouse in a compromise gesture, once some of the families' secrets are revealed.

Various types of mother-tongues structure *Cold Harvest*. As is common in Janaczewska's plays, English is only one of several languages spoken. Korean and Polish words pepper the play, sometimes translated directly or by context, and sometimes not. More importantly, just as the "language" of painting becomes an important means of communication for Armand, the characters in *Cold Harvest* speak most confidently through a language of food. The chorus of the "countdown for the wedding cake" weaves through the play as each parent contributes to the recipe for the perfect wedding cake, to the bemusement of the bride and groom (17). Food marks their difference from the Anglo-Celtic culture that the children once longed to emulate; that difference also represents a point of intersection between the two families. Whenever the conversation gets tense, someone brings it back to the polite, safe territory of food.

The two families, moreover, joke about how Australian multiculturalism is frequently equated with food. Myong-Hwa complains that the immigration officials constructed her as an item of food that the Anglo-Australian Jack was "buying" to take back to Australia (17). Franciszka talks about emigration as a process of shedding all that she brought with her, including her name which an immigration official changed from Barszczewska to Coles, after the Australian grocery store (26). Food even comes to mean fitting into Australia, and Kasia and her fiancé recount her father's desire to find the answer to one of his "secrets":

Yong-su: How can you have the best of both worlds?
Kasia/Yong-su: How can you have your cake and eat it?" (28)

"Fatherlands and Mother-tongues" 357

For the older generation, this symbolic construct of food-related "languages" also has associations with the fatherland. Yet, for Kasia and Yong-su, finding the fatherland or—in this case, "the best of both worlds"—entails a different process than for their parents. So much has been shed in her parents' arrival in Australia that Kasia feels that she does not have enough ingredients to construct herself: her response is to accrue as many subject positions as possible. Both Kasia and Yong-su decide that the best way to gather relevant subject positions from which to create their identities is to visit their parents' birth countries. While they complained as children about the idea of anything homemade (which was quintessentially un-Australian), they now want a "homemade" identity, even if it is construed as a new form of fatherland. However, they find their return to their parents' fatherlands disappointing: Kasia complains about "the mythology of the homeland package tour," which is an unexpected "Disney-fiction" created for people who have migrated to other countries (38). From another perspective, Kasia's aunt bluntly expounds that the idea of children of migrants returning "home" to rediscover what happened years ago does not appeal to Poles living in Poland:

> No one here gives a damn what happened years ago, we're too busy making half a cabbage and a scrap of meat last the week. Yes, that's the unpalatable truth of the matter. And if someone's made a new life in another country well good luck to them, but it won't fix our rickety economy or my leaky roof. Do you want to know what I think? I think it's you, not us. You, the children of those who left, who can't let go of the past (25).

Kasia is not yet in a position to let go of the past, because her parents have held on to it too tightly, keeping it even from her. Kasia asks Yong-su, "Do you think we're overshadowed by our parents' histories?" (39). Her question is answered when she returns to the storeroom. Throughout the play, Kasia witnesses fragments of an argument between her mother and her aunt which culminates in a large jar of preserves falling and shattering. The storehouse keeps more than food: it also represents a preserved form of culture, past and secrets. It preserves a combination of mother-tongue and fatherland, while the shattering of the jar releases the secrets. Once she knows the origin of her parents' migration to Australia, Kasia in particular is able to piece together the possibilities for her identity and then to choose a combination of elements that suit her. The families then seem willing to make room for the past, this present and—in terms of Kasia and Yong-su—the mix of cultures. *Cold Harvest* does not stage the wedding between Kasia and Yong-su as a naive figuration of the harmony of cultures. The play focuses on the desire of the second-generation to decode the clues to fatherland and mother-tongue that are crucial to their identity formation. As the families move to bridge the space between the confines of the storehouse and the wider culture in Australia, it seems that Kasia and Yong-su might achieve their goals.

Marty Chan's comedy, *Mom, Dad, I'm Living with a White Girl*, pursues some of the absurdities of families and multiculturalism through the construction of a Lacanian fantasy world. In his attempts to break from the family bosom, Mark is caught between his Chinese-Canadian family and his partner, a Canadian of undisclosed (Anglo-Celtic) cultural heritage, Sally. Mark's mother is suffocating, while his father is determined to make him join the family business, acupuncture, even though Mark is an auto mechanic. The play's narrative traverses two worlds, a naturalistic one and a fantasy world that dramatises obvious stereotypes from both the Chinese and Canadian experiences, each as absurd as the other. *Mom, Dad, I'm Living with a White Girl* inverts culture and intercultural misunderstandings with the deliberate aim of misrepresenting families, cultures, and the relationship between different cultures.

This fantasy world is depicted as Mark's nightmare. Sally works as a film script editor and Mark reads one of her scripts, "Wrath of the Yellow Claw," which he finds amusing in its play with stereotypes.[21] It becomes the basis for the fantasy narrative, although at times it seems hard to discern the boundaries between the naturalistic world of Mark, Sally, and Mark's parents, and the fantasy world of the Yellow Claw, "an Oriental warlord bent on world domination" (98). Yellow Claw is determined to conquer, not merely infiltrate, the decadent world of Vancouver. The weapons that this "inscrutable villain" (99) uses include opium-tipped shurikens, lengthy acupuncture needles, truth serum, deadly judo chops and kung fu; the B-movie genre's trench coats, fog, spies, double agents, double-double agents, and labyrinthine plot twists abound. In the fantasy world, Sally's code name is Agent Snow Princess, while Mark is referred to as Agent Banana.[22]

---

[21] Mark does not dismiss the stereotypes purely on racist grounds, because he finds many of them entertaining and not necessarily derogatory. Sally, however, finds the script racist and *clichéd*. One could also consider their discussion about the script in terms of the psychoanalytic joke. For an explanation of the risk of the joke and the personal-social dichotomy that it sets up, see Elizabeth Wright, *Psychoanalytic Criticism: Theory in Practice* (London: and New York: Routledge, 1984): 179.

[22] Colour also operates as a communicating tool for each of the two opposing fatherlands: anything Chinese is yellow (and connotations of the Yellow Peril are intended), while anything Canadian is white. Agent Snow Princess engineers a way to disguise Agent Banana by covering his skin with white cream and powder. When he

"Fatherlands and Mother-tongues" 359

As in *Cold Harvest*, the language of the mother-tongue is figurative: in addition to the filmic language that structures the fantasy world, Chinese stereotypes become the language for both parts of the play. This is the "Chinese language" that communicates to those who do not speak Cantonese or Mandarin. Mark refused to learn Chinese as a child, but Sally has taken lessons in Cantonese, even if she fails to recognise just how limited her understanding is. Every *cliché* of Chineseness can be found here, including Confucian-style aphorisms, ritual death connected with honour, Chinese restaurants, MSG, Chinese laundries, Bruce Lee, mathematical skills, inability to say "l" as in Yellow Craw, David Carradine, feng shui, yin/yang, ping pong, and eating the cat for dinner.

Two warring fatherlands underscore both narratives. The stereotyped Chinese world comes across clearly enough. The Chinese culture that Mark's parents represent in the naturalistic narrative is open to scrutiny, particularly since they leave him no choice in matters concerning his future. The play also critiques two levels of Canadian culture through the well-meaning Sally. In the naturalistic narrative, Sally seems to try to acquire cultures as if they were available to anyone for ready consumption. At her first meeting with Mark's mother, she asks if she could get some pointers on how to "make authentic Chinese tea" to which Li Fen responds "You pour hot water on tea leaves" (105). In the fantasy world, Canada receives as much critical attention as the stereotyped China, particularly when Mark declares in mock patriotism to Yellow Claw, "I have an adopted mother now, and her name is Canada" (133). The play puts a stereotyped Canada on par with a stereotyped China, making ridiculous that which is always stereotyped and daring to stereotype that which is more frequently seen as sacrosanct. Canada's multiculturalism in particular is thrown open to parody. As a representative of Canada—championing Canada and whiteness against everything the Yellow Claw represents—Sally defends a nominal multiculturalism in a manner that Mark cannot tolerate. She explains to Mark's father that "We will treat him with the dignity that we treat all our immigrants. Even the Native Indians" (124).

With Sally's inability to compromise, the relationship ends as Mark rejects both the position that Sally represents and his mother's essentialist one.[23] Mark claims to want independence from his family (and

---

discovers this fiendish trick, Agent Snow Princess declares, "Assimilation is the only way. No longer will you be Mark Gee, minion of the Yellow Claw. Now, you'll be Sven Olafsen, Swedish shoemaker" (146). Not surprisingly, the dye wears off.

[23] This is the revised version of the script. In the original version (published in *Canadian Mosaic II: 6 Plays*, edited by Aviva Ravel (Toronto: Simon and Pierre, 1996), Sally and Mark conclude the play in a filmic "happily ever" after closure.

from Sally), but he decides that he must find a way for elements of his two worlds to co-exist. The fantasy world, where in Lacanian terms, the two parts of the Oedipal construction are finally integrated, is shown to be more nightmare than gratification. Mark refuses to accommodate the integration of signifiers of "China" and "Canada" if that integration effectively amounts to assimilation (to Sally) or essentialism (to Li Fen). His mother and his girlfriend seem to require him to perform their versions of their cultural imaginary, rather than allowing him the autonomy of self-definition. In *Mom, Dad, I'm Living with a White Girl*, mother-tongue and fatherland act as extremes from which Mark will develop his construction of selfhood, based on a selection of somewhat compatible signifiers that will enable him to represent himself.

These plays dramatise what Hage calls "real multiculturalism" or "a deep commitment to a more far-reaching multiculturalism.[24] In fact, a multicultural praxis already occurs in these staged versions of multiculturalism. The four plays suggest a reconfiguration of mother-tongue and fatherland (in addition to the more standard mother/father roles) to reject many of the standard definitions of identity-determining structures that may have suited their parents and/or other Australians/Canadians. The constructions favoured by the second-generation subjects carefully recognise their complex subject positions. More than demonstrating split subjectivity or multiple subject positions, these plays exhibit several of the processes whereby this takes place, as unconventional and visual languages merge with tangible and intangible patrimonies. The characters in *Mother Tongue* find ways through the drowning effects of language and the versions of the jingwei bird story. Armand learns how to structure himself in terms of his various fathers, his several claims to homelands, and the accretion of ghosts and history that necessarily define his fatherlands in *My Father's Father*. *Cold Harvest* provides a different order of language—food—to translate the repressions engendered by the previous generation into the forms of subjectivity that are crucial to the second-generation characters. Finally, *Mom, Dad, I'm Living with a White Girl* explores the language of *cliché* in both Chinese and Canadian terms in an attempt to expose essentialist and assimilative forms of culture for what they are.

The subjects in these plays are not naïve enough to search for a mythical wholeness: while Lacan's construction of the fully-functioning self reduces two units (father/mother) to one (child), these second-generation children refuse to accept any predetermined definition of self

---

Canada, in effect, triumphs over the Yellow Claw. The revised edition, in which the relationship terminates, offers a more nuanced and politically strategic ending.

[24] Hage, *op. cit.*: 26.

according to cultural outlines. These subjects also refuse to speak for an entire community or nation, preferring to reshape the possibility of fantasy spaces for themselves, spaces which may be relevant to others in their communities/audiences. They cannot construct a fantasy national space for an entire country in Lacanian terms. It is perhaps not surprising that when Hage himself attempts such an endeavour in *White Nation*, he imputes to nationalists the very essentialism that he opposes in figurations of multicultural communities. Rather than simply performing the gatekeeping function, contemporary Australian and Canadian multicultural family plays attempt to reformat cultural boundaries to remove some of the restrictions experienced by second-generation subjects and to explore some of the useful complications that such a position affords.

Works Cited

Balodis, Janis. *My Father's Father*, in *The Ghosts Trilogy* (Sydney: Currency, 1997).
Bennett, David, ed. *Multicultural States: Rethinking Difference and Identity* (London and New York: Routledge, 1998).
Berry, J.W. and J.A. Laponce, eds. *Ethnicity and Culture in Canada: The Research Landscape* (Toronto: U of Toronto P, 1994).
Bissoondath, Neil. *Selling Illusions: The Cult of Multiculturalism in Canada* (Toronto: Penguin, 1994).
Blonski, Annette. *Arts for a Multicultural Australia: An Account of Australia Council Policies, 1973-1991* (Strawberry Hills: Australia Council, 1992).
Castles, Stephen, Mary Kalantzis, Bill Cope, and Michael Morrissey. *Mistaken Identity: Multiculturalism and the Demise of Nationalism in Australia* (Sydney: Pluto, 1992).
Chan, Marty. *Mom, Dad, I'm Living with a White Girl*, in *Ethnicities: Plays from the New West*, ed. Anne Nothof (Edmonton: NeWest, 1999): 99-167.
Chan, Marty. *Mom, Dad, I'm Living with a White Girl*, in *Canadian Mosaic II: 6 Plays*, ed. Aviva Ravel (Toronto: Simon and Pierre, 1996): 99-163.
Diamond, Elin. "The Violence of 'We': Politicizing Identification," in *Critical Theory and Performance*, eds. Janelle G. Reinelt and Joseph R. Roach (Ann Arbor: U of Michigan P, 1992): 390-98.
Gunew, Sneja and Fazal Rizvi, eds. *Culture, Difference, and the Arts* (St. Leonard's: Allen and Unwin, 1993).
Hage, Ghassan. *White Nation* (Sydney: Pluto, 1998).
Hutcheon, Linda. "'A Spell of Languages': Introducing *Other Solitudes*," in *Other Solitudes: Canadian Multicultural Fictions*, eds. Linda Hutcheon and Marian Richmond (Toronto: Oxford UP, 1990): 1-16.
Janaczewska, NoNlle. *Cold Harvest* (unpublished manuscript, 1997).

Khoo, Tseen-Ling. "Banana Bending: Asian-Australian and Asian-Canadian Literature" (University of Queensland: unpublished Ph.D. thesis, 1999).
Lyssiotis, Tes. *A White Sports Coat and Other Plays* (Sydney: Currency, 1996).
MacCannell, Juliet Flower. *Figuring Lacan: Criticism and the Cultural Unconscious* (London and Sydney: Croom Helm, 1986).
Quan, Betty. *Mother Tongue* (Victoria: Scirocco, 1999).
Reinelt, Janelle G. "Psychoanalysis Introduction," in *Critical Theory and Performance*, eds. Janelle G. Reinelt and Joseph R. Roach (Ann Arbor: U of Michigan P, 1992): 383-89.
Rossi, Vince. *The Last Adam* (Montreal: NuAge, 1995).
Rossi, Vince. *The Chain* (Montreal: NuAge, 1989).
Shakespeare, William. *King Lear*, ed. Kenneth Muir (London: Arden, 1964).
Tompkins, Joanne. "Inter-referentiality: Interrogating Multicultural Drama in Australia," in *Our Australian Theatre in the 1990s*, ed. Veronica Kelly (Amsterdam: Rodopi, 1998): 117-31.
White, Patrick. *Voss* (Ringwood: Penguin, 1960).
Wright, Elizabeth. *Psychoanalytic Criticism: Theory in Practice* (London and New York: Routledge, 1984).

APPENDIX

Garden of Drama: Talking to John Harding

MARYROSE CASEY

La Trobe University

A performance poet, playwright, screenwriter, ex-actor, stand-up comedian and activist of Torres Strait Islander descent, John Harding was born in an inner city suburb of Melbourne, Australia in 1961. One of seven children, Harding's brothers and sisters include a number of well-known visual artists, actors and dancers such as Destiny Deacon and Clinton Nain. A born entertainer with lots of "street cred," good humoured charm and nervous energy, Harding's passionate concern about the challenges facing Aboriginal and Torres Strait Islander people is never far from the surface.

When he was fourteen Harding's family moved to Lalor, an outer western suburb of Melbourne. In an attempt to deal with his feelings "about what it was like to be the only black in about twenty kilometres," Harding started to write poetry. In a piece of characteristic humour, his first book of poetry, entitled *John Harding's Little Black Book of Poems*, is pocket-sized and doubles as an address and telephone book.[1]

Through his mother, the late Eleanor Harding, an important community leader and activist, Harding's first theatrical experience was the premiere production of Kevin Gilbert's play *The Cherry Pickers* in 1973, produced by Nindethana Theatre Company.[2] Eleanor Harding was a member of Nindethana, one of the first Koori Theatre Companies in Australia. Harding's first forays into writing for performance were usually on the run. To mark the end of the 1985 National Aboriginal Education Conference in Adelaide, representatives from every state had to put together some form of performance. So in one hour, Harding wrote his first play *Blackman and Sobbin,* a fifteen-to-twenty-minute sketch. Then, when he was co-ordinating a series of plays for Radio 3CR, he wrote a radio play *Land Rights Rally*. The play was later picked up by ABC Radio and broadcast nationally. In 1990 Harding was commissioned by the Aboriginal Housing Commission in Victoria to write a training video,

---

[1] John Harding, *John Harding's Little Black Book of Poems* (Richmond, Victoria, n.d.).

[2] Nindethana was a Victorian Koori theatre company established in 1971; it continued through a number of major changes until 1973, when it was dissolved.

Not just Bricks and Mortar, for non-Indigenous officers to sensitise them to Aboriginal issues.

In 1990, with his then partner Kylie Belling and other members of the Victorian Koori community, Harding was involved in establishing Ilbijerri, Aboriginal and Torres Strait Islander Theatre Co-operative. ("Ilbijerri," a term found in a Melbourne area Aboriginal language, means "an occasion for socialising.") Since its inception in 1990, Ilbijerri has been totally Aboriginal and Torres Strait Islander initiated and controlled. It was formed with the aims of providing a performing arts base for the Victorian Indigenous community and to raise awareness of important issues in the wider community. Ilbijerri's inaugural production in 1991 was John Harding's *Up The Road*, directed by Kylie Belling.[3] It was hailed as a step forward for intercultural understanding. Peter Weiniger, in a review for *The Age*, summed up a general feeling when he wrote: "Thank you, for the first time I felt like I was peeking through the venetians [blinds] of Aboriginal homes, you weren't doing it for me."[4] *Up the Road* has since been produced and co-produced by a number of major companies as it has toured Australia.

The play originated from John Harding's desire to "challenge the view that all Indigenous Australians are a large homogenous group." As Harding stresses, Indigenous Australians "are a dozen Europes," not one single group with one single voice or culture. *Up The Road* was originally a one-act play that ran forty minutes. It was then workshopped at the Australian National Playwrights Conference (ANPC) and at Belvoir Street Theatre. Through the workshopping process, the play was developed to full length.

The story of *Up the Road* is that of a young man's return to his community after years of working as an Aboriginal bureaucrat in Canberra. Harding's play examines what at times appears to be the only three pathways or choices for young male Indigenous Australians: "one gone fishing, one gone to bureaucracy and one dead." *Up the Road* is an example of contemporary work by Indigenous Australian artists developing innovative and humorous ways to bridge the gulf of ignorance, guilt and fear that continually undermines the process of reconciliation between Indigenous and non-Indigenous Australians. As Harding says, "Salvation may be just up the road, but we'll never know until we get there and create it. It doesn't mean we can't have a good laugh getting there." *Up the Road* was nominated for both the Victorian and NSW Premiers' literary awards. Harding's other credits include the works for television *Lift Off* and *Blackout*, as well as the development and production of the Aboriginal sitcom *The Masters*.

---

[3] John Harding, *Up the Road* (Sydney: Currency Press in association with Playbox, 1997).

[4] Peter Weiniger, "Aboriginal Theatre Company Has Promise of Bright Future," *The Age* (27 September 1991): 14.

Garden of Drama

The following material has been edited from interviews and discussions with John Harding conducted while he was in Melbourne in 1997 for the Playbox/Belvoir Street co-production of *Up the Road*.[5]

CASEY: You were involved in setting up Ilbijerri, Aboriginal and Torres Strait Islander Theatre Co-operative in 1990. What was the original motivation for establishing the company?

HARDING: Ilbijerri came out of frustration of no Aboriginal people being seen in the theatre ... [The company] came out of my anger, because there was nothing in Melbourne Victoria, the so-called cultural capital of Australia ... for Aboriginal people. Occasionally, you know, someone from the MTC [Melbourne Theatre Company] would ring up looking for a *didjeridu* player, but that was about it. And so we had all these people who had a lot of experience in film and television, but nothing ever happening in terms of theatre supporting Aboriginal people in Victoria ...

And so out of frustration I just thought, well let's just start our own theatre company. [It was the only way] we were going to get anywhere and start training facilities for our young people who ... aspire to be actors, technicians, stage managers, and directors and writers. So really that was just out of all that frustration of nothing being there, out of the cultural desert. Yet it was supposed to be a cultural capital, it was quite ironic ... So I rang the Aboriginal Legal Service and said how do I go about setting up a co-op, and I got a solicitor on board and started running with it. Started thinking about the fact that I needed a group of young people to be on the board, started selecting people who were interested ... Archie Roach and Ruby Hunter were on the original committee ... When we were setting it all up ... there were musos [involved] as well, not just actors ... We got support from all over the place in terms of the Aboriginal community.

Then [once] we set it up ... we thought "Oh gee, what are we going to do for our inaugural production? We haven't got a play." ... We forgot about that in the fervour of all this political [process of] setting [the company] up. And we thought "Oh God, what are we going to put on?" So people said, "Well Johnny you're a writer, write a play." So I wrote *Up the Road*. I just picked up a poem called *Pinstripe Blues*.[6] I wrote the poem seven years before all this, and just dug it out of the cobwebs and saw it. I was searching for inspiration going through my poetry, I suppose. And I saw it and I thought, "Oh there's a story in this." And I created Ian, who is an

---

[5] Playbox Theatre Company is a Melbourne-based company with the primary artistic focus of producing new Australian plays. Belvoir Street Theatre and its resident company, Company B, are based in Sydney. Company B is dedicated to producing innovative theatre, drawing on Australian and classical texts.

[6] The poem "Pinstripe Blues" was written after Harding worked for the Federal Department of Aboriginal Affairs. "It came out of that experience in the public service. It was about serving two masters."

alter ego of myself, really. Out of that really evolved *Up the Road*, which we toured for four weeks around Melbourne. We went to all the universities and Trades Hall, Footscray Community Arts Centre. Probably about, I don't know the exact figures, but it would have been say somewhere between two and a half to three thousand people saw it. It did quite well ... We took it to the Aboriginal Advancement League in Thornbury, that's where it opened. A lot of people saw it. We got a lot of great commentary, it got a fantastic review in the *Age*, for the first production of a new theatre company ... and that was the beginning of *Up the Road* really ...

CASEY: Since then *Up the Road* has been through a lot of changes, not the least being the development of a one-act play into a two-act play. Do you think in the process the intention of the work has changed?

HARDING: ... [Despite] the fact that *Up the Road* went from a community production to a mainstream production, [and the] 1995 Playwrights Conference in Canberra added considerably to its development ... I don't think any of the substantial issues have changed ... The same points are being made. We didn't have the six or whatever they are songs in 1991, it was just a straight narrative but it was still, I think, it was funny then it's funny now. The same points that [Helen Thompson] makes astutely [in this review],[7] I was making in 1991. They are still there obviously or it wouldn't be written in the review. So it really hasn't changed in terms of the points that were being made as a story and what you share with the audience and want to educate the audience about. Especially about reconciliation ... When we first started the word reconciliation hadn't ever really been on the agenda. Yet that's what it was about in 1991 ... We were trying to promote reconciliation before the Federal Government was. And I suppose the [other] thing [the play is] about— because I write very much for my own people—when we start to put each other in categories, "you're a Koori bureaucrat, so you're an arsehole," "you've lost touch with your people and you're a coconut," then we are dehumanising ourselves. The whole point of, I thought, of the political struggle of our people was to humanise us again. We are seen as this generic thing at the moment. They were the original reasons and they still are, and Neil Armfield the director [of the 1996-97 Belvoir Street production] has seen all these things and he has just basically embellished ... them ...

CASEY: What do you see as the major themes in your work?

HARDING: Peace, really, and justice are my two big themes. I think [for] most people, [most] Indigenous playwrights around the world, [the] two biggest themes are justice and peace. That's all they want ... I just keep trying to work out [approaches], I look at different situations whether it be the Olympic games or reconciliation or the anniversary of Federation, the republic ... and I look at them and analyse them and think "OK what are [these events] going to mean to this country and how are they going to affect black/white relations?" ... That's what I do ... All

---

[7] Helen Thomson, "Going Home to Love and Loss," *The Age* (10 March 1997): C5.

Garden of Drama

these political things happening and I think "Is that going to help us find peace or is it going to drive the wedge in even further?" ... Because of that, as a playwright, there's always a great garden of drama. It's easy to find drama in there because you have the hypocrisy, the unconcern about Aboriginal and Torres Strait Islander people, by white Australia. You have all those things, and yet you know that we still own the country, because there has never been a treaty. So there's this beautiful garden of drama until the treaty's signed ... All I try to do with my work is to push towards the treaty really. And peace and justice, that's what's going to push us towards a treaty, because we won't sign the treaty otherwise ...

CASEY: What sort of changes do you think have occurred since you first wrote and produced *Up the Road*? Do you think the environment and reception for your work has changed?

HARDING: We were disappointed then about the lack of action on the treaty under the [Bob] Hawke government, the Compact they were calling it then, and now we still haven't got a treaty ... I am not going to hold my breath for [John] Howard to make it happen, and so I don't think much has changed ...[8]

[In fact the] situation has got a lot worse [especially in terms of services and support for Indigenous communities]. The irony of *Up the Road* is that it is even more relevant six years later. [As I wrote in the program for the Belvoir Street production], they are still treating the grandfathers of the planet like little children, not realising there is all this wealth of knowledge of how to look after your community. That they are taking even less notice of than they were six years ago ... If anything, it has gotten a lot worse, and it's going to affect our children's chance of any future again ... We're back where we started again in the 80s. Not back where we started, but it was getting better and now it's gotten worse again ...

CASEY: What impact do you see this having on your writing?

HARDING: ... The biggest thing that stops reconciliation is fear. What the Federal Government doesn't address through the Council for Reconciliation and stuff is the fear ... which is what *Up the Road* does in many ways, and that's part of its strength and interest for people both white and black, it does in an innovative way challenge that fear. I really think unless they start addressing issues like that and finding innovative ways to address it, until they start challenging the fear, the Federal Government and the country itself, it's always going to be "the blacks are doing this," "the blacks are drunks" ... "The blacks are over there and we are over here." And yet I pay taxes, I worry about issues concerning immigration. I worry about all the same issues everyone else is worried about, not just Aboriginal deaths in custody. I worry about everything else in the news as well. And you have to show white Australia all these commonalities that we have. A large percentage of Aboriginal and Torres Strait Islander people live in the same cities as white people. And once

---

[8] Robert J. Hawke was Prime Minister of Australia from 1983 to 1992. John Howard is the current Prime Minister.

[non-Indigenous Australians] start realising that the "only true Aboriginals" aren't just in Arnhem Land or Central Australia or the Northern Territory, then that's to me how you confront the fear by showing the commonality. As Helen Thompson's article said, [*Up the Road* is] not only about this Aboriginal family. It's about issues about class. [It's] about members of the family becoming upwardly mobile, then coming back and having to deal with the members of the family who haven't changed because of economic circumstances, because of where they live, in regional Australia. [It's about] all those things and its [about the commonality] between us ... If you look at Ian as a character, he's many many different strands of men and women who have experienced those things of being apart and coming back and trying to fit in again. That's one of the major themes of the play, it's not just about race.

CASEY: What was your primary intention when you were writing *Up the Road*?

HARDING: I suppose I was trying to find an innovative way to make Australia see the universality of the issues. I think a core part of reconciliation is if people can see that it's not just us and them. We need childcare, they need childcare. It's not Aboriginal childcare, white childcare, it's childcare, and all those same issues of economics and social welfare affect us just as much ... All the things people worry about the Australian government doing, we worry about. ATSIC [Aboriginal and Torres Strait Islander Council] is just one issue in our lives. Once white Australia realises that we won't have to just live and march under the Aboriginal flag every time we have an issue ...

CASEY: You mentioned finding innovative ways to engage with material. Do you have any preference for styles of writing, for particular ways of presenting your work?

HARDING: I'm a big sucker for comedy ... I think comedy is one of the best ways to educate people because ... how long would you stand in the Bourke Street Mall and listen while someone on a soapbox is screaming about what white people have done to black people? You'd stand there for only two or three minutes, then you'd go and buy something. You wouldn't last too long, I wouldn't last too long ... [Even] if it was someone standing there screaming about what Australia's done to East Timor, something I'd find interesting I'd still ... if they were up there for half an hour, after ten minutes I'd switch off because I'm a human being ... We have a short concentration span ...

[If] that guy or that woman who was on that soap box turned what they were saying into a performance piece, I'd be fascinated and I wouldn't move, so long as it was good performance, of course. So I see the theatre as another medium, another soapbox, but a very, very effective, subtle soapbox to hold an audience, to hold people there so that they can get the whole message, so they don't walk off and buy something ... That's what I see theatre as. I mean we're the oldest exponents of theatre in the world: people forget that, the *corroboree* is the oldest form of theatre in the world, older than African, Indian, American. It's the oldest form in the world.

Garden of Drama 369

Because we never had pens and paper, we had to rely very much on oral traditions, history and story telling, and that made us very good at it. We've had a hundred thousand years of rehearsals ... We know how to hold the story ... And what we've never been given until the last twenty or thirty years—no not even thirty years—is the opportunity in modern Australia to [have access to a] theatre and stage in which to do it, a stage that white people are coming to. We're not just talking to our community around the campfire, or in a community centre, we're actually now getting into theatres. All this essentially is a development, an adaptation in the twentieth century of the same skills of how to pass a story on so that people not only get the point, but are enthralled and want to hear it, and want to stay there and want to do something about it ...

CASEY: In other forums you have spoken out against the restrictiveness of labelling work as "Aboriginal," citing as an example that if an Aboriginal company toured a play by Chekhov, it would only be discussed as an Aboriginal play. Do you think that's changing at all?

HARDING: I don't think it actually has, to tell the truth. The first line of the first review of *Up the Road* read "This was the best Aboriginal theatre in the Perth Festival." I thought "Yeah, but what about the other twenty-five plays in the Festival?" We were the only Aboriginal play, us and *Runamuk*, Yirra Yaakin.[9] And [the critics] really only compared us to them, [they were] not comparing us to the others, it was ghettoising us again ... Yet I had Neil Armfield, the best mainstream [non-Indigenous] director in Australia, yet it's still classified as "Aboriginal theatre." So you know if the main critic in WA was doing it still then, obviously not a lot has changed. I didn't get compared to anything else in the Festival except *Runamuk* as the best Aboriginal theatre ...

Melbourne was good ... they don't say that. [My work is] discussed as theatre. In the last line of one review it says, "it's not just a play, it's a living breathing theatrical event." It doesn't say "not just an Aboriginal play." That's fantastic ... It makes me feel that things are changing ... in Perth it was all comparisons with Jack Davis and Jimmy Chi and everything else they've seen like Richard Walley, but not comparing [my work] to any white theatre work ... So when John on the street reads that, he just goes, "Oh yeah, another Aboriginal play." It may be a good one, but it's still "just an Aboriginal play," so it's not really relevant to him. That's a bit disheartening even though they were fantastic reviews in WA ... The Melbourne ones give a sense of hope, because they haven't classified us as Aboriginal ...

... Why can't I or any other Aboriginal playwright be compared to David Williamson?[10] [The critics and commentators are] saying "You're not in that world." Even though we both write plays and he's had plays on at Playbox and I've had

---

[9] *Runamuk* was presented by Yirra Yaakin Noongar Theatre for the Festival of Perth in 1997.

[10] David Williamson is one of Australia's most eminent and popular playwrights.

plays on at Playbox. We're not in the same world. And I want to say "Why aren't we? Why can't you compare my play to his, in terms of dealing with Australian issues?" But they don't think about things like that they just keep ghettoising ...

I want people to see [my work] as theatre. [When my play is discussed as theatre rather than labelled and ghettoised], it gives me hope that people will be treated with the same respect ...

CASEY: As a playwright, what styles, traditions or streams do you see your work within or parallel to?

HARDING: I saw Chekhov last week at Belvoir, *The Sea Gull* with Noah Taylor, Cate Blanchett and Richard Roxborough. It was fantastic. It was hilarious, and yet it was so similar to *Up the Road*, and this play was written so long ago. It's funny how Aboriginal theatre has only been able to flower for the last thirty years, and yet if I was allowed to flower, we'd be doing Chekhov ... It's ironic ... *The Seagull* was so much like *Up The Road*. They both had the same director sure [Neil Armfield], but the script of *The Seagull* by Chekhov was hardly touched, it was all ... His irony, his comedic [*sic*] irony ... the way he saw history just through a family. The way he touches on politics, the way he touches on the interests of the time. He touches on many of the same things *Up the Road* touches on. To me that's a great irony, that's beautiful, that's the so-called classics, even some of the best qualities of Shakespeare are the same qualities that Aboriginal playwrights like Jack Davis have been writing about for thirty years. So [as] I see it, that if anything ... if [my writing] is going to fit in any style, then I want it to be classic ... and show the universality in the world ... That's why those plays can go to any country in the world ... Everyone can find something that they can connect with ... That's part of why *Up the Road* was getting such good reviews. As Helen Thomson said in *The Age*, it's about any rural family ... Just because [I'm] black, I made the family black. If I was a white country boy from Tocumwal, I would have written the same play, but it would have been a white farmer and his wife sending their son off to Melbourne Uni, and then he came back a doctor for a funeral and couldn't fit in again. It's exactly the same thing. So, if anything, my aspirations are that [my work] will be classic in the same sense as those guys, William and Anton ...

Works Cited

Harding, John. *John Harding's Little Black Book of Poems* (Richmond, Victoria, n.d.).

—— *Up the Road*, (Sydney: Currency Press in assoc with Playbox, 1997).

Thomson, Helen. "Going Home to Love and Loss?" *The Age* (10 March 1997): C5.

Weiniger, Peter. "Aboriginal Theatre Company has promise of bright future," *The Age* (27 September 1991): 14.

Notes on Contributors

Robert Appleford teaches Native Literatures and Canadian Drama at the University of Alberta in Edmonton. He has published numerous articles on Native Canadian performance and contributed to the volume *Native America: Portrait of the Peoples* (1994). Currently, he is at work on a monograph entitled *The Indian 'Act': Tactics of Performance in Native Canadian Theatre*.

Franca Bellarsi is assistant to Marc Maufort at the Université Libre de Bruxelles, where she is currently helping him to convene the conference "Crucible of Cultures: Anglophone Drama at the Dawn of a New Millennium" (May 2001). Her affinity for theatre partly derives from her interest in American performance poetry. She has also contributed several articles on the Beat Generation writers.

Tom Burvill heads the Department of Critical and Cultural Studies at Macquarie University, Sydney. He has written extensively on Australian community and radical theatre and alternative performance forms, as well as co-published with John Tulloch on the production and reception of Anton Chekhov in English-speaking cultures. He maintains a close association with Sidetrack Performance Group, based in Marrickville in Sydney, with which he has collaborated as *dramaturg* and co-writer.

Maryrose Casey is a performer whose fiction has been shortlisted for a number of literary awards. She also lectures in Theatre and Drama at LaTrobe University, where she has undertaken a Ph.D. examining the history of production and critical reception of theatre texts by Indigenous Australian artists.

Alan Filewod is a professor of Drama in the School of Literatures and Performance Studies in English at the University of Guelph. His books include *Collective Encounters: Documentary Theatre in English Canada*, three anthologies of Canadian drama, and the forthcoming volumes *Workers' Playtime: Studies in Theatre and Labour in Australia, Canada and the United States* (with David Watt) and *Performing "Canada": The Nation Enacted in the Imagined Theatre*.

Peter Fitzpatrick is Associate Professor of Drama at Monash University in Melbourne, where he heads the Centre for Drama and Theatre Studies. He has published widely in the field of Australian theatre, most notably in his critical books *After "The Doll"* (1979), *Williamson and Stephen Sewell: The Playwright as Revolutionary* (1991), and in the award-winning double biography, *Pioneer Players: The Lives of Louis and Hilda Esson* (1995). He is also a published novelist, theatre director and a writer for film.

Reid Gilbert is a College Professor in the Department of English at Capilano College, Vancouver, Canada. He has published a play, articles and reviews, as well as articles on popular culture in the most prestigious journals in the field. He has published *A Short Guide to Writing Essays about Literature* (1997) and he is a member of the Editorial Board of *Theatre Research in Canada* and of the Advisory Board of *Canadian Theatre Review*. He also acts as theatre advisor to the McClelland and Stewart *Canadian Encyclopedia Plus* (CDRom).

Albert-Reiner Glaap, Professor Emeritus at the Heinrich-Heine-Universität, Düsseldorf and Honorary Officer of the Order of the British Empire (OBE), has written extensively on modern and contemporary English, Canadian, New Zealand and Jamaican literature and drama. His recent books include *Onstage and Off-stage: English Canadian Drama in Discourse* (1996), *Stimmen aus Kanada: 25 kanadische Dramen für deutsche Bühnen* (1997), *A 50th Birthday to Willy Martin Russell* (1997), and (with Nicholas Quaintmere) *A Guided Tour Through Ayckbourn Country* (1999).

Helena Grehan has a Ph.D. in Contemporary Performance and teaches in the English and Creative Arts programme at Murdoch University in Perth, Western Australia. Her areas of research include: performance theory, race and representation, cultural geography and interculturalism. She has published articles in *Intersections, Australasian Drama Studies* and *Theatre Research International*. With a colleague, she is currently working on a manuscript tentatively entitled *Shakespeare, Performance and Interculturalism*.

Ric Knowles is Professor and former Chair of Drama, as well as founding member of the Centre for Cultural Studies at the University of Guelph. He co-edits the *Canadian Theatre Review* and edits the journal *Modern Drama*. He is the author of *The Theatre of Form and the Production of Meaning: Contemporary Canadian Dramaturgies* (1999).

Jacqueline Lo teaches in English and Theatre Studies at the School of Humanities, Australian National University. She is currently seconded as postdoctoral fellow to the Centre for Cross-Cultural Research (ANU). She has published widely in the areas of Asian-Australian cultural politics, postcolonial literature and performance, and Malaysian and Singaporean theatre.

Paul Makeham is Coordinator of Theatre Studies in the Academy of the Arts at the Queensland University of Technology. His work, which has been published in Australia and internationally, has particularly investigated representations of landscape in Australian drama. His other areas of interest include theatre criticism, community theatre and theatre for young people. In 1999, he convened the Australian Drama Studies Association conference "Industrial Relations," addressing the links between theatre scholarship and professional theatre practice.

Marc Maufort teaches English, American and postcolonial literature at the Université Libre de Bruxelles (Belgium). He is the author of *Songs of American Experience: The Vision of O'Neill and Melville* (1990), as well as the editor of *Eugene O'Neill and the Emergence of American Drama* (1989) and *Staging Difference. Cultural Pluralism in American Theatre and Drama* (1995). Within the framework of his current research in contemporary American, Canadian and Australian drama, he is convening the conference "Crucible of Cultures: Anglophone Drama at the Dawn of a New Millennium" (May 2001).

Anne Nothof is Professor of English at Athabasca University, Canada, where she has written and instructed courses in Canadian, modern British drama and theatre history. She has published essays on Canadian and British playwrights and edited three theatre texts for NeWest Press. A monograph on Sharon Pollock is in press with Guernica. She is currently president of the Association for Canadian Theatre Research.

Robert Nunn, until his retirement in 2000, was Professor in the Theatre and Dramatic Literature Program of the Department of Fine Arts at Brock University. He has published a variety of articles on Canadian theatre and drama. He has served as co-editor of *Theatre Research in Canada/Recherches théâtrales au Canada*. He is on the editorial board of that journal and of *Essays in Theatre/Etudes théâtrales*.

Bruce Parr edited *Australian Gay and Lesbian Plays* (1996) and is the author of a number of articles on the plays of Peter Kenna and gay/lesbian/queer theatre. He has worked as an actor, director, and arts administrator, and has taught theatre studies at the Universities of Queensland, Southern Queensland, New England, and the Queensland University of Technology.

Susan Pfisterer is a cultural historian and playwright who teaches Australia Studies at the Menzies Centre, King's College, University of London. She is the co-author of *Playing with Ideas: Australian Women Playwrights from the Suffragettes to the Sixties* and the editor of its sister play anthology, *Tremendous Worlds*. Her collection of plays, *Griefbox*, will be published in 2001.

Peta Tait is a Senior Lecturer in the Theatre and Drama Department at La Trobe University, Australia. She is the author of *Converging Realities: Feminism in Australian Theatre* (1994) and *Original Women's Theatre* (1993). With Elizabeth Schafer, she has co-edited *Australian Women's Drama: Texts and Feminisms* (1997). She has also edited the forthcoming *Body Show/s: Australian Viewings of Live Performance* (2001).

Helen Thomson is a senior lecturer in the English Department of the School of Literary, Visual and Performance Culture at Monash University. Her teaching and research fields include Australian literature, particularly the writing of women, and Australian drama. She has been a theatre critic for *The Australian* newspaper for over twenty years. As a critic, she is also currently writing for the Melbourne newspaper, *The Age*.

Joanne Tompkins teaches drama and literature at the University of Queensland. She has co-authored *Post-colonial Drama: Theory, Practice, Politics* (with Helen Gilbert, 1996) and *Women's Intercultural Performance* (with Julie Holledge, 1996). She is, moreover, a co-editor of *Modern Drama*. She publishes widely on post-colonial, multicultural, and intercultural theatre, with a particular emphasis on Australian and Canadian theatre and their construction of theatrical and social space.

Gerry Turcotte is the Founding Director of the Centre for Canadian-Australian Studies at the University of Wollongong. Besides numerous articles and pieces of creative writing published internationally in the most prestigious journals, he is also the author of several books, including *Jack Davis: The Maker of History*, *Neighbourhood of Memory* and *Writers in Action*. He has, moreover, recently co-edited *Canada-Australia: Towards a Second Century of Partnership* (with Kate Burridge and Lois Foster). His new novel, *Flying in Silence*, will be published in Canada and in Australia in 2001.

Robert Wallace is Professor of English and Coordinator of Drama Studies/Etudes d'art dramatique at York University's Glendon College in Toronto. His books include *The Work: Conversations with Canadian Playwrights* (1982, with Cynthia Zimmerman), *Quebec Voices* (1986), *Producing Marginality: Theatre and Criticism in Canada* (1990), *Making, Out: Plays by Gay Men* (1992) and *Theatre and Transformation in Contemporary Canada* (2000), which he wrote as the Robarts Chair for Canadian Studies at York University, 1998-1999.

Ann Wilson is an Associate Professor in the School of Literatures and Performance Studies at the University of Guelph. An editor of *Essays in Theatre/Études théâtrales* and *Canadian Theatre Review*, her research interests focus on social identities, particularly intersections of gender, sexuality, race and class in relation to issues of nation.

Dramaturgies

Texts, Cultures and Performances

This new series will publish innovative research in the field of twentieth century dramaturgy, primarily in the anglophone and francophone worlds. Its main purpose will be to re-assess the complex relationship between textual studies, cultural and performance aspects at the dawn of this new multicultural millennium. The editor will welcome manuscripts dealing with the following topics: reconsiderations of established playwrights in the light of contemporary critical theories, studies of the interface between theatre practice and textual analysis, drama and multiculturalism, studies of marginalised theatrical practices (circus, vaudeville etc.), postcolonial drama, new modes of dramatic and theatrical expressions and comparative drama studies. Works on dramatic theory (including theatre semiology) will also be considered. Manuscripts, written in English or in French, will comprise monographs, collections of essays, revised doctoral theses, high-quality *Festschrifts* and bibliographies.

The Series Editor, **Marc Maufort**, is Professor of English literature and drama at the *Université Libre de Bruxelles*.